The Joy of Coaching

To all the incredible, hardworking teachers out there who leave light, learning, and love in their wake every day. You never cease to elevate and inspire me. What a privilege it is to work with you to better the lives of children, teens, and young adults.

Teachers are my heroes!

The Joy of Coaching

Characteristics of Effective Instructional Coaches

Rebecca Frazier

CORWIN

For information:

Corwin
A SAGE Company
2455 Teller Road
Thousand Oaks, California 91320
(800) 233-9936
www.corwin.com

SAGE Publications Ltd.
1 Oliver's Yard
55 City Road
London EC1Y 1SP
United Kingdom

SAGE Publications India Pvt. Ltd.
B 1/I 1 Mohan Cooperative Industrial Area
Mathura Road, New Delhi 110 044
India

SAGE Publications Asia-Pacific Pte. Ltd.
18 Cross Street #10-10/11/12
China Square Central
Singapore 048423

Program Director and Publisher: Dan Alpert
Senior Content Development
      Editor: Lucas Schleicher
Associate Content Development
      Editor: Mia Rodriguez
Project Editor: Amy Schroller
Copy Editor: Will DeRooy
Typesetter: Hurix Digtial
Proofreader: Dennis Webb
Indexer: Integra
Cover Designer: Scott Van Atta
Marketing Manager: Maura Sullivan

Printed in the United States of America

Library of Congress Cataloging-in-Publication Data

Names: Frazier, Rebecca, A. author.

Title: The joy of coaching : characteristics of effective instructional coaches / by Rebecca A. Frazier, PhD.

Description: First edition. | Thousand Oaks : Corwin Press, Inc., 2021. | Includes bibliographical references.

Identifiers: LCCN 2020021912 | ISBN 9781506333786 (paperback) | ISBN 9781506334967 (epub) | ISBN 9781506334950 (epub) | ISBN 9781506334943 (ebook)

Subjects: LCSH: Executive coaching. | Leadership. | Northouse, Peter Guy.

Classification: LCC HD30.4 .F73 2020 | DDC 658.3/124–dc23

LC record available at https://lccn.loc.gov/2020021912

This book is printed on acid-free paper.

20 21 22 23 24 10 9 8 7 6 5 4 3 2 1

Table of Contents

Chapter 8: Trustworthy

I can be counted on.

Chapter 9: Planned

I organize and facilitate teacher growth using a variety of quality tools and processes.

Chapter 10: Models

I find ways to *show* teachers how to be successful.

 Visit the companion website at
https://resources.corwin.com/JoyofCoaching
for downloadable resources.

Foreword

By Jim Knight

As I write these words, I am, like most people in the world, quarantined at home during the COVID-19 crisis. As a researcher, I've found this to be a very interesting time to study coaching. Although coaching is usually understood to be a face-to-face activity, social distancing has brought an end to that. What I have seen played out on social media and in many Zoom conversations during this pandemic, is that coaches are rising to the challenge of doing all they can to help teachers with their professional learning needs.

As one teacher posted on Twitter, "we are all first-year teachers now." Even though coaches, like teachers, must feel like they have a whole new job, they have done incredible work helping teachers master a completely new form of professional practice. In part, this means that coaches have had to demonstrate incredible emotional intelligence as they help teachers who must teach in entirely new ways, sometimes with the parents of their students also watching their lessons online, and sometimes also trying at the same time to teach their own children at home. To provide the best support, coaches have had to learn at a ridiculously rapid rate, developing their playbooks for remote learning, finding new ways of reaching more students during remote learning, and indeed finding better ways to support teachers.

Coaches have met the challenge and then some. At a time when educators need to learn so much so fast, coaches have proven themselves to be essential. Coaches have shown when it comes to turning ideas into practice, they are indispensable resources in schools. That's why am I so grateful for Dr. Rebecca Frazier's, *The Joy of Coaching*. She shows all of us how even the best coaches can get better.

This is a beautiful and inspiring book that will help any coach improve her or his craft. Most impressive to me is Dr. Frazier's courage in speaking out strongly for caring and compassion and, what she refers to as "the L word," *love*. The best coaches are genuinely committed to doing the best for the good of others. This isn't just a nice idea; this is who they are.

Dr. Frazier doesn't just tell us how to care for each other. She gives us the tools so that we truly can become more caring people. Each chapter ends with self-assessments to push us (they certainly pushed me), to reflect deeply on our beliefs and actions. If we take this book seriously and really think about what Rebecca is asking us, we can't help but be better coaches, in fact better people. A simple self-assessment statement such as, "I think about others at least 50% of the time" can lead us into real insights into who we are, and this book contains dozens of provocative statements just like that.

At the same time, the book is more much than an inspiring publication about love and caring. The book is filled with practical, powerful tools to ensure that teachers are caring <u>and</u> competent. The old strategy of "fake-it until you make it," Rebecca says, is not a good strategy, and coaches who don't know their stuff will be found out. Teachers expect coaches to help them reach more students, so coaches need to have the tools that help teachers have greater impact.

Frazier gives coaches those tools by expanding what I refer to as the big four of planning, assessment, instruction, and classroom management to include a fifth component H.O.P.E. (health, organization, positivity, and encouragement). Then she offers many suggestions on where coaches can find resources they can share with teachers so that teachers are even more skilled at empowering students.

Each of the other 10 characteristics in this book help us better understand what instructional coaching is, and more importantly, how coaches can get better. Frazier, for example, provides a clear and practical definition of authentic leadership and outlines six helpful characteristics of authentic leaders. She also articulates, for example, the importance of coaches being inspirational, clear communicators.

Finally to support her claims, Dr. Frazier shares the research she conducted that led to these findings including a quantitative study analyzing 279 evaluative surveys of 43 coaches, 15 qualitative interviews, and growth results for 69 coached teachers. She also provides ample references to other studies and works we can look at if we want go deeper into any of the 10 characteristics she describes. Yes, this is a book about the joy of coaching. However, it is also a well-researched publication, a book that coaches and coaching leaders need to pay attention to.

This quarantine we are experiencing will pass. Teachers and students will return to schools, and while some aspects of school may be forever changed, one thing that will not change is the need for teachers to keep learning. As I like to say, when teachers learn, students learn, and at least some of the time, the opposite is also true. That is why we need coaches who partner with teachers to help them flourish. And that is also why I am so grateful for Dr. Frazier's book. *The Joy of Coaching* will help any coach become more competent and caring. The book also holds the potential to help anyone become a better person. That's certainly the impact I believe it should have on me.

Acknowledgments

My Students,

If I hadn't loved teaching, I don't think I would have been able to fully embrace the coaching and leadership roles that are now my world. Almost every day, I recall with happiness those beautiful days in the classroom as I watch my former students, now adults, bless this world with their talents and love. Currently, my mornings begin with a Principal Power Walk, then singing and playing games with about 300 students from many nations at an international language academy. You beautiful students have my heart—we do it all for you!

Gary Frazier,

Thank you for being my rock: strong, loving, kind and patient. We are going on 39 years, and I would not have accomplished anything worthwhile without your unconditional love and encouragement. Gary, thank you for always being there—life works because of you.

Mike, Elizabeth, Jeff, Lizzy, and Jon Frazier,

Kids, thank you for so many happy moments and memories and for teaching me important life lessons so I have the opportunity to become better. Thanks too for your encouraging words and thoughtful notes and gifts that I always keep near me. Your support, kindness, and attention mean so much!

Nancy Shanklin and Kate Shannon,

You two are the best teammates and friends anyone could ever have! Your encouraging ways and extensive knowledge continue to bless my life and the lives of so many. This book could never have been written without you. Our shared situations and struggles working to better the lives of teachers and students have become a deeply treasured part of my journey. Much love always.

Dr. Marcia Bader, Linda Ward, and Marilyn Luoma,

From the time my children were students during our PTSA days, to being my inspiring leaders and teammates during my teaching years, you have always stood by me and supported my work. This has meant more than you could ever know, thank you for being the incredible people you are. You have all blessed the lives of many children and teachers. Thank you for including me in the beautiful worlds you create just by being you!

Judy Williams, Ronda Schimpf, Dr. Mary Thurman, and Dr. Janeen Demi-Smith,

You had my back, allowed me space to be creative, opened doors, and supported my passion for teaching and coaching. I hope to be the kind of leader who creates the conditions for dreams to come true, like you have for me.

Dr. Jim Knight,

This book was not even a thought in my mind before you put it there. When reading your books or listening to you speak, I internalize encouragement, understanding, structures that work, intelligence, and, above all, kindness. I also have never seen anyone be able to quote so many people and apply the quotes perfectly to any given situation! You are inspiring, period.

Bobbie Halpenny and Dora Haslinger,

Once you two added your artistic touches, the book began to feel alive and complete. Thank you for your talents and for all our meaningful conversations. You both know how to see the world in creative ways that expand perspectives and illuminate understanding.

Debbie Goldsberry, Liz MacDonald, Miriam Stay, Sharon Johnson, Nancy Strawderman, and Dawn Eastman,

Life would seem harsh without you, my dear friends and sisters! Thank you for all the reassurance and inspiration, and for listening without judgment. It was and is absolutely necessary for survival! You are incredibly loved by me and so many others.

Dr. Dick Carpenter,

You were right about the PhD. It was worth the work, though I had my doubts! Your expertise, incredible teaching and writing gifts, and scary high intelligence ensured quality control and credibility. This book is based on our work together. You rock!

Dr. Paul Medina,

My data partner! Thank you for sticking with me as we spent many months analyzing and organizing data, then running statistical studies. Your expertise, tenacity, and attention to detail made the work doable and the results reliable.

Dan Alpert,

How did you do it? You were able to instill confidence even while suggesting changes! You are a true gift in my life. Thank you, Dan. Through your wise and thoughtful support, we finally finished. How did I luck out and get the best of the best?

Lucas Schleicher, Will DeRooy, and the Corwin team,

Thank you, Lucas, for helping me understand the production process and for getting all those pictures and permissions figured out! Your positive take on life and your organizational skills made everything work. Will, your attention to detail and positive comments have been wonderful gifts at the end of a long journey. Who knew copy editing could be enjoyable! Thanks too, to the Corwin team, for all the help you have given me over many years during conference presentations and discussions, always giving thoughtful support and encouragement. The Corwin team handles details professionally with unexpected heartwarming touches. You are exceptional!

Max, Fox, Lucy, Finn, Jude, and Theo,
thanks for keeping life fun and full of love and adventure!

Love, Gramzy

Publisher's Acknowledgments

Corwin gratefully acknowledges the contributions of the following reviewers:

Angela Becton
Director of Advanced Learning
Johnston County Public Schools
Smithfield, NC

Brian E. Fernandes
Reading Specialist
Hampden Meadows School
Barrington, RI

Marta Ann Gardner
Teacher, Instructional Coach,
    Literacy Expert
Los Angeles Unified School
    District (Retired)
Half Moon Bay, CA

Kendra Hanzlik
Instructional Coach
Prairie Hill Elementary School,
    College Community School District
Cedar Rapids, IA

Margaret Harris-Shoates
Instructional Coach
Isle of Wight County Schools
Smithfield, VA

Melanie Hatch
Instructional Coach
Oskaloosa Community School District
Oskaloosa, IA

Shelly Kelly
Curriculum and Instructional Coach
Great Falls Public Schools
Great Falls, MT

Laura K. Linde
Educator
District 77
Mankato, MN

About the Author

 **Rebecca Frazier, PhD,** has centered her professional career around learning and sharing how to become an effective coach in a variety of situations. When teachers feel encouragement and love as well as being supported by a technically skilled and competent coach, both the positive energy to persevere and the skills needed to meet difficult challenges are produced. This holistic way of delivering coaching, that includes a focus on personal development, benefits all involved in the process: students, teachers, coaches, and leaders. Rebecca's doctoral research included a qualitative and quantitative study dedicated to answering the question, "What makes an effective instructional coach?" which became the foundation for this book, *The Joy of Coaching: Characteristics of Effective Instructional Coaches.*

Her years as a classroom teacher, an instructional coach, trainer of instructional coaches, district facilitator for coaching program development, and a K–8 principal have provided her with a multi-tiered perspective of the coaching process. Rebecca sees coaching as the "go to" professional development strategy that, when delivered with warmth and power, can inspire joy and professional success.

Find Rebecca Frazier at CoachHappy.com or coachnteachhappy@gmail.com.

Introduction and Overview

Joy. A natural side effect of learning.

I reflect often upon my first memory, one saturated with all the glorious colors and emotions associated with the pure joy of learning. I was three, sitting by myself on a semi-springy dark blue and green plaid loveseat in a small student apartment in Laramie, Wyoming. I was intently looking past the scab on my knee toward my foot, trying my best to tie my shoes the way Mom had shown me. *The rabbit goes around the . . . under, through . . . why can't I make this work? Maybe if I make two rabbits?* I decided to keep trying even though it was frustrating, and it took a while—but oh, the incredible feeling of joy and satisfaction I experienced in that moment. My shoe was tied!

My immediate reaction to this success was to jump up, scream with delight, then throw the screen door open and run like crazy down the street to tell my mom and brother (hopefully not tripping on the laces of the other shoe, which was not yet tied). I can still feel the intense happiness that permeated my being as a result of building personal capacity in something that really mattered to a 3-year-old. And now, I was set up to feel that happiness again and again, because I could help my siblings and friends learn how to tie their shoes. I experienced the benefits of being coached, the incredible joy of learning, and then the magnified joy of using that learning to coach others very early in life. I have the opportunity to feel similar joy every day as I coach teachers.

What is joy? The online dictionary Lexico.com describes it as "a feeling of great pleasure and happiness." Synonyms include "triumph," "gladness," "exhilaration," "elation," and "delight."

When I think of joy, I think of it as being a step up from happiness: happiness+! When I have experienced joy, it has been something that sinks deeply into my soul. It penetrates, it stays with me longer, it is incredibly meaningful and encouraging, and most often it has come into my experience in one of two ways: (1) after some level of effort has been put into obtaining it, similar to the shoe-tying experience, or (2) when I am in the presence of and connected with someone who inspires, encourages, and cares about me.

Can we experience joy in a coaching role? Absolutely! What a wonderful job coaching is! We are able to continually learn, grow, and build our personal capacity, filling our toolboxes and our interpersonal skill sets with a variety of useful strategies to support teachers. We grow as they grow. We have the incredible opportunity to be where we're needed—in the trenches with teachers, collaboratively developing and sharing skills and strategies to show them how to be successful.

As we progress toward becoming more effective coaches, we continually build our outward competencies in coaching, teaching, and leading. Concurrently, our internal world and delivery of support is refined as we work on becoming the type of inspiring person people want to listen to. We are striving to develop the presence and skills to effectively make a positive difference in the lives of teachers and students.

As coaches, we can help teachers and students experience the joys of learning and teaching through not only building, engaging, and enlarging their competencies, but also encouraging their hearts through the inspirational application of our own balanced growth. Since I started coaching about 10 years ago, I've realized the need to intentionally work to develop my heart and mind in ways that would make my coaching contributions inspiring, meaningful, and effective. I've had to be more caring, more competent, more collaborative, and authentically so. I've needed to become a better communicator; act in ways that build trust; and be more flexible, more planned, and able to model or find models to demonstrate excellent instructional practice. In short, for the past 10 years, I've needed to work on being a better version of myself to become a more effective coach.

In the encouraging words of Harvard Business School professor Fanny Frei, in her recent TED Talk (2018): "I believe that there is a better version of us around every corner."

We are not going to be able to do coaching (or much of anything) perfectly; that is a part of humanness we must accept. Though it is true we are all works in progress, coaching provides us with many opportunities to move forward. It is in our serving, learning, striving, struggling, connecting, and overcoming that we find joy within ourselves and in our collaboration with others. Remember that, though perfection is elusive, we can still (even if the other shoe is not tied yet) experience deep and satisfying joy as we continue loving and learning. It is that intersection between authentic caring and competency—the merging of love and knowledge shared—that brings joy into the coaching relationship.

What is the basis of this book?

This book is based on the findings of a mixed-methods (qualitative and quantitative) study, "Characteristics of Effective Instructional Coaches" (Frazier, 2014), conducted as an initial study to begin to fulfill doctoral requirements during the years 2011–2014. It was designed based on a simple question I had as the newly hired coordinator of a coaching program called Teachers Coaching Teachers: "What makes an effective instructional coach?" While reading on the topic of instructional coaching, I had been able to find information on processes, steps to take, and ways of increasing student learning, but only a few pieces here and there that focused on coaches themselves. What were the qualities and characteristics needed to be successful in this important role? I wanted to find out more about the importance of the person doing the coaching. I was hoping to find what I needed to be a better trainer and leader of instructional coaches. As noted previously, I was not able to locate enough detail in the articles and books I read to adequately address something I had found to be very true: Individual teacher progress and coaching programs, in general, live or die depending on *who is doing the coaching*. In the words of Instructional Coaching Group president Jim Knight, "Without question, the most important factor relative to the effectiveness of a coaching program is 'Who is the coach?'" (Knight, 2011, p. 122).

Though a major component of teacher success surely rests on how willing a teacher is to change (Fillery-Travis & Lane, 2007), it had been my experience that many, if not most, teachers could and would make changes if they had someone competent and caring to assist them. I wondered, then, *What characteristics reside within the person, the "being" of effective coaches?* If I could figure out what qualities effective coaches possessed, I would have something valuable to use when deciding how to train the coaches on my team.

My study included a quantitative analysis of 279 evaluative surveys regarding 43 instructional coaches in the System for Teacher and Student Advancement (TAP) who provided a variety of coaching supports for teachers. The evaluative surveys were completed by teachers being coached, lead teachers, and administrators. Qualitative interviews were also conducted with 15 coaches. The definition used for "effective" in the study was an adaptation of Peter Northouse's (2010, p. 12) definition of leadership:

- Positively influences another individual, or group of individuals, to achieve a common goal

- Inspires and facilitates meaningful change

The dependent variable in the statistical study (linear regression) was the mentoring section of the survey. This section referenced some relational parts of coaching including caring words, such as "support" and "guides." The independent variables determined to be predictors of the mentoring section included more technical aspects of coaching, including staff development and instructional supervision, along with community involvement. The results showed that the three independent variables were predictors of higher results in mentoring. In other words, when coaches were ranked high in mentoring, they were also ranked higher in the other areas. One important finding of this research was that when people perceived they were being effectively supported/mentored/cared for by a coach, the teacher, administrators, and other coaches considered the coach to be successful in technical areas as well. The reverse was also true: A coach who was rated low in mentoring skills was also rated lower in technical coaching skills. Fifteen qualitative interviews were also conducted, and patterns within the scripts were analyzed, first manually and later through the use of NVIVO, a computerized tool that could identify when characteristics were mentioned within the interview scripts.

Who are the coaches involved in the studies, and why were they chosen?

The "Characteristics of Effective Instructional Coaches" study (Frazier, 2014) was explained previously as the foundation for the characteristics model. The results of this study caused me and the coaching team I was leading (at Teachers Coaching Teachers) to engage in a great deal of reflection, which inspired us to change our coaching practices to balance heart and mind more meaningfully. After analysis of the findings was completed in 2014, adaptations were made to the Teachers Coaching Teachers (TCT) program, based on findings showing the need for a more balanced coaching approach. For us, this meant incorporating more caring, human connection, and relational pieces into our practice. We had always been pretty good at data analysis, alignment, using best practices, and sharing strategies. As coaches, we were relational people, but we were not consciously intentional about incorporating more abstract things, like love for and understanding of the individual people we were coaching, into our coaching processes. Since adding these elements (see Chapter 9), we are experiencing more sincere connections with teachers, which speeds up our work as we partner with them to accomplish coaching goals.

During school year 2016–2017, the effectiveness of the TCT coaching program was analyzed through multiple dissertation studies to determine whether it was effective at increasing teacher competency, job satisfaction, and student growth when compared to control groups of teachers not coached. The results were stunning, showing approximately four to five times as much growth compared to non-coached teachers in the areas of planning, instruction, assessment, classroom environment, professional growth, and even more in job satisfaction (Frazier, 2018). The Northwest Evaluation Association (NWEA), also known as MAP testing, indicated NWEA student growth results of teachers who accessed the TCT program over a five-year period, when MAP results were available, as almost half a year more than students in control groups. Detailed statistical results are found in Appendix B. Coaching experiences, quotes, and meaningful scenarios experienced by coaches, teachers, and students involved with the two coaching programs are shared throughout this book.

The coaches involved in both studies (my initial study and the study of the resulting changes at TCT) performed as a regular part of their work most, if not all, of the roles and responsibilities of coaches as defined by Joellen Killion and Cindy Harrison (2006). These roles included resource provider, data coach, instructional specialist, curriculum specialist, classroom supporter, learning facilitator, mentor, school leader, catalyst for change, and learner. Much was required of these coaches, as is the case in many schools and districts. Multiple analyses of the effectiveness of the interactions of 31 coaches over 10 years in the generalist, K–12, district-level coaching program Teachers Coaching Teachers (TCT), and the 279 evaluations of 43 coaches and interviews of 15 who were chosen as master and mentor teachers in the Teacher Advancement Program (TAP), included within their roles, a wide variety of support options available for teachers (Killion & Harrison, 2006). This coaching support was provided in a large, urban school district (50-plus schools and approximately 25,000 students) that housed multiple socioeconomic levels and diverse populations. Because of the many roles and responsibilities embedded within the coaches' jobs and the variety in the populations they were serving, the likelihood of the findings being applicable to many coaching situations is enhanced. For more information on the studies, you can access the original papers on Google Scholar or at Coachhappy.com (see the references).

In writing this book, I referenced seven coaching publications and synthesized the information they contained with my research findings (statistical study and scripted interview pattern results) to create a model that identifies 10 characteristics of effective instructional coaches. In summary, an effective instructional coach is one who is:

- collaborative (Chapter 1),

- caring (Chapter 2),

- competent (Chapter 3),

- authentic (Chapter 4),

- a quality communicator (Chapter 5),

- inspirational (Chapter 6),

- flexible (Chapter 7),

- trustworthy (Chapter 8),

- planned (Chapter 9), and

- able to provide models (Chapter 10).

Authors whose ideas I accessed include Jane Kise, Kathryn Kee, John Daresh, Jim Knight, Karla Reiss, Paula Rutherford, Beth Tatum, Patti McWhorter, Jean Boreen, and Donna Niday.

Who is this book for?

This book is for those interested in expanding their personal capacity to inspire and support teachers. It is for those who believe partnering with teachers to improve instruction and intentionally cocreating bright spots of hope and happiness will make a lasting, positive impact on students. It is for coaches, educational leaders, teachers, and friends of teachers everywhere.

Through this book, it is my hope that coaches, teachers, and educational leaders will find resources to hone their coaching skills, as well as the strength to radiate possibility and happiness when faced with long days and difficult circumstances.

As indicated above, each chapter of this book will address an important characteristic of effective coaches. It is interesting to note that "caring" and "competency" were mentioned with very high frequency by authors in the field of coaching and by the coaches interviewed in my 2014 study. These two characteristics were referenced in all interviews and often mentioned in the same breath by coaches as they responded to interview questions about what it takes to be an effective coach. For example:

> Effective means I'm human enough to understand what's happening with them [the person being coached] and empathize with that. I'm professional enough to have the expertise to offer them help, whatever the help might be, and I'm student-centered enough to understand that out of my coaching and out of their good practice will come improvement for our kids.
>
> Coach #11

> So I think that compassion and empathy [are what it takes to be an effective coach] and really knowing your stuff.
>
> Coach #13

> [I think that being effective means] recognizing areas of need and being able to gently guide and direct people into that area without making them feel like they're failures.
>
> Coach #15

Within the characteristics model, caring and competent are incorporated into one central theme and will be considered *inseparable and incomplete* without each other. Your ability as a coach to effectively merge these two traits and share them with the person you are coaching creates wholeness and joy in the coaching relationship (see central section below).

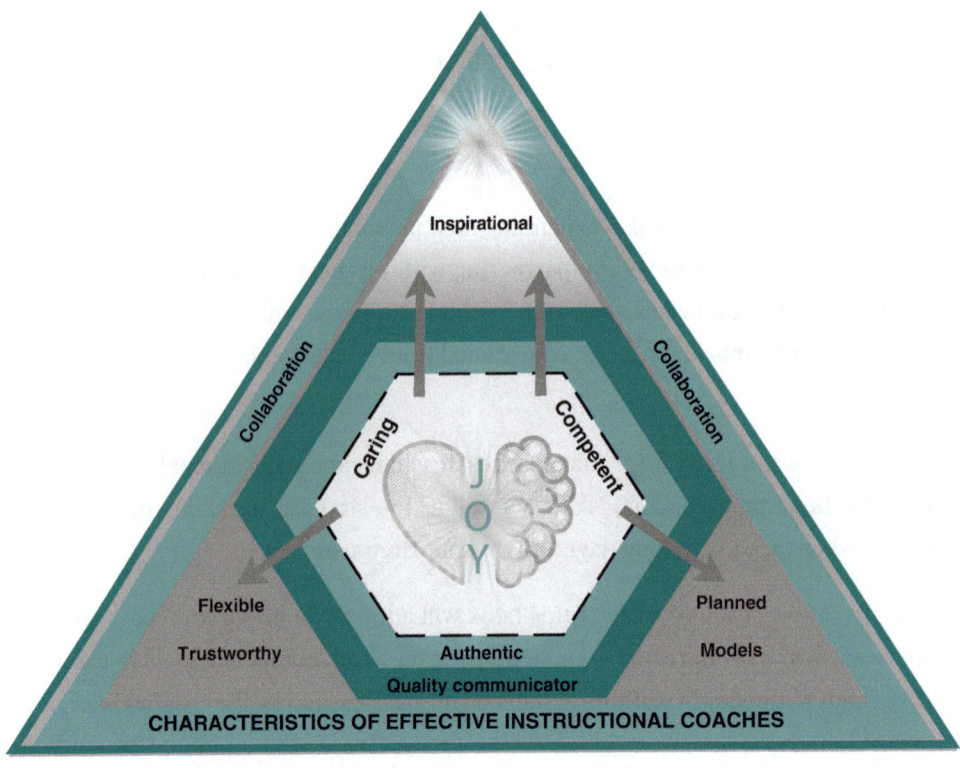

CHARACTERISTICS OF EFFECTIVE INSTRUCTIONAL COACHES

The model suggests that the characteristics of effective instructional coaches are surrounded and protected by the shelter and structure of *collaboration*. A coach's capacity to address individualized details associated with being *caring* and *competent* are magnified when coaching is delivered and filtered through the connecting power of *authenticity* and the skills of a *quality communicator*. The model, when split in half vertically, shows the left side incorporating characteristics related to being *caring*, including being *flexible* and *trustworthy*, and the right side incorporating characteristics related to being *competent*, including being *planned* and being able to provide *models*. The arrows pointing from the center section of the model up to the characteristic of being *inspirational* indicate that we consider people inspiring for a variety of reasons, and those reasons can typically be traced back to one or both of the basic characteristics of being *caring* and *competent*.

Why is what we do so important?

Embedded in our roles and in our hearts as teachers, coaches, and educational leaders is a deep and personal commitment to protect and nurture children and teens. Yet very rare are lives or environments in which traumatic events do not or have not happened. Taking on these roles now requires more of us than in days past. We are striving to be warriors, capable of emotionally managing and fighting against the confusing, often incomprehensible actions of others. Random shootings—many times at schools—kids considering or committing suicide, poverty, teachers being beaten up by students, and bullying of students on social media (Ruedy, 2008) are just some of the unsettling things we face, along with lagging student achievement (Cohen & Moffit, 2009; Lee, 2006).

Many children, teens, and teachers are unhappy and depressed (Markow, Macia, Lee, & Harris Interactive, 2012; MetLife, 2012; National Center for Injury Prevention and Control, 2018). This is happening all over the world. A recent study indicated 1 in 10 teachers in the United Kingdom are on antidepressants because of excessive workloads, student behaviors, and working conditions (Pells, 2017). Teachers are leaving the profession, creating shortages (Aragon, 2016; U.S. Department of Education, 2015), and young people do not want to take on the role because of the lack of respect for the profession and low pay (National Center for Education Information, 2011). Teachers who are doing all they can to stand strong in difficult situations are experiencing or are at risk of experiencing compassion fatigue or vicarious/secondary trauma (Sizemore, 2016).

So what if our heroes are run off and we run out of them? Has society considered the cost of losing the influence of wonderful teachers, particularly in such challenging times? What will our children and teens do if they have fewer and fewer quality teachers to whom they feel like writing notes like these?

> You have taught me so much about school and about life. With you, I learned to set goals and strive to achieve them no matter how difficult it is. You were and are the greatest teacher I have ever had, and I am still learning from you. Having you

> as my teacher has been a blessing, and we have had many wonderful experiences. Thank you for being my teacher and teaching me so much.

> You are the best teacher ever. I love you. When I am around you I feel like I can do everything. You will always be in my heart.

And this one, from a parent:

> I thought that only a parent could be a child's best advocate; but you proved me wrong. You have been a blessing to our family. You have promoted our son to greater heights and you've provided him the opportunities to reach the stars. . . . But yet, we see that you have done this for many others. You have allowed children to see and feel the dream. To feel accomplishments in their lives. Many are born to this world . . . but some people make the world special just by being in it. Thank you for being a part of [my son's] life and ours.

Children need heroes, and adults do too.

How do we hang on to and help our teacher heroes triumph?

We coach (Bush, 1984; Frazier, 2018; Killion, Harrison, Bryan, & Clifton, 2012; Knight, 2007; Marzano & Simms, 2013; Podolsky, Kini, Bishop, & Darling-Hammond, 2016; Ross, 1992). And we do it in an authentic, balanced way that values the hearts and minds of teachers.

This book is designed to identify and explain key characteristics of effective instructional coaches and to provide:

- a framework and structure to work within to develop the characteristics of an effective coach;

- a variety of activities, exercises, experiences, examples, stories, measures, and ideas for actions to support a person striving to become an effective coach; and

- resources for encouragement and renewal.

Why do we need to learn about balanced coaching?

Coaching is about guiding and supporting people through the process of change. A singular focus on data and the details of instructional processes designed to increase test score results does not acknowledge, allow for, or incorporate basic elements of humanness. Understanding human motivation and providing meaningful support that includes both caring and competency is central to the work of coaching. Coaches want and need to know how to provide effective support that acknowledges and values both the mind and heart of the teachers they work with. There is currently not enough information available to coaches on how to increase their effectiveness through structured personal growth.

Why now?

This is the time to voice the need for balance—to stand up for what it is to be human, to move forward in matters of the head (including what we have learned about best teaching practices), and also to get to the heart of what matters. Emotions rule the day for us all, according to Nobel laureate Daniel Kahneman (2011). Since we have had lackluster results over the past 30 years focusing on strict accountability, let us now strive for a better balance and seek to understand and validate matters of the heart.

Authors who have begun to express the need for balance and to call for ways to help teachers and coaches internalize what they need to "be" to become effective include Michael Fullan, in *The Six Secrets of Change* (2008, p. 23):

> I have centered my own work around the moral imperative of raising the bar and closing the gap of achievement for all children, so I am an advocate of the sentiments expressed in these policies [No Child Left Behind, Every Child Matters, and Children First]. But there is one problem: Secret One ["Love your employees"] tells me that the children-first stances are misleading and incomplete.

Kevin Cashman, in *Leadership From the Inside Out* (2008, p. 178):

> Coaching is the art of drawing forth potential onto the canvas of high performance. It's the gentle yet firm hand of leadership guiding the way like a caring friend, helping the "coachee" to steer clear of danger or set a more positive course.

Margaret Wheatley, in *Leadership and the New Science* (2006, pp. 69–70):

> We live in a universe where relationships are primary. Nothing happens in the quantum world without something encountering something else. Nothing exists independent of relationships . . . we participate in the creation of everything we observe.

Elena Aguilar, in *The Art of Coaching* (2013, p. 77):

> But the greater goal is to gain the client's trust. This is a challenging end point to evaluate, as it resides almost exclusively in the subjective and volatile realms of emotions and beliefs.

Parker Palmer, in *The Courage to Teach: Exploring the Inner Landscape of a Teacher's Life* (2007, p. 3):

> In our rush to reform education, we have forgotten a simple truth: reform will never be achieved by renewing appropriations, restructuring schools, rewriting curriculum, and revising texts if we continue to demean and dishearten the human resource called teacher on whom so much depends . . . [nothing] will transform education if we fail to cherish—and challenge—the human heart that is the source of good teaching.

Joellen Killion and colleagues, in *Coaching Matters* (2012, p. 28):

> An effective coach: Has good interpersonal relationships, wants to be part of a team, fosters trust, communicates effectively, [and] listens skillfully.

and Jane A. G. Kise, in *Differentiated Coaching* (2006, p. 161):

> Further, because Feeling types . . . want to stay harmonious, they may remain silent when Thinkers overlook the Feeling concerns.

It is my desire that this book will provide clarity and understanding about what characteristics need to be incorporated within the person of an effective coach and provide practical ideas showing how to make that happen. Coaching supports that address both Thinking and Feeling types of personalities and provide specific ways coaches can thrive as they work through sometimes joy-crushing schedules, societal issues, and pressures that exist in education today will be included in the text of this book.

Within the book, two icons will be used to show Practical Applications and Professional Development ideas:

Some sections within book chapters will be formatted specially. These include the following:

- Reflect and Connect: These activities to connect the chapter focus to individuals' roles and situations could be used for personal reflection, coach trainings, or professional development activities.

- Characteristic Self-Assessment: Near the end of each chapter, a self-assessment will be provided to help you determine how well you are incorporating the chapter characteristic into your daily life. You will informally evaluate yourself on a Likert scale, to get an idea of your current level of skill in each of the areas before and after implementing some of the practical suggestions.

- S.O.A.K. (Stress-free Opportunities to Absorb Knowledge): Located at the end of each chapter is a one-page multisensory/avenues document for you to easily reference when you need a positive, rejuvenating boost. It's like a mini-poster to help coaches/teachers/educational leaders easily incorporate the coaching characteristic they are focusing on into their daily lives. Sometimes in our cerebral world of data analysis—breaking down complex standards into daily learning targets, designing formative assessments, and the like—we teachers and coaches forget to connect with the healing power of music, the balancing breath of laughter, the comforting stories of those who have achieved, the piece of art that takes our breath away, the inspiring quote, or the uplifting thought. I hope you use this section when you need a laugh, are looking for easy ways to focus on a characteristic, and need to hear in a variety of ways, "You can do this!"

As noted previously, many authors are acknowledging and writing about the importance of balance, and with society taking a good look at the basically nonexistent results of being overfocused on accountability and using hard-nosed tactics to help students and teachers improve, educators and many stakeholders (including parents and children) are looking for more peaceful and effective ways to learn, teach, and coach.

A few years ago, I created an activity for our coaches to use with teachers to figure out where the teachers they were working with were coming from emotionally and what their desires for themselves and their students were. I purchased rocks that had the words "Strength," "Courage," "Peace," "Hope," "Inspire," "Dream," and "Believe" engraved on them (and provided blank rocks and a felt-tipped marker in case they wanted to choose another word). on them. Then I asked the coaches if they would ask the teachers they worked with two questions:

1. In one word or so, what would you like your students to come away with, gain, feel, or incorporate into their lives as a result of your teaching this year? In other words, what would you like your influence in general to be on your students?

2. In one word or so, what would you like to have or what do you need in your life right now (added later—that would help you convey that influence with students)?

The number-one thing that coaches said teachers across our large urban district felt they needed in their lives at that particular time was peace. The top responses for what influence teachers wanted to leave with students were a mix of "Inspire," "Believe," "Courage," "Confidence" (both personally and academically), "Peace," and "Happiness."

The feedback from coaches after they had used this process was that it saved a lot of time (the consensus was about six weeks!) because the process established trust and purpose with the teacher very quickly. This happened because teachers' heartfelt desires for students were brought to light, and often these core desires were connected to why they had chosen to become educators. Often those internal motivators, those treasures that carry with them so much power and energy, had been buried beneath minutiae and needed to be located and excavated. This process was and is incredibly useful to identify teacher purpose and motivation, allowing coaches the opportunity to adjust their coaching to support teachers' core desires and needs.

When I saw how well this "touchstone process" (see Chapters 6 and 9 for details) worked with teachers, I decided to reword it and use it with coaches in the TCT program (this activity is included as part of the *Finding Home* process in Chapter 6). After I asked the questions to one part-time coach (who was also a classroom teacher), she remained silent for a bit, then picked up a marker and carefully wrote "Joy" on a blank stone. She said she wanted joy for both herself and her students.

I had originally planned to include the word "joy" as part of the engraved stone options but had run out of money. How symbolic! Isn't that what happens every day in our classrooms, in our districts, in our legislatures? Joy is pretty much basic and universal, we all want it, and it likely doesn't cost more than other important things, but how often we forget to include it or seek after it! This book is organized to help you create joy in your coaching relationships by incorporating characteristics into your life that will help you deliver coaching in a balanced way. Joyful coaching honors and values both the heart and mind of the person being coached, addresses our beautiful and complicated humanness, and brings wholeness and happiness to our work.

For me, being able to work as an instructional coach has been a wonderful gift. It hasn't always been easy, though—it has inspired and sometimes demanded personal change in order to be most effective—and I'm still happily in process. Teachers need coaches who can help them weather the storms of our time. How fortunate we are to have the chance to help others teach with inspiration and accuracy; how meaningful the opportunity to expand our influence and bring caring and competent support to teachers who daily make foundational contributions to the future of our world. Coaching: It's awe-inspiring!

Let's do it well.

Following is an overview of the 10 characteristics determined to positively impact effective instructional coaching (Frazier, 2014). Within it, each of the characteristics is explained using two statements. The first is a summary statement, and the next is an internalizing statement which is meant to help you internalize the characteristic by speaking the words out loud or reading through and thinking about them often. Then, synonyms and specifics from the research study or book text are included. Finally, a visual image is provided, to bring to mind a picture or possible metaphor of the characteristic. These words are also incorporated into a simplified model found at the beginning of each chapter, and the overview is available for viewing or download on the book's companion website (https://resources.corwin.com/JoyofCoaching)

An Effective Instructional Coach is . . .

COLLABORATIVE

Summary Statement	Internalizing Collaborative	Synonyms	Visual
I believe every person is of value and that students benefit, difficult challenges are overcome, and friendships are forged through meaningful collaborative work.	I embrace as important the thoughts and opinions of others. I come to collaborative situations prepared and willing to share my best thinking. I understand that when I engage in focused collaborative work with my colleagues, great things can happen for students, and I can often find shelter and support as I face the challenges of teaching/coaching/leading.	partnership; cooperation; synergy; allies; support; relationships; teamwork	Aspen trees Their roots grow together, creating greater stability, beauty, and longevity.

CARING

Summary Statement	Internalizing Caring	Synonyms/Specifics From Research (Frazier, 2014)	Visual
I continually refine my motives, speech, actions, and heart so that I can genuinely care for those I coach.	The people I coach know and feel I am interested and invested in their growth and happiness. I show my love and caring in a variety of ways. I take the time to get to know the people I coach and provide personalized support that matters to them.	empathetic; loving; welcoming; gentle; encouraging; open; unselfish; kind; supportive; patient; sensitive; respectful; compassionate; understanding	

COMPETENT

Summary Statement	Internalizing Competent	Synonyms/Specifics From Research (Frazier, 2014)	Visual
I know, understand, and apply current instructional best practices and coaching techniques.	The people I coach can trust that I am experienced, knowledgeable, and continually learning. They can count on experiencing professional growth through their committed efforts and my quality coaching.	knowledgeable; experienced; can provide ideas for next steps to better teachers' instructional practice; aware of and shares current data and research; respected resource	

(Continued)

(Continued)

AUTHENTIC

Summary Statement	Internalizing Authentic	Synonyms/Quote	Visual
I like who I am.	I strive to be congruent and consistent with my core values in thought, word, and deed. I seek to inspire those I coach with pure intention by regularly cultivating my highest thoughts and ideals.	real; genuine; credible; pure; true "In the last analysis, what we are communicates far more eloquently than what we say or do. We all know it." —S. R. Covey	

a QUALITY COMMUNICATOR

Summary Statement	Internalizing Quality Communicator	Synonyms/Specifics From Research (Frazier, 2014)	Visual
I connect and empower.	The teachers I coach are empowered by the words I speak, my knowledge and preparation, my sincere desire to understand and help, and the consistent support I provide.	listens; creates a positive relationship; understands needs; clearly defines roles and work; uses positive, clear, and intentional language; gives specific feedback that clarifies; shares instructional strategies	

INSPIRATIONAL

Summary Statement	Internalizing Inspirational	Synonyms/Specifics From Research (Frazier, 2014)	Visual
I desire and prepare to be an inspiring person.	I am dedicated to personal and professional growth and enjoy learning with and encouraging others. I spend time caring for my body, mind, and spirit so that I can function at my best. I smile, learn new things, and passionately and courageously go about my work. I strive to deliver joyful, inspired coaching by being humble, quick to laugh and celebrate, and by modeling enthusiasm. I tenaciously stand in service to and authentically believe in those I coach until the goal set is the goal met!	courageous; tenacious; passionate; encouraging; enthusiastic; humble; involved in school community; experienced; respected; lifelong learner	

FLEXIBLE

Summary Statement	Internalizing Flexible	Synonyms/Specifics From Research (Frazier, 2014)	Visual
I can adapt and create positive change.	The teachers I coach and the colleagues I work with know they don't have to look, act, or think exactly like me to be accepted and respected. I tailor my coaching to individual teachers' needs and do not assume my past experiences will always be the right solution for their situation.	willing to look at alternatives; able to tailor instruction to a variety of situations; able to see multiple perspectives; culturally sensitive and aware	

TRUSTWORTHY

Summary Statement	Internalizing Trustworthy	Synonyms/Specifics From Research (Frazier, 2014)	Visual
I can be counted on.	The teachers I coach know their reputations and their hearts are safe with me. I do what I say I am going to do.	integrity; confidentiality; honesty; ethical	

PLANNED

Summary Statement	Internalizing Planned	Synonyms/Specifics From Research (Frazier, 2014)	Visual
I organize and facilitate teacher growth using a variety of quality tools and processes.	The teachers I coach are confident I will come to each coaching session with personalized resources and coaching structures that are relevant and meaningful. I use targeted data collection to inform individual coaching goals and to provide reportable feedback on coaching effectiveness.	collaboratively determines specific and measurable goals with timelines; prepares for individual coaching sessions; prioritizes needs using data; uses evidence-based strategies; utilizes quality coaching tools tailored to individual situations; references and reinforces content standards; checks in with teacher and follows up on action plans frequently	

(Continued)

(Continued)

able to provide MODELS

Summary Statement	Internalizing Models	Synonyms/Specifics From Research (Frazier, 2014)	Visual
I find ways to show teachers how to be successful.	As a coach, I am continually learning and looking for opportunities to refine my own teaching. I can and do provide modeling personally, through videos, co-teaching, observations of other teachers, and in other ways to show the teachers I coach what quality instruction looks like.	demonstrates excellent instructional practice; models rigorous analysis of instruction and self-reflection; embodies personal characteristics that lead to great coaching	Modeling shows teachers how to get from where they are to where they want to be.

Characteristics of Effective Instructional Coaches, © Rebecca Frazier, 2018. Illustrations: Bobbie Halpenny

Note From the Publisher

In addition to numerous templates, tools, and references, full-page printable versions of the following items are available to download from the companion website for your practical use:

- "An Instructional Coach Is . . . " table: an overview of the ten characteristics determined to positively impact effective instructional coaching

- The self-assessment tools from each chapter

- Full-sized copies of the "S.O.A.K." tables (Stress-free Opportunities to Absorb Knowledge)

- Templates for Unit and Daily Lesson Plan Sequences

- The "Go Fish . . . Coach" card game, including instructions and printable playing cards

- The Instructional Survey and Survey Results

- The four-page Coaching Planner:
  - Teacher Information,
  - Human Connection,
  - Action Plan, and
  - Tracker

- Time Distribution Tool

- Teacher Observation Note Catcher

 Visit the companion website at
https://resources.corwin.com/JoyofCoaching
for downloadable resources.

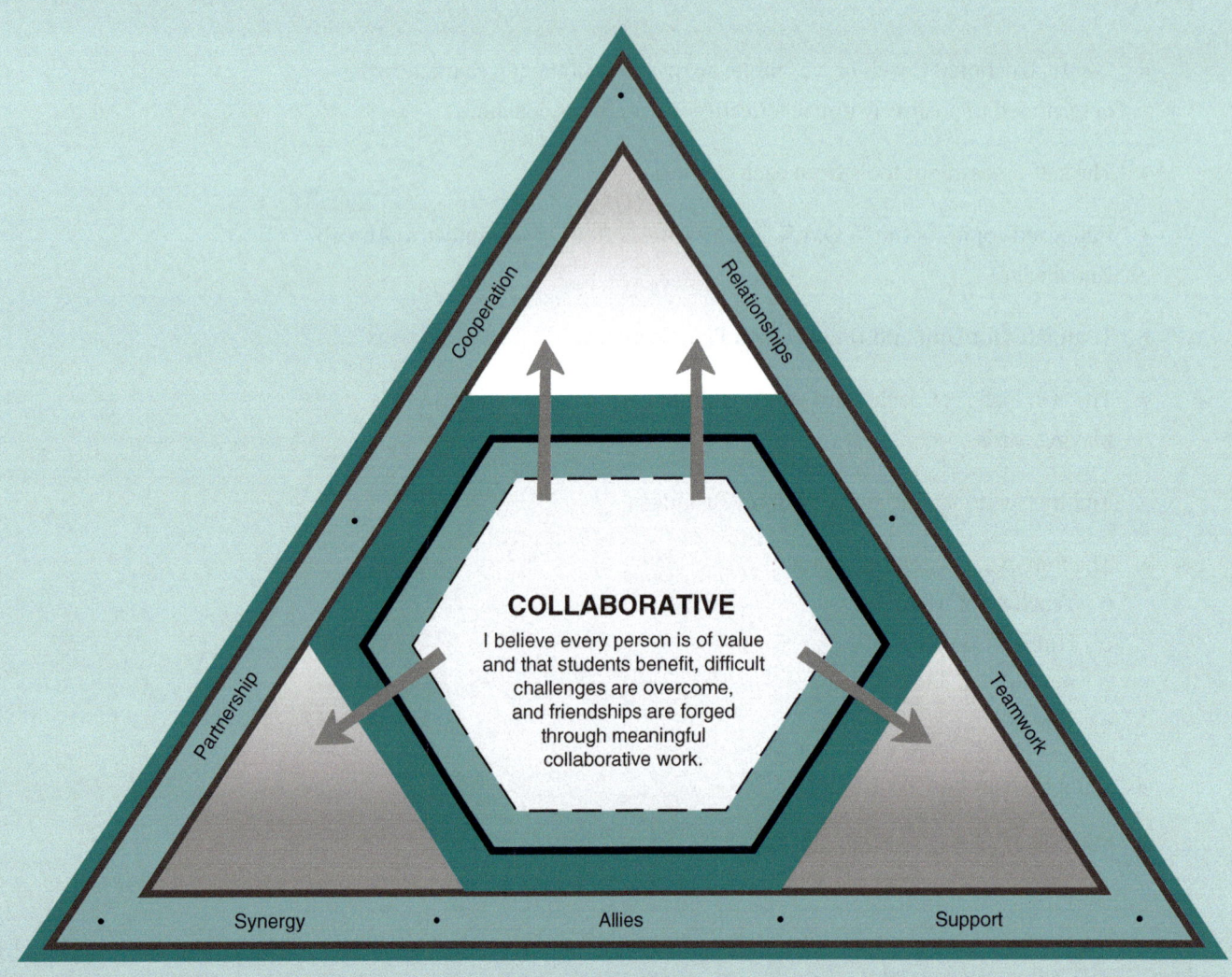

COLLABORATIVE

I believe every person is of value and that students benefit, difficult challenges are overcome, and friendships are forged through meaningful collaborative work.

Cooperation

Relationships

Partnership

Teamwork

Synergy · Allies · Support

I embrace as important the thoughts and opinions of others. I come to collaborative situations prepared and willing to share my best thinking. I understand that when I engage in focused collaborative work with my colleagues, great things can happen for students, and I can often find shelter and support as I face the challenges of teaching/coaching/leading.

Collaborative

1

Coaching is obviously, but also inherently, collaborative. The triangle structure represents collaboration as a powerful and protective concept that provides foundational structure and shelter for all other characteristics of effective coaches. Visually similar to an A-frame home, this portion of the characteristics model suggests that when we are willing to enter into the welcoming structure of collaboration, we can create enjoyable interactions and experience increased success as we partner with others.

Collaboration Can Provide Shelter and Support

As a teacher, it took me some time and practice to jump on the collaboration bandwagon. I was wondering, *How (when I don't even have time to walk up the hall to the restroom) can I be expected to give up planning time to attend more meetings?* I figured since I alone was going to be held accountable for the assessment results of certain students, it was going to be me who determined what needed to be done to ensure my students grew academically; I did not want to trust their success or failure to anyone else. This was after I had taught a few years and felt confident in my skills. At the beginning of my career, I wanted someone who knew what to do and cared enough about me and my students to help me!

As I look back now, I realize it was arrogant and selfish on my part to not quickly consider the positive possibilities of working with others, but in my mind the lack of time available to complete everything required of me was putting me (and my students) in a precarious situation. I felt myself sinking into survival mode, trying to protect my planning time because I was afraid I seriously might not survive in the profession without dedicated time to accomplish the many "duties as assigned" required of me (besides teaching) and still be able to accomplish my family goals.

In my current coaching work, when teachers are in a place where they feel completely overwhelmed and wonder how to squeeze in coaching on top of so many other duties, I am reminded of a dreary, bitterly cold winter day during my first year of teaching. During a rare quiet moment before the start of the school day, a colleague walked by my room. She peered through the small rectangular window to wave hello. But I had my head on the desk, sick to death with an awful cold.

I had felt I couldn't take a day off, because there was too much to be done, and I would have had to go in at 5:00 a.m. anyway to write detailed sub plans so that the sub would totally understand what to do so no academic time would be lost, so I might as well just try to make it through the day. I was caught basically sobbing my heart out because I wanted to be a good teacher but didn't think I could do "all this stuff" anymore. This colleague took the time to come in and check on me. I was embarrassed that someone finally knew how I was really feeling, but because she knew, there was no keeping up appearances. It was obvious I was a mess, so I thought I might as well express what I was feeling and be open to receiving her encouragement and support. She coached me with pure intention for my welfare both personally and professionally.

Miraculously, within just a few minutes, I felt listened to, I felt understood, and it all seemed doable again. She was my shelter, she was my support—and because of her awareness and compassion, I kept going. When teachers are feeling this way (unfortunately, this is not uncommon), coaching that begins with a fire-hose approach (identifying deficits or things that need to be changed immediately) can be counterproductive, especially when the real-life world and emotional landscape the teacher is traversing is not even considered. Using a teacher-friendly, gentle, but organized and consistent approach using meaningful data, goal setting with measures, and discussion that includes identifying supports to help teachers be successful both personally and with students inspires teachers to have the desire to collaborate. This type of process is explained in more detail in Chapter 9.

 Can you think of a way to remind yourself to notice those around you? Maybe be quick to say hello, provide a kind word, give up a few minutes to listen, and offer a shoulder to lean on when someone needs it? If you worry about the time needed for you to do this, be assured it often doesn't take very long to brighten someone's day. Who knows? That person may remember you years later for it!

For example, here is a coaching experience shared by an instructional coach who attended the 2015 Teaching Learning and Coaching Conference (TLC). It is her success story about facing a challenging coaching situation. She asked to remain anonymous.

> The teacher [I was working with] was absent extensively but within district protocol. However, she left early in addition to taking other sick days. The teacher told me her mother was battling cancer but she didn't want to "burden" her team and administrators [with this information]. Together, we found a way for her to be vulnerable and yet safe. [I stayed with her] as she shared her reasons for the time off with her team and administrators. Her family situation was met with care, concern, understanding, and the necessary emotional and classroom support, enabling her to teach successfully and care for her mom.

This teacher felt she could be real with her coach, which resulted in her receiving the help and support she needed both personally and professionally. We want to be with people who have our backs, who exhibit compassion and use their problem-solving skills to benefit us. When we feel supported, we are much more likely to put in the work required to move forward, allow that work to flow freely with little resistance to needed change, save time because we are focused on collaboratively determined priorities with support built into the process, and continually progress in a way that feels natural and fulfilling.

However, when the collaborative work of coaching is forced, based mostly on what the teacher is not doing—or what the teacher is doing wrong—the energy surrounding those interactions is prone to being stilted, negative, and full of fear and sadness. If coaching is delivered in a punitive way by someone who is seen as being given orders to "fix" the teacher because somehow that teacher is lacking, coaching is not as likely to create positive synergy and the energy needed to solve challenging problems. Can teachers, coaches, or educational leaders ensure that the children or adults they are working with will do anything a certain way (even if it's a great idea) when not under supervision? Unless coaches or educational leaders can supervise 24/7 and handle being disliked during the process, it's likely better to decide on coaching goals and measures together in ways that generate positive energy so that the teacher will be internally motivated to implement changes and continue with them over the long term. Both teachers and coaches want their work together to be positive and happy, not leave a nasty aftertaste. How we set up our collaborative structures is important. If people feel they are being treated as "less than," then, at the very least, coaching will be seen by teachers as something to fear rather than to embrace.

I still remember my colleague coming in that day and basically gifting me with the strength to move forward. That was 15 years ago. She made a lasting impact in my life. I'm thinking if someone tells us or implies in some way that we aren't very good teachers/coaches/educational leaders, we might remember that person, but it would not likely be fondly, and we wouldn't feel a great desire to implement that person's suggestions. People do not enjoy relationships in which they are looked upon as damaged or someone's "project."

During the last 10 years, it has been my experience as an instructional coach that almost all teachers have a sincere desire to improve their teaching practice. Many teachers also already feel they know what they need to work on, because possible areas of instructional focus have already been determined through classroom assessments, students' grades, students' pass/fail rates, state and/or district test results, interim benchmark assessments, grade-level data, PLC data analysis, and/or teacher evaluations. There is a lot of data available. The last thing teachers need is to believe that coaching is going to be another beat-down, especially if their data and evaluations point to the need for extra support. There are only so many times a person can hear "You're terrible" in so many ways before shutting down.

I needed my colleague that cold winter day to provide me with fuel to rekindle my waning desire to continue on my path. She understood the job and the workload, she had worked through similar emotions, and that day she showed up for me. Coaching delivered in a way that includes compassionate support, along with the exciting components of effective instruction, can produce satisfying and lasting interactions that positively impact the lives of all involved; the coach, the teacher, and both current and future students.

Coaching is satisfying and meaningful work when it is communicated in ways that support and value both the heart and the mind of the teacher. Taking time to honor the humanity of those we serve while building technical expertise and heartfelt connections addresses both academic and foundational human needs.

Valuing Others

Collaboration becomes essential when a coach and teacher and/or a collaborative team are faced with complex problems that can be addressed effectively and creatively only by accurately describing the current situation, brainstorming, and looking at a variety of solutions from multiple perspectives. Collaboration can be especially powerful when members of a team do not think exactly alike and the team has autonomy and authority to determine solutions and put them into practice. When working to solve challenging problems, different perspectives can help the team get to a more accurate assessment of the problem and identify solutions that could work in a variety of situations.

A friend of mine, Dr. David Lee, is an engineer who works on global GPS systems. Here is a paraphrased version of his explanation about how GPS systems work (personal communication, August 27, 2018):

> Out of 30 satellites in space, the GPS receiver picks the best four satellites to be used by where they are in the sky. The most accurate destinations are determined when one satellite is overhead and the other three are on the horizons with good separation. If the satellites are clustered together overhead, a place of destination could be determined, but it would likely not be correct.

Think about how much more accurate and interesting an understanding of and the posing of solutions to problems of practice could be when we start from the higher ground of valuing and accepting differing perspectives rather than only accepting or listening to

BAD GPS GEOMETRY

GOOD GPS GEOMETRY

"Navigation satellites with poor geometry for Geometric Dilution of Precision (GDOP)" and "Navigation satellites with good geometry for Geometric Dilution of Preicision (GDOP)" by Javiersanp (https://commons.wikimedia.org/wiki/User:Javiersanp) is licensed under CC BY-SA 3.0: https://creativecommons.org/licenses/by-sa/3.0/

those who think the same way we do. We can listen with the intent to find the best destination, solution, or accurate information regarding the problem based on the synthesis of the two perspectives shared in a typical one-on-one coaching situation or with multiple perspectives when collaborative teams work together to solve complex problems such as "Why don't our seventh-grade students understand how to balance equations, and what can we do about it?" Valuing different opinions and being okay with everyone not producing the same signal can result in innovative and effective problem solving.

Do we really value others' opinions or thoughts? What happens when we automatically discount, dismiss, or exclude people for any reason?

As players in the field of education, we rely on our knowledge. It's our brains that got us here. We have all been to college; we've had to prove we understand things; we've had to take tests. *Educator.* The word means someone who knows things and then tries to help others learn the things he or she knows. Members of knowledge-based professions may mistakenly assess their personal worth or the worth of others by giving too much attention or credence to who is the "smartest," who is the fastest thinker, or who has produced the best results.

Do we buy into the thinking distortion that we are smarter than those we work with and, thus, how could it possibly be worth our time to collaborate? Or, do we have the opposite thinking distortion: that we could never be as good as Mr. or Mrs. Amazing Teacher/Coach/Leader, so what could we have to offer when we get together to collaborate—better just keep our mouths shut?

At times there is an unspoken hierarchy in the teacher ranks. There are those who are considered the "really good" teachers, or the ones who have gained respect through student test scores, their amazing relationships with students, the extracurricular work they do, or the amount of attention shown to them by administrators. After that, there are the okay teachers: solid, but classified as not capable of doing anything amazing. And then there are those classified as somehow struggling—they may have some issues. Regarding this last group, there is fear they may bring everyone down, scores will be negatively impacted, their participation will not be helpful, and, because of them, the state will take over the school or there will be some other unwanted consequence.

There are serious problems with this human tendency to categorize our fellow workers. Number one, people cannot be accurately classified within a complex system where all information is not public. For instance, maybe the teacher with the lowest student test scores has been teaching a struggling population. Maybe the high-school students in his or her foundational math classes are court-ordered to go to school, are not interested in math, and are planning to drop out of school as soon as they are of age. Is it fair to classify that teacher as not able to share anything of worth during a team meeting or during coaching because he or she has no street credibility? Of course not, but there is an even deeper problem with this labeling. In our subconscious minds, we may be considering other people to be less than us, somehow unworthy of our attention or consideration.

This principle of valuing those we work with (and, in this case, specifically educational leaders and instructional coaches treating teachers as equals in a coaching relationship) is expressed by Instructional Coaching Group president Jim Knight (2007) in the following quote:

> The central idea behind instructional coaching is the central idea behind most democracies and republics: the belief that all people are created equal. We say we believe in equality, our votes count equally, and we share equal rights and responsibilities. . . . If teachers are truly equal, then their ideas must count. Equality does not mean that coaches and teachers have equal knowledge of every topic, but it does mean that the collaborating teacher's opinions are as important as the coach's, and both points of view are worth hearing. Teachers who work with instructional coaches should walk away from all interactions feeling like they are valued and that their opinions matter.

> (pp. 40–41)

An essential component of being an effective collaborator is to accept that *every* person is important and worth our time. This is a basic element that can be missed or swept under the rug when meeting with others, because we don't often say, "Okay, do you believe in equality and valuing everyone in the room equally? If not, you need to, or this isn't going to work." We don't say things like that, but a belief in equality is necessary. It is not possible for true collaboration to be present if we feel certain people aren't worth listening to, because we won't hear a word they say.

Collaboration Can Strengthen Individuals

Referring back to the GPS analogy, each satellite emits its own, individual signal, and the more diverse or unique the signals, the more accurate the GPS location. The reality is that usually it is one teacher alone with often 30-plus students most of the day, every day. Including ways to build strength and confidence in individuals within our collaborative structures supports the strength of both the individual and the coaching relationship or team interactions. Individuals want to feel safe when they share who they are and what they feel. When we create environments where each person feels included and important and is comfortable sharing insights from a place of confidence and acceptance, we honor, empower, and strengthen each individual.

In collaborative situations, one important norm to identify early in the process is balanced participation. We all know how irritating it is when the same person keeps talking incessantly during coaching sessions or team meetings. If protocols are put in place for everyone to have pretty close to equal opportunities to participate, and each person is considered able and is expected to formulate and share ideas, individuals will come to know and understand that their individual input is acknowledged and critical to the success of the work. This helps them build self-confidence, which can then spread to other areas of their lives, including their classroom instruction.

Don't Give Up on Collaboration, Even When It's Challenging

Sometimes collaboration feels great and produces amazing team synergy, resulting in high levels of excitement, productive energy, and seamlessly integrated work, resulting in breathtakingly positive student achievement, with high-fives and fist-bumps all around. Other times, it can feel like an exhausting, painful slog through knee-deep mud as conflicting personalities enrage and/or disengage at will, producing chaos, frustration, wasted time, and unhappy coworkers. It is likely we have all experienced both extremes at times and probably some middle of the road, mediocre collaborative situations that produce minimal amounts of excitement or student/teacher success. At times, we can experience all these things with the same people or even in the same meeting!

We may find we have to fix, patch, or at times rebuild our shelters and structures of collaboration, but we must not lose hope that the ongoing construction is worth the time and effort required. During collaborative situations, we can give ourselves permission to be real and bring our best, real selves (honest, respectful, kind), allowing and encouraging others to do the same. This may be uncomfortable at times, because often people don't agree easily or quickly. This is where general goodwill, assuming others' positive intentions, and structures and norms for participation become critical.

We may want to avoid judging a person's whole life and future opportunities for positive contributions by the limited time we may have had with them, especially if our interactions with that person were negative. People grow and change. The bad thing that happened when we were interacting with that person last week, or even years ago, will never be a comprehensive example of how that person might act in every situation, so we can't accurately say with surety, "That's just how he/she is." Whether family members or colleagues, it creates more space for growth and less drama within us and around us to grant people the time, space, and opportunity to grow out of our limited current perceptions of them, and hopefully they will grant us this grace as well. (This does not mean we should remain in situations where we are being mistreated; it means that we should recognize that the process of life, which includes physical and social maturation, typically wears away at our worst personality flaws.)

There is a protective and creative power within the concept of collaboration that would not be possible to generate on our own. Collaboration can offer us shelter and a variety of supports that can warm our bleakest days and help us regain our strength, reignite our purpose, and multiply our power. We are at our collaborative best when we are sincerely "with" others and enter collaborative situations with an open heart and open eyes, knowing that when you get a bunch of different people together, it's not always going to be utopia. We may need to be willing to attend extra meetings or stay in the room and listen to things we might not completely enjoy at that moment, because collaborating is well worth weathering the seasons and storms that may accompany addressing tough problems with a variety of personalities, agendas, and circumstances. And who knows, maybe just the opportunity to work through personality and situational difficulties will provide us with critical life lessons that will prove helpful to us in future teaching/coaching/leading opportunities. At TCT, our coaching has improved when we have faced challenging circumstances. For example, here is an anonymous comment from a teacher who participated in team and individual coaching during school year 2017–2018:

> My coach is an amazing professional. She never gave up on us even when faced with difficult personalities, teaching us to mesh and work together. Her show of love, faith, positive attitude and tenaciousness are what make her an amazing coach and person. I look forward to always seeing her and having her push me in ways without feeling rebellious. BEST EVER!

Educators are on the front lines, working to counteract the negative effects difficult societal issues have on children. Educators can help each other mount an effective defense against these challenges. There is the issue of poverty that makes life feel hard and hopeless to so many of our students, their parents, and to the educators themselves, who may be struggling to support their families on a teacher's salary. There are the challenges of technology: How do we help our students use it as a tool and empower them to not let it take over their ability to think on their own? In the words of former sociology professor Nicholas Carr (2011):

> One of the greatest dangers we face as we automate the work of our minds, as we cede control over the flow of our thoughts and memories to a powerful electronic system, is the one that informs the fears of both the scientist Joseph Weizenbaum and the artist Richard Foreman: a slow erosion of our humanness and our humanity. It's not only deep thinking that requires a calm, attentive mind. It's also empathy and compassion.
>
> (p. 220)

Mental illness, evidenced by the rising number of suicides, has also become a major concern (Klass, 2018).

Coaches can and do serve as lifelines, helping teachers address these challenging issues. One topic that has come up often in our coaching practice is "How can we balance the instructional focus of coaching with the need to support teachers who are struggling with mental illness? How can we provide what is needed without moving into the world of counseling, which we are not qualified to do?" The following story is an example of one way to handle this type of challenging situation:

> One teacher I worked with was struggling with serious depression. She began to take a lot of days off, even when she had important work to accomplish. Together we had determined specific coaching goals that she seemed very excited about, but she was able to complete only a few of the action steps. Some days she couldn't seem to manage anything at all. The little encouraging quote clipped on a wire

place-card holder that read, "I have hope, and I know how to use it!" and the "Believe" bookmark I had given her were on her desk every time I came to visit. Those little things meant a lot to her.

There were numerous difficult issues in her personal life: continual betrayals, separation from family, the death of a pet, so much loneliness. One day she told me she felt suicidal. I didn't know what to do. I had signed a confidentiality agreement and didn't want to break it. I comforted her the best I could, encouraged her, and did my best to empathize with the deep level of despair she was experiencing. We had built a good relationship over time. I loved her and felt badly she was going through so much hardship.

I considered what to do, and then knew I had to report what was happening. The principal of the school and the district handled the situation wonderfully. On a particularly bad day, the HR department came to the school and kindly arranged for her to take time off to work through the situation with professionals who could help her. As a result, she was able to regroup, then return to work and finish the year successfully. I felt relieved and thankful for how it all turned out. The situation was beyond my expertise; it was necessary for me to collaborate with people who could add their signal to the mix, so that we could calculate the best course of action to accurately meet her needs. I was grateful she didn't hold it against me that I had shared my concern with my boss and HR. She thanked me often, and we parted friends. I could have just let it go, thinking it was just a passing thought, that she didn't really mean it, but I'm glad I didn't.

How I wish people never felt this way, but many do. Love and concern expressed in a variety of ways will never be regretted, no matter how a mentally ill person deals with his or her situation.

The following professional development activity is designed to help teachers/coaches/ leaders identify current challenges they are facing and then determine how collaboration can help them face those challenges. The next step after identifying challenges and how collaboration could help solve them would be to choose to implement one idea that was generated.

Reflect and Connect

You can complete this activity individually or on poster paper with others. On the outside of the triangle, identify and record current storms or difficulties educators face (or personalize this to your situation). Then, on the inside of the triangle, note how collaboration can help you weather these storms. The point of this activity is to recognize that together we can survive and thrive, no matter what difficulties come our way!

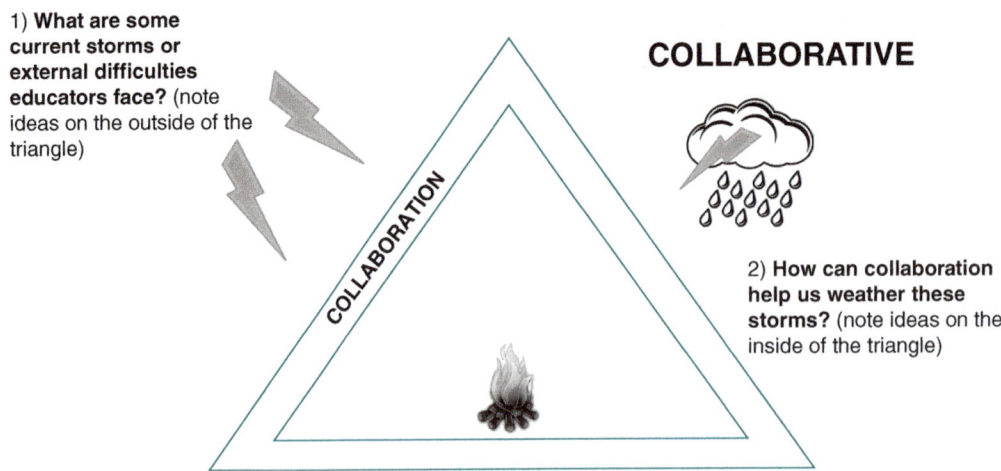

1) **What are some current storms or external difficulties educators face?** (note ideas on the outside of the triangle)

COLLABORATION

COLLABORATIVE

2) **How can collaboration help us weather these storms?** (note ideas on the inside of the triangle)

Examples from participants at the Teaching, Learning, and Coaching (TLC) Conference 2014.

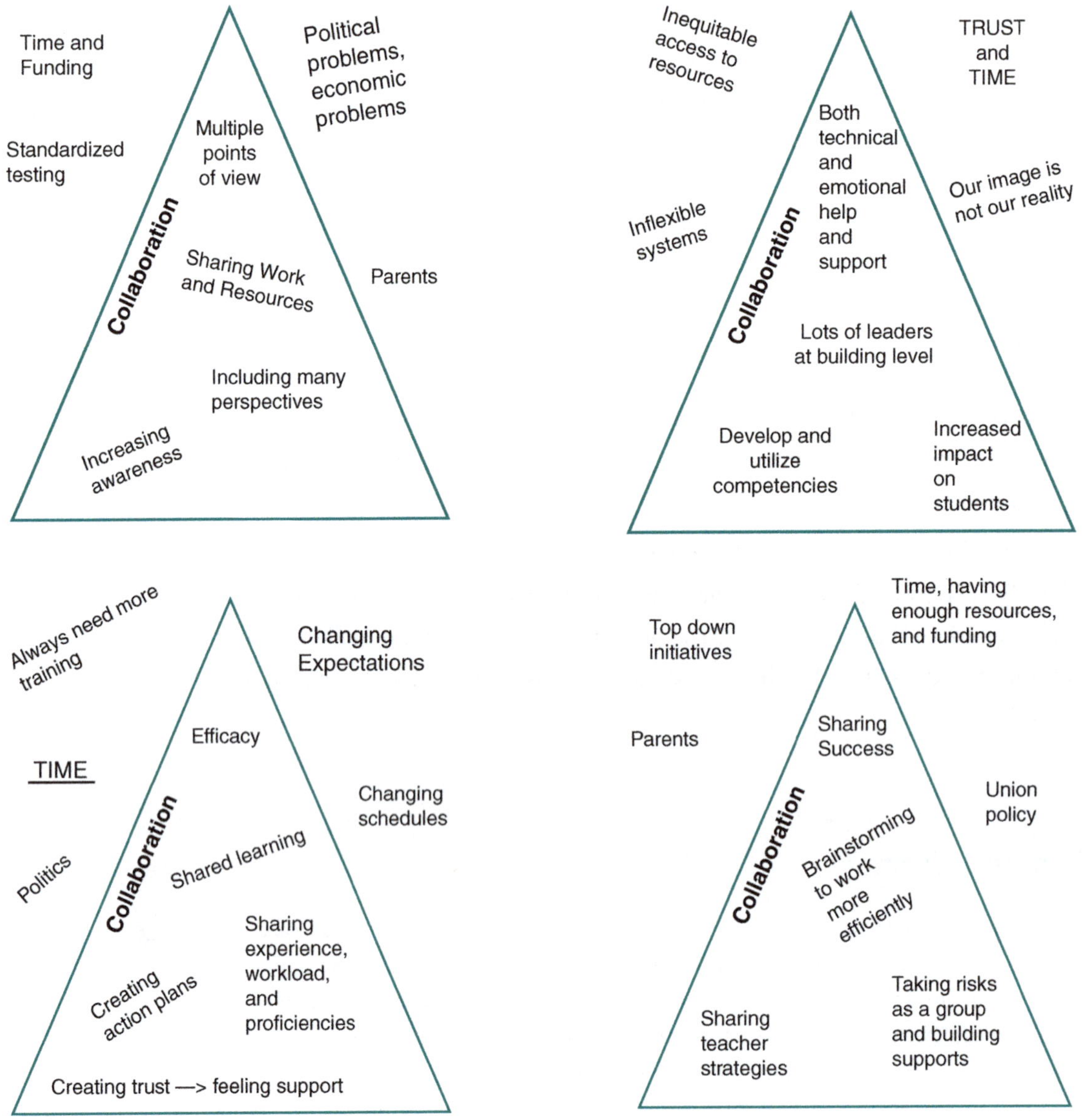

Triangle 1 (top left)

Time and Funding

Standardized testing

Political problems, economic problems

Parents

Collaboration

Multiple points of view

Sharing Work and Resources

Including many perspectives

Increasing awareness

Triangle 2 (top right)

Inequitable access to resources

Inflexible systems

TRUST and TIME

Our image is not our reality

Collaboration

Both technical and emotional help and support

Lots of leaders at building level

Develop and utilize competencies

Increased impact on students

Triangle 3 (bottom left)

Always need more training

TIME

Politics

Changing Expectations

Changing schedules

Collaboration

Efficacy

Shared learning

Sharing experience, workload, and proficiencies

Creating action plans

Creating trust —> feeling support

Triangle 4 (bottom right)

Top down initiatives

Parents

Time, having enough resources, and funding

Union policy

Collaboration

Sharing Success

Brainstorming to work more efficiently

Sharing teacher strategies

Taking risks as a group and building supports

Collaboration gives us strength, shelter, and hope knowing that together we can overcome whatever challenges are placed in our path. With our colleagues (who can become our friends) as we stand shoulder to shoulder fighting for kids against difficult circumstances, we create havens where we can work in safety and joy.

We can find support and shelter within the structure of collaboration.
Together, we can change environments of fear and stress to havens of hope.

We do this by:

- Believing in each other and in our profession

- Coaching each other to provide: 1) Higher levels of academic and personal success for students, and 2) Rejuvenating support systems for teachers that address both academic and social/emotional needs

- Being willing to whole-heartedly join our colleagues in constructing external structures and internal commitments to produce collaboration with enough power to ignite positive change

If you're not quite ready to believe wholeheartedly in collaboration, I get it. I found it hard to want to spend the time, be willing to listen to others, and share my own ideas. Yet it was and is well worth the effort. Hearing different perspectives, acquiring useful resources, and gaining a greater understanding of where we (our grade level, school, district) were and where our best destination could be were wonderful benefits of collaboration. For me, some of the most important benefits were the hope and friendship I found when I wholeheartedly jumped in. I gained lifelong friends, forever connected as we passionately pursued the same goals: to create enjoyable and meaningful opportunities for kids, empowering them to be happy and successful in school and in life. There is joy and freedom inherent in the work of teaching, coaching, and leading when many are sincerely and creatively working together to benefit the lives of children, teens, and young adults.

Collaborative Self-Assessment

1. Take this self-assessment before you set an intention to consciously find ways to become more collaborative.

2. Implement some of the practical application (PA) or professional development (PD) ideas found throughout the chapter and in the section following this self-assessment. You could also reference some of the collaborative S.O.A.K. supports found on the mini-poster at the end of the chapter or generate your own ideas.

3. In a month or so, take this self-assessment again to see whether you have been able to improve your thoughts, motivations, and behaviors surrounding the important coaching characteristic of being collaborative. Reference the following synonyms as you personally determine what being collaborative is and determine how to make it a more conscious part of your daily life: *partnership, cooperation, synergy, alliance, relationships, teamwork* (Frazier, 2014).

	Strongly Disagree	Disagree	Neutral/ Not Sure	Agree	Strongly Agree
	1	2	3	4	5
I see collaboration as a powerful way to generate new ideas and creatively solve problems.					
I come to collaborative situations (coaching, teamwork) prepared and willing to share my best thinking. I have courage and confidence to share my thoughts, see myself and others as equals, and have prepared any homework needed to add depth to the discussion.					
I can set aside my ego and unhelpful biases when working in collaborative situations. I listen with respect to people who may not share my opinions.					
I research, organize, implement, and adhere to structures designed to maximize collaborative time.					
I am sincerely interested in what the person I coach and/or my colleagues have to say.					
I practice basic courtesy in collaborative situations. I use positive language, do not interrupt, stay on topic, and keep the overarching focus on student learning.					
Column Totals:					

Grand Total: _____

What totals mean: 26–30 = Collaborative Rock Star, 21–25 = Very Collaborative, 16–20 = Sort of Collaborative, 11–15 = Some Collaboration Is Happening, 6–10 = Could I Step It Up? 0–5 = Would Becoming More Collaborative Be a Useful Goal?

Practical Application Ideas for Collaborative

For Coaching

A professional agreement is a great way to begin the collaborative structure of instructional coaching on a solid foundation.

Here are some ideas of what to include:

- Share the purpose of your coaching program. (Maybe something like this: "To deliver instructional coaching in a way that values and strengthens the hearts and minds of teachers resulting in quality instruction for students.")

- Determine the frequency of services and time commitments expected or possible for both teacher and coach.

- Share that continuation of coaching services would be based in part on the implementation of collaboratively determined action steps.

- Clearly explain that coaching assistance and paperwork are not part of a written evaluation by administration.

- Note that the coaching program is not legally responsible for advice or the outcome of teacher evaluation or employment, either positive or negative. Coaching can help teachers score higher on their evaluations or even play an important role in helping teachers retain their jobs. Most situations turn out positively, but not every time with every teacher. A way to explain this is that the teacher being coached takes ownership of and responsibility for the decision to implement suggestions offered. Implementation of suggestions and use of resources provided are subject to personal instructional delivery preferences and style. In other words, we don't take credit for all the great strategies the teacher implements, or the things that might not go as well. This has not been a problem at TCT, because goals are collaboratively developed, so whether the implementation of the agreed-upon strategies goes well or not, the goal is still worked on typically until completion. However, it's good to state this up front.

- Explain the tools used to provide evidence of teacher and student growth and coaching impact (e.g., surveys, assessments, feedback, engagement data).

- Explain coaching delivery options (action plan conferences, observations, reflective feedback conferences, modeling/co-teaching, analysis of video, analysis of student work, analysis of assessments, lesson planning sessions, etc.).

- Determine levels of confidentiality. It could be stated like this: "Assistance is confidential between parties involved." Stated this way, the level of confidentiality coincides with what the teacher prefers. For instance, teachers may want to have the coach include team members or a principal in the coaching process, or they may want discussions with the coach to be in complete confidence. The level of confidentiality is determined up front.

- Include any district, state, or federal laws that may apply to coaching situations. For example: Videotaping of special education students and students whose parent permission is not granted will be excluded from view.

- Set professional expectations for both the coach and teacher, such as "E-mails will be responded to within ___ hours."

Both the coach and teacher sign the agreement. The agreement can be referenced as needed throughout the coaching process. Personally, I have never needed to refer back to it, and it always scares me a little bit to address some of those possibly sticky things at or near the start of coaching, but it benefits both the coach and the teacher to start out with clarity and address any possible uncomfortable situations or problems up front. I can remember only one person who refused to sign the agreement, and in that situation, it was probably a good thing.

(Continued)

(Continued)

For Teams

Establish norms for team discussion (take care of your needs; balanced participation; professional management of electronic devices; stay on topic; use positive, professional language, etc.).

A favorite tool at TCT for checking in with team members (just as teachers do with students) when working toward determining a course of action is a three-sided table tent to see where each team member is in his or her thought process. One side of the table tent reads "YES"; another side reads "NO"; and the final side reads "MAYBE, or NOT SURE." Stopping the discussion and asking for everyone to share where they currently are in the decision-making process works well, because then individuals think through what they have heard and mentally summarize briefly before they flip their table tent to the appropriate side. This simple, novel, and sometimes funny process is a quick way to get to the meat of a discussion. It works because each team member shares his or her YES, NO, or MAYBE/NOT SURE, then is given the opportunity to explain why he or she feels that way, so that the team can benefit from all perspectives. Sometimes one person realizes he or she is holding up the process unnecessarily or, alternatively, defends his or her point so successfully that others change their minds. Sometimes it turns out that everyone agrees or disagrees on a course of action, and a lot of time is saved!

Collaboration Killers: The following list could be used as a check-in with team members. The leader of the team could ask team members to anonymously circle any roadblocks to effective collaboration they are noticing. Then, the topics most noted could be addressed.

- There is no meaningful purpose for taking the time to meet.

- Students are not central to the work or conversation.

- Real issues that matter (elephants in the room) to those called to the meeting are habitually ignored or intentionally avoided.

- Meeting has no organizational structure, no plan/agenda, no professional norms or protocols, so time is wasted on off-topic or less than productive conversations.

- Goals/plans with action steps and timelines are not determined.

- Individuals do not have or are not willing to take on specific assignments.

- Individuals do not complete their part of the work.

- The same individuals end up doing the bulk of the work.

- No follow-up plans are created to ensure progress.

- Leadership's and team members' roles and responsibilities are unclear. (How much power does the team lead have, and what is he/she responsible for? Can this be collaboratively determined up front? Job descriptions?)

- There is no time built into meetings to get to know people and build relationships/few celebrations/little opportunity for connection/no fun ☺

When teachers ask for help implementing structures for group work with their students, the most common concern I hear is this: "When I was in school, I hated collaborative groups, because I always got stuck with all the work. Because of this, I don't like to use them with my students." Unfortunately, this problem is not always resolved when adults work together in teams. Part of choosing to enter structures of collaboration that offer shelter and support includes being willing to shoulder one's fair share of the "chores." Everyone must take on a reasonable amount of the workload, as people may dislike working with the people who don't pull their weight.

Conclusion

Collaboration demands the best that is in us. We can be that shelter, that support for others, if we are willing to reach out and show up when things get tough. We can learn new, exciting teaching strategies that propel our students to new heights; we can get better when we work together. If we want collaboration to work, we should come to it striving to be our best selves, checking our egos at the door, losing the need to have our brilliance shine the brightest, honoring and valuing others' opinions, sharing things in respectful ways that are energizing and thoughtful, and always keeping our students' best interests in mind to provide that central overarching focus everyone can agree upon.

We can conquer the challenging issues we face when we are dedicated to finding ways to combine our intelligence and hearts to benefit both the child (or teacher, or teammate) standing next to us and others who might need our support somewhere within our world as a whole. Compassion, empathy, and caring are powerful beyond measure. Not only do they create a better world for those on the receiving end of actions taken because of them, but they are the stock, the base, of a kind of comforting internal soup, simmering with gentle, creative thoughts and contemplations of kindness where we can live peacefully. In the words of Stephen Post (2011), director of the Center for Medical Humanities, Compassionate Care, and Bioethics at Stony Brook University:

> So the heart, and not our location on the face of the earth, is ultimately the place where we dwell. The key to hope is focusing our minds and hearts inwardly on the ways and power of love so as to reflect this focus in our relationships with others. It does not take too much time to hear the call of our hearts, and it is the only call that makes our species worth struggling for.
>
> (p. 159)

COLLABORATIVE ~S.O.A.K. ~ Sometimes learning penetrates best when we are relaxed and not trying too hard to make it happen.

Stress-free Opportunities to Absorb Knowledge   Choose what works for you. (Like a "Collaborative" Bath Bomb infused with personalized nutrients)

Quotes
- "Alone we can do so little, together we can do so much." —Helen Keller
- "It is literally true that you can succeed best and quickest by helping others succeed." —Napoleon Hill
- "None of us, including me, ever do great things. But we can all do small things with great love, and together we can do something wonderful." —Mother Teresa
- "It's amazing what you can accomplish if you don't care who gets the credit." —Harry Truman
- "You can make more friends in two months by becoming interested in other people than you can in two years trying to get other people interested in you." —Andrew Carnegie

Music
- "It Takes Two" Rob Base & DJ EZ Rock
- "Takin' Care of Business" Bachman-Turner Overdrive
- "Lean on Me" Bill Withers
- "Yellow Submarine" Beatles
- "What a Wonderful World" Louis Armstrong
- "That's What Friends Are For" Dionne Warwick
- "All for One" High School Musical
- "Olympic Fanfare and Theme" John Williams

Statements affirmations
- For coaches: My work with teachers creates positive forward movement in teacher efficacy and student growth.
- I recognize and value the inherent worth of each person despite challenging personality quirks.
- By choosing my thoughts, I create a warm and peaceful internal world full of goodwill and kindness.
- Coach to teachers: Your interactions with students leave them inspired and empowered!
- Student voices are honored and respected in your presence.
- For teachers: I design opportunities for students to work together, so that they can practice academic and interpersonal skills that build confidence.
- "Teamwork makes the dream work!" —John C. Maxwell

Books poetry stories
- "It Couldn't Be Done" Edgar Albert Guest
- "Working Together" Janice Walkden
- "The Bundle of Sticks" Aesop
- The Teamwork Fable—"4 Oxen & the Lion" Charlie Scott
- Stone Soup Jon J. Muth
- Horton Hears a Who Dr. Seuss

Art
- Aerial Flamingos The holy grail of wildlife photography: Bobby Haas
- And the Symbol of Welcome Is Light Norman Rockwell
- Cake Baking African American Art
- Summer: Harvest Time Pieter Brueghel
- Reach for the Stars Millie134 (Kindergarten Auction Project from the Oak Hill School)
- Head of the Charles (Silk screen print)
- Connie Crosby

Videos movies
- Don't Be So Defensive (TED Talk) Jim Tamm
- Zootopia (2016)
- Effective Collaboration: 1:57 clip from the Big Bang Theory Funny; available on YouTube
- Union is Strength Together We Aspire Together We Achieve Marlon Modeste (YouTube)
- Toy Story (1995)
- Wonder Woman (2016)
- The Last Jedi (2017)
- The Mighty Ducks (1992)
- Monsters Inc. (2001)

Movement other ideas
- Wide-Legged Standing Forward Fold — With a yoga partner, mirror the pose, grasping the partner's hands between their legs.
- Chair — Stand back-to-back with a yoga partner and do a chair pose with backs touching to support one another.
- Oil: lavender
- Stones: blue calcite; amazonite
- Color: lime green

What new beauty and adventures await us when we merge our thoughts and gifts in service to others.

NOTES

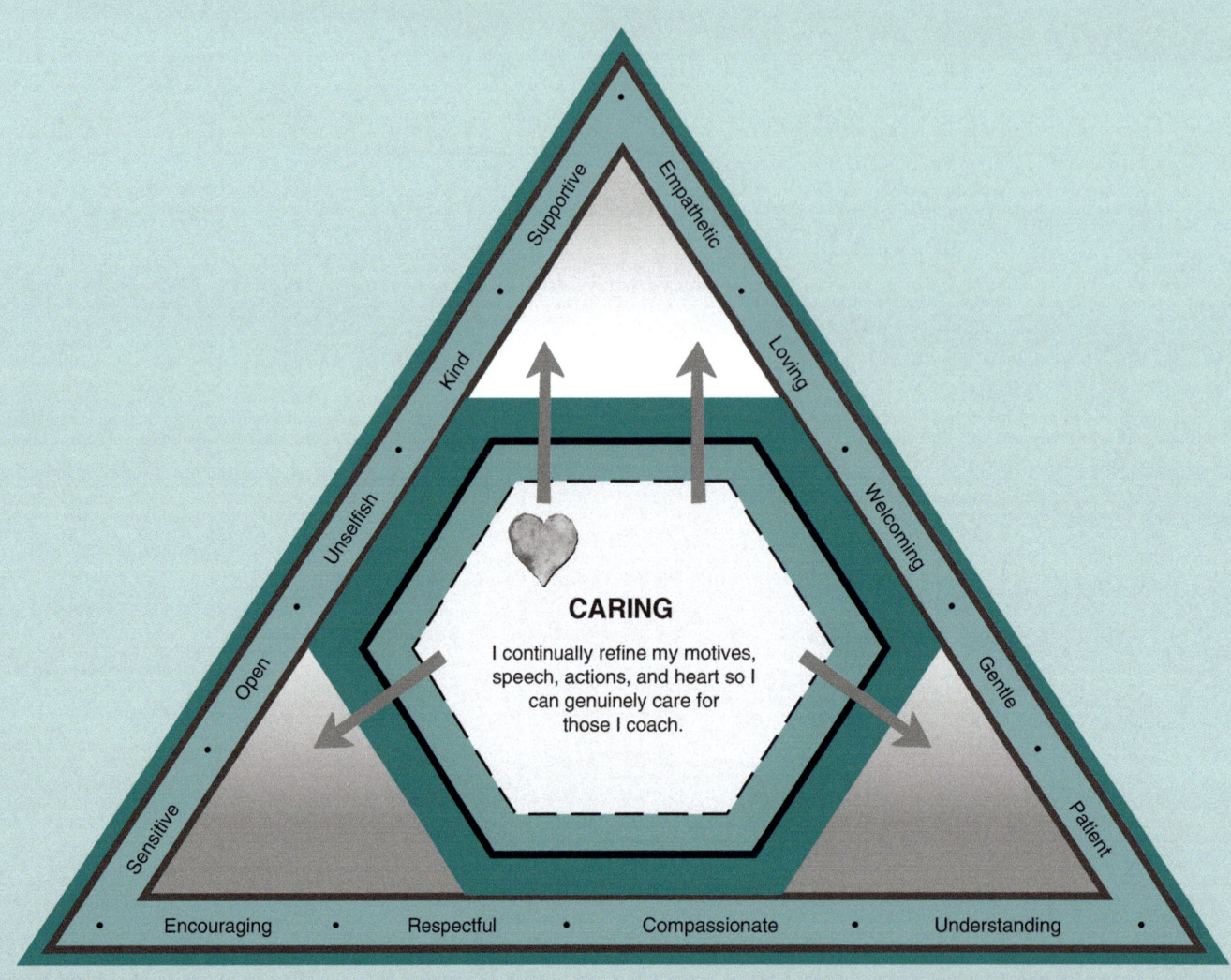

The people I coach know and feel I am interested and invested in their growth and happiness. I show my love and caring in a variety of ways. I take the time to get to know the people I coach and provide personalized support that matters to them.

Caring

2

Love is the learner's balm, smoothing and softening sharp edges that may exist in presentation or personality, allowing learning to be deeply absorbed.

Gifted With a Halo

We are judged to be better than we deserve when people know we care about them.

I live in the mountains of Colorado. One teacher wanted to meet for our coaching sessions extremely early in the morning before school many miles from my home. I was late, more than once. Sometimes I schedule coaching appointments too close together. I'm not always on time. Yet, 100% of the people I coached a few years ago (2013–2014) gave me a perfect score in the area of promptness. This makes no sense (see below)—or does it? Why would a person be scored highly on something he or she didn't do very well? Similarly, no coach could be as good as the survey below indicates. What happened here?

TEACHERS COACHING TEACHERS
2013 – 2014 Teacher Survey
Coach & Teacher Effort Survey
Your feedback is important to us!
Please take a minute to rate the effectiveness of the support you received and your effort for change and growth. Thank you!

COACH EFFORT FOR	Weak to Strong	COACH EFFORT FOR	Weak to Strong
Professionalism	1 2 3 4 ⑤	Professionalism	1 2 3 ④ 5
Courteousness	1 2 3 4 ⑤	Courteousness	1 2 3 ④ 5
Promptness	1 2 3 4 ⑤	Promptness	1 2 3 ④ 5
Resources	1 2 3 4 ⑤	Resources	1 2 3 ④ 5
Strategies	1 2 3 4 ⑤	Strategies	1 2 3 ④ 5
Teacher Change, Growth	1 2 3 4 ⑤	Teacher Change, Growth	1 2 3 ④ 5

Compliments	Suggestions	Why did you rate yourself this way?	How can the coach support you for increased change?
• Knowledgeable • Professional • Kind spirit • Creative • Intuitive and supportive	Keep being such a great, professional, and helpful person!	There's always room to improve, grow, and change.	If you could keep working with me (forever?), that would be very helpful! haha

Daniel Kahneman (2011), a Nobel Prize–winning economist, might describe what happened in this way. System 1, the emotional, intuitive, and automatic part of the brain, took over and dismissed the logical evidence that System 2, the rational and controlled part of the brain, could provide about the number of times Rebecca was late. System 1 deemed this evidence located in memory as irrelevant because of the emotional frame developed within the teacher's mind from memories of positive experiences she had experienced with the said Rebecca. System 1, because of the positive emotional frame of mind surrounding Rebecca, could quickly refer to the frequency and emotional impact of positive experiences with Rebecca and conclude that the evaluation was really more of a reflection of the relationship, so the need to numerically analyze and be completely accurate about the evidence to the contrary regarding promptness at coaching appointments by Rebecca was minimal.

If this is not a reason to just *be nice* and do caring things for people, I don't know what is. Here is a way to be cut a little slack, which is an awesome find because none of us is perfect! (Note to self: Do as many caring things as possible for husband, kids, and grandchildren so their brains will automatically ignore my faults!) I'm not exactly sure what specific actions could have biased those teachers' responses toward System 1, but, like many coaches, I feel love and concern for those I work with and try to do small things that matter to them (specific ideas are included at the end of this chapter). I deeply appreciated the "halo" that was gifted to me in this situation. I like the way Stephen Post and Jill Neimark (2007), in their book *Why Good Things Happen to Good People*, defined being nice (aka civility): "Civility is doing small things with great kindness" (p. 156). Coaching is the "how," it is the sharing of small things that provide the necessary bridge between theory and practice, it is the nuts and bolts of success, and we are loved for doing it well.

Research on Caring

As mentioned in the introduction, the research that prompted the development of the model upon which this book is based (Frazier, 2014) included an analysis of the evaluations of 43 instructional coaches (279 evaluations) by other coaches, the teachers they served, and their administrators. The results indicated that coaches who were ranked high in mentoring skills (as being supportive, guiding, and a knowledgeable resource) were also ranked high in the areas of instructional supervision, staff development, and community involvement.

Let's think about this for a minute. It does not exactly follow that a person who supports and guides people well could be considered good at almost everything, but that is what the study showed. The community involvement section of the survey could be accounted for very visually and logically—for instance, did the coach show up to school events or not? Could System 1 have triggered an override of System 2 again? Could the halo effect be a factor here as well? Coaches who did not score high in mentoring skills—or, in other words, did not offer effective support, guidance, and coaching—also scored lower in other areas of the evaluation.

The research, both mine and Daniel Kahneman's, indicates that if evidence of caring is not shown during interactions with others (i.e., if the people you coach are not provided enough positive emotional experiences in order to develop an automatic positive mindset surrounding the essence of "you"), you might be branded as less than what you actually provide.

What motivates teachers to engage in and stay in a coaching relationship, especially if it is voluntary and there will be work involved? Well, one of the reasons is that it is natural to want to work with people who are likable. In a 2005 study by Tiziana Carsciaro and Miguel Sousa Lobo, employees in four organizations (including a university, a technology company, an IT corporation, and a global luxury-goods corporation) were asked to choose whether they would prefer to work with a lovable star, an incompetent jerk, a competent jerk, or a lovable fool. As expected, everyone wanted to work with a lovable star, and no one wanted to work with an incompetent jerk. The results became interesting when employees had to choose between a lovable fool and a competent jerk.

Consistent results for all organizations showed that if they had a choice, people would typically choose to work with someone who had greater likability (the lovable fool) over competent skills provided by a jerk. People who are considered "inherently attractive (lovable) . . . are considerate, cheerful, generous" (Carsciaro & Lobo, 2005, p. 4). They are the ones we want to work with; they are the people we like. Looks like getting the job done is not all there is or all that matters. Most of our time is spent in process. We typically don't linger for long in the fleeting moments of success, and if the working process bites most of the time because we are working with a jerk, most of our time spent at work will be less than enjoyable.

Rushworth Kidder (1994) and colleagues at the Institute for Global Ethics conducted lengthy interviews with 24 international "ethical thought leaders," including writers, university presidents, religious leaders from many nations, United Nations officials, and heads of state. From these interviews, eight core values emerged as values that were shared the world over. The number-one value was love. It was defined in this way, as recorded by Craig Johnson (2012): "Love: Spontaneous concern [caring] for others, compassion that transcends political and ethnic differences" (p. 394).

Why do people in our educational environments still try to sweep love and caring under the table? Are they embarrassed by it, is it not scholarly to care? Are they not sure how to verbalize or validate it? Does it not fit well within our systems and structures, our previous NCLB or current ESSA requirements?

I vividly remember the vertical team meetings we had every couple of weeks when I was a new teacher in 2002. We would meet before school, and a teacher who had produced some of the highest test scores in the district would inform us how to prepare students for state assessments, so that our school could do well and no one would have to worry about the state taking us over. The woman was scary, and the situation was scarier. After those meetings, my stomach hurt, and I wanted to quit. At home, I referred to the meetings as "Vertical Scream" meetings because I felt like screaming when I went to them. I was so afraid that I could never measure up and do all the things she did in order to have students score well on the state tests. As a staff, there were times when fear reigned in our halls and in our hearts. We taught bell to bell with rigor, with discipline, and with data. My teammate jokingly said one day, "I wouldn't be surprised if I had to record a data point every time I go up the hall to visit the restroom."

As I began getting to know the scary teacher better, I learned she had been an art teacher and was creative and student-focused along with being extremely capable of making sure her students were ready to be assessed in the 5.5 months she had to get them there. In her grade, the state assessments began in February. She was a stellar teacher. I would go after school to see her teach extra classes organized for students whose data showed they needed extra support. She was amazing. She was the cream of the crop, an outstanding teacher with the highest of test scores. Naturally, we were all in shock when she decided one year to just quit. So successful, so done.

She explained to me that she didn't like what she had become, a taskmaster every second of every day in order to get students to where they needed to be for a test. Gone were the social studies and science lessons (the untested subjects), the projects, the creative extensions, the joy. There wasn't time to care; the focus was on numbers, not people, because the numbers would determine our survival as a school.

During this time in education, it became unprofessional to spend time doing "touchy-feely" things like having class discussions to solve problems; taking time to explore, extend, and enjoy content; or finding out how students were doing. Colleagues were exhausted and stressed trying to keep up with the data demands and preparing for the never-ending testing. Since then, it has just gotten worse. Recently, one of the people I coached showed me her school's testing schedule. From March through May, there were high-stakes assessments scheduled almost every day.

In the words of Nel Noddings (2005), professor emerita of child education at Stanford University:

> Students spend weeks—even months—preparing for and taking tests. Many of us believe that these are weeks that should be spent exploring new ideas, discovering new interests, extending established ones, and expressing thoughts in art, drama, music, and writing. In particular, we believe that students should be given opportunities to learn how to care for themselves, for other human beings, for the natural and human-made worlds, and for the world of ideas. This learning to care requires significant knowledge; it defines genuine education.

(p. xiii)

Making time to locate reliable resources and act on foundational best practices of human interaction—as summarized in one sentence by Nel Noddings, "The living other is more important than any theory" (p. xix)—is still not a daily priority in education. This does not make sense, because people are what education is about!

Most educators know the brain does not function well under stress, for students or for teachers. I'm surprised my students learned anything the first year I taught, because I felt so much pressure all the time. When I heard the squeal of the brakes on the school bus each morning, my stomach tied itself into knots. Our brains are not designed for stress that lasts over 30 seconds (the amount of time it would take to quickly react to a predator's attack). Stress does damage, serious damage, to all kinds of cognition. It damages executive functions and memory and can hurt motor skills. Long-term stress negatively affects performance (Medina, 2014).

Unfortunately for many educators, thinking about trying to remedy this serious fight-or-flight conflict creates a "resistance is futile," hopeless type of dynamic in schools because damaging requirements for students, teachers, and leaders are often embedded within systems. Educators, particularly those who teach in urban environments and poor communities, are exposed to survival-level stress on a regular basis because of how schools may be penalized if their students don't perform well (on standardized tests). Why are our systems set up to add more destructive stress to the difficulties that poverty already exacts from our students?

We need to care, and we need to be cared for. It is necessary, it is foundational, yet we sometimes find ourselves in situations that don't support the implementation of caring actions or even allow the topic to be credibly discussed. In 2014, I was facilitating a team of 10 representatives from different organizations, schools, and coaching programs in our district. We were designing a district peer-coaching program. During the process of determining a purpose for our work, I introduced caring as a key component of coaching. Immediately, a firestorm of emotions erupted that lasted through parts of two meetings. It was something I felt strongly about, but a few vocal others didn't feel it was necessary to mention it as a guiding value. As the facilitator, I didn't want to be too pushy or show my emotions too much. I was surprised by the backlash against caring and felt blindsided by the response. My internal voice was saying: *Seriously, you don't think coaches who are helping others improve need to care? Why then, would teachers, who must sometimes make uncomfortable changes, be motivated to listen to the coach if the coach doesn't care about them?*

I was very tempted to go off on all the research and interviews I had recently conducted and become a major competent jerk, which I probably did to some extent. But luckily, less vocal people eventually spoke up, and "caring" was kept in our purpose statement. I have since thought of this situation many times. I have a running joke with the person who most loudly opposed adding "caring": We bring up funny situations now and then about how she should care more and how I care too much.

Why is it so hard to talk about this? A friend of mine who occupies a leadership role in a large school district in our area said talking about caring is difficult because there are many who think caring is something we do at home, not at work: It doesn't belong there; it's inappropriate in the workplace. Yet is it even possible to disengage from being human? Why is it easier for some people to show care and feel cared for? According to Daniel Goleman (1995), one of the reasons that it is hard for some people to understand how others feel is that "People's emotions are rarely put into words; far more often they are expressed through other [nonverbal] cues . . . tone of voice, gesture, facial expression, and the like" (p. 96). Goleman suggests that people who "have no idea what they feel themselves, are at a complete loss when it comes to knowing what anyone else around them is feeling . . . for all rapport, the root of caring, stems from an emotional attunement, from the capacity for empathy" (p. 96). The benefits of being able to read emotional cues are extensive.

Harvard psychologist Robert Rosenthal and his colleagues (1977) gave 7,000 people throughout the world a test of empathy (caring), the PONS (Profile of Nonverbal Sensitivity). In this test, a young woman expressed a wide range of feelings through a series of videotapes. The videos were edited so that one or more types of nonverbal communication were eliminated. The test subjects, who viewed the videos, had to determine the woman's emotion from the other nonverbal cues that were still present. The findings for those who could read emotional cues well were that they were more popular, more sensitive, more outgoing, and better emotionally adjusted. When a similar test was given to 1,011 children, those who showed skill at reading nonverbal emotional cues did better in school, even though their IQs were not higher than those of children who did not read nonverbal cues well. They were also more popular and emotionally stable.

There is an aspect of reputation associated with successful (or unsuccessful) coaching. If a coach is considered "popular" or someone others want to work with, it's probably because they've developed, among other things, the ability to create "rapport, the root of caring," as described by Daniel Goleman (1995, p. 96).

 If we can summon the guts to say words like "love" and "caring" at work, we should go ahead and say them and see what happens. If we do, we can positively change our working climates by verbally acknowledging their importance in our human interactions. Carrying a torch for caring may take some courage. Yet, we can be tough enough to weather the frustrations of people who may have trouble getting verbally in touch with their emotions, those who are uncomfortable with this "softer side." Maybe we can share with them how wonderful it can be to be gifted with a "halo" because of the kind things we have done, so that we are not vilified when we do make mistakes.

Could a substantial part of the problem be that many educational leaders and legislators either have not taken the time or do not as yet have the capacity to understand, communicate, or value teachers' and students' emotional needs? If this is true, important emotional and social components of academic and personal success for students, teachers, and leaders have been and are being ignored.

I believe that at some point, the importance of empathy and caring in education will be acknowledged (some educational communities already embrace this research wholeheartedly), but not if people who understand its importance keep quiet. Who knew educators would have to fight for the concept of caring within their own profession? Unfortunately, many educators do not understand or cannot give voice to what a positive impact understanding and implementing the ethic of caring can have. It can increase our effectiveness as leaders, teachers, and coaches in our interactions with students, colleagues, parents, and others within our school communities.

The importance of caring can be backed up with research; it is not just fluff. We can look to Daniel Kahneman, Tiziana Carsciaro and Miguel Sousa Lobo, Nel Noddings, Rushworth Kidder, Robert Rosenthal, John Medina, and Daniel Goleman, the authors and researchers mentioned above, along with the research and model used in this book to communicate the need for caring in our educational environments. We may need to explain with data and in a scholarly manner to effectively make the case for caring. It has strengthened my confidence and resolve to know I have a foundation of credible research to support caring, one of the central components of the Characteristics of Effective Instructional Coaches model.

In coaching situations, it is particularly damaging to come off as uncaring or "holier than thou." Jim Knight, in *Focus on Teaching* (2014), described this as people feeling "one down" (p. 12). If we come off as dismissive and elitist, there is zero chance that we will be effective. Rob Anderson and Kenneth Cissna, as recorded in the book *Meeting the Ethical Challenges of Leadership* by Craig Johnson, poignantly described what *not* to think or be like when listening to teacher concerns while coaching or in any other situation where a continuing relationship is desired:

> It's not that your position is weak, or that I disagree, or that you are wrong, or that you are unethical, or that you are ignorant or insensitive. It is that *you* are actually beneath response. Your points are self-defeating and patently absurd; they don't have the force necessary to stimulate reply. Yet I reply anyway, demonstrating my largeness, my open-mindedness, my commitment to dialogue. I reply anyway, to dispense with the argument, characterizing it so that other audiences, less astute than I, will not be taken in.
>
> (p. 288)

Sadly, I have experienced being treated like this, and you probably have too. What is really damaging is when these types of people (those who have internally concluded they are inherently better than other people because they have demonstrated greater capacity by the fact that they are in the position of leader, or maybe they've had more schooling, they have a superior work ethic, or whatever they may use as faulty evidence) occupy leadership positions in companies, schools, and families. Let's make sure we, as teachers, coaches, and leaders, do not give off a dismissive and counterproductive vibe of fake caring and superiority.

The following quote, by business professors Rabindra Kanungo and Manuel Mendonca (1996), sums up the essence of the stories and results of the research noted in this section:

"Leaders [and coaches] are truly effective only when they are motivated by concern for others" (p. 35).

One of the best ways I know of to remind myself what caring looks like, and to remember why I chose a nurturing profession, is to think of the people who had the biggest positive influences on my life. The following story is about my favorite teacher.

Remembering Why

"Hey, Tomato." "We want a pitcher, not a belly itcher!" My throat was dry, my lips chapped from licking them nervously preparing for this, the first fast-pitch softball game of the season for the Franklin Dragons. It was my inaugural experience on the mound, and I didn't want to let my teammates down. We had practiced so hard, but we really weren't very good, so if the other team hit too many balls, it was going to be a long afternoon in the dirt for us. I threw the grayish, worn softball into my mitt a few times for good measure, put my feet together on the plate, and prepared to let the first pitch fly. Then, the worst taunt I could have imagined as a preteen just starting to worry about her looks was heard from behind the backstop: "Hey, toothpick legs, you can't pitch." This one hurt because it was kind of true; other people thought so too, and they snickered. I was 10. I was scared and hurt. Why were people so mean? I looked toward our side of the field, hoping for some kind of support. There he was, Mr. Bush, my coach and fifth-grade teacher, with his twinkly eyes, white goatee, and rigid posture. He gave me the nod, his nod, which consisted of one slight dip of his chin accompanied by continuous, rock-solid confident eye contact. My heart took courage. *If he knows I can do this, then I can—he wouldn't lie to me.*

Mr. Bush was a World War II veteran. No one who knew him would disagree that he should be classified as a stellar representative of the greatest generation. He had trouble writing on the board, because his arm was shot up and full of shrapnel. He taught us to love our country and the flag and understand that people had died for us so we could go to school and learn. He took us on field trips, brought in disgusting animal organs so he could "show" us science, played movies backwards just for fun, and took us sledding at his home in Black Forest, where his wife made us fried doughnuts. In short, he loved being a teacher, and he loved us. To those who hadn't experienced his love, he may have (from the outside) looked to be a crusty, old, and rigid man, but Mr. Bush had earned my love and trust. And when he said to my mom, "That girl can do anything," I believed him, even if I didn't believe it myself.

I threw the first pitch, a high ball, then settled down and threw three strikes in a row. The batter never had a chance. Mr. Bush was an authentic influence in my life; he was real; he cared. I knew it rationally, because of the things he did for me and for the other kids. I knew it in my heart, because of how he made me feel and what I could accomplish because of it.

Some people come into our lives and leave without a trace. Others leave footprints on our hearts and we are never the same.

—Flavia Weedn (1999)

Some of the greatest sessions I've had the opportunity to facilitate with teams of teachers and coaches have been when we have taken the time to connect with why we went into teaching and coaching in the first place. Who influenced us to take on these giving, busy, and sometimes difficult roles?

It has been my observation that teachers who were not able to identify a person they had connected with in some way, someone who had modeled how to care—maybe a parent, a friend, or a former teacher who had demonstrated how to teach or how to "be" a force for good—often struggled to form positive relationships with students and colleagues. How much they needed someone to show up for them in this way and, in the process, facilitate the healing of their hearts. How important it is that we find ways to access and share the best parts of ourselves as we strive to effectively do this work of coaching—which, as Elena Aguilar (2013) wrote, "is at its essence a nurturing structure" (p. 15).

Reflect and Connect

Three Words

This activity was designed to provide an opportunity for PD participants to identify and connect with role models and mentors from their past or to be inspired by others' experiences to elevate their teaching/coaching/leading. The activity begins with the presenter asking the following question: "Has there been someone who was able to positively impact your choice to be involved in education, to the point that you have never forgotten the contribution he or she made to your life?" Then the presenter asks the participants to go through the following steps:

1. On the card provided below, participants note whether the person was a family member, a friend, a teacher, or another type of person, by circling the category that applies to their situation.

2. Participants are then asked to think of three words or phrases that trigger a visual memory of the person chosen. (For me, it would be Mr. Bush, Franklin Elementary School Baseball Field, and Toothpick Legs.) Participants then record the three words on the lines provided at the bottom of the left side of the card.

3. Participants then record some details about the experience on the right side of the card.

4. After participants record their thoughts, they are asked to move to a corner of the room labeled with the appropriate category (family member, friend, teacher, or other); then they are asked to find a partner and share their story. *(Continued)*

(Continued)

Who Influenced Your Choice To
Be Involved in Education?

Circle One: Author, Historical Figure, Situation

FAMILY   FRIEND   TEACHER   OTHER

3 Word Journal
By Randal A. Wright

Thoughts and Feelings about this foundational experience:

_____

Choose 3 words That Trigger a Memory:

_____

- The words need not make up a phrase or sentence

_____

- If possible, always include a person, place, or thing in your three-word summary

_____

_____

- Choose three words that refer uniquely to that particular experience

_____

_____

_____

_____ _____ _____

_____

Sometimes it is what we do, the small caring things, that can open the door to communication and connection with those we coach, our students, and our families. Often, what connects our coachees, students, or family members to us is our meaningful responses to their situations and feelings and how we address needs they may have. Connection is also strengthened when there is a personal desire on the part of the coachee, student, or family member to make changes (Fillery-Travis & Lane, 2007; Schein, 2002). Similar to my need for support in a new situation as an inexperienced pitcher being made fun of by the crowd, I needed Mr. Bush right then, and he was there. In that moment, the mix of my pressing needs and his authentic desire to be a good coach and support my well-being merged, and a lasting connection was forged.

Not every opportunity to work with others will result in lifelong relationships, but as coaches, teachers, parents, and leaders, we would do well to pay attention to how people feel, show up then in some way, and provide support that demonstrates an understanding and acknowledgment of the person's needs and/or situation.

Remember and Acknowledge What's Happening in the Lives of Those You Coach

When a coachee mentions something that is around the corner in his or her professional or personal life, write it down after the session, then send a note or leave a message on their voice mail wishing him or her success in the upcoming situation. Staying current with what your coachees are doing shows you are paying attention and lets them know that even after you've walked out the door, you are still thinking about them and wishing the best for them.

For example, have you ever been in the hospital or needed support when you couldn't take care of yourself? Do you remember who showed up for you? I still remember a delicious pork roast surrounded by baked apples seasoned with cinnamon and nutmeg that Joan Wixom brought to my home. It was perfect timing: I had just returned home from the hospital after surgery, was extremely hungry, and had no food in the house. Joan, whom I didn't know very well and had never done anything nice for, brought me that roast 19 years ago, yet her influence, the love I have for her, and even the flavor, texture, and aroma of the roast remain with me. Let's first "observe, then serve" (Burton, 2012). As we consider and reflect upon situations we see teachers struggling with, we can make an educated guess as to what is truly needed and then act. By doing this, we can make the most of situations that would magnify the impact we could have, enhance relationships, and make life better for those we coach.

More Reasons to Care

Teachers often mentally dwell in a land of exhaustion, trying to decide over and over again (depending on the demands of the day) whether they have the tenacity to provide strenuous, dedicated effort over time for higher purposes determined by others. For example, the mantra of a useful program presented for teachers in our district goes like this: "Our kids are worth whatever it takes!" (Rogers, 2011). Though this is heartfelt and true much of the time, the reality is that our priorities change based on circumstances we face. Health becomes a priority over detailed lesson planning when a teacher has a chronic disease. Attending professional development offerings after school becomes a lower priority when a teacher needs to be home to regularly engage with a teenage child beginning to have a drug problem.

Leaders and coaches whose opportunities to influence others' attitudes of commitment to bottom-line issues such as student learning or enrollment numbers would do well to remember the automaticity of Daniel Kahneman's (2011) System 1. If people have had positive emotional experiences with a teacher, a coach, a school leader, or even a school in general, their brains will search for what is good about that person or situation, to reinforce their automatic "good" assumption. The brain will be lazy and avoid searching for negatives (even if they exist) about the school, teacher, or coach.

Schools, districts, and education in general must change the no-nonsense "work till you drop and it will be worth it" or "accountability at all costs" attitude or risk ending up bankrupt, dysfunctional, or closed for business, similar to many of the high-accountability, no-nonsense firms in Jim Collins's 2001 best-seller *Good to Great: Why Some Companies Make the Leap—and Others Don't*. The push for accountability and a "one size fits all" mentality has pressed many key stakeholders in the field of education (principals, students, and teachers) to the point of unhealthy stress. We cannot force people (students, teachers) to participate in systems that are not set up to value them and expect them to be happy, motivated, and highly productive. What have we been leaving out of our action plans that could help us be more effective and happy as leaders, coaches, and teachers? Here are a few ideas:

> Love is an extreme case of appreciation. However, as leaders we don't appreciate enough, much less love enough. In fact, we have banned the "L" word . . . in spite of the fact that the "L" word is the substance that unifies teams, builds cultures, fosters commitment, and bonds people to an organization.
>
> (Cashman, 2008, p. 99)

> In our rush to reform education, we have forgotten a simple truth: reform will never be achieved by renewing appropriations, restructuring schools, rewriting curriculum, and revising texts if we continue to demean and dishearten the human resource called teacher on whom so much depends . . . [we cannot] transform education if we fail to cherish—and challenge—the human heart that is the source of good teaching.
>
> (Palmer, 2007, p. 3)

Research is taking us a different and better way, guiding us down a path of emotional and heart awareness, bringing us to the truth that positive emotional connections and climates nurtured by individuals, schools, and districts engender loyalty, motivation, and forward movement over time. We all want work to be something we look forward to every day, not something to dread.

In *Firms of Endearment*, by Rajendra Sisodia, David Wolfe, and Jagdish Sheth (2014), companies that showed they valued all stakeholders (including employees) by creating opportunities for social, emotional, experiential, and financial support *outperformed* (by large margins) firms analyzed in the book *Good to Great* whose basic values were more rigid and focused on no-nonsense strategies and numeric accountability. Over time, firms that acknowledged, accepted, and put strategies in place that met stakeholder needs (including the needs of employees) to "be in love," as summarized by Michael Fullan in *Six Secrets of Change* (2008, p. 26), stayed strong over time and continued to prosper. One notable example was the comparison of Wal-Mart (marketed as a great choice for better prices and convenience, but with a less than stellar track record of employee support) and Target (focused on providing a quality experience for customers and staff, with classy products and competitive prices). Wal-Mart stock had been stagnant for five years, whereas Target stock had grown by nearly 150%.

A new term, the "helper's high," has been coined to bring attention to the benefits that occur not only to the person who is the recipient of a kind, thoughtful, or altruistic act, but also to the helper (Post, 2011, pp. 33–35). Along with increased longevity, better pain management, and lower blood pressure, helping others (which is central to coaching) results in happiness for the helper. When we engage in acts of kindness, or support others in some fashion, the reward center of the brain produces the neurotransmitter dopamine, which elevates our mood. Taking on the role of coach provides us with unlimited opportunities to show we care, and to be there for others during the highs and lows of their professional and personal lives, thus giving us many chances to enjoy the positive effects of supporting others: good moods, living longer, less pain, lower blood pressure, and more joy! We just have to be careful that we don't overdo it and forget to take care of ourselves (self-care ideas are listed in the Practical Applications section at the end of this chapter).

Legacy

Mr. Bush took the time to be a true lifelong friend, coach, and teacher, who continued to check in on me throughout my life. He came to my wedding and gave me a beautiful gift when I was in my 20s; he invited my boys to go sledding at his home when I was in my 30s. When I was in my 40s, he and his wife attended a special event my fourth- and fifth-grade students put on called, "Thanks, America!" and he brought me flowers. He was even thinking of me when he went on a vacation to Hawaii after he had retired. While he was there, he sent me a small tile with my name on it in Hawaiian: "Peke," for Becky. He showed me what it meant to authentically love and what a powerful influence for good that caliber of love could make in my life.

None of us is perfect, but Mr. Bush's imperfections went unnoticed or were quickly dismissed in my young mind and heart. I was willing to give him the benefit of the doubt when difficult situations arose (like when he didn't take us to A&W after a game we played really well but didn't win—a tragic occurrence to a 10-year-old who loved root-beer floats), because I knew he genuinely cared about me.

What Mr. Bush likely didn't realize was that because he showed me how to care, he had provided a pure example for me to refer back to when building relationships with others. He had no hidden agenda or ulterior motive. Test scores were not a focus, though my classmates and I excelled under his direction. Sometimes I remember how he did it, and sometimes I forget all the details, but I never forget how important and strong I felt because of his influence.

Caring Self-Assessment

1. Take this self-assessment before you set an intention to consciously find ways to become more caring.

2. Implement some of the practical application (PA) and professional development (PD) coaching ideas and/or caring S.O.A.K. supports found in the body of the chapter and below, or use some of your own ideas.

3. In a month or so, see whether you have been able to improve your thoughts, motivations, and behaviors surrounding the important coaching characteristic of caring. Remember the synonyms of caring, identified by coaching authors and by coaches like you, as you define what caring is and determine how to make it a more conscious part of your daily life: *empathetic, welcoming, unselfish, supportive, sensitive, respectful, loving, encouraging, gentle, patient, open, kind, compassionate, understanding* (Frazier, 2014).

	Strongly Disagree	Disagree	Neutral Not Sure	Agree	Strongly Agree
	1	2	3	4	5
I think about others at least 50% of the time.					
In the past week, I've done at least three things for others that were not expected or required.					
People often express their deep appreciation for specific things I've done for them.					
I express my love and appreciation daily in a variety of ways.					
My motives are pure and include others' best interests.					
I contribute money and/or volunteer my time to charitable causes that make life better for others.					
Column Totals:					

Grand Total: _____

What totals mean: 26–30 = Caring Rock Star, 21–25 = Very Caring, 16–20 = Sort of Caring, 11–15 = Some Caring Is Happening, 6–10 = Could I Step It Up? 0–5 = Would Becoming More Caring Be a Useful Goal?

PA

Practical Application Ideas for Caring

Show You Care Through Creative Notes

Give teachers ideas of how they can show students they care about them. As part of TCT coaching protocols, teachers have the opportunity to survey students to collect feedback about their teaching. One pattern we have seen repeatedly over the past six years—district-wide, and particularly in middle school—is that students do *not* feel that their teacher (1) Shows in a variety of ways that he or she likes them and (2) Shows an interest in them and the things they like. Little things mean a lot. It is not extremely difficult to greet students at the door and ask them how the game went, notice their new haircut, or provide a positive word or inspirational note for them. When teachers do these things, they provide evidence to students that they are liked and valued. This is important for adults as well. The following note ideas can be personalized to provide positive messages to coaches, teachers, or students:

Creative Note Ideas to "Lift" Others:

- I mint to tell you . . . (specific feedback on a slip of paper with a mint attached).

- Your influence/your kind deed/your quality work/your leadership/your extra effort/your thoughtfulness can never be erased from my heart (note with an eraser attached).

- The difference between ordinary and extraordinary is the little "EXTRA" effort you showed/provided for your students/teachers! (Attach a stick or pack of EXTRA gum.)

- You are a JOY to work with! (note with a mini-Almond Joy candy bar)

- Thanks for providing MOUNDS of inspiration to your students/teachers/coaches! (note with a mini-Mounds candy bar)

- For a very POPular student/teacher/coach (Pop Rocks or can of pop).

- Thanks for chewsing to grow! (gum)

- I'm not an Airhead (Airhead candy), thanks to you ☺

- Your implementation of _____strategy/professionalism with colleagues/positive presence/positive communication with _____/attitude/effort/behavior/ability to pay attention today was SWEET! (sweet treat)

- Nothing is impossible; even the word itself (with a few little adjustments) says, "I'm possible."

- If Plan A doesn't work, the alphabet has 25 more letters—stay cool. (mint, popsicle, or alphabet soup)

- Things fall apart so other things can fall together. Trust in the growth process of life. (small puzzle that fits together to form the word "Courage" and/or a small plant)

- Believe in What We Do, Believe in Kids, Believe in You!

The Importance of Self-Care

Good people need to know how to draw boundaries around themselves so they can have time to take in nature, exercise, enjoy friends, and get away . . . learn to say "enough" and entrust others to take over for a while. . . .

. . . We have our own unique physical and psychological limits. We all have certain fundamental needs to be loved and cherished, to be secure and respected. Helping others is not at all about getting rid of these needs, but rather about fulfilling the universal need to give and live better. . . .

(Continued)

(Continued)

. . . We still have to look after ourselves, get some rest, eat well, and organize our lives to be effective in the long run. . . .

. . . When it comes to cultivating generosity and kindness, however, do it all the time.

(Post, 2011, pp. 49–51)

Self-care is an integral part of being a caring person. If it is not included as part of a caring persona, the coach or leader runs the risk of limiting opportunities due to neglect of the instrument, the body and soul of service, you! It is, obviously, a good idea to avoid a drooping persona. When we can't think straight because we are exhausted, because we look and feel haggard, worn, and unhealthy, it's difficult to do much of anything.

We, as coaches, would like to model what it means to be a healthy, dynamic individual. By making time to keep ourselves healthy, we provide the means for quality coaching to be accomplished. For example (this situation is referred to over and over, but that's because it makes the point so well), think of oxygen masks in an airplane. Adults are directed to put their mask on first, in order to help children. This may seem counterintuitive, because our instinct would be to make sure the child was okay before we worried about ourselves. However, if we try to help someone else while we're gasping for breath, we run the risk of not being able to help at all, thus limiting future opportunities to coach, lead, or parent. Our health is necessary. We must find a way.

During the past 10 years, I have been extremely busy and at times overfocused on trying to be the perfect boss, the perfect coach, the perfect parent, and a straight-A student. Many days, I have run myself ragged to stay on top of everything at my job and at school and to meet the needs of those in my care. While working full-time, I obtained two master's degrees, earned national board certification, volunteered regularly, and began a doctoral program. During this intense time in my life, I was also grieving the passing of my mother, who had always been there for me and had provided daily loving support to me throughout my life. I gained 60 pounds. I felt terrible. I made a conscious decision two years ago to put my health first, even though it might mean I would not be putting in as much time at work or school.

As a result, I narrowed my focus to the most important elements of my coaching and leadership responsibilities—I found this also allowed *others* to breathe, because they didn't have to keep up with all my extra stuff. I was amazed that even in spending less time on my homework, I was still able to do well in the most difficult doctoral classes. The benefits of taking time to change my diet and increase the amount of exercise I was getting resulted in my having more energy, endurance, and mental speed. I also ended up giving myself permission to have more reasonable timelines. I was honestly kind of shocked that the world didn't fall apart when I decided to let my doctoral work take longer than I had originally planned. Self-care applies not only to our bodies, but to our minds as well.

One of the best ways to illustrate a healthy mental attitude of self-care (or, in other words, self-kindness) is for me to share a story about my boss. She is extremely professional and inspiring. Everyone I know loves and respects her for her kindness and integrity. Plus, her clothes and outfits are always elegant, and her presence exudes a sense of being completely put together at all times. Recently, she was experiencing an exceptionally busy time as the head of the professional development department in our school district and had to arrive at work very early. About halfway through the day, someone pointed out to her that she had two different large and dangly earrings on. My boss laughed and said: "There was a time when I would have been mortified that I had not noticed that and would have taken them out. Now I can leave them in and not worry about it—even wear them as a badge of honor." The acknowledgment that life gets hard at times and sometimes we are not at the top of our game is reality—how refreshing it is to have a leader who understands that! Sometimes we just get to be human and let things go. At our next meeting, a number of women wore mismatched earrings in her honor.

Love is the learner's balm, smoothing and softening sharp edges that may exist in presentation or personality, allowing learning to be deeply absorbed. I began this chapter with the thought above. I wrote it while trying to encapsulate the essence of caring in education. We absorb learning best when we feel cared for and supported—when we know that our coach, the person imparting his or her thoughts and wisdom to us, understands and wants the best for us and is willing to take specific, meaningful actions to help us internalize the learning and grow as a person and as a professional. I hope you feel this way about what you are learning as you read these pages. It is my wish for you to know and feel your worth and to understand the nobility and power that is inherent in quality teaching and coaching. Know that you have an imperfect friend who is walking this path with you. Together we can become better every day.

> Just remember what it's like to walk a mile in their shoes, because as an instructional coach, you're coming in and you're correcting perceived things they may be very self-conscious about . . . it's that understanding of what the people you're coaching are going through. I think that's the most important aspect of coaching.
>
> Coach #15

Images by https://www.istockphoto.com/portfolio/fizkes

CARING ~S.O.A.K. ~

Stress-free Opportunities to Absorb Knowledge

Sometimes learning penetrates best when we are relaxed and not trying too hard to make it happen. (Like a "Caring" Bath Bomb infused with personalized nutrients)

Choose what works for you.

Quotes	Music	Statements affirmations	Books poetry stories	Art	Videos movies	Movement other ideas
"Love is an extreme case of appreciation. However, as leaders we don't appreciate enough, much less love enough. In fact, we have banned the 'L' word . . . in spite of the fact that the 'L' word is the substance that unifies teams, builds cultures, fosters commitment, and bonds people to an organization." —Kevin Cashman	"Just Put Some Love in Your Heart" Lionel Richie	**For coaches:** I have the strength to lift others. I quickly see and internalize what is positive and create more of it through my awareness. I am conscious of others' needs. I lead a purposeful life that influences many.	"If I Can Stop One Heart From Breaking" Emily Dickinson	A Flower for the Teacher Winslow Homer	Look on YouTube for short clips, or immerse yourself in "Caring" by watching the whole movie!	Cobra Pose
	"Lean on Me" Club Nouveau					
	"You've Got a Friend in Me" Randy Newman and Lyle Lovett		"Song of Life" Charles MacKay	Mother Playing With Her Child Mary Cassatt		Fish Pose
	"Angels Among Us" Alabama and Demi Lovato		The Challenge to Care in Schools Nel Noddings	Sharing Is Caring Bill Holkham	Big Miracle (2012)	
	"True Colors" MattyB				Charlotte's Web (1973 or 2006)	Camel Pose
"If there is any kindness I can show, or any good thing I can do to any fellow being, let me do it now, and not defer or neglect it, as I shall not pass this way again." —William Penn	"Testify to Love" Wynonna Judd	**For teachers:** I believe in teachers! I bless the lives of students every day with my love, dedication, and preparation.	"The Little Boy and the Old Man" Shel Silverstein	The Good Samaritan Vincent Van Gogh	Frozen (2013)	
	"Love, Oh Love" Lionel Richie					
	"I'll Be There" Jackson Five		"The Lion and the Mouse" Aesop	Caring-Girl [With Dog] Rudi Monterroso	The Blind Side (2009)	Oil: melissa
"Never let a problem to be solved become more important than a person to be loved." —Thomas S. Monson	"Love Can Move Mountains" Celine Dion	My positive influence paves the way for student success.		Auguste Reading to Her Daughter Mary Cassatt	Despicable Me (2010)	Stone: rose quartz
	"Wind Beneath My Wings" Bette Midler	My daily work is of immense value.	"Outwitted" Edwin Markham		The Grinch Finally Cares (2000)	Color: bright pink

Love is the learner's balm, smoothing and softening sharp edges that may exist in presentation or personality, allowing learning to be deeply absorbed.

NOTES

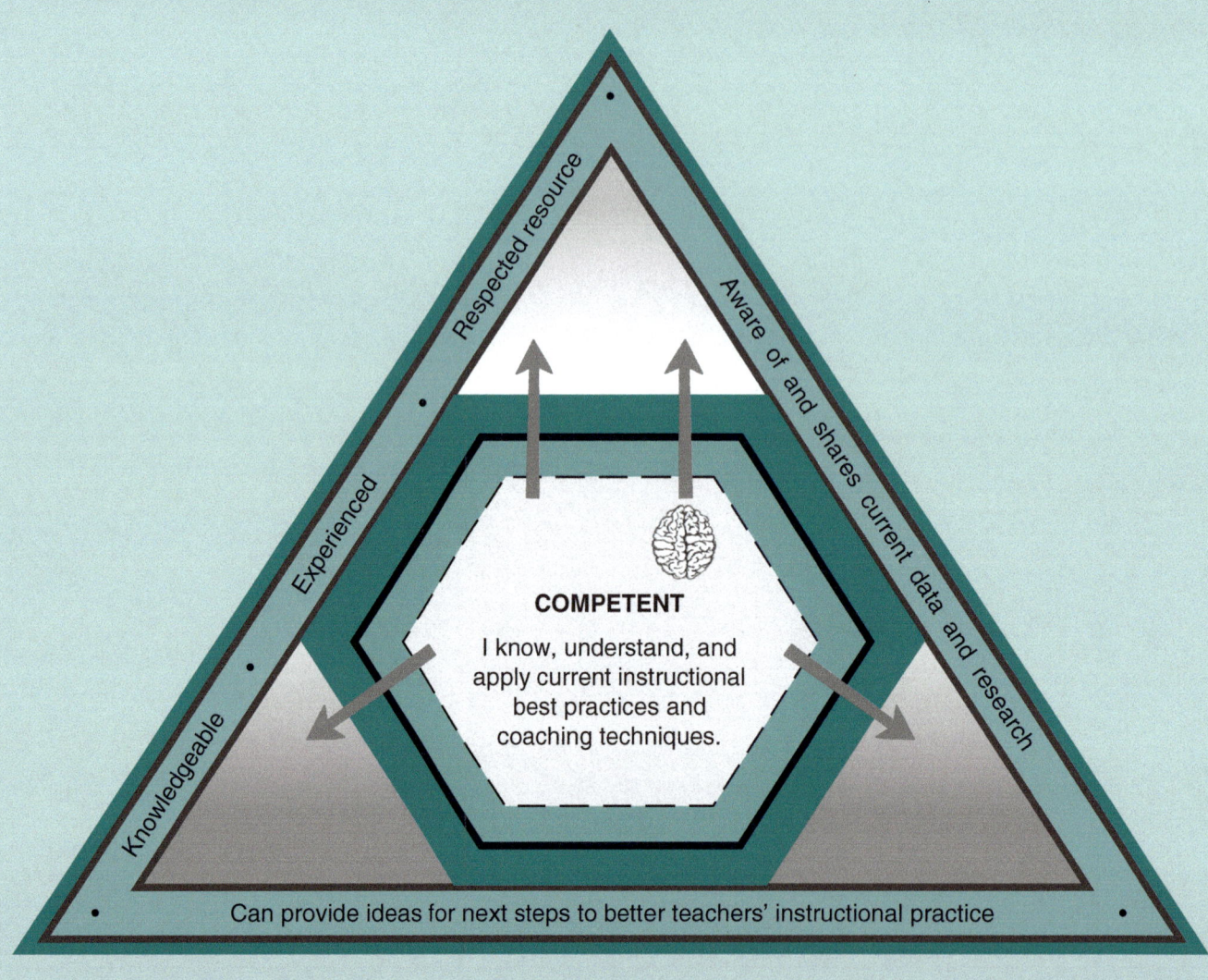

Respected resource

Aware of and shares current data and research

Experienced

Knowledgeable

COMPETENT

I know, understand, and apply current instructional best practices and coaching techniques.

Can provide ideas for next steps to better teachers' instructional practice

The people I coach can trust that I am experienced, knowledgeable, and continually learning. They can count on experiencing professional growth through their committed efforts and my quality coaching.

Competent

3

///

Having the necessary ability, knowledge, or skill to do something successfully.

English Oxford Living Dictionaries, s.v. "competent"

The definition of competent in this situation does not mean minimal or adequate, as some alternate definitions of the word might imply.

The characteristic "competent" occupies the right half of the central section of the model. Providing coaching that includes both competence and caring creates wholeness in the delivery of coaching, resulting in joyful coaching relationships that produce positive results.

What does it mean to be *competent*?

Yes	No
• Knowledgeable • Experienced • Respected—has a history of successes • Can break teaching into manageable chunks and share with teachers how to move forward step by step • Understands and applies current research and evidence-based practices and can facilitate the classroom application of current educational topics • Knows where to find quality resources • Can model effective instructional practice • Plans for coaching success • Provides a variety of instructional supports and processes for teachers to use as needed • Values, respects, and encourages each teacher • Exemplifies exceptional effort and commitment	• Knows everything • Is perfect • Provides minimal support only when it's convenient • Confident in past skills and successes, but not interested in continually learning or keeping up with new resources or technology • Figures it's okay to just be a caring friend who throws in some ideas now and then that worked in the past

In other words, when you are a competent instructional coach, *you* **and** *your colleagues* know that you:

1) know, understand, and apply current instructional best practices and coaching techniques;

2) can plan for, show, and share effective processes and practices; and

3) have a track record of success meeting the needs of students and teachers.

Being competent means that you have the instructional knowledge to plan and demonstrate quality teaching and coaching. It does not mean that you know everything.

The definition of a competent instructional coach can mean different things to different people. To a teacher, it may mean the coach has enough experience to help with the nuts and bolts of teaching and understands how to guide and support the teacher to move forward in his or her teaching practice. To a principal, it may mean a coach sees to it that school-based initiatives are supported and that students in the classes of teachers who are coached learn better than they did before the teacher had a coach (and there is data to prove it). To students, it might mean that their teacher does a better job explaining information and is nicer and less stressed.

Since coaches cannot know everything, how can we consider ourselves competent when situations arise that we have never encountered before? It's this simple: *Believe* you can figure out how to solve problems, just as you have with students in the past. Know that it is likely that—through meaningful collaboration, accessing quality resources, and good old tenacity—you and the teacher you are working with will be successful. You can trust in your ability to access quality resources and resource people, and remember that you weren't asked to serve in the role of facilitating educational problem solving for no reason. Typically, coaches are chosen based on proven academic success with students and their ability to work and play well with adults. Trust in those who put their trust in you to hire you to this role, and know you can always grow in your coaching abilities over time.

We have all heard the old saying, "fake it till you make it." In the role of instructional coach, this typically does not work. It's like trying to fake you can diagnose and treat a medical problem without the appropriate schooling and training, or trying to ace a competency-based exam on the details of programs in Microsoft Office without knowing how to use a computer. However, because coaches can't possibly know everything and haven't taught every grade and subject, they sometimes feel and/or are treated as less than competent. Sometimes coaches are considered by teachers to be administrator spies; and, when categorized this way, coaches can be treated unkindly, particularly by teachers who feel coaching has been forced upon them in some way. Teachers will try to find ways to protect themselves, sometimes by focusing on perceived deficiencies in someone who is genuinely trying to help them.

This happened to me a few times when I was asked to work with teachers whose grade level and/or subject I had not specifically taught. At times, when my competency was questioned, my first instinct was to fight back—to try to defend myself and explain how much I did know about students of that age; that I was a mother of three, understood about quality K–12 teaching practices, had been coaching for many years, had two master's degrees, was an NBCT, almost had my PhD, and had already successfully worked with many teachers (in almost all content areas, at all levels)—and I wanted to scream, "I'm not a rookie, and I'm not incompetent!"

Do not go to this place.

Sometimes we, as coaches, are put in situations where people feel inadequate just because they are being coached. A teacher trying to make a coach feel "less than" is making a natural attempt to equalize the professional and personal playing field. Teachers, especially those who did not volunteer to be coached, may be hesitant or resistant to accept a coach's help, because they feel they must justify that, as teachers and people, they are "good enough to be valued and respected."

Thomas Allen and Jeffrey Sherman (2011) found that when the human ego is threatened, bias toward others is increased, particularly for groups that the person feeling threatened is not part of or already has a bias toward. Have you ever heard teachers say, "Those kids can't learn because of their terrible home lives," or frustrated coaches say, "Some teachers are so resistant—I just wish they would listen and do the things I'm suggesting," or educational leaders say, "If some teachers were more intelligent, I wouldn't have to spell out everything they need to do." Maybe these individuals really believe their biased thinking; however, it is likely they are feeling unable to successfully complete the challenging work they are being asked to accomplish.

Roy Baumeister, Laura Smart, and Joseph Boden (1996) noted the fragility of the human ego when events or situations shed negative light on a person. Being more apt to share unhelpful biases toward others may stem from a need to boost self-esteem (Fein & Spencer, 1997; Sinclair & Kunda, 1999; Tajfel & Turner, 1986). Understanding this natural tendency to "kick people when *we're* down" can help us be more emotionally aware and avoid making sweeping biased judgments or blaming others when feeling personally vulnerable. We can also understand that a teacher may not be at his or her communicative best when feeling threatened.

The best thing to do when a teacher is critical of your competency as a coach is to not allow yourself to become defensive, but keep your focus on the teacher and on understanding and identifying what he or she would like to accomplish through coaching. In this situation, I like to think of Stephen R. Covey's (1989) fifth habit of highly effective people: "Seek first to understand, then to be understood" (p. 235). Once a teacher feels authentically heard, once he or she feels valued as an equal, and after one or two teaching goals have been met, the initial abrasiveness toward the coach due to the teacher feeling "less than" often naturally dissipates.

If you don't have the knowledge and/or experience necessary to help a teacher with a specific goal, be upfront about wanting to take some time to research the topic and look for strategies considered to be effective. Using your own and others' professional wisdom and looking for empirical (experimental and practical) evidence (Whitehurst, n.d.), you can usually find workable options for teachers. Great coaches are also great students. "Coaches can deepen their knowledge of teaching practices by devouring reading material about the teaching practices they share. Instructional coaches should read, reread, create mind maps of what they are learning, write notes, and create checklists" (Knight, 2011, p. 123).

Our own feelings of fear or inadequacy when facing uncharted waters are normal. Some of the best advice from an experienced, successful coach and educational leader, Judy Williams (2010), about helping teachers tackle problems the coach hadn't faced before, was "Think of what you would do in your own classroom if you faced this problem with your own students, then you'll know what to suggest." Modeling self-trust or a *competent state of mind* can provide a great example for teachers. To summarize Carol Dweck's (2014) takeaway for successful learning or moving forward in any endeavor, we focus on the word *yet*: I may not get it, I haven't learned it, I haven't succeeded at it, or I haven't figured this out . . . *yet!*

> *"As you believe,*
>
> *So shall you lead."*
>
> (Cashman, 2008, p. 55)

As the model suggests, *competent* coaching support can be accepted and shared effectively through the filters of *authenticity* and *quality communication*. A genuine desire to listen, to learn, to be real, and to access and provide valuable resources for the people we coach will facilitate teacher growth. Adults have automatic shut-off valves when listening to top-down advice that someone is trying to force upon them couched as help or support (Sparks, 2009). If coaches fail to communicate their expertise in a way that can be heard or accepted, it doesn't matter how much a coach knows, because that expertise will be discounted or not heard at all. Coaching requires emotional and social awareness to communicate components of quality teaching. No one likes to be told what to do, and adults will resent even competent support when it is presented poorly.

Being a competent coach involves desire and effort to learn about and understand education's big-picture topics and recurring day-to-day themes. Appendix A, "Competent Cliff Notes," provides a quick overview of current educational movements, policy innovations, professional learning, legislation, and research developments.

The rest of this chapter is designed to provide information about and help coaches support teachers when addressing the five most frequently requested/addressed/needed topics the Teachers Coaching Teachers (TCT) team has tackled over the past five years.

Why Teachers Need H.O.P.E.

Instructional coaches are in an influential position to help keep good teachers from quitting. Richard Ingersoll and Thomas Smith (2003) reported that 40%–50% of teachers leave within their first five years of teaching. A more recent study by the National Center for Education Statistics (Gray & Taie, 2015, p. 3) found the percentage to be lower, at 17% (with higher salaries and mentors/coaches being two of the main reasons teachers stayed). Either way, many teachers have had enough of teaching after only a few years in the profession.

There are many reasons for this, but following are three frustrations teachers face:

1. There are so many things, both physical and virtual, to keep track of and on top of, many of which have relatively little to do with direct "teaching" and being with students.

2. There is a stressful and constant expectation to perform at a high level (no matter how much experience you have), even though the teacher has limited control over many variables and is sometimes not made aware of what standardized student assessments look like.

3. Teacher evaluations and assessments for students are often analyzed in a way that illuminates deficiencies but expects proficiencies, leaving teachers and students feeling discouraged because when they did something well it was just briefly noticed, or maybe it was not noticed at all because it was an expectation.

If teachers feel that one year of bad scores could result in their letting their teams down, being part of the reason for intense scrutiny of their school by the district or state, losing their reputation or street cred, or even possibly losing their jobs, they may understandably experience high levels of stress, experience burnout, and want to quit.

In the 2012 MetLife survey of American teachers (Markow, Macia, Lee, & Harris Interactive, 2012), consisting of interviews of 1,000 teachers and 500 principals, teacher job satisfaction was shown to have dropped 23 points since 2008. The number of very satisfied teachers decreased from 62% to 39%, the lowest in 25 years.

Teaching is complex and layered. The landscape is always changing, and there are many parts and pieces to be understood, addressed, sorted, and synthesized to create the best learning possible for students. Gathering and organizing information so that it can be found and utilized after being buried deeply beneath the sediment of professionally complicated and sometimes emotionally heavy days is a skill coaches can help teach. On many teachers' desks and desktops, towering stacks of papers or e-files representing the leftover sediment of eras of the school year when each new initiative, copies of school or district policies that could be looked at later, stapled pages of computer program click paths, or handouts from brief half-day PD encounters—Cambrian, Jurassic, Cretaceous—we have all seen, experienced, and probably helped create the burdensome and rocky classroom landscape teachers must climb.

The impact of new requirements in many states where teacher and principal evaluations are now tied to student achievement results places the burden on individual teachers and principals to prove their worth or employability on, at times, seemingly endless rubrics. This has attuned some educators' internal GPS to locate the educational landscape at the bottom of Abraham Maslow's hierarchy of needs (1954)—in other words, they may find they are positioned in a not so healthy or happy place. When in this situation, individuals can conclude that teaching might not be able to provide them with the basics of life, safety, or opportunities to belong and be respected. These fears can impede educators' ability to reach self-actualization, the highest level—where, according to Maslow, positivity and happiness reign (Maslow, 1987, p. 22). The impact on teacher health and longevity in a sometimes "gotcha" type of environment, where many variables are outside an individual teacher's control, is difficult to measure, but when "Teacher ain't happy, ain't nobody happy," especially students!

What would happen if coaches could include, as part of their menu of options, support that would help teachers last in and love the profession? What if we intentionally built a competent, resilient mindset by teaching skills to inspire hope? This need for the components of H.O.P.E. (health, organization, positivity, and encouragement), as voiced by hundreds of teachers over the last five years, will be explained in further detail in Chapters 6 and 9. The coaches in our program have found that working on these pieces can significantly improve teachers' well-being and help teachers create both an internal and external environment that supports longevity and joy while facing the challenges that are part of the current teaching landscape. At TCT, we often receive feedback about how much these H.O.P.E. supports have positively affected the teachers we coach. Our inclusion of these sometimes hidden, yet commonsense, pieces of quality coaching have helped our coaching team achieve an average 99% customer satisfaction rating from about 60 to 70 teachers each year for the past five years.

Now let's begin our exploration of the most common coaching topics addressed by coaches in the TCT program over the last five years.

Each of the following "Frequent Five" categories could be the subject of its own book. What is shared here are ideas that have worked. This information is not meant to be all-inclusive, and it hasn't been determined through extensive research to be "the best possible coaching info ever." It is a collection of helpful, current support ideas from a successful coaching program.

- H.O.P.E. (expanded upon in Chapters 6 and 9)

- Classroom management

- Planning—with teacher (Coach planning will be addressed in Chapter 9.)

- Instruction

- Assessment

H.O.P.E.

H.O.P.E. stands for health, organization, positivity, and encouragement.

- Health
  - Use the Human Connection page in the four-page Coach Planner in Chapter 9 to help teachers identify ways to stay healthy both physically and emotionally.
  - Encourage good nutrition, sleep, exercise, and the use of stress-management techniques. Provide support resources as needed.

- Organization
  - Share suggestions and tools to help teachers take control of the physical classroom environment. Teachers need to find and implement useful systems to organize information (both paper and electronic), their desks, and student materials. Teachers will also need easy access to relevant calendars and resource documents.
  - Prepare a menu of organizational options for teachers who are working toward becoming effective at prioritizing workloads and managing their time, both in the pacing of lessons and in effectively structuring planning time.
  - Help teachers organize protocols for how students will respond, both verbally and in written form, including the organizational structure of student notebooks, student reference materials, and grading procedures. Attending to these details will help teachers experience the benefits an orderly environment brings. It is much easier to be confident when we can find what we need and when we have determined structured ways for students to participate in and receive feedback regarding their learning.

- Positivity
  - Guide teachers to identify their core purpose and motivation for teaching. To do this, take individual teachers through the "touchstone" process on the Human Connection page of the four-page planner in Chapter 9.
  - Model and provide supports to help teachers intentionally choose positive thoughts and words. Help them remember to laugh, cultivate joyful awareness and gratitude, connect to core beliefs, and use empowering words. Both the words in our minds and the words that come out of our mouths create the emotional atmosphere that surrounds us. Learning to master what thoughts we allow to stay in our minds and to intentionally choose the words we speak is a key component to becoming an inspirational and happy person.
  - Gather resources that build professionalism, capacity, longevity, resilience, and happiness in both teacher and students. Personalize your positive supports, and record your efforts on the Tracking page of the four-page Coach Planner found in Chapter 9.

- Encouragement
  - Help teachers surround themselves with good influences and rally support by encouraging them to cultivate relationships and communicate regularly with supportive family members, friends, mentors, teammates, coaches, parents, leaders, and community members.
  - When observing, identify and share teacher strengths. Use the "Strengths Reference" coaching hack in Chapter 9 to help.
  - Access and share ideas to encourage teachers by referencing the "Stress-free Opportunities to Absorb Knowledge (S.O.A.K.)" sections at the end of each chapter.

Classroom Management

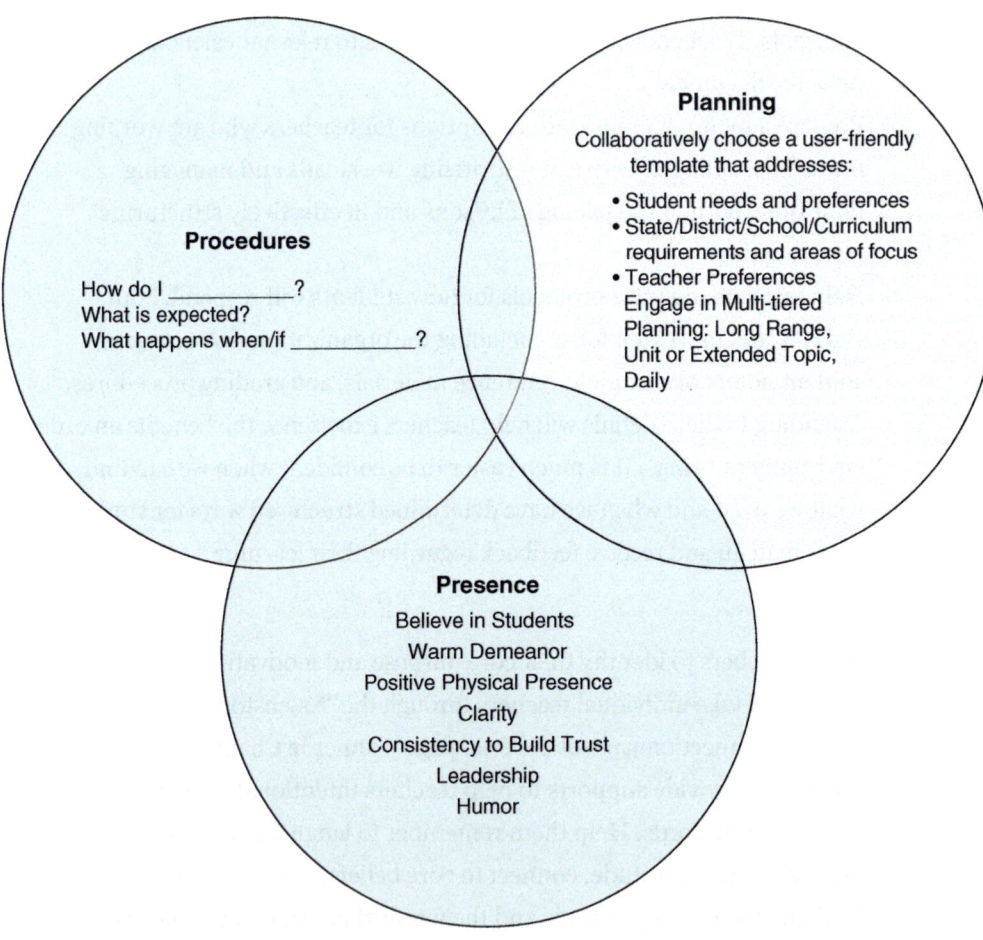

At TCT, for the past five years, coaching support for what is most often referred to as "classroom management" has been what teachers have requested most. It has been helpful to organize this topic into three areas: presence, planning, and procedures. Presence and procedures will be addressed in this section of the chapter, and planning will be addressed next, as its own section. Planning is integral to classroom management and is included as an important piece here, but it merits its own section as one of the "Frequent Five" coaching support topics.

Presence

Presence—or how a teacher's essence, persona, or personality is perceived by students—is a complex matter, since every teacher is unique. Teachers with good presence typically exhibit the following traits: believing in students, a warm demeanor, a positive physical presence, clarity, consistency, leadership, and humor.

Believing in Students

As part of preparing an entry to become national board certified, I worked in a school where 95% of the students qualified for free or reduced lunch. My previous teaching experience had been in a school with about 35% free and reduced lunch–status students. I was afraid it might be a lot harder to work with students who were experiencing extreme poverty, and I thought I might not be able to get the results I had been able to get in the school with more privileged students.

This was not the case. If anyone out there reading this doubts that children of poverty (which often means children of color) can be successful, just know that students who come from difficult circumstances *can learn* at high levels! I am so grateful for the opportunity I had to work with students whose parents were in jail, or whose parents had been deported, or who experienced horrific violence before they arrived at school in the morning. It was likely the most important lesson I learned working in a district that spans both urban and suburban areas, so that I didn't become a coach (or a person, for that matter) who wasn't sure whether "those" students could really be successful in school or in life.

Students in high-poverty schools have the capability to learn as well as those in more affluent environments. Following are five attributes teachers who are willing to take on such meaningful work need:

1) Love for all students

2) An understanding of quality teaching practices and the wisdom to intentionally choose and deliver them, based on student needs

3) Confidence/belief in themselves and in the students

4) A solid classroom-management/environment plan that they are comfortable with and are able to be consistent with

5) Tenacity to persevere in a challenging, but deeply meaningful and soul-satisfying cause

A Warm Demeanor

Teachers with good presence value and build relationships. Their students can sense and interpret through their words and actions that they like them and have their best interests at heart. They smile, speak welcoming words, are enthusiastic about learning, and have a default setting of "Encourager" rather than "Enforcer." This does not mean that when students do not follow expectations, consequences aren't "enforced"; instead, consequences are administered in a way that will not be interpreted as carrying hatred or disrespect. Students know the teacher wants to work "with" them to help them learn.

A Positive Physical Presence

Teachers with good presence:

- have a strong, calm voice—not too soft or wimpy; not screechy, preachy, or screaming (Practice this; use a mirror and video; ask for feedback from colleagues, mentors, and/or leaders. This is really important!);

- carry themselves confidently (no cowering; chin is up, but not to where it looks arrogant; neck is over shoulders, not forward);

- keep their back straight, not bent over;

- keep their shoulders down, not in a stressed position up by the ears;

- are as healthy as possible (get sufficient rest, nutrition, and exercise);

- have a relaxed and friendly smile that they use often;

- are mobile during class, not planted at a desk or lecturing up front the whole period;

- are showered; wear deodorant; have clean, styled hair; are manicured;

- if female, wear appropriate makeup to present a professional appearance; and

- wear relevant, appropriate clothing.

In seventh grade, I was put in Mr. Buque's (not his real name) pre-algebra class. There were serious concerns among the students that Mr. Buque was, in reality, a vampire. He had extremely long, dirty fingernails; his breath was horrible, as though he had been in a coffin for a *very* long time; and he stood hunched over, as if he was about to become a bat at any moment. He wore an ancient, stretched-out brown jacket that smelled of mothballs. He called me Becky Bump, because I sat there, in his words, "like a bump on a log." This was humiliating. The reason for my behavior was that I definitely did *not* want to attract any attention, because I was afraid he might come over and try to help me (in the eyes of a teenager, he was just totally gross), and I didn't understand a word he was saying, since all he did was write problems on the board, explain a little bit, and then expect us to work the problems the rest of the class period and just ask for help as needed.

In the words of Craig Boykin (Educating Children of Color Conference at Colorado College, January 14, 2017), "What message are we sending when kids see the dope dealer drive a shiny, clean Escalade, the professional athlete a Jaguar, the rapper a Mercedes, and then they go out to the school parking lot and see their teacher's car is an old, beat-up, dirty junker?" In the same vein, why would kids want to be taught by people who don't take care of themselves, who smell, or who present themselves as less than inspirational? This is not to say we as educators must have the best cars or best clothes, or that we must do all we can to come across as fake sappy happy, but it is to say that taking pride in our appearance and in how we present ourselves is likely to be more inspirational to students, to ourselves, and to everyone else. Helping teachers see this as an important part of their ability to manage a classroom and help students learn more effectively can be tricky, but it does matter.

Clarity

In these teachers' classrooms, instructions and explanations, both verbal and written, are clear and concise. Processes and procedures are explained, regularly referred to, and often visually displayed with such clarity that they cannot be misunderstood.

The following story is an example of the importance of verbal clarity when teaching. Two teachers were facilitating the same review activity, in which students worked in teams and chose problems to solve at stations around the room. After one teacher had intentionally assigned partners based on a personality profile and told them at which station they would begin, the teacher explained the activity like this:

> There are 10 numbered stations around the room. On each green paper located at each station, there are three problems. You and your partner will choose one of the problems and solve it. You will each need to turn in your own paper at the end of class today, but you can work on solving the problems together. Each of you will show your work next to the station number on your graphic organizer. Answers to the problems are provided under the blue card at each station. You will be scored on the accuracy of the process you used to get the correct answer. By the end of the class period, you and your partner will have answered 10 questions. You will have approximately five minutes to solve the problem you choose at each station. You will know when to move to the next station when you hear this sound [then the teacher played the sound]. I will be moving around the room to help you if you need support. Are there any questions? You may begin.

The second teacher explained the activity like this:

> Get with your partner, and start at a station. Choose one problem from each station. Do you think we should time this? No? Okay, just take as long as you need. Try to get to all the stations. The answers are there.

Most students in the first class completed the work with their partners at an 80%-plus accuracy level. How many students in the second class do you think used the power of collaboration to improve the accuracy of the process they used to find the given answers and complete the work? Right . . . not as many. Not even close.

The importance of verbal clarity surrounding directions, processes, procedures, expectations, and time limits cannot be underestimated. If students know exactly what to do and by when, it is much more likely they will do it.

Consistency

Teachers with good presence consistently support students in ways that *build trust* by:

- regularly showing a genuine interest in students by finding time to learn about and talk with them about interests/activities/talents that are important to them;

- delivering instruction that is accurate, prepared, and meets student needs;

- providing and/or co-developing meaningful expectations and procedures that create a safe, organized learning environment; and

- consistently following through with expectations and procedures, including rewards and consequences when applicable.

Teachers who struggle with classroom management often think being "nice" means changing expectations whenever a situation arises that is uncomfortable or that ditching expectations is appropriate when there is a conflict. This may be true in an emergency or some other extreme situation, but typically it happens far too often and undermines students' trust in any type of classroom-management plan or anything else the teacher is trying to accomplish with students. Helping teachers understand that doing what they say they are going to do, no matter how uncomfortable it is—or, in other words, "walking their talk"—is a key element of effective classroom management. One common violation of this occurs when teachers are frustrated and make random threats they can't carry out—for instance, "If you can't be quiet, I'm going to keep you all after school" (even when the teacher knows half the class takes the bus), or "No one's paying attention, so everyone's going to get an F and I'm going to call *all* your parents" (right, like that's going to happen), or "Go to the office; I'm sure Mr./Mrs. _____ will suspend you for that," or (a teacher I know sheepishly admitted she had said this when trying to get her class to behave) "I'm going to call the police, and they are going to come and arrest you all for being out of control in class."

Helping teachers design a clear classroom-management system (with meaningful expectations and reasonable plans for what happens next if expectations are or aren't followed), then providing coaching support to help the teacher follow through consistently, will help teachers avoid high frustration levels that can result in random outbursts and nonproductive threats that create doubt about whether the teacher really means what he or she says. The biggest bonus of consistency is that it builds students' trust in the teacher's ability to lead and manage a classroom.

Leadership

Teachers incorporate leadership skills into their teaching practice by developing a presence that includes the confidence to set high expectations and ensure procedures are clear and consistently followed. Teachers gain respect as leaders in many ways, but definitely through their organization and professionalism related to their knowledge of and ability to create plans based on state/district areas of focus, content standards, and student needs, developmental levels, and interests. Students are never without something meaningful to do and are considered by the teacher to be partners in learning. Students need to be able to trust in the leadership of the teacher, that he or she is ultimately in charge of leading the learning and is completely capable of doing so in ways that honor and respect students. Planning and pacing of lessons, students' interactions with each other, student responses to material being presented, learning activities, and practice work are intentional when a teacher is truly leading learning. The teacher accepts that responsibility and accountability are naturally embedded in the mantle of leadership.

Leadership has many facets, but working to achieve instructional goals by organizing and designing step-by-step pieces of learning, with the intention to help students engage authentically in ways that produce specific instructional results, is central to creating a great classroom environment with minimal disruptions.

Remember early (or maybe current) attempts at implementing "personalized learning"? An inaccurate assumption of some teachers was that students would just play on the computers or iPads and "create their own learning," so teaching would be a lot less work. Learning was also at times "flipped" or "blended" in some haphazard way that ended up creating an unappetizing and ineffective classroom stew, leaving students and parents scratching their heads as to what learning was actually happening. As coaches, we know that being "the guide on the side, rather than the sage on the stage" requires a great deal of outside planning, which is why there is still (cue music) "a whole lot of lecture going on."

Leadership in the classroom is about learning to plan for and maximize instructional results within time limits—using intentionally chosen instructional delivery methods that meet the needs of students, provide for meaningful feedback to and from students, and administer targeted formative assessments so that instruction can be modified as needed to ensure that as many students as possible master the standards. It also means doing all this in ways that inspire students to participate. No easy task. And . . . why don't we pay teachers more?

Humor

Teachers with good presence understand that everything is not super serious, and they find ways to bring fun and joy into the classroom environment. They enjoy interactions with students and find ways to use humor to enhance learning and defuse stressful situations.

They are okay with laughing at themselves when mistakes are made. They steer clear of trying to be funny by using cutting, sarcastic remarks that could hurt or injure students (they laugh *with* students, not at them).

Humor is an underutilized, yet extremely powerful, tool that can assist teachers as they strive to connect with students. Humor can also increase students' knowledge and comprehension (Hackathorn, Garczynski, Blankmeyer, Tennial, & Solomon, 2011). We all like to be around people who can "bring the fun" to lighten our burdens, even if it's only for a moment. One effective teacher I know started every day with a joke or an interesting, funny story. When he retired, he gifted me with many books that had funny jokes and interesting short stories. This was a great lesson to me as a new teacher. I tended to be super serious about getting all the content and all the standards taught; there was *no* wasted instructional time in *my* classroom. I wonder now how many kids I scared into lower levels of enjoyment and understanding. More learning can be accomplished when our brains are happy and not in a heightened "fight or flight," stressful state. According to John Medina (2014), the ability to concentrate, remember, solve problems, and process language can be negatively affected by stress: "In almost every way it can be tested, chronic stress hurts our ability to learn" (p. 65). Another great reason to help teachers develop and use a sense of humor is that it strengthens teacher resilience and longevity by promoting good health (both mentally and physically), and it enhances relationships with colleagues and students (Bobek, 2002). If you or teachers you are working with struggle to incorporate humor into their teaching or even their daily lives, try researching some ideas together and give them a try! Collect resources from books or videos, or observe a funny teacher to get ideas. This is one way to help teachers avoid coming across as or even feeling boring, and that is definitely worth some serious effort!

Helping teachers improve their teaching "presence" has been one of the biggest challenges the TCT team has faced over the years, because sometimes people have to acknowledge and address parts of their personalities that don't support quality teaching. Jay provides a good example of this.

After retiring from the military, Jay (not his real name) wanted a meaningful second career. Coming from his military background that included immediately following the orders of his commanding officer, and his own old-school days of how students should (and often did) just "sit and listen," Jay was baffled as to how to get his middle-school math students to learn. He was very good at just standing in front of the class and expounding on pretty much any topic, because he was very knowledgeable, but he couldn't seem to get the students to listen to him for any length of time. This upset him, resulting in some outbursts of concern and inconsistent consequences. The reality was that his classes, especially the big ones, were out of control.

Using a team approach involving the school's administration and instructional coaching, clear expectations and procedures were determined, and Jay was able to rein in the shouting, throwing of papers and pencils, students walking around, students sitting on desks, constant talking, and so on. But the students still did not seem to want to listen to him.

Here is how a typical class period went: Jay would write a topic on the board, and then he would talk for most of the period about the topic while modeling how to do the math on the board (with his back to the class) and tell the students to take notes however they wanted to on what strategies came to him in the moment. Sometimes he would present a slideshow while he was talking, and then the rest of the class time would be left for students to basically fend for themselves. Explaining relevancy or hooking students into the lessons, meaningful pacing with a variety of instructional strategies, and structures for student responses and group work were missing in his instructional delivery. Students rarely worked through problems with the teacher, and Jay was not aware of the power of checking in regularly with students to informally assess their levels of understanding. In his defense, Jay was teaching with an alternative licensure and had never had the opportunity to learn in-depth how to manage a middle-school classroom.

After addressing the management pieces, planning more variety into his instructional delivery, and creating different opportunities for student participation and responses (including the modeling of a specific note-taking process), Jay began experiencing better teaching days. During one coaching session, he said something like "You know, I've been realizing that I have to fight my personality to do this job well. I tend to be lazy and too laid-back, letting the kids do whatever as long as they aren't beating each other up, and I can't be that way if I'm going to be successful in this job. I'm finding it's a lot of hard work to be prepared and consistent." Jay admitted he had thought that teaching, as a second career, would be easy: "Hey, I'll share my knowledge by talking to well-behaved kids all day, get off at 3:00 p.m., and have the summers off—sounds great, right?" Not so much. The good news is, he figured it out. We all have to sometimes check the less-than-helpful parts of our personalities at the door in order to be our best for students.

Procedures

Classroom procedures create structure and provide necessary information and boundaries students need to make sense of the classroom environment. They also help students understand how to operate successfully within the classroom, and they create a safe and productive learning environment.

When coaches are called into a classroom-management situation that needs immediate changes, it has worked well to begin by helping teachers clarify, communicate, and implement procedures with consistency, then focus on the other two Ps: presence and planning. Of course, if a teacher's demeanor is offensive and unproductive, presence and procedures would need to be focused on simultaneously. The following is a process we at TCT have used to help teachers organize procedural pieces to quickly get the classroom environment under control.

1. The coach observes the class and then meets with the teacher to determine what classroom-management strategies are already being used and to understand what the current issues are.

2. The coach provides exemplars of management plans and discusses ideas with the teacher. The teacher and coach collaboratively come up with a plan to present to the school administrator(s) that incorporates the building PBIS system (if there is one), the school or district's behavioral processes/systems, the age and interests of the students, and the teacher's philosophies on management and discipline. In the examples below, the teachers have organized behavioral plans using a theme and have clearly identified expectations or rules (written as observable behaviors). Included in the plan are specific procedures for what happens both when the expectations are met and when they aren't met. These plans are designed for individual situations and are based on philosophies and processes the teacher can be consistent and happy with.

The following sections of a classroom-management plan would be developed collaboratively with the coach and teacher, and students could also be included, as appropriate:

- *A reason or purpose*—an explanation and discussion with students about why an orderly environment with predictable routines is needed to maximize student learning
- *An inspiring theme with a visual image* to support the purpose (e.g., "We can conquer even the toughest math problems when we can focus!" A picture of a rock climber reaching the top of a mountain could be used, or something that the teacher and students would consider inspiring, maybe a mascot or symbol representing the class.)
- *Student ideas* incorporated into the plan (when possible)
- *Clear expectations* (with principles such as Respect clearly defined as observable behaviors)
  - *Celebrations*—positive consequences, incentives, intrinsic reward focus with supports (perhaps affirmations about how successful learning experiences now are paving the way for long-term success)
  - *A step-by-step process* of what will happen if students do not follow expectations (Talk this through with the principal if he or she would be involved.)
- *A tracking system*. If a teacher/school/district has a plan for action when students do not follow expectations that includes a hierarchy of consequences—such as (1) a warning, (2) a phone call home (Level 1 referral), (3) the student leaves the class (Level 2 referral)—there must be a way to track the consequences so that the teacher can consistently implement the planned steps. Here are some ideas:
  - Print off a class list, and make tally marks by a student's name under appropriate dates.
  - Print off student pictures by class, put them in a plastic sheath, and put dots, numbers, or tally marks on the picture.

○ Record consequences on a spreadsheet in the computer (some school/
district PBIS plans require this).

- *A procedure board.* Explanations of procedures regarding bathroom breaks,
pencil sharpening, handing out papers, cell-phone use, and so on are visually
available for easy reference. These basic classroom procedural pieces *are not
included in the expectations* or else the expectation list would be too long,
but they are posted so that they can be referenced as needed. One teacher
prepared a visually appealing procedure board and then purchased a laser
pointer. She then attached her laser pointer to her badge lanyard and used it
to point to the appropriate procedure when necessary, rather than explain the
bathroom or other procedures over and over.

3. The classroom-management plan is taught in depth and regularly reviewed.

4. The teacher follows the plan consistently.

Here are a few examples of how this was done:

Second-Grade Plan	Eighth-Grade Math Plan

Soaring to Success

Flying Expectations
for Listening During Instructions

- Hear the Signal and Respond
- Eyes on the Speaker
- Voices are OFF
  - No Blurting, Arguing, or Side Conversations
- Follow Directions and Procedures Quickly
- Remain Seated

Clip Your Consequence

- Outstanding –followed Expectations and Flew the Extra Mile (Gold Mustang Ticket)
- Good Day –Followed Expectations and Helped Other Students Learn (Blue Mustang Ticket)
- Ready to Learn –Following Expectations
- Stop and think (Warning)
- Teacher's Choice (Loss of Recess, IB Reflection, Time Out, Loss of Privileges, etc.)
- Parent Contact/Principal/Referral

The King's Plan
The Class Environment Action Plan for
Miss Donnell's Class

"Faith is taking the first step even when you don't see the whole staircase"

Martin Luther King, Jr.

"I have a dream that my four children will one day live in a nation where they will not be judged by the color of their skin, but by the content of their character."

Martin Luther King Jr.

The King of Beasts
The lion is the largest and the most powerful of the wild cats; no wonder it is called the king of the jungle. It is regarded as the symbol of power and strength in almost all the countries of the world. We often hear strong people being referred to as lion-hearted. Also, the figure of the lion is engraved on many shields awarded to players. Even some flags carry the picture of a lion. The ancient Egyptians believed lions were a sacred animal.

**What can you be the King of?
And how would you demonstrate leadership?**

(Continued)

(Continued)

Celebrations

- Table Slap
- Mighty Yay!
- Pinky Woop!
- 10 Second Party
- Pat Yourself on the Back
- Round of Applause
- Watermelon Cheer
- Fab Friday –90% of students at **Ready to Learn** or above M – F = **TREATS!!**

Procedures

- Lining Up Outside
- Walking Down the Hall
- Breakfast
- Entering the Classroom
- Pencils
- Bathrooms
- Moving to the Carpet and Back to Desks
- During Small Group Instruction (Independent Work)
- What to Do if You Finish Early

Lining Up Inside and Out

- Line up in number line order
- Toes to heels and heels to toes
- You are Straight, Safe, and Silent
- Always be thinking (Where does my back go? Do I have homework to turn in? Do I have notes for the teacher?)

K – KEEP
I – INSPIRING
N – NEW
G – GROWTH

Be the King of your own rock.
Rely on your confidence and knowledge.

FOCUS

How to Show Respect and Responsibility in Class

1. Hear or See the Signal and Respond
2. Follow Directions Quickly
3. Raise Hand to Speak
4. Use Voice Appropriately
   - Maintain requested voice level
   - No blurting, arguing, cussing, or side conversations
5. Hands to Self
6. Stay on Task and On Topic

Classroom Rewards and Consequences

Rewards

- Fun Food After 10 Good Days (see chart)
- A Good Day = No Visual Warnings Given

Consequences

1. Verbal Warning
2. Visual Warning
3. Assigned Seat
4. Level 1 Referral –Parent Contact
5. Office

Science Teacher K–5

 Come in and sit down

 Active listening

- **Eyes on teacher**
- **Pencils down**
- **Voices off**

 Follow directions

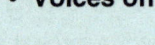

 Do your best work/stay on task

 Line up quietly

Rodgers

5-Star Class Program
The 5 Star Ornaments Represent 5 Expectations

Each class could earn up to 5 stars per day. At the end of class, students shared how well they felt they had followed the expectations using a "fist of five." Star ornaments were added to the chart if most of the students and the teacher agreed they deserved a 5. The class could earn 5 points for each star they earned. When 50 points were accumulated, the class would have a "5-star party" (star lights were turned on), with a treat. This teacher also had a hierarchy consequence system for individual students, which was (1) Warning, (2) Reflection Form, (3) Office.

Because this teacher taught science to six different grades, she changed the rectangle to the appropriate teacher's name for each class session.

Helping a teacher create a personalized classroom-management plan is a great way to provide competent coaching support. A plan provides clarity for both the teacher and students. Organizing down to the nitty-gritty details helps teachers figure out what they do expect and what that looks like. Does this always work? Well, it works most of the time. Here are a few problems that sometimes show up:

1. The teacher communicates expectations and procedures but does not implement them consistently, implements them in an angry or unproductive way, or uses the behavioral plan to try to make kids be quiet all the time when there isn't much interesting instruction going on. These types of problems are the ones that surface most frequently, and they typically indicate the teacher and coach have a lot of work to do with presence and planning.

2. The administrator(s) and teacher are not on the same page. When a difficult management situation is occurring, coaches absolutely need to work with both the teacher and administrator(s) to come up with a plan everyone agrees with. Even when a collaborative plan has been determined, once the coach is no longer on-site to provide immediate support, things can take a turn for the worse, especially if the situation has gotten to the point where there are quite a few extreme student misbehaviors that need to be addressed through the office. Sometimes administrators or counselors are not available—then what do we do? Sometimes teachers and/or administrators don't follow through—then what? Troubleshooting and discussing these possible issues ahead of time with all parties is a proactive way to avoid some very difficult situations.

3. The classroom has been mismanaged for way too long, and the kids like it the way it is. We sometimes see this when the teacher accesses the coach very late in the school year, after students have gotten used to running the show. Over time, students have developed a lack of respect, or even a great dislike, for the teacher (usually because of a presence issue) and have decided to work together to undermine whatever the teacher says or does. Once, after observing a disruptive middle-school class (where students were standing on the chairs and tables, yelling, and throwing stuff), I had to call security, the one and only time in ten years that I did so. After security was called and things settled down, the teacher showed me a note he had found on the floor. It read, "What should we do today to make his life miserable?" In this type of situation, administrator support (and, possibly, the removal of some students) might need to be considered.

4. Some students have extremely challenging behaviors related to diagnosed (and sometimes undiagnosed) conditions, such as attention deficit disorder; attention-deficit/hyperactivity disorder; conduct disorder; oppositional defiant disorder; acute stress disorder; and depression. Parents, a behavioral specialist, medical doctors, specialized support personnel, and the school administration may need

to be accessed to work through these issues to maximize instructional time. The best resource I have found to help with these types of situations is Martha Tate's *Shouting Won't Grow Dendrites* (2014), chapter 19, pages 125–137.

The plans shared above have worked very well. Here's what some teachers who used this type of personalized system for organizing a behavioral plan have said:

> I have been teaching for 26 years and I finally know what I am doing with classroom management. I like teaching again; this has saved my career and given me the strength to continue. I enjoy the kids so much more.
>
> Primary elementary teacher

> This was my first year teaching, and without this I think I would have quit; the difference is [like] night and day.
>
> Middle-school math teacher

> Why didn't I learn how to do this somewhere? I have read a bunch of books and gone to a lot of classes over the years, but this puts everything together.
>
> Intermediate elementary teacher

Planning

Planning involves ways to help teachers organize and "chunk" instruction into manageable pieces that address state/district/school/curriculum expectations and student needs. I recommend that you create, compile, or organize a menu of planning template options, so that your teachers can develop or choose personalized planning structures based on their learning modality preferences and preferred tools. Set aside time to assist each teacher as he or she plans at the following three levels: long-range planning, unit planning, and daily planning. Include team teachers, if possible/applicable.

Long-Range Planning With Sequencing

Pick one course or subject to work on first. Acquire both a school and district (and maybe a personal) calendar that notes professional development days, assessment days, intervention schedules, personal vacations or occasions, and any other events the teacher is aware of that might interrupt instruction. This will not cover everything that will come up, but it is a good start.

Compile and organize content standards, available curriculum resources/overviews, assessment data and assessment categories, evidence outcome information, or any other support documents available from your school, district, and state. Administer, analyze, and look for patterns in student surveys, such as learning modality preferences and interest survey results, for easy reference during the long-range planning process. The coach and teacher/team of teachers can collaboratively organize a reference notebook that makes all necessary planning information easily accessible.

Begin prioritizing standards, topics, or units by referencing standards, applicable student data, and prioritized assessment categories (if available) and by locating information on frequently occurring student misconceptions for the course or subject. Next, collaboratively determine what is most important, using a structured process (maybe something as simple as copying, enlarging, and taping up the standards and/or evidence/learning outcomes on a wall and collaboratively prioritizing, using a marker to write "1," "2," or "3" beside each standard. Or, perhaps a more involved structured process, such as a Tregoe Decision Analysis, could help team members collaboratively determine the most important criteria to be addressed when determining priority standards for current students.

Fit the most important standards, topics, or units within the days available, adjusting as needed (this usually means shortening some units or topics and expanding others, depending on their importance). Some districts have pacing guides that can be referenced during this process. Typical course lengths are divided into quarters (9 weeks) and semesters (18 weeks), though some schools do have trimesters or other organizational structures. Having a big calendar posted or projected that everyone can see and work on together is very useful at this stage.

Help teachers understand that organizing at this big-picture level is very important. They are intentionally using their professional judgment to decide what content, in what sequence, will provide students with the best education possible. Sometimes, teachers who have been married to long units that focus on personally preferred content rather than skills or standards will have to make tough choices. In districts where teaching to a specific curriculum with fidelity is required, because the district has determined the curriculum hits all the standards needed, this level of planning may not be necessary or may have been done by district leaders. However, it is difficult to ensure that a specific curriculum covers everything, and going through this process with teachers helps to clarify their work and build confidence in their professional judgment. It also supports a deeper understanding of the content, builds team awareness and alignment, and provides a meaningful flow and sequence for the teacher(s) and coach(es) involved with the planning.

This is where reality hits. Teachers typically cannot easily cover everything they are being asked to address within a reasonable amount of time. Thinking through and making conscious, intentional choices to give more time to some standards, skills, topics, or units than others is critical, and the gathering of all needed resources—the mental focus, organization, teamwork, and brainpower needed to synthesize so much information into what is best for students—is what separates competent teachers (and coaches) from peers who would rather avoid productive struggle.

Unit/or Extended Focus Area Planning

After the general units/topics have been decided upon for the quarter, the semester, or the school year, and the amount of time has been allotted for each unit/topic, it is time to divide the unit/topic into smaller parts that fit within the allotted time limit for the entire unit. Remember that everything isn't set in stone. As you go through and figure out the details, some of the big-picture timelines can still be altered, though the teacher/team should have a solid instructional reason for making changes. Perhaps new student data might provide enough evidence for a change in plans? However, it is best when learning a new planning system to not try to address too many variables, or else it can get really confusing and both the teacher and coach will want to quit. Getting started is the most important thing. There must be something there to edit or improve upon! Help teachers quickly record their best thinking at that point in time, and, if editing needs to happen, it can be done later. Try to rein in perfectionism (for both you and the teacher), or else this will take way too long.

Graphic organizers or templates are very helpful at this stage. Offer choices, or collabora-tively develop one based on school/district pacing guides or planners, the teacher's learning modality preferences, or his or her favorite tools. For instance, would the teacher prefer an electronic planning template or a color-coded process with sticky notes organized on poster paper? Let's look at some examples of how to organize at the unit/topic level. The following color-coded template was designed for a teacher who preferred kinesthetic and visual tools. This unit/extended topic planning process (one option from a bank of options) was chosen often by teachers in TCT's district.

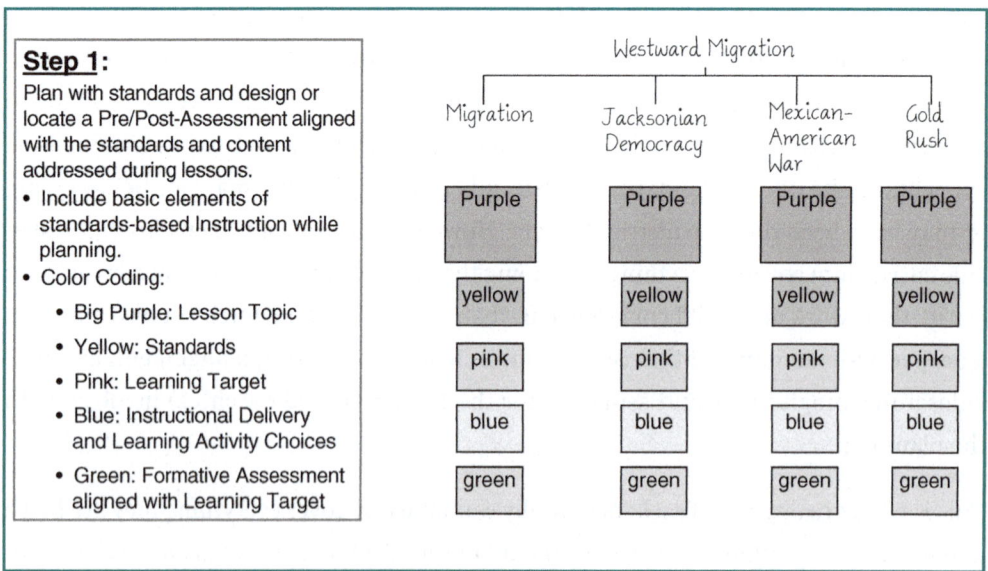

Daily Planning

A basic skeleton of daily plans can be incorporated into a Unit Planner, showing general sequencing and the major parts of the lesson, to include (1) the standards addressed; (2) the instructional goal/objective/learning target; (3) the instructional delivery method chosen;

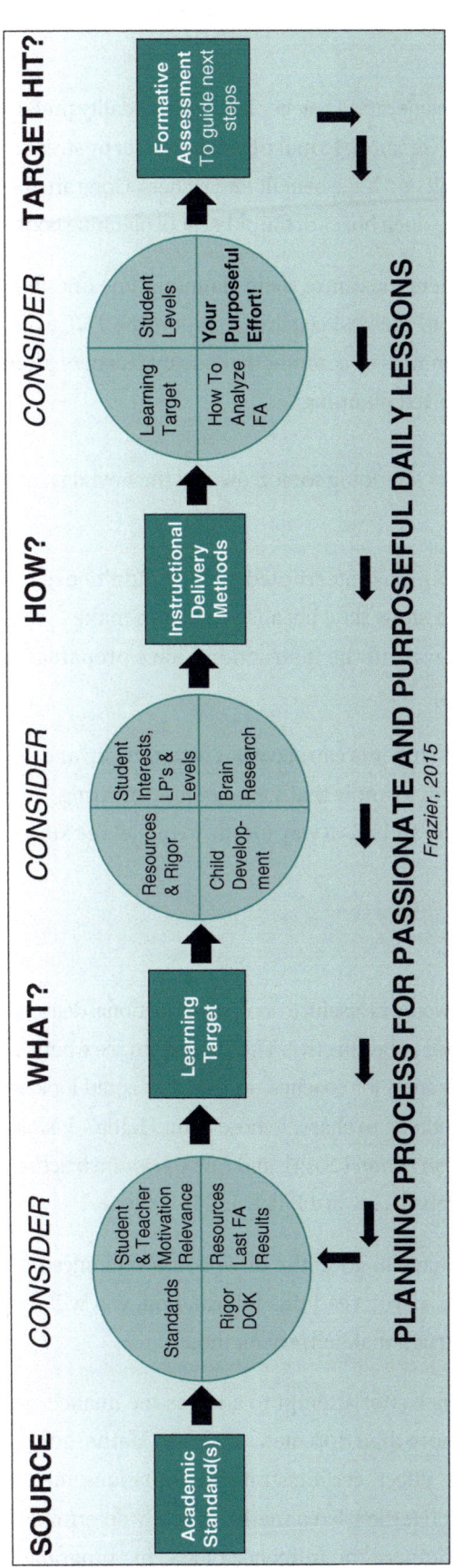

PLANNING PROCESS FOR PASSIONATE AND PURPOSEFUL DAILY LESSONS

Frazier, 2015

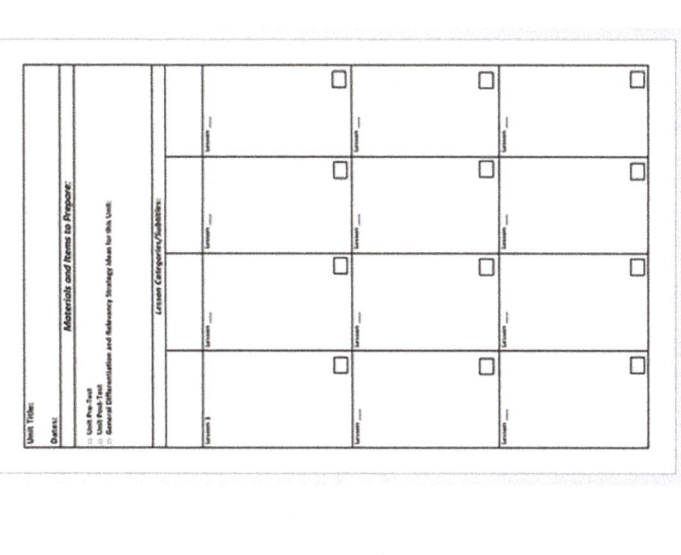

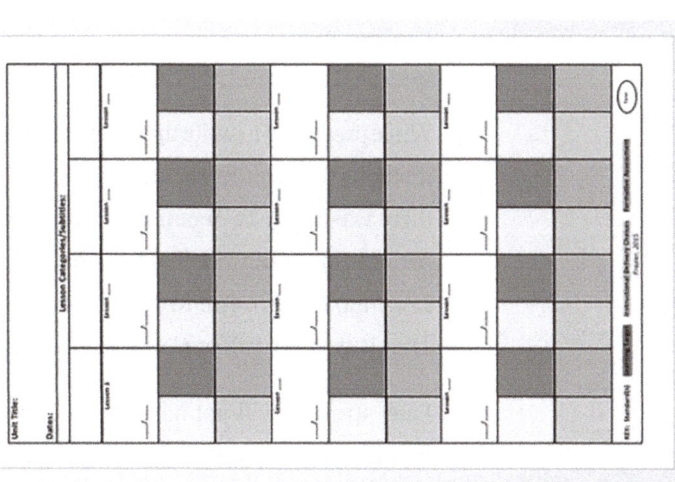

Full-sized resources are available for download from https://resources.corwin.com/JoyofCoaching

and (4) the formative assessment. Other pieces may include a hook or inviting start to the lesson and plans for differentiation.

Creating or finding a template that takes into consideration teacher learning-modality preferences can make planning manageable. Anything we can do to make teaching easier by streamlining and personalizing the planning process will be a huge benefit for teachers. Gone are the days of fitting our plans for an entire day into the 1-inch boxes of the old-school planning book.

Offering concrete planning tools to help teachers maximize their planning time and find *their* "how" for planning has resulted in some of the best coaching support the TCT team has been able to provide. Here are a few summaries of comments made by teachers after they experienced coaching sessions that supported planning:

- "Now I can sleep at night. I know what I am doing tomorrow and the next day, and next month—it's such a relief!"

- "I used to not really care if my teaching was interrupted, since I didn't have a good plan. Now, I don't even want a snow day, because I want to make sure my students are able to benefit from all the instruction I have prepared for them!"

- "I leave my planning poster up, so that students can see what is coming up and how it all fits together. It's good for them to know that I am not just throwing their lessons together at the last minute, and it is a way for me to model the kind of effort I want to see from them."

Instruction
Instructional Delivery Methods

While preparing to write this section, I thought it would be useful to look at instructional delivery methods that prominent authors have determined to be effective. The idea was to see whether there was a way to organize and provide information for coaches, so that they could look at patterns and prioritize instructional delivery methods to share. I chose John Hattie's *Visible Learning* (2009), Jim Knight's *High-Impact Instruction* (2013), and *Classroom Instruction That Works* (2012), by Ceri Dean, Elizabeth Hubbell, Howard Pitler, and B. J. Stone.

Each strategy will not be explained—you will have to go to the three books referenced to find that level of detail—but it is my hope that as you read this information, you will see patterns that will help you identify quality instructional delivery methods.

Hattie's research in *Visible Learning* (2009) does not attempt to address the nuances in individual classrooms, but it is a synthesis of more than 800 meta-analyses (Hattie, 2009) organized into categories to show what level of "effect" certain strategies, situations, methods, or programs had on student achievement. Hattie used a mathematically determined effect size to create a user-friendly scale to compare the influence of specific programs, strategies, or statistics in five different domains (student, home, school, teacher, and curricula) on student achievement. "An effect size provides a common expression of the magnitude of study outcomes for many types of outcome variables" (Hattie, 2009, p. 7). Hattie determined that an effect size of .40 or above would make enough of a difference to merit a change in current practice to include the strategy.

Jim Knight's *High-Impact Instruction* (2013) is a user-friendly resource, based on research that explains a variety of best teaching practices and how to implement them in actual coaching practice. It includes online checklists and resources. The specificity for identifying detailed practical changes using the checklists and the suggested next steps, which would include organizing the most effective strategies into a coaching instructional playbook, have greatly influenced our coaching at TCT. This book has been one of our favorites, and we have utilized some of the checklists and resources provided.

Classroom Instruction That Works (2012) has been a popular and influential resource for educators since the first edition was published in 2001. The second edition has foundational pieces included in the first edition written by Robert Marzano, Debra Pickering, and Jane Pollock. In an effort to give credit to all seven authors, I will be referencing this information under the designation Marzano et al. Both editions were designed to support teachers as they purposefully decide what instructional delivery methods to use. This continues to be an important topic, as teachers work to deliver instruction in the best ways possible and effectively pace their instruction to design instructional delivery in ways that will result in student mastery of as many standards as possible within limited amounts of time.

The following table (see page 82) is organized to show the authors' *similar* thoughts, research, and categories related to the question, "What helps students learn best?" This information from some of our most respected researchers and leaders, with a few additions thrown in from coaching experience, can be summarized as follows:

Teachers can positively impact students' academic success and classroom environment experiences if they (1) create a caring environment where behavioral and learning expectations, procedures, and instructions are clear, (2) learn where students are in their cognitive development and choose lessons and materials accordingly, (3) show in various ways they believe in and like students, and (4) plan and deliver instruction with clarity and variety to include specific learning goals and visible ways for students to practice and show mastery (with a plan to intervene when students do not learn or already know the material).

Or, for the details enthusiasts:

Teachers will do well if they . . .

1. Believe in themselves and in students and are determined to help students believe in their academic potential and personal worth.

2. Learn where students are in their cognitive development, and choose lessons and materials accordingly.

	What Instructional Delivery Choices Help Students Learn Best?		
	Categories named by Hattie, Knight, and Marzano et al:		
Book	**Visible Learning** An effect size of .40 or above makes enough of a difference to merit a change in practice	**High Impact Instruction**	**Classroom Instruction That Works 2nd Edition**
Author	**John Hattie**	**Jim Knight**	**Marzano et al.**
Authors' *similar* thoughts, research, categories about: **What Helps Students Learn Best?**	• Piagetian programs (1.28) • Comprehensive interventions for students with learning disabilities (.77) • Teacher clarity (.75); Reciprocal teaching (.74) • Spaced vs. massed practice (.71) • Direct instruction (.59) • Mastery learning (.58) • Worked examples (.57) • Goals (.56) • Visual perception programs (.55)	• Planning • Authentic learning	• Setting objectives and providing feedback • Assigning homework and providing practice • Cues, questions, and advance organizers
	• Questioning (.46)	• Guiding questions • Effective questions	• Generating and testing hypotheses • Cues, questions, and advance organizers
	• Concept mapping (.57)	• Learning maps	• Nonlinguistic representations • Cues, questions, and advance organizers
	• Meta-cognitive strategies (.69) • Self-verbalization/self-questioning (.64)	• Thinking prompts • Freedom within form	• Generating and testing hypotheses • Summarizing and note-taking • Identifying similarities and differences

	• Teacher-student relationships (.72)
	• Classroom management (.52)
	• Classroom cohesion (.53)
	• Motivation (.48)
		• Community building:
		  o Learner-friendly culture
		  o Power with, not power over
		  o Freedom within form
		• Witness to the good
		• Fluent corrections
			• Reinforcing effort and providing recognition
			• Setting objectives and providing feedback
			• Cooperative learning

• Providing formative evaluation (.90) • Feedback (.73)	• Formative assessment	• Setting objectives and providing feedback
• Cooperative learning (.41) • Peer tutoring (.55) • Peer influences (.53) • Small group learning (.49)	• Cooperative learning • Freedom within form	• Cooperative learning
• Expectations (.43)	• Expectations	• Setting objectives and providing feedback

3. Provide clear verbal and written instructions and concise explanations when teaching content.

4. Like kids and value relationships. They will show this by taking time to get to know students and by creating a positive and structured classroom environment so that students feel safe, valued, and cared for.

5. Make sure classroom expectations and procedures are clear, visible, and full of common sense.

6. Plan quality instruction for the students in the room by using relevant data and knowledge of students to make instructional delivery choices and researching and choosing from evidence-based instructional delivery methods.

7. Know and show exactly what they want students to learn and produce (aligned with standards). Whenever possible, they show, demonstrate, or list what needs to be done to successfully meet the learning goal and what mastery looks like (exemplars, modeling, etc.).

8. Use a variety of instructional delivery methods—banish boredom!

9. Check in often with students to see how they are doing, and ask for their feedback in a variety of ways (checks for understanding, formative assessment, progress on rubrics).

10. Intentionally ask meaningful questions at a variety of levels, and provide opportunities for students to think, infer, generate hypotheses, and ask and answer questions.

11. Choose strategic, spaced step-by-step student practice over massed practice.

12. Provide specific academic feedback when students do not understand, and, when needed, choose another way to get the concept across.

13. Ask for specialized support and/or seek new knowledge when situations arise that are beyond the teacher's expertise.

14. Don't give up! Keep going and organize ways for students to enjoy the lesson and help each other until students (with few exceptions) can demonstrate mastery of the instructional goal/objective/intention/target.

While thinking through these ideas, I was intrigued with Hattie's #1 meta-analysis result (not included in the table above) regarding students. It was entitled "Self-reported grades," or students estimating their own performance based in part on their past educational experiences. This topic netted a huge effect size (1.44), noticeably bigger than all others. I believe the takeaway from this result is that most students know at what level they have achieved in the past and perform about as well as they think can (Hattie, 2009, p. 43). This is bad news for students who do not have confidence in their ability to learn.

Helping teachers organize instruction in ways that provide students with many opportunities to receive frequent, meaningful feedback (.73) and formative evaluation (.90) can improve students' perceptions of their ability to learn. Addressing specific student needs (identified through formative assessments) by intentionally planning and focusing instruction to help students be successful one small step at a time is a powerful way to increase students' skill levels. Being this detailed with what students need, and filling those needs, not only works as an academic intervention, but also can be a factor in improving academic self-confidence and increasing students' personal expectations for achievement. This approach is a logical way to address the incredibly scary truth that if students don't believe they can achieve, they won't.

Understanding Inconsistent Educational Vocabulary

One of the most confusing pieces in instruction today is the inconsistent use, interchangeability, and conceptual overlapping of the words "goals," "objectives," "learning intentions," "learning targets," and "learning outcomes." The hope is that when teachers have communicated the goals/objectives/intentions/targets/outcomes desired, along with aligning their instructional delivery, materials, student work, and assessments to those goals/objectives/intentions/targets/outcomes, clarity and connection to the learning (for both students and teachers) will be created. At TCT, we have learned that teacher clarity (ranked #8 on Hattie's list) is one of the most important characteristics of a successful teacher, so it is reasonable to assume that the people who coach and lead teachers must do so with clarity to be effective. This is not always easy, given the many ways these concepts are explained in educational literature.

It's likely that every instructional coach and educational leader has wrestled with which words, authors, and resources to use and how to best organize and explain similar concepts. When I think about how to organize and explain educational vocabulary important to coaching, it helps to think of going on vacation. (Don't we all feel like taking off when things don't make sense?) What I mean is that I think of the purple luggage set I use to carry everything I need when I'm traveling by plane. The set looks great, and each piece stacks neatly inside each other when stored in the closet. Shall we head out together on an educational adventure?

Before we get started, let's take a look at the word "goal." "Goal" could be used for all levels of instructional organization; we could just differentiate the levels by saying "overall course goals," "unit goals," "quarter goals," "weekly goals," "daily goals," and so on. Setting a goal means we identify something we want to accomplish, and we recognize that we can consciously decide to move forward with actions that will help us reach the goal (Locke & Latham, 1990). So, in a way, the word "goal" is always appropriate. We just need to determine how big the goal is and how to break it down into smaller and smaller mini-goals until we get to what needs to be done each day during each lesson. Much of the educational vocabulary on this topic has been created with that idea in mind: to help teachers sequence and break instruction down into small pieces, so that they can be as effective as possible every day.

So, back to our trip and my four-piece set of purple luggage.

Overall Goals
- Content Standards
- General Unit Goals
- Key Conceptual Understandings to be learned by the end of instruction
- Overall Guiding Questions
- General Learning Outcomes Expected

Objectives
- Typically smaller pieces of standards written in professional language for teacher use
- Used to connect and sequence instruction

Learning Targets
- Short-term learning topics taken from standards, written in student friendly language. Synonym: **Learning Intentions**

Success Criteria and Formative Assessment:
- How will students do the work?
- How will levels of student mastery be determined?

In this analogy, the overall goals of a unit or topic of study are represented by the biggest piece of luggage and include bigger-picture or more long-term knowledge or understandings, such as content standards, general unit goals, or key conceptual understandings. Objectives would be the next piece, the second-largest suitcase. I still have to check it with the airline; it's a bit smaller, yet still able to hold quite a bit of information. It contains what teachers want students to know and understand within shorter time periods. Objectives are based on standards and are used to pedagogically connect and sequence instruction. They are typically written in professional language for teacher use. Next comes the carry-on bag, representing learning targets (Moss & Brookhart, 2012) or learning intentions (Hattie, 2009) organized for shorter periods of time. These daily targets/short-term learning intentions incorporate the teacher objectives but are written in language that students can understand and relate to. They focus on what students will be learning during a lesson or "chunk" of content (Leahy, Lyon, Thompson, & Wiliam, 2005; Moss, Brookhart, & Long, 2011). A lesson can incorporate targets/intentions that take more than one class period, but it is important to understand that providing clarity for small chunks of instruction is one of the main reasons for breaking down the learning to this point, so it wouldn't be effective to use the same target/intention for many days at a time. These targets/intentions are what we carry with us each day and keep close (in the overhead bin).

The implementation of learning targets/intentions into daily instructional practice has helped teachers organize their thinking about how to explain the learning in ways their students can understand. The concept has helped coaches support teachers to increase clarity surrounding what the instruction will entail, how the learning activities and formative assessments will align with the target/intention, why the learning will be important for students, and how it connects with previous and future learning. A learning target would include "what students will be able to do; what ideas, topic, or subject is important for them to learn and understand so they can do it; how they will show they can do it; and how well they will have to do it" (Moss et al., 2011, p. 67.) Moss et al. (2011) also suggest writing age-appropriate descriptions that answer each of these questions when targets are introduced. Writing learning targets that include all components, when teachers have many targets to write each day (particularly if they are new teachers or have a new grade level or subject to teach and haven't had time to strategically plan), can become difficult to manage. In situations like these, coaches can provide a lifeline by collaboratively writing learning targets with teachers and demonstrating how to access standards and quickly turn them into targets. Sometimes curriculums have targets aligned with standards already incorporated into daily lessons.

The final piece of my four-piece luggage set is the personal item that I stow under the seat in front of me. In this analogy, it would contain specific information about how students would show mastery of the learning target/intention and whether or not students had met the defined target or intention, and at what level, so that next steps could be determined. Hattie's concept of learning intentions can be explained as "What do I want students to know, understand, and be able to do?" Learning intentions "describe what it is we want students to learn in terms of the skills, knowledge, attitude, and values within any particular unit or lesson" (Hattie, 2009, p. 162). Success criteria—similar to the detailed pieces of learning targets, such as the "How will I show I have met the target?" pieces—are described by Hattie (2009) as "What are we looking for?"

Success criteria can be codeveloped with students. They are used to create clarity surrounding what students will be doing and how their work will be formatively assessed. Levels of performance on success criteria (possibly using rubrics, exemplars, or modeling to further define what success looks like) provide specific information for students and teachers, letting them know to what extent the target/intention of the lesson(s) has been met. Success criteria would be generally considered the same as formative assessment criteria (Education Services Australia, n.d.). Both learning target details indicating how students will show they have met the target and success criteria can be represented by the final piece of the four-piece purple luggage set. This final part of the luggage set is the personal item that we keep close, so that we can access it frequently. This is often a forgotten piece in our planning, yet it holds the keys to clear and effective teaching, showing students what their part will be in learning the content and at what level the content has been mastered. Keeping these pieces in front of us allows the teacher and coach to intentionally plan next steps, based on how students are progressing.

If we can coach teachers to understand the patterns and concepts that exist beyond the words, we can save them a great deal of misunderstanding and stress. We can't count on educational terminology to be consistent, so is it fair to expect teachers (especially inexperienced ones) to be able to understand that different words often used in the field of education can mean close to the same thing? The confusion created by an overabundance of words or strategies with similar meanings or structures in the field of education sometimes borders on the ridiculous. For instance, think of a basic outline structure for a paragraph that includes a topic (I), subtopics (A, B, and C, if needed) that back up the topic, and details (1s, 2s, and 3s), finishing with a wrap-up of the topic (I) in a different way (conclusion). This structure can also be taught using color codes for the topic, main points, details, and conclusion. It has also been explained using a variety of graphic-organizer formats, including the "hamburger," the "house," the "chicken foot," and the "tree." Scholars, authors, and the teacher down the hall coin phrases or use certain words, models, or visuals to explain concepts and introduce or expound on educational topics of interest. This is one reason why research results can be interpreted and explained in many ways, with different verbiage, and why we see great teaching strategies coming back 20 years later with different names. As coaches, let's help teachers understand this by becoming knowledgeable enough to point out patterns and empower teachers to make informed professional choices, so that they have a better understanding of what is being asked of them and why.

I am fascinated by the remarkable creativity I see and experience regularly as I visit classrooms, read educational literature, and attend professional development classes. We are all working in the best ways we know how to help students and colleagues succeed in a complicated world, one with challenging and ever-changing technology, complex people, and innumerable variables. There are many roads that can help students and teachers be successful—and that is a good thing, as long as we can conceptually make enough sense of it all to teach, coach, and lead with clarity.

I have found that it really doesn't matter much what teachers call their reason for spending 50 minutes or more on a topic, whether the "lesson purpose" (there's another phrase used by Fisher & Frey, 2014, p. 4) is called a goal, an objective, a target, or an intention—but what is important is that there *is* one, that it is aligned with standards, and that it is broken down into small chunks that can be easily understood and quickly assessed by both teacher and students as the learning progresses. Coaches will want to learn about and find ways to make sense of the current language and concepts being addressed in educational literature—the four-piece luggage analogy is one way to do this.

To simplify planning details for both teacher and student use, we could help teachers organize daily learning for each period of instruction in student-friendly language in three sections, like this:

What? Goal/objective/target/intention/purpose for the class period or for a short time aligned with standards	
1.	
How: Success Criteria/Formative Assessment: Details explaining how students will participate and how they will show they have understood/ met the target/intention:	**By When:**
1.	
2.	
3.	
4.	

Communicating time limits for pieces of instruction supports long-range sequential planning and helps teachers make sure time is left for all prioritized standards planned to be taught. It is always wise to include some wiggle room here and there, to allow for student input on timelines, student accommodations, interventions, and unexpected events. We don't want to create a stressful and completely rigid classroom climate. However, one of the biggest complaints I've heard from administrators when they are concerned about teacher effectiveness is the poor pacing of lessons and teachers taking too long to get through concepts. Usually this is due to a lack of intentional long-term planning. If we don't know what's next, why worry about how long it takes to get through a topic?

As I write this, I am recalling deer-in-the-headlights looks in the eyes of teachers (particularly new ones) as they courageously took on this productive struggle to be organized, to be intentional, to be competent. Educational thought leaders write about the important theoretical underpinnings of comprehensive, intentional, rigorous, instructional practice, and it would be great if every teacher could achieve that level of detail with every lesson every day. However, we know this does not happen easily, especially if a teacher tries to go it alone. Good curriculum resources can help, and teams can organize their work to maximize time. Seasoned, successful teachers may have already broken standards down into small "how" chunks and have success criteria and formative assessment ideas they use regularly but just haven't written down or shared with others. Accessing their knowledge could significantly shorten the time it would take to drill down to the detailed level of what specific student and teacher actions would produce the highest levels of mastery. Analyzing student data (both formative and summative), and noting when specific instructional practices were employed and what the results were, is an effective way to determine future instructional choices (Love, Stiles, Mundry, & DiRanna, 2008).

Teachers may ask: "Why do I need to do any of this, since it's all right here in the book? I'll just follow the book, because the amount of work required to take all this apart is extreme." In some school districts, this might work if district leadership prefers teachers to follow the books they have purchased with fidelity. There are some advantages to this from a systems perspective, particularly when considering alignment of curriculum, both vertically (with grades above and below) and horizontally (with grade-level or subject teams).

However, as I have shared previously, there's always going to be a downside to an overly strict focus of rigidly adhering to a curriculum at the expense of honoring the professional expertise of teachers on the front lines. This is because no curriculum covers all the standards perfectly or effectively meets the needs of all students who are in front of a teacher every day. A curriculum can't know a student, but it can provide wonderful, helpful resources. Similarly, there is not much collaboration or teacher motivation to be had when the opportunity to use professional judgment, problem solve, dig deeply and creatively into content, or discover new ways to adjust for individual student needs is surrendered. With the increased use of professional learning communities (PLCs), teachers are being asked to engage in discussions and interactions with colleagues that delve into instructional details that matter. Are teachers professionals or technicians? If we believe they are professionals, they must have authority to act in the best interests of the students they serve, along with balancing the need to effectively teach curriculum that relies on grade-level concepts being mastered before students move to the next grade.

The devil is in the details, in all professions. The Parable of the Oranges, told by Randall L. Ridd (2015), is a story I often think of when I begin to tire of details. I will paraphrase it for you:

> A young man wanted to work for a prestigious company. He was hired at an entry-level position and then set his sights on a supervisor position. He completed the tasks he was given and often came in early and stayed late so his boss would see that he put in long hours. After five years, the supervisor position opened up, but another employee who had only been at the company for 6 months was given the job. The young man was very angry over this situation and went to ask his boss about it.
>
> The wise boss said: "Before I answer your questions, would you do a favor for me? Would you go to the store and buy some oranges? My wife needs them." The young man agreed and went to the store and bought some oranges. When he came back, the boss asked him how much they cost. The young man said he wasn't sure, and gave his boss the receipt.
>
> Then, the boss called in the employee who had received the promotion and asked him to do the same job. He readily agreed and went to the store. When he returned, the boss asked, "What kind of oranges did you buy?" "Well," he replied, "the store

had many varieties—there were navel oranges, Valencia oranges, blood oranges, tangerines, and many others, and I didn't know which kind to buy. But I remembered you said your wife needed the oranges, so I called her. She said she was having a party and that she was going to make orange juice. So I asked the grocer which of all these oranges would make the best orange juice. He said the Valencia orange was full of very sweet juice, so that's what I bought. I dropped them by your home on my way back to the office. Your wife was very pleased."

"How much did they cost?" the boss asked.

"Well, that was another problem. I didn't know how many to buy, so I once again called your wife and asked her how many guests she was expecting. She said 20. I asked the grocer how many oranges would be needed to make juice for 20 people, and it was a lot. So, I asked the grocer if he could give me a quantity discount, and he did! These oranges normally cost 75 cents each, but I paid only 50 cents. Here is your change and the receipt." The boss smiled and said, "Thank you; you may go."

He looked over at the young man who had been watching. The young man stood up, slumped his shoulders and said, "I see what you mean," as he walked dejectedly out of the office.

A teacher, coach, or educational leader who is determined to access the best information and resources available, and who is willing to dig to the level of detail that will provide crystal-clear clarity, will be able to achieve an impressive level of excellence, as the story suggests.

We will want to remember, however, that even such a great cause as this can be overdone to the point of sapping our energy and negatively affecting our health. Notice how the guy who received the promotion wasn't focused on staying late or making a good impression; he was focused on finding out as much information as he could from a variety of sources and using that information to do the best job possible. It was more a state of mind—it was about being curious and quickly doing what was needed to accomplish a goal.

We all have 24 hours in a day, and that's it, so anything we, as coaches, can do to help teachers streamline their work is always greatly appreciated. Administrators will want to look for ways to provide supports with scheduling, encouragement, and flexibility for teachers and teams willing to put forth a great deal of effort to be their best for students. The process of mining this deeply to unearth all the small pieces of each quality lesson and fit them together to best meet the needs of students takes focused intention and time. Thinking through these detailed processes showcases a foundational piece of becoming a competent teacher and coach—hard work. Vince Lombardi said it this way: "The only time success comes before work is in the dictionary" (BrainyQuote, n.d.).

More Ways to Deliver Instruction

It is helpful to have at our fingertips different ways to deliver quality instruction, especially when we may find that some teachers tend to use the same methods every day. Teachers don't want to resort to "think, pair, share," "popcorn," "choral response," and lecture all the time; it's just that these methods come to mind quickly in the heat of the moment, since they don't involve much prep. Helping teachers understand—and sometimes just remember, when they are stuck in a rut—that there are many ways to deliver instruction and then supporting them as they decide which methods would work best for them and their students is a vital coaching skill. Compiling the results of interest surveys and learning modality preferences are easy ways to access useful information when determining which instructional methods to choose.

One year, when 19 out of 26 of my students showed by survey they preferred instruction delivered in kinesthetic ways, I decided to move the small-group teacher desk to the middle of the room and planned a variety of teaching strategies and stations that facilitated movement throughout the day, so that my students could be active as they learned. The academic and social growth of those students was exciting, and I didn't have to waste instructional time telling very active students to sit down and stop distracting others, because they were engaged in the learning. It was active; it was mobile; it was designed for them. Helping teachers access and analyze meaningful information about students so that instruction can be adapted to meet their needs is competent coaching.

 The following ideas for instructional delivery are organized into categories. There is not room in this book to go into great detail about each idea, but there are a few examples within each category. These instructional delivery ideas are meant to provide a coach with specifics to help a teacher plan *how* students are going to learn and to be intentional about what the teacher and students are going to do during the lesson. When choosing instructional delivery methods, don't forget to make sure their use supports content standard(s) and learning targets.

Go-To Processes

Organize academic procedures, processes, and protocols to provide students with the "how" to quickly identify, analyze, and understand a skill or standard in context. When students already know how they will be participating and how to record information they are learning, they can focus on the concept being modeled or explained without being bombarded with too many variables to consider at the same time. This allows for greater understanding and retention of the core concept. If students are continually trying to figure out how they are going to record, analyze, or interact with the information being presented, it is difficult for them to focus solely on the point the teacher wants to make. Creating *protocols for participation* allows for intentional organization of content, to facilitate easy access for review. Having a plan students are familiar with, to facilitate their participation, saves a great deal of time and allows for focused practice and access to previous content taught.

Detailed protocols can be found in a variety of educational literature and can also be collaboratively developed at the school or team level. Students could help design the protocols or choose from different options. Here are a few ideas:

- Color-coded paragraph analysis protocol

- Poetry analysis process

- Color-coded parts-of-speech analysis protocol

- Note-taking templates

- Writing rubrics

- Warm-up routines

- Writing conference protocols

- Student-to-teacher or teacher-to-student feedback protocols

- Writing-plan templates

- Science notebook structures, with table of contents

- Math notebook structures, with table of contents

- Student reference and results (R&R) notebook, organized with tabs by subject or topic to include anchor charts, exemplar papers, rubrics, and reference materials for easy access at home and/or online, with opportunities for students to record data and track their progress on a variety of skills, standards, or tests over time

- Student question-creation flipbook (using Bloom's Taxonomy or Webb's Depth of Knowledge), with a graphic organizer for analyzing questions within text and formulating new questions at different levels

- Flow maps

- Learning maps (Knight, 2013)

- Science-experiment plan

- Choral-reading protocol

- Lesson conclusion or wrap-up protocol

- Review processes

Go-To Desk/Chair Configurations

When students are familiar with a few desk/chair configurations and can organize their desks/chairs into those formations quickly, it becomes easier to facilitate different types of group work. Students learn ways to split up for group work and practice moving their desks/chairs within a time limit to facilitate different types of instruction.

- Small groups:
  - Dyad (2 students)
  - Triad (3 students)
  - Quad (4 students)
  - Pent (5 students)

It is important to take the time to teach students the details of how to put the chairs/desks together and where to put them back after the group-work section of the lesson is complete. Demonstrate, and then take some time for students to practice moving to each configuration, possibly using a signal or sound and a timer. This saves instructional time in the long run and lets students know the instruction will be presented and experienced in a variety of ways.

- Larger groups:
  - U shape—allows teacher easy access to each student and room to meet in the middle
  - Dice pods (pods of four to six students, organized visually like the number 5 on a die—can accommodate up to 30 students)
  - Inner and outer circle—students in each circle participate in a specific way
  - Speed learning (like speed dating—straight rows, with students facing each other; students on one side move every few minutes; questions are provided and discussed with each "date")

When organizing large-group configurations, it helps to project a visual seating chart showing where each student will be sitting, so that desks/chairs can be moved quickly and the teacher can decide where individual students would learn best for specific lessons, topics, or units. One important piece to remember when doing this is to plan for traffic flow into, out of, and around the room. The coach can help the teacher design these formations so that the teacher can easily access students to provide support or redirection. Two resources the TCT team uses for desk configurations are Fred Jones (2007) and Spence Rogers (2013).

Creating Support Stations (Rogers, 2013), Reference Posters, Anchor Papers, and Exemplars

A powerful way to provide support for students, allow them to move, and encourage them to take ownership of their learning is to have support stations and helpful reference items available in different areas around the classroom. These materials could also be provided for teams or individuals at their desks or tables. These support documents and materials could provide access to specific content to answer questions; they could be experiential activities to support a differentiated approach to understand a concept; they could be posters with information students can easily reference, papers, or specific areas on the board that explain to students the details they need to know or accomplish to move forward in their learning for the day; they could be anchor papers or exemplars of completed student work scored at different levels, with rubrics provided for students to analyze. The idea is to provide clarity and support. The message is: "You don't have to guess, get lucky, or figure this out completely on your own. All the support, structure, and examples you need to be successful are provided. You can do this!" Other support stations could address the basics of school life, such as a station with Kleenex, bandages, and hand sanitizer, or maybe a station with snacks, water bottles, and pencils (with a bowl for students to pay when they can).

Go-To Celebrations

Cheers or expressions of encouragement can positively influence student motivation. For example, when something goes well, let loose with a five-second party or happy dance (dance with reckless abandon); do a table slap with a catchy rhythm to honor a person or a group that has done well; have the class do a slow-motion celebratory fist pump, a "raise the roof" motion, or group dance moves (could be something the whole class decides upon together); bow to a student who achieved something great; sound the gong when something good happens; have the class join in a resounding "Yes!" "Nice!" "Awesome!" or "Yay"; or play a short segment of a song, such as "Celebrate, good times, c'mon!" when something wonderful happens. It's amazing how little time it takes to "focus on the happy" for a moment. Small, positive actions implemented regularly can shape an entire classroom culture. Let's acknowledge what goes well, so that students want to produce more of it!

The teacher can draw a relevant visual (e.g., a blue ribbon, a trophy, a scroll) on the board, where each student adds points he or she has earned on an assignment toward a class goal, resulting in a reward when the goal is met (this is also an informal way to formatively assess as students record their scores).

For team acknowledgments, the teacher might place the Einstein/Emerson/Inspiring Team trophy or some other type of easily visible team award in the middle of a high-functioning team's pod after the team has had some type of success. Perhaps the team that earned the most points during a class period could receive a fun award. It could be a little quirky; kids could decide (it's relatively easy to find an old trophy and decorate it). Team or individual points for a variety of purposes, including progress toward an incentive or goal completion, could also be kept track of digitally and projected.

Finally, the teacher might keep postcards ready to send home for exceptional work and effort. Positive phone calls home, birthday cards, or small gifts are also good ways to celebrate.

Student Response Strategies

Increasing the opportunities students have to respond, rather than having one student answer at a time, encourages all students to think and participate. The following are great tools to have in your teaching or coaching toolbox:

- *Response tools.* The key is to make it easy for the teacher to process responses from many students in a short amount of time, honor students as partners in learning, and add a bit of novelty into the mix. Use cups, cards, popsicle sticks, or paper stoplights, allowing students to indicate by color or number their choice of answers (A, B, C, D) or how well they are understanding the lesson (red: "I don't get it—stop!" yellow: "I sort of get it"; green: "Got it; let's go on").

- *Whiteboards.* It's almost unlimited what can be done with these. Whiteboards are so helpful when students are tasked with a specific problem to work on; then, when students finish the problem, they can hold their boards up (it helps to have a protocol in which students hold them up at the same time). The teacher can then quickly visually assess progress toward the learning goal—this supports spaced versus massed practice (Hattie, 2009). Whiteboards allow for numerous back-and-forth interactions between students and the teacher during direct instruction and are a useful tool for short segments of meaningful practice.

- *Apps.* There are many useful applications for tablets, smartphones, and other devices that allow students to respond. Some allow for all student responses to be visually acknowledged, compiled, and assessed quickly.

- *Gestures.* Teachers can use gestures to indicate many things. For instance, if used for quick checks for understanding, an "okay" sign held up high above the head can mean "totally okay," half covered with the other hand can mean "sort of okay," and completely covered can mean "not okay" or "I do not understand." For younger children, the class expectations might have gestures associated with them to help remind students how the class runs and to allow the teacher to prompt students to remember the expectations without speaking.

Music, Movement, Art, Plays, Rhymes, Mnemonics, Memorized Sayings, or Quotes

Teaching in these ways supports brain-friendly, active learning (Harmin & Toth, 2006; Medina, 2014; Tate, 2012) and allows multiple intelligences to be addressed (Gardner, 1993). By coaching teachers to use a variety of methods to deliver instruction, we can help tune their teaching to the key that will help students learn best. Variety is the spice of life! When students at an alternative high school in TCT's area filled out a multiple-intelligence survey, musical intelligence was the top result.

Videos and Technology

Short video clips are great ways to provide examples, illustrate points, or explain processes. Computer programs, games, apps, and interactive presentations using SMART Boards that support the learning intention are great ways to teach effectively in this relatively new digital world. Students living in this digital age are being exposed to "an unprecedented level of interaction and immediate feedback" (Kelly, McCain, & Jukes, 2009, p. 15). Students' ability to process visual information at lightning speeds due to their interaction since birth with technology, and their preference for multimedia that includes rich graphics, sound, and color rather than just text (Kelly et al., 2009), is an amazing development that is shaking up the educational landscape. Students' brains today work differently because of technology, and there is no going back to the pre-digital age. The more we can effectively use technology in schools, the more relevant we can make our teaching for our digitally savvy students.

Demonstrations

I've never forgotten a horribly effective science lesson. Our teacher somehow secured a cow lung from a local slaughterhouse. When he brought it into the room, he laid it on the smooth, black table next to me and blew it up with a bicycle pump. Then, he cut the lung and showed us the little air sacs, or alveoli (I still remember this word), all filled up. OOOOHH! Terrifying and fascinating. It was bloody and kind of scary for a squeamish preteen who had never met a cow she didn't like. Obviously memorable, though. Demonstrations can be powerful!

Modeling

The best modeling is sequential, structured, and focused on one skill or strategy at a time. The "gradual release of responsibility" instructional framework (Fisher & Frey, 2014)—sometimes called "I Do, We Do, You Do"—incorporates a modeling opportunity during the "Focused Instruction" section for teachers to show students how work is to be accomplished. After the teacher has modeled what needs to be done, the teacher works with students, and then the students work together—this is the "We." At the end of the lesson, the student practices alone and, by the end of the lesson, has had enough types of practice to show mastery of the "learning purpose" (which is the term Fisher & Frey use instead of "goal," "objective," "target," or "intention").

For some reason, probably to save time, the modeling piece is often left out of instruction and coaching. I see this often! Showing *how* is so powerful, in both teaching and coaching. It can save time in the long run if learners know exactly how to do things because they've seen them done. One way to ensure students or teachers remember the modeling piece is to allow learners to video-record the modeling section of the teaching or coaching, so that they can refer to it as needed. If there is an opportunity for the coach to model an instructional practice with a teacher's students, discuss the modeling results with the teacher, identify any roadblocks, and then provide feedback while/after the teacher tries the strategy, that would be ideal. If not, coaches can look for videos or find other teachers to observe who effectively implement the strategy and provide them as resources for the teacher. This "gradual release," or scaffolding of instruction that includes modeling, provides support for students (and for teachers) throughout the learning process as they work to individually master a specific skill.

Games

Let's not forget to play! It's easy to make school fun for students (and the teacher), by incorporating instructional games that support the learning target/intention of the lesson. There are many resources that provide ideas for instructional games. Story Wars is a favorite! Here's how it goes:

1. Divide students into two teams.

2. Students read and take notes using a writing plan or graphic organizer for fictional or informational text. The quality of note-taking is important, because details about the reading will be asked during the game.

3. Organize questions from the reading text: Factual Questions (3 points), Inferential Questions (5 points), and Bonus Questions (difficult, creative questions posed by the teacher, possibly with universal applications) (10 points).

4. After students have read the story and filled out the plan or graphic organizer, play the *Star Wars* theme and have the two teams line up facing each other. Students may bring their notes to the game.

5. The first two students in line from each team face each other, and the first question is asked. The first student who hits a "buzzer" with something (maybe the "buzzer" is a tall stool, and the student hits it with a fake light saber) is allowed to answer the question.

6. If that student answers incorrectly, the other team has 30 seconds to collaborate to figure out the correct answer. This process holds individual students accountable for their reading and note-taking and also facilitates useful collaboration.

7. A scoreboard is started, and the appropriate number of points is given to the team that answered the question correctly.

8. The students who have just had a turn go to the end of the line, and the next two students step up to be asked a question.

9. The winning team is determined when a certain score is reached; or, when the allotted time is up, the team that is ahead wins.

Incentives for winners could include extra recess time, art time, homework passes, treats, and so on. In practice, the competition, and the novelty of the *Star Wars* theme, was enough to make the game a favorite with students.

Differentiation Ideas

Here are a couple of my favorite ideas for facilitating differentiated instruction:

- *Leveled notes for students at different levels and those who might need accommodations.* The teacher creates a full version of notes to be used when teaching the lesson; then the teacher cuts a few details out and creates a version with less information and blanks for students to fill in some of the concepts or vocabulary; then he or she creates another version with less information, if there is a need for four levels; and finally the last version is an outline, for students who will not struggle to summarize and record the concepts. Thank goodness for computer programs that make this editing doable!

- *Dinah Zike's Foldables.* A Foldable is typically used as a type of interactive graphic organizer. They are helpful kinesthetic tools that can be used to support the learning of specific skills in all subjects at all levels. I visited a middle school in Japan in 2011, and classes there were using Dinah's Foldable ideas. The need for inexpensive and easy-to-use kinesthetic tools and activities to organize and support learning is universal. Visit the website of Foldables' creator at www.dinah.com.

Cooperative Learning/Group Work Tips

Following are a few general guidelines for cooperative learning or group work:

- *Have a reason for grouping students in a certain way.* A teacher could consider organizing groups based on personality styles, multiple-intelligence survey results, interests, mixed or similar ability levels related to the learning intention, or behavioral considerations. Another method is to match students who need extra support with students who can and would like to provide that support. These are only some possible considerations to be thought through when group work is chosen as an instructional delivery method. Competent teachers have a reason for grouping students a certain way, and it's not to just to keep Joe away from Nicky.

- *Every student has something to do for the entire time.* This could be a role (speaker, recorder, artist, leader, etc.) that includes specific tasks, or it could involve detailed steps for each team member during the learning activity. Team work could be organized by role or based on which number students receive in the group. For instance, in each group, each student is given a number from 1 to 4, so, for this activity, number 3 will be doing _____.

- *Each team member can visually access what he or she needs to be doing throughout the activity.* It helps to have what each student will be doing easily visible. This information could be projected on a screen or SMART Board, in large print on the whiteboard, or—even better—organized as a checklist on each table or pod for students to check off as each piece is accomplished.

- *Time limits are communicated.*

- *Accountability for completing group work within the time limit is built in.* For instance: The speaker will report the findings from a group lab or discussion to the whole class, the recorder will turn in the notes he or she took (show exemplars of high-quality notes to the recorders before the group work begins, so that students don't think it's okay to turn in work that is less than what is expected), the artist will create some type of poster or large visual for the speaker to refer to when presenting—this large visual will be a synthesis of the notes (and each team member can add his or her own thoughts to the poster in a "My Take-Away" section of the poster, with a different colored marker). A quick search on Google or Pinterest can provide many ideas of roles that could be used. I have found that the often-mentioned timekeeper role (making sure the team uses the time well) and leader role (making sure everyone does their jobs) are not that effective when defined in those ways, because there isn't anything specific to do in those roles except nag others. You might incorporate within the leader role the timekeeper, the materials provider, and keeping everyone on track by checking off the whole-group tasks as they are completed on a checklist. Or, maybe the leader introduces the speaker and summarizes what was shared in his or her own words, or perhaps this person suggests an application of what was learned after the speaker presents. Just a thought, because I've seen way too many kids lose interest if their role or assignment didn't really keep them thinking and doing.

- *The teacher is mobile and regularly checks in with groups.*

- *The work counts in some way.* Maybe the group work is of value because the information generated can be captured on cell phones and referenced on an upcoming test, or each student receives a grade based on how well he or she fulfilled his or her part of the group work. Maybe there is a group incentive, such as groups that received the highest ratings on a peer-presentation rubric after all groups have presented their work get that Einstein trophy, or maybe those students get to go to lunch early, or they receive a certain number of points toward a reward, or they get to enjoy something positive that is meaningful to them.

Assessment

The familiar struggle with vocabulary is found in this arena as well. There are so many words associated with assessment that it becomes difficult to give teachers an overview of the different levels/parts/types of assessment in a way that includes most of the vocabulary they have heard.

Understanding an Assessment Range

I have organized an Assessment Range Table (see below) with information and some vocabulary from the book *Learning by Doing* (DuFour, DuFour, Eaker, & Many, 2010), a district-level presentation by Tom Many (2016), Yahya Al Alhareth and Ibtisam Al Dighrir's (2014) formative assessment continuum, and Joan Herman and Kilchan Choi's 2008 CRESST report. Before you look at this table, please understand that the amount of time it takes to address different units or focus areas of study will vary. For instance, depending on how a unit is organized, it could take three weeks or three months to complete. The main idea is that when planning for instruction, teachers make intentional and meaningful choices for assessment as the learning progresses, so that by the time the final summative assessments are given, the results should not be a surprise to the students or the teacher.

The table first lists opportunities for pre-assessment. Sometimes final assessments or interim assessments included in curriculums or collaboratively developed by teams are given to students before a unit of study begins. This is done to see how much the class already knows about the topic, so that differentiation can be applied and planned instruction adjusted as needed. Pre/post data using the same test can also be used to provide evidence that students have learned specific information on a topic the teacher has taught. Data of this sort is often necessary to provide numeric information for administrators to review, so that they have what they need to complete teachers' evaluations. Some school districts purchase a standardized assessment system that includes a pre-assessment for the beginning of the school year, followed by mid-year and end-of-year assessments, to help teachers identify weaknesses and strengths as students prepare for the annual state assessment.

One issue with pretests is the problematic task of motivating students to give their best efforts when they often know next to nothing about the topic and cannot answer most of the questions. When conducting a pre-assessment that a teacher feels students wouldn't know anything about, it could be helpful to make a connection to the relevance of the test results for students and communicate that doing their best will allow them to see an accurate measure of their growth after instruction. Maybe even some type of incentive could garner more student effort. It would be natural for some teachers to think that the lower students score on the pre-assessment, the better the teacher will look, particularly if the pre/post data counts on his or her evaluation, right? This is where gaming comes in, and often the losers are kids. If teachers, administrators, and states are serious about pre-assessment being used to adjust a unit of instruction to match the needs of students and for the results to be used to effectively differentiate, then pre-assessments should definitely be used. If their use is to just to check a box and the data will go to waste, we might as well not put students through it. Let's do whatever we can to avoid wasting students' time and killing their motivation.

There are many ways to conduct assessments without turning them into burdensome old-school "tests." Most assessments that coaches can help teachers be prepared to give are formative in nature, structured to monitor and guide instructional delivery choices and to provide useful feedback and information for both teachers and students. Following the Assessment Range Table, "on the fly" (Al Alhareth & Al Dighrir, 2014) or "In the Moment" ideas (often referred to as checks for understanding)—along with planned informal, or short-cycle lesson-based, formative assessment ideas—will be shared.

Great teachers regularly assess in a variety of ways to see how well students are learning, so that they can both give and receive meaningful feedback. This also speaks to the importance of clear goals/objectives/targets/intentions, backed up with strategically chosen instructional delivery methods, so that all learning is logically linked and the assessment can provide targeted information to inform course corrections and ensure that the learning that was planned actually happened. When using learning targets/intentions and success criteria, the levels of completion (possibly organized through rubrics) for each success criterion would be a type of formative assessment, or a measure of how close the student is to successfully achieving the learning target/intention.

Planning with this level of focus has had the positive effect of (a) reeling in teachers who tend to get off topic and (b) keeping students aware of their learning goals and how they are progressing toward them. Thinking of assessment as a continuum, with some methods of assessment being primarily *for* learning and some used as measures *of* learning within specified timelines, has been a useful visual when searching for ways to best deliver coaching on this important topic (DuFour et al., 2010).

A few years ago, I was privileged to work with five district-level coaches: Kristy Feldman, Toby Lefere, Jean Rice, Nancy Shanklin, and Lisa Wolf. We collaboratively defined, discussed, categorized, and compiled most of the following resources from a variety of sources to share with teachers we coached. We felt a need to define and share ideas about these two types of informal "for" learning assessments. The important thing is that we came to an agreement about how to be clear when explaining these concepts. Different teams and school districts may define these topics differently or disagree on the length of time, whether details should be recorded, and so forth, but at least six of us were on the same page, and I'm sure the teachers we jointly interacted with were appreciative! Many of these ideas can be found in the book *Explicit Instruction: Effective and Efficient Teaching*, by Anita Archer and Charles Hughes (2011), and in an online PowerPoint presentation of the same name, created by Dr. Archer.

Assessment Range Table

More Formative		More Summative
Short Cycle Small Chunks of Instruction (Assessments **FOR** learning)	**Medium Cycle** Moderate Chunks of Instruction	**Long Cycle** Massive Amounts of Instruction (Assessments **OF** Learning)

◄————————————————————————►

Informal Formative	Formal Formative	
In the Moment	Planned	Curriculum-Embedded

Checks For Under-Standing	Short Cycle Planned	Weekly Quizzes or Mid-Unit Tests	Common Formative Assessments	End of Unit Tests	District Mid-year Standardized Benchmark Tests	Final Exams	Annual Standardized Tests
(On the Fly, Minute by minute)	(at the end of each lesson)	**Interim Assessments** found in curriculum resources **Formative Assessments of:** Performance Tasks, Projects, Products, Exhibits, Portfolios (formative assessment designed to provide meaningful feedback on progress toward expectations typically found on a rubric. Could include student, peer, and teacher review)	created by teacher teams (about every 3 weeks) to include students' mastery level of standards **Interim Assessments** found in curriculum resources **Interim Assessments of:** Performance Tasks, Projects, Products, Exhibits, Portfolios (more formal formative assessment to provide meaningful feedback on progress toward completion of learning intentions)	to indicate students' final mastery level of content standard(s) addressed during the unit Standards addressed within the unit could be included on the end of quarter or semester final exam	used to compare to beginning-of-year standardized test results to assess student progress and prepare for summative annual standardized test	(at the end of a quarter or semester) typically for middle- and high-school students to include all units addressed during the quarter or semester **Final Assessment of:** Performance Tasks, Projects, Products, Exhibits, Portfolios End-of-Year Standardized Benchmark Tests	**State Required Annual Assessments** **PARCC** Partnership for Assessment of Readiness for College and Careers **SBAC** Smarter Balanced Assessment Consortium

Pre-Assessment Possibilities

- District Beginning-of-Year Standardized Benchmark Tests
- Teacher Choice:
- Pre-Daily or Short Cycle chunks of instruction
- Pre-Weekly Quiz
- Pre-Mid-Unit Tests
- Pre-Common Formative Assessment
- Pre-End of Unit Tests

Checks for Understanding

Teachers frequently check in with students to quickly assess their continual progress toward understanding the instruction that is occurring in the moment. This information is not recorded and may or may not include all students. Checks for understanding are used to give teachers a mental awareness of which students are grasping the instruction in the moment. Teachers then use this information to adjust instruction.

Teachers can use a variety of quick (less than 30-second) checks to assess levels of student understanding, and they can do so frequently throughout the lesson. Following are some examples.

- *Student summary of another student's answer.* In order to promote active listening, after one student has volunteered an answer to the teacher's question, the teacher asks another student to summarize the first student's response. Many students hear little of what their classmates have to say, waiting instead for the instructor to either correct them or repeat the answer. Having students summarize or repeat each other's contributions both fosters active participation by all students and promotes the idea that learning is a shared enterprise. Given the possibility of being asked to repeat classmates' comments, most students will listen more attentively to one another.

- *Turn to your neighbor.* After students complete a learning task, the teacher asks students to compare ideas with their neighbors (elbow or knee partners, spaghetti and meatball partners, even and odd partners, etc.). Students signal (thumbs up, down, or wiggly; yes or no in sign language; etc.) to the teacher to share whether their answers are the same as or different from their partner's.

- *Whiteboards.* These are a visual platform for student responses—for example, drawings, words, symbols, or math problems. Students can show answers when they are ready, or they can hold up their answers at the same time, and the teacher can note and address student error patterns in the moment.

- *Response cards or tents.* Students hold up cards (3 × 5 or bigger) or other objects that indicate their level of understanding of a concept or an answer they have chosen. The teacher might like to use red, green, and yellow cards or cups, with red indicating the student does not understand, yellow meaning the student sort of understands, and green indicating it's okay to go on because the student understands. Or the teacher might ask a multiple-choice question that is projected on a screen, and students put their finger next to the answer A, B, C, or D, which is written in large letters on the left side of a card. Or the teacher asks a question, and students can respond with cards that read "Yes," "No," and "Maybe" (we use this in our TCT team meetings to get an idea of how people are leaning on the way to making a decision). When teaching the parts of speech, the teacher can show an example, and students can answer with the appropriate card that has the correct part of speech ("noun"/"verb"/"adjective"/"adverb") on it.

- *Thumbs up ("I agree or understand"), thumbs down ("I disagree or do not understand"), thumbs wiggly ("I'm not sure").* Have students show this signal close to the body for more valid results; this helps students avoid cueing off others' signals. This strategy has been taking a lot of hits lately, especially when teachers are trying to use it instead of a more structured formative assessment, but it can still provide useful information, especially if students feel safe showing a thumbs-down.

- *Choral responses.* In this method of checking for understanding, all students respond at the same time; the teacher uses a gesture, so that they know when to respond; responses should be short; 100% participation is expected; and the teacher monitors student participation.

- *Four corners.* The teacher gives students a question and then asks students to move to a corner of the room based on their answer. For example, the teacher designates the four corners of the room as A, B, C, and D and asks a multiple-choice question with four possible answers.

- *Hot potato.* The teacher asks a student a question to test the student's understanding of content. If he or she gets the answer right, that student gets to ask a different question that tests another student's understanding. The student asking the question must know the answer. This game could be played in groups, to involve more students. The teacher would pose the initial question to a particular group member (defined either by role or by number), and then the teacher would move around the room, checking in with groups to hear students' questions and answers and asking new questions when needed.

Formative Assessment

The formative assessment allows all students to show their current level of mastery aligned with the instructional goal/objective/learning target/intention (all student responses are reviewed to determine next steps). It can be administered in a variety of modalities (usually takes less than five minutes) and is used by teachers to determine levels of content mastery and inform instructional next steps. The formative assessment is typically given at the end of a lesson that usually takes one to two class period(s) or block(s) of time. Following are some examples of formative assessments:

- Exit tickets: written responses to questions designed to directly address the learning target or intention

- Targeted questions answered in written form, possibly using a template the teacher has prepared

- Whiteboards (for answering questions or solving problems to visually "show" to the teacher)

- Quick quizzes (small sampling of content taught that day based on the learning target; three to five true-or-false, fill-in-the-blank, or multiple-choice questions)

- Clickers/plickers/apps that allow for all student responses to formative assessment questions to be posted and quickly analyzed

- Summarizing or paraphrasing in written form

- Informally recording levels of understanding as students work—student work related to the learning target is observed and recorded, used for adjusting instruction and to show student progress over time

- Use of kinesthetic tools to formatively assess young learners (or older learners), so that they can demonstrate their understanding of the learning target (E.g., give kindergarten students the numbers 1–10 and have students put the numbers in order; or give them four numbers, then have students organize them from least to greatest, then greatest to least.)

- Fill in a graphic organizer (or portions of a graphic organizer) related to the learning target as a quick assessment.

Finally, there may be time for some formative assessments to be given orally to individual students while other students are working on another activity related to the learning target.

Conclusion

We are working in a knowledge-based profession. There is a lot to think about, to learn, and to remember. Let us bring to our coaching the "I can do this" kind of attitude that prompted Leonardo da Vinci (2016) to write, "Learning never exhausts the mind."

To recap: The chapter began with a comparison of what competent coaching *is* and what it *isn't* and then moved to the importance of believing that we, as coaches, can make a difference. Then, current big-picture topics were listed, and more details about them were provided in Appendix A, "Competent Cliff Notes." Next, the "Frequent Five" were introduced. These were the five situations most often requested/needed/addressed over the past five years in a successful coaching program located in a large, urban school district. They were:

- *H.O.P.E.*, addressing health, organization, positivity, and encouragement (many of these details are also explained in Chapters 6 and 9)

- *Classroom management*, in the three-pronged structure of presence, planning, and procedures

- *Planning,* long-range planning with sequencing, unit or extended focus area planning, and daily planning

- *Instruction,* with a comparison of best instructional delivery choices, a discussion about educational vocabulary, the four-piece luggage analogy, and a list with definitions and explanations of 12 instructional delivery methods

- *Assessment,* including an assessment range table and ideas for checks for understanding and formative assessments

Use this chapter and Appendix A as reference support stations when looking for a quick way to get up to speed on important information and ideas, both big (scholars, authors, movements, programs) and small (daily applications by coaches). The information shared in both these places has been designed to support competent instructional coaching.

Reflect & Connect

What Do You Need to Know to Be Considered Competent?

What are you being asked to be on top of globally, nationally, in your state, in your district, in your school?

• Personal Expectations	• Outside Expectations (colleagues, administrators, evaluation documents, coaches, etc.)
_____	_____
_____	_____
_____	_____
_____	_____
_____	_____
_____	_____
_____	_____
• Goal 1	• Goal 2
_____	_____
_____	_____
_____	_____

Competent Self-Assessment

1. Take this self-assessment before you set an intention to consciously find ways to become more COMPETENT.

2. Implement some of the practical application ideas, coaching resources, and/or competent S.O.A.K. supports found in the chapter and below (or use some of your own ideas).

3. In a month or so, see whether you have been able to improve your thoughts, motivations, and behaviors surrounding the important coaching characteristic of being competent. Remember the synonyms of "competent," identified by coaching authors and by coaches like you, as you define what competent is and determine how to make it a more conscious part of your daily life: *knowledgeable, experienced, knows what to look for to determine next steps to better teachers' instructional practice, aware of and shares current data and research, a respected resource* (Frazier, 2014).

	Strongly Disagree 1	Disagree 2	Neutral Not Sure 3	Agree 4	Strongly Agree 5
I believe that, with my support, the teachers I work with can make positive changes to their instructional practice and students will benefit. I believe in my ability to make a difference.					
To continually develop my coaching skills, I regularly attend classes and read professional articles and books related to current best teaching and coaching practices. Through my studies, I maintain an awareness of current educational policies, hot topics/movements, and influential authors. I give myself time to process and synthesize this information and determine how to most effectively share it with teachers I coach.					
I know what the goals of my state/district/school/teacher are and I incorporate those goals into my coaching processes.					
I share quality resources with the people I coach, and the strategies I share are evidence based (based on reliable evidence).					
The people I coach can trust that I am experienced, knowledgeable, and continually learning. They can count on experiencing professional growth through their committed efforts and my quality coaching.					
I cultivate humility and seek opportunities to learn from and make connections with school and district leaders, content facilitators, and other coaches.					
Column Totals:					

Grand Total: _____

What totals mean: 26–30 = Competent Rock Star, 21–25 = Very Competent, 16–20 = Sort of Competent, 11–15 = Some Competence is Happening, 6–10 = Better Step it Up, 0–5 = Would Becoming More Competent Be a Worthwhile Goal?

Practical Applications Ideas for Competence

Competent Coaching Resources From Coaching Authors

Jim Knight, Marti Elford, Michael Hock, Devona Dunekack, Barbara Bradley, Donald D. Deshler, and David Knight authored the article "3 Steps to Great Coaching," found in the February 2015 *Journal of Staff Development*. We at TCT have found the eight questions on Page 12 of their article to be a great way to help teachers set meaningful goals and then identify strategies that would support the goals. We use some of these questions in our own protocols (with permission). I have every Jim Knight book and reference them often. When I read his words, I can feel his respect for educators and his personal commitment to support them and make their daily experiences better. He and his colleagues teach with optimism, clarity, and gentleness. They keep the focus on what matters most: the positive effects teachers and coaches can have on students. I treasure all his books.

Appendix A of the book *Differentiated Coaching* (2006, p. 184), by Jane Kise, is entitled "The Sixteen Types: Strengths, Beliefs, and Needs During Change." If teachers and coaches know their four Myers-Briggs Type Indicator Tool (MBTI) personality type letters, this is an amazing resource. It helps coaches get to know the people they are coaching by listing, for each personality type, their associated strengths and stressors, times when they are at their best when teaching, and their needs during times of change. It also has specific coaching suggestions, based on growth areas for each personality type. Another useful table is entitled "Tips for Coaching Someone With Different Personality Preferences" and is located on Pages 144–145. I also am a fan of the 2017 second edition of *Differentiated Coaching*.

Joellen Killion, Cindy Harrison, Chris Bryan, and Heather Clifton wrote *Coaching Matters*. Want to quickly find references for a lot of coaching research? Just check Pages 10–12. There is also another useful table on pages 18–19 that explains different types of coaching. I reference this book quite a bit, for a variety of reasons. It contains a lot of good coaching information, is well organized, and is easy to follow.

COMPETENT ~S.O.A.K.~

Stress-free Opportunities to Absorb Knowledge

Sometimes learning penetrates best when we are relaxed and not trying too hard to make it happen.
Choose what works for you. (Like a "Competent" bath bomb infused with personalized nutrients)

Quotes	Music	Statements affirmations	Books poetry stories	Art	Videos movies	Movement other ideas
"Skills make dreams happen." —Emi Iyalla	"Don't Stop Believin'" Journey	**For coaches:** I trust in my ability to persevere and solve even the most challenging problems.	"The Village Blacksmith" Henry Wadsworth Longfellow	*Playing School* Harry Brooker	*The Pursuit of Happyness* (2006)	**Warrior II Pose**
"I have no idols. I admire work, dedication, and competence." —Ayrton Senna	"Girl on Fire" Alicia Keys	My past efforts and willingness to seek wisdom and knowledge allow me to provide meaningful support.	*High Impact Instruction: A Framework for Great Teaching* Jim Knight	*Hard Working Man* Cameron Hampton	*A League of Their Own* (1992)	
"If you were born without wings, do nothing to prevent them from growing." —Coco Chanel	"Gonna Fly Now" (Theme from *Rocky*) Bill Conti	I am confident in myself because I study, learn, and continually grow in my instructional capacity.	*Visible Learning* John Hattie	*The Girl Planting* (Bodypainting art) Johannes Stoetter	*Soul Surfer* (2011)	**Triangle Pose**
"Always believe in yourself and always stretch yourself beyond your limits. Your life is worth a lot more than you think because you are capable of accomplishing more than you know. You have more potential than you think, but you will never know your full potential unless you keep challenging yourself and pushing beyond your own self-imposed limits." —Roy T. Bennett	"Ain't No Mountain High Enough" Marvin Gaye & Tammi Terrell	I have the knowledge, experience, and expertise to be of benefit to teachers. I believe in myself and in teachers!	*Classroom Instruction That Works, 2nd Edition* Marzano, et al.		*Chariots of Fire* (1981)	
	"Fight Song" Rachel Platten		"The Stars in the Sky" William Bennett		*Mr. Holland's Opus* (1995)	
	"We are the Champions" Queen	**For teachers:**	"Hercules and the Wagoner" Aesop	*Diminish and Ascend* (Sculpture) David McCracken	*Stranded* (Documentary, 2007)	
		My hard work shows the respect I have for the students I work with and it will pay off!	"Can't" Edward A. Guest		*Dead Poets Society* (1989)	**Oils:** peppermint; basil
	Symphony No. 5 Beethoven		"Success" Henry Wadsworth Longfellow	*Mustangs Sculpture* Robert Glen	*Music of the Heart* (1999)	**Stones:** agate, aquamarine
					Happy (Documentary, 2011)	**Color:** gray

I trust in and celebrate the competencies I have developed. I am learning to masterfully research, sort through, and categorize resources tailored to teachers' individual needs. I intentionally share information with teachers in ways that can be easily understood and implemented.

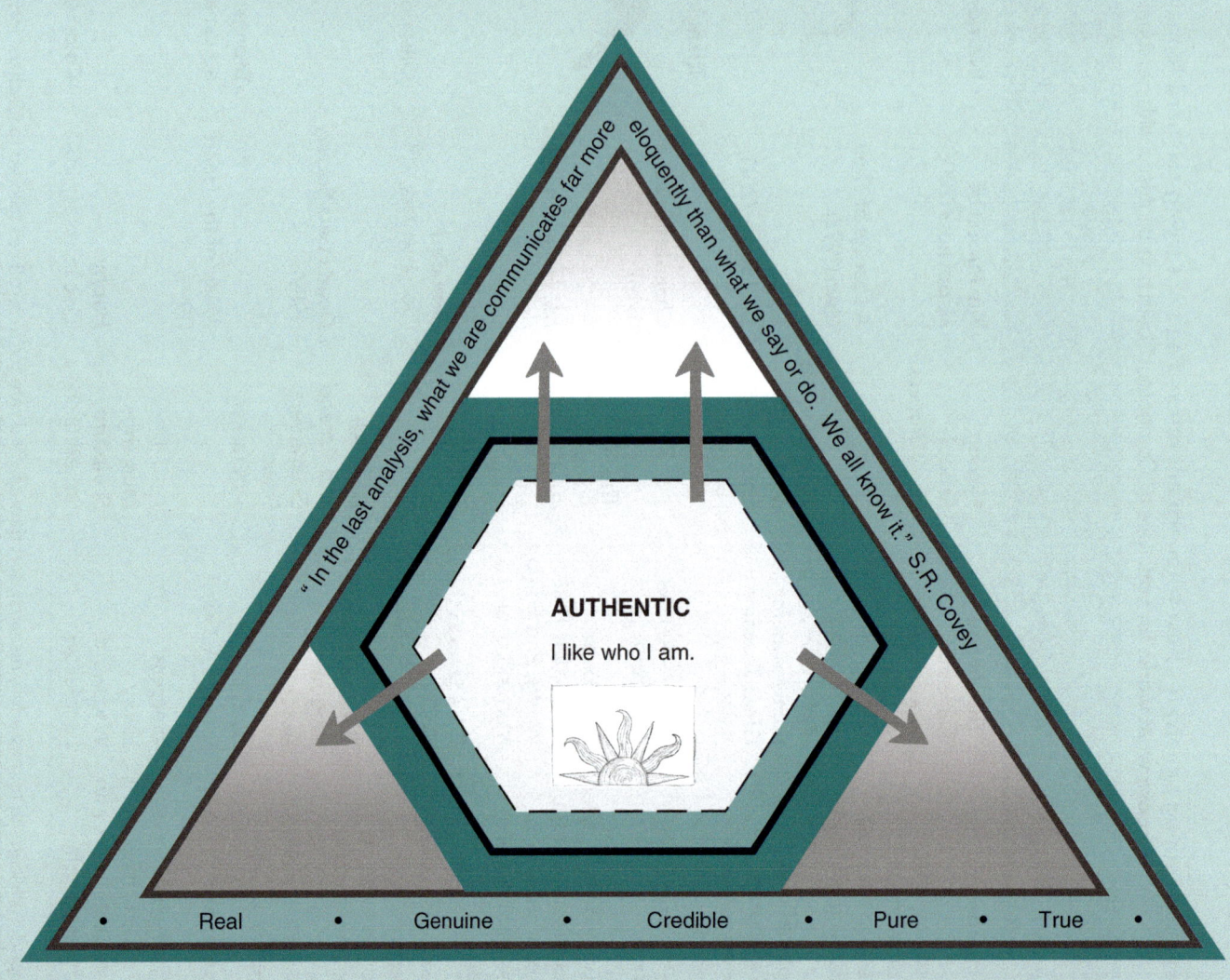

I strive to be congruent and consistent with my core values in thought, word, and deed. I seek to inspire those I coach with pure intention by regularly cultivating my highest thoughts and ideals.

Authentic

4

///

In the last analysis, what we are communicates far more eloquently
than what we say or do.
We all know it.

—Stephen Covey

As we look at the center section of the characteristics model, a hexagon shape is seen surrounding "caring" and "competent." This is the first filter of a refining process we go through when working toward being more effective coaches and/or leaders. This is the filter of authenticity. Are we really caring? Are we really competent? It's hard to fake competency—it's smarter for us to just say, "I don't know how to do that," because, at some point, it will become clear we don't know what we're talking about. Similarly, people can sense whether we really care or not. It's also easy to see in some ways. Do we avoid mingling with certain people because they aren't at our pay grade? When we're talking with someone, do we immediately drop our conversation with that person when someone else walks by, or when the phone rings or buzzes with a text? Or, do we respect the person we're with enough to find a way to work through interruptions without discounting him or her, sincerely listen, finish the conversation, and then follow up with things we said we'd do? Are we who we profess to be? If we can use this filter to our advantage, and work on becoming more authentic, hopefully others will not discount our ability to support them emotionally or technically. When we lack authenticity, we are punching a ticket on a very fast train headed toward a loss of respect, trust, and a willingness to listen to what we have to say. This chapter is designed to support parents, teachers, instructional coaches, and educational leaders of all types as they work to develop the important characteristic of being authentic.

Educational leadership is multifaceted and multileveled. Most of us work as leaders or followers in a variety of situations. Parents are positioned to be a child's fundamental leader and need to be respected and listened to. Teachers are powerful and important leaders who can make a life-changing difference for students as they form meaningful relationships and effectively teach empowering content that opens doors of wonder and opportunity. Coaches are catalysts for growth in teachers' instructional capability, resulting in higher levels of student learning. Coaches can also increase teachers' job satisfaction, efficacy, resilience, and longevity. Principals, district- or state-level executives, superintendents, and all those whom we typically think of as educational leaders can provide the encouragement, direction, and support needed for all other levels to succeed.

Coaches are in an interesting and often coveted role. Are they leaders? Yes. Evaluators? Not usually. Responsible for facilities, solving parent concerns or dealing with severe disciplinary situations? Not very often. Coaches are often able to experience the satisfying and empowering parts of educational leadership as they witness teachers they work with becoming successful with students, without having to be responsible for many of the difficult challenges other educational leaders face. This is one reason I often receive inquiries into the number of openings available for coaching positions in TCT's school district and am asked to keep people in mind or let them know when an opening might be available. Though instructional coaching can be structured as a separate job (if we're fortunate), all educators' daily realities include opportunities to be both leaders and coaches. In many situations, both at work and at home, leadership and coaching skills are blended together in interesting ways as part of our life and career roles. We set the expectations (leadership) and then help others successfully reach them (coaching).

Whatever leadership and/or coaching role we find ourselves in, it is the universal desire of those who have chosen the service-oriented profession of educator to see that our children succeed, both personally and in society generally. We know this will require giving the gift of our best selves, our best thoughts, our best efforts. We also know we can be most effective by becoming people who can be trusted to be real, to share our stories—including how we have overcome difficulties—and to always be striving to better ourselves. We can be living proof that through effort and acting on our best intentions, the finest leadership and coaching traits can be manifested.

Instructional coaches play a sort of unsung, middle-manager type of position when it comes to leadership. They are boots-on-the-ground leaders, leaders who prepare teachers to effectively weather the various types of winds and even the typhoons that are inherent within the current teaching climate. Coaches are incredibly influential. We can increase our ability to influence those we coach by growing in authenticity.

Since he was a young teen, one of my sons has been interested in politics. He was granted time off during high school to work for a state legislator, has spent many hours helping with local and presidential campaigns, and even ran for office at a very young age. One day, while trying to give insightful parenting advice to my budding politician, I suggested that he make sure he was always being authentic (not just accepting others' ideas or trying to always be "politically correct") when he shared his views. He replied, "What does that even mean?" I have thought a lot about that question. It is a good question. My thoughts while trying to answer that question resulted in a paper for a doctoral leadership class. Much of what I will share throughout the remainder of this chapter comes from that paper, for which I researched and, in some ways, redefined the term "authentic leadership."

Recognized as a leadership style that inspires trust and confidence, "authentic leadership" has a variety of definitions, depending upon researchers' points of emphasis. Attributes that appear frequently in leadership research as components of authentic leadership, or leadership qualities a person must possess to be considered authentic, will be categorized during the remainder of this chapter, and a framework for understanding authentic leadership will be proposed.

I have defined "authentic leadership" as an amalgam of the following attributes: spirituality and values, grouped under the heading "Look Up"; integrity and personal mastery, forming the category "Look In"; and vulnerability and relationships, combined under the term "Look Out." Leaders who possess these interrelated qualities are in high demand in the current climate of difficulty and uncertainty.

> *Disruptive elements seem to be afoot, gathering strength in air masses that spiral over oceans or in decisions that swirl through the halls of power. The daily news is filled with powerful changes, and many of us feel buffeted by forces we cannot control.*
>
> *(Wheatley, 2006, p. 137)*

Leadership in our day has become complicated. With a myriad of variables regarding situation, location, culture, personalities, crises, and so forth, can leaders be expected to be prepared for or effectively respond to every scenario? During a time when previously unimaginable amounts of information must be processed, and constantly shifting levels of uncertainty abound, how do leaders gain and consistently retain the respect and trust of those they lead?

The need for authentic leaders has increased. Economic instability, concerns about educational funding remaining a priority, political scandals, terrorism, and unexpected natural disasters are happening at an unprecedented rate worldwide. People are feeling less secure and are looking for people of character who can be trusted with leadership roles (Northouse, 2010).

When leaders lead, they do so from what they are in that moment. Their leadership becomes the visible expression of authenticity (Eriksen, 2009). Powerful leaders who last a long time and *can inspire followers to support them without coercion* are not superficial. Oprah Winfrey (as quoted in Roberts, 2007) explained this concept:

> When you get me, you are not getting an image. You are not getting a figurehead. You're not getting a theme song. You're getting all of me. And I bring all my stuff with me: my history, my past, Mississippi, Nashville.
>
> *(p. 335)*

What characteristics do those who are recognized as authentic leaders possess? Why do we so desperately need these leaders now?

Look Up

> *We all face times when answers are elusive, when we need a better way, a higher purpose, a wiser approach. "Look Up" symbolizes the universal desire to elevate our view to access soul-satisfying hope and help from a source greater than ourselves.*

Spirituality

Deepak Chopra (1994), in his book *The Seven Spiritual Laws of Success*, stated, "Each of us is here to discover our true Self, to find out on our own that our true Self is spiritual" (p. 97). If what Chopra says is true, where can a leader find that wise self, that sacred internal ground to travel to for respite when seeking insight to the difficult problems of our day? An ancient legend retold by Jack Canfield (2005) describes this sometimes confusing search:

> There was a time when ordinary people had access to all the knowledge of the gods. Yet time and again, they ignored this wisdom. One day, the gods grew tired of so freely giving a gift the people didn't use, so they decided to hide this precious wisdom where only the most committed of seekers would discover it. They believed that if people had to work to find this wisdom, they would use it more carefully. One of the gods suggested that they bury it deep in the earth. NO, the others said— too many people could easily dig down and find it. "Let's put it in the deepest ocean," suggested one of the gods, but that idea was also rejected. They knew that people would one day learn to dive and thus would find it too easily. One of the gods suggested hiding in on the highest mountaintop, but it was quickly agreed that people could climb mountains. Finally, one of the wisest gods suggested, "Let's hide it deep inside the people themselves. They'll never think to look in there." And so it came to be—and so it continues today.
>
> *(p. 314)*

The idea of looking inside ourselves to find wisdom and spiritual strength is the subject of many leadership books and articles. The tendency to avoid looking for ways to access the "knowledge of the gods," to relegate time in reflection and retreat to the bottom of our to-do lists, is acknowledged in leadership literature. Stephen R. Covey's (1989) focus on "Sharpening the Saw" suggested prioritizing time to focus on spiritual pursuits that are important but not urgent, and Jack Canfield's (2005) Success Principle 47—"Inquire Within"—encourages leaders to trust the "still, small voice within" (p. 315). These are examples of pieces of leadership literature that stress the importance of finding inner strength through spirituality. They recommend taking time to connect to a greater wisdom than can be easily accessed during hectic situations. Kevin Cashman (2008) explained this concept in the following way:

> For most leaders, the most innovative ideas and creative solutions usually arise, not during traditional work hours, but during the quiet, inner moments while swimming, running, walking, gardening, or meditating. The mind is loose, settled, relaxed, and able to comprehend the parts and the whole at the same time.
>
> *(p. 151)*

Spirituality is not only the search for insight within an individual, but also the ability to connect to a greater source of wisdom that provides answers when internal searches come up short. Do imperfect people hold inside themselves all the knowledge of the gods? Even if we are, as Chopra (1994) stated in his law of Dharma, "a god or goddess in embryo that wants to be born so that we can express our divinity" (p. 98), would an embryo know how to address rapidly changing needs in complex situations? Leaders who desire to become spiritually enlightened "Look Up" to a greater source, to powers beyond their own, to help them manage chaotic situations flexibly and wisely (Fry, 2003).

> Spirituality is the basic belief that there is a *Supreme Power, a Being, a Force*, that governs the entire universe—there is a purpose for everything and everyone. . . . It asserts that there is a *transcendent Power* which is responsible for the creation and care of the universe. . . . Thus, God, or a Higher Power, is also imminent in the world.
>
> *(Mitroff, 2003, pp. 379–380, emphasis in original)*

Religions provide frameworks and information for those who seek access to this higher power. Mark Kriger and Yvonne Seng (2005) compared leadership as exemplified in five major world religions:

Table A   Comparisons of Leadership in Judaism, Christianity, Islam, Buddhism, and Hinduism

	Judaism	Christianity	Islam	Buddhism	Hinduism
Leader as:	Teacher & question-asker	Role model	Servant of God and His creations	Teacher and role model	Role model of the gods
Exemplars:	Abraham	Jesus	Mohammed	The Buddha	Rama/Krishna
Core Vision:	Oneness	Love	Surrendering to God	Wisdom & compassion	Liberation from duality

Kriger, M., & Seng, Y. (2005). Leadership with inner meaning: A contingency theory of leadership based on the worldviews of five religions. *The Leadership Quarterly, 16*(5), p. 149.

William Bennett (1993), in *The Book of Virtues*, stated, "Faith is a source of discipline and power and meaning in the lives of the faithful of any major religious creed" (p. 741). All five major religions incorporate into their theology the necessity of looking to someone or something that is more than what we are now, to move to higher ground to become spiritually enlightened, to "Look Up." Religions also play a role in helping people determine moral values to incorporate into their lives. Texts such as the Bible, the Torah, and the Qur`an contain guidance about values that, when incorporated into the life of leaders, guide their lives and subsequently affect the lives of followers. Taking time to focus on spirituality can lead to the development of moral values that can be the "basis for moral leadership" according to Kriger and Seng (2005).

Values

William Bean (1993) expanded on the importance of leaders having personal and organizational values: "Every enterprise is driven by its leaders' individual and collective values, whether those values are consciously understood or unconsciously influential, spoken or unspoken, written or unrecorded" (as cited in Russell, 2001, p. 78).

According to Stephen R. Covey (1989), research on leadership collected 150 years before World War I was based on character and included a focus on traits, such as integrity, humility, fidelity, courage, justice, patience, and industry. After the war, what constituted success was determined more as a function of personality. The problem with placing a leadership emphasis on what Covey called secondary greatness—which he defined as being related to personality or social prowess—rather than primary greatness, which is related to character, is that a lack of fundamental character eventually becomes evident in long-term relationships when real motives are revealed and superficial smoke screens dissipate. For anyone to remain an effective and authentic leader over time, character (i.e., the embodiment within a person of basic human values that inspire trust) is a necessity.

Examples of values a society deems important can be found in what children are taught. For instance, the Girl Scout organization has the following values:

> I will do my best to be honest, fair, cheerful, friendly and considerate, respect authority, be a sister to every Girl Scout, to help where I am needed, to use resources wisely, to protect and improve the world around me, and to show respect for myself and others through my words and actions.
>
> *(as cited in Bennett, 1993, p. 218)*

In organizations, one of the most important responsibilities of leadership is to facilitate the "coming together" of workers at all levels within the organization to support a shared purpose. According to Joyce Huth Munro (2008), overall ideals should include the common values and ideas about the mission and purpose of the business, the quality of goods and services produced, and the rights and duties of group members. Leaders must be clear about what they value, the followers they lead must be congruent with the values of the leader, and the behavior of the leader must also be congruent with these values. Robert Goffee and Gareth Jones (2006) stated, "Unless you are clear about your purpose and your values and are doing something that you really care about, it is difficult to act as a leader" (p. 73).

Religious groups that involve businesspeople who pray and focus on spirituality are on the rise, and most leaders of organizations in the United States have a belief that spirituality has supported them in their ability to lead (Driscoll & McKee, 2007). Striving to seek access to wisdom from sources considered divine and clarifying values can support leaders as they strive to become authentic in times of confusion and chaos. "When my heart is overwhelmed: lead me to the rock that is higher than I . . . the rock of my strength and my refuge is in God" (Psalms 61:2, KJV).

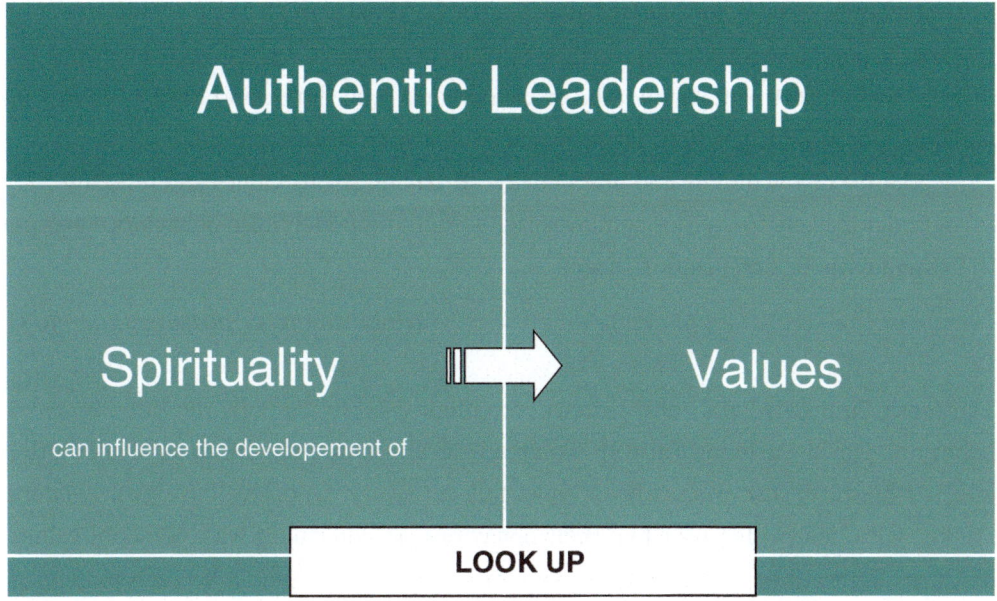

Authentic Leadership

Spirituality
can influence the developement of

Values

LOOK UP

Spirituality and values combine to define authentic leadership. Spirituality can influence the development of values.

Look In

A better me awaits, so I sacrifice the ease of stasis. I succeed, and sometimes fail, but never give up. As my actions match my values, I experience internal peace, and the trust of others in me is magnified.

Integrity

Once leaders have determined their values, it is critical that they live in harmony with them. Margaret Wheatley (2006), author of the book *Leadership and the New Science*, advised, "We must say what we mean and seek for a much deeper level of integrity in our words and acts than ever before" (p. 57). Integrity is a recurring topic in current leadership trainings. In the book *RESULTS Coaching* (Kee, Anderson, Dearing, Harris, & Shuster, 2010), which focuses on training educational leaders to be successful, the first S in the acronym RESULTS stands for Seek Integrity. Seeking integrity according to this model includes being honest, sincere, and upright.

> A leader shows integrity when his actions match his purpose, values, and beliefs; there is alignment between who the leader is (or is becoming) and the behaviors or actions he is taking. The leader's expectation is to be "real" and to be authentically present in all interactions.
>
> *(Kee et al., 2010, p. 176)*

The book *True North*, by Bill George, is a compilation of authentic leadership attributes of 125 successful leaders. In one review of this book, the following statement was made.

Oftentimes, leaders mistakenly believe that subordinates must respect a title and not the person serving in the position. Such leaders act in a way that is not consistent with departmental standards or policies and procedures, and have a "do as I say, not as I do" position. These managers are not effective and often oversee a workforce of low morale and productivity. By having strong values and integrity, a leader is likely to oversee employees who aspire to model those behaviors consistent with the organization's values.

(Robinson et al., 2010, pp. 307–308)

The words "integrity" and "authenticity" are often used to describe the same types of behaviors. Kevin Cashman (2008) explained, "Commonly referred to as 'walking the talk,' authenticity also means being your talk at a very deep level" (p. 36). Leaders are known to have integrity when their behaviors are congruent with personal values or values determined within corporations or groups. Integrity is a key component of authentic leadership.

Personal Mastery

William Bennett (1993) described integrity as something that "human beings need to practice over time . . . and until they have achieved such a state, they may do all sorts of things that prudence tells them had better be concealed" (p. 599). Personal mastery is the amount of consistent strength a person can produce to make his or her behaviors consistent with his or her values, or to be congruent in action with what integrity compels him or her to do.

Most people experience times when they feel confident they know what the best choice for handling a situation would be, and yet, they choose not to take the most effective course of action. For instance, why do many of us choose to avoid exercise when we know it is necessary for good health? Why do we often choose procrastination over dealing with situations that clearly need to be addressed? According to Richard Daft (2011), our mind filters choices in two ways when dealing with these internal conflicts that cause a disconnect or lack of follow-through between knowing and doing. Daft referred to the older, "elephant" part of the brain that automatically takes us through our days and keeps us safe. However, when the automatic elephant brain is not in line with our better intentions or the knowledge a leader has acquired that would improve leadership performance, those old negative habits that had protected us—such as being reactive, finding fault, being resistant, not following through, and showing impatience—die hard. The wiser "CEO/executive" part of the brain, as Daft called it, can override the elephant, but it takes practice.

An awareness of these two parts and making a conscious choice to make the "CEO the master and the elephant the servant" (Daft, 2011, p. 33) is what is needed for leaders to consistently have the strength to master themselves and make better choices even when it is difficult to do so. Authenticity requires a high level of self-awareness and a willingness to look at weaknesses. This level of introspection could seem counterproductive to the self-protecting elephant brain. Developing personal mastery is the process of bringing our actions in line with our most productive and inspiring thoughts, and this is how leaders demonstrate integrity.

Authentic leaders are willing to "look inward" to determine whether their actions match their values. They are aware when their actions are out of line with what they believe, and they work to correct breaches of integrity. They look for ways to be congruent with their spirituality and values, and they strengthen their conscious mind to choose solutions that may be personally difficult but necessary.

Look Out

"Looking Outward" involves being willing to honestly share struggles and successes that are part of our life story. It also means that we intentionally use our gifts and skills to enhance or "look out" for others' well-being so they can feel the warm embrace of our love.

Vulnerability

Can we expect leaders to know everything? What if a leader isn't right? In times of uncertainty or crisis, what if a leader does not know immediately, with conviction, what is best when facing uncharted waters? Is being right the most important quality of being a leader? An experience retold by Kevin Cashman (2008), of an executive named Craig, seems to dispel the notion that leaders must always be "right." After feeling for many years that if any of his workers knew he had any faults, they would see him as weak or not worthy of the mantle of leadership, Craig had a change of perspective. He stated: "I thought my power was in being *right*. Now I understand my power is in being *real*" (p. 44). "What happens to us when we are around people who are real and open about themselves, warts and all? We trust them" (Cashman, 2008, p. 44).

It is interesting that in the process of letting go of perfectionism—acknowledging and allowing "warts" to exist—we can, at least in part, release the anxiety and pressures of leadership. If leaders can be transparent and authentic in relationships, which means being open and honest in presenting their true selves to others and "includes showing both positive and negative aspects of themselves to others" (Northouse, 2010, p. 218), then they will more likely be accepted as "real" and will be able to inspire higher levels of devotion and loyalty from those they lead.

Trust, as defined by Megan Tschannen-Moran (2004), is "one's willingness to be vulnerable to another based on the confidence that the other is benevolent, honest, open, reliable and competent" (as cited in Kee et al., 2010, p. 176). Being good trumps being perfect. Followers want a leader who can be trusted with sensitive topics, perhaps situations that involve embarrassment or failure. Being willing to talk about and acknowledge problems—even though doing so could put members of the group, and often the leader, in a vulnerable position—is part of developing a healthy work environment.

Stephen M. Covey (2006), in his book *The Speed of Trust*, described this as being willing to confront reality. "It's about sharing the bad news as well as the good, naming the 'elephant in the room,' addressing the 'sacred cows,' and discussing the 'undiscussables.' As a leader does this, he or she "builds trust—fast" (p. 185). This willingness of leaders to share and learn from personal challenges can enhance the working environment. Bill George, Andrew McClain, and Nick Craig (2008) explained this concept in the following way.

> One of the most effective ways to break down barriers and create a deeper level of trust and honesty is to talk about the challenging experiences you have faced, the times when you have made mistakes or failed, and how you learned from these times to succeed in the future. By admitting your mistakes and explaining what you learned from them, you give others permission to do the same.
>
> *(p. 137)*

Acknowledging limitations, faults, or failures can spark rallies of support and provide nurturing energy, awareness, and cooperation needed to ameliorate and resolve difficult problems within a school or company. Walt Disney (1992), founder of the so-called happiest place on earth (that materialized after a bankruptcy), said, "There is great comfort and inspiration in the feeling of close human relationships and its bearing on our mutual fortunes—a powerful force, to overcome the 'tough breaks' which are certain to come to most of us from time to time" (p. 3-C2,1).

In most work and home environments, we have opportunities to be leaders and to be followers. To be human is to be imperfect. It's also to be tired, to become ill, and to have family issues. When people intent on keeping their values find themselves falling short, they may believe they have let themselves and others down, and sometimes this can lead to painful discouragement. We, as followers, can help get things back on track through our encouragement and support. When we find ourselves in the role of a follower, let us be not overly critical of, but benevolent (as Tschannen-Moran mentioned) toward, those who are sincerely trying to lead with integrity but may (and likely will) fall short at times.

Relationships

"I sought my soul, but my soul I could not see, I sought my God, but my God eluded me, I sought my brother, and I found all three."

(William Blake, quoted in Bennett, 1995, p. 744)

For some leaders, it is in the process of working with others that they develop authenticity (George, 2006). In the article "The New Public Service: Serving Rather Than Steering," Robert Denhardt (2002) explored a change of focus from being an entrepreneur, or the only one who steers, to a more inclusive leadership model for a public leader. We need leaders who desire to empower others to express their concerns and to solve problems through collaboration. One of the main points of the article is that public service leaders can be effective "by valuing people, not just productivity. Public organizations and the networks in which they participate are more likely to succeed in the long run if they are operated through processes of collaboration and shared leadership based on respect for all people" (p. 556).

In this time of trying to keep up with fast-paced changes in technology, and with teachers trying to overcome the negative effects of poverty on children, tumultuous financial situations, pandemics, and natural disasters, we need leaders who can be trusted and who can trust others to share leadership burdens. This willingness to acknowledge the necessity of interconnectivity is an important component of being an effective leader in the sometimes chaotic current environment. In the past, leaders have focused on fixing just the parts of organizations that were, in a mechanistic sense, breaking down. They did not see problems as they related to the whole of the organization. Now, in order to survive, schools, districts, and businesses must "work with webs of relations, not with machines" (Wheatley, 2006, p. 145).

One of the most difficult challenges we face worldwide is how to prepare for and keep ourselves and our children safe from terrorism (both foreign and domestic). Though their numbers may not be impressive, terrorists have been effective because of their structure. They have a clear intention, everyone is allowed access to information, they are allowed freedom to do what they think is needed, and they do not completely rely on top-down commands to accomplish their objectives. The U.S. Army is changing to a similar "network" structure by incorporating more special forces in an effort to be "as adaptive, nimble, and smart as the insurgents" (Wheatley, 2006, p. 180).

It is important for organizations to have structural designs that allow for breakdowns in parts, but the parts must have a way to knit themselves back into the organization together through relationships. Margaret Wheatley (2006) postulated that when organizations are focused on a clear intention, and all parts (both human and subsystems within organizations) have an understanding of how they relate to the whole, an environment of resiliency, creativity, and freedom can be established. "We must understand that we lose capacity and in fact create more chaos when we insist on hierarchy, roles, and command and control leadership" (p. 186).

The six attributes of authentic leadership. Spirituality influences the development of values. Values provide a framework for integrity. Integrity is strengthened through personal mastery. Striving for personal mastery can expose vulnerability. Vulnerability allows for "real" relationships.

In these challenging times, leaders must acknowledge the critical nature of relationships and respect the inherent value and necessary contributions of each employee. They must also find ways to solicit feedback from everyone within an organization so that the whole organization can set a course for its mutual benefit rather than just focusing on fixing broken parts. Bill George et al. (2008) added their statement to the body of evidence that suggests that in the current upheaval of our day, leaders must find ways to involve all members of organizations in the development of organizational principles and encourage an open environment that allows individuals and groups freedom to offer solutions to problems as they arise: "In the 21st century, the saying 'People support what they help create' is truer than ever" (p. 138). When leadership is focused on building relationships within an organization, shared intent is strengthened, human needs are nourished, and schools, districts, and companies can more easily respond to challenges.

Conclusion

As leaders strive to develop these six qualities (spirituality, values, integrity, personal mastery, vulnerability, and relationships), they will be able to lead with greater authenticity. "In the last analysis, what we *are* communicates far more eloquently than what we *say* or *do*. We all know it" (Covey, 1992, p. 58). Becoming authentic is something that happens over time (George et al. 2008; Northouse, 2010).

It consists of finding ways to spiritually connect to higher, wiser sources and to determine values (Russell, 2001) that will inspire trust and confidence in oneself and one's followers. The process of "Looking Up" supports leaders as they strive to lead wisely and honorably.

Once leaders decide on their values, living those values with integrity becomes important, as followers look to the leader to model personal and school/district/company standards (Kee et al., 2010). This "Looking In" allows leaders to strengthen their integrity by working on personal mastery, noticing where they fall short, and being willing to acknowledge failures and imperfections. As leaders become aware of their vulnerabilities and failures and find ways to share how they have worked (or how they are trying to work) through them with followers, they become "real" to those they work with (Cashman, 2008). This authenticity, coupled with a desire to continue to strive for higher levels of personal mastery, inspires others to continue trying, and it helps them not become discouraged even though people and situations will not always be perfect.

This choice to "Look Out" to learn about and support others through relationships—both human relationships and relationships among parts of organizations—produces a deeper understanding of followers and a more holistic view of the school, district, or company in general, increasing the likelihood that the leader will grasp how parts of a company contribute to the whole (Wheatley, 2006). Taking time to focus on relationships reminds leaders that all members of the organization are valuable and that it is more effective for organizational goals to be developed in ways that motivate everyone on the team to achieve them.

Bill George (2006) summarized leadership in tumultuous times in the following way.

> What, then, is the 21st-century leader all about? It is being authentic, uniquely yourself, the genuine article. Authentic leaders know who they are. They are "good in their skin," so good they don't feel a need to impress or please others. They not only inspire those around them, they bring people together around a shared purpose and a common set of values and motivate them to create value for everyone involved.

(p. 52)

Andrew Halpin and Don Croft (1966) identified authentic leadership as "behaving in such a way that professional roles remain secondary to whom the individual is as a person" (as cited by van Dierendonck, 2011, p. 1234). Teachers, coaches, or school/district leaders who are able to positively influence others are people who have intentionally built internal reserves they can dip into during times of trouble. They offer a wellspring of goodness that inspires trust. What a leader brings to the table or the workplace each day is all he or she can offer and is what is available to the teacher/school/district/company in times of distress. Therefore, when we "Look Up" by seeking spiritual wisdom and defining values, "Look In" by adhering to values with integrity and developing greater personal mastery, and, finally, "Look Out" by being vulnerable enough to share lessons learned and make relationships matter, we will be known as authentic and will be better prepared to meet any challenges we may face.

Reflect and Connect

Read~Rotate~Reflect

1. Choose 6 to 12 short poems, excerpts, quotes, or stories, each of which will fit on one page, to express components of authenticity. Pages with a font size of 12–14 work well. Each reading should take about one minute to read through.

2. Split participants into groups, and put enough readings out for each group member to have one or maybe two readings, depending on the size of the group and the amount of time allotted for the activity.

3. Each person in the group begins reading. When finished (after about a minute), each person passes the reading they have just finished to the person to the right or left, and then the next session of reading begins, until all the readings are read by each group member or until time is up.

4. After each of the readings have been read, then rotated, each member of the group is given the opportunity to reflect on a favorite reading, why it was a favorite, how it touched him or her, and maybe why and what it has to do with being authentic.

5. Finally, all group participants have the opportunity to join in a discussion about what it means to be authentic.

The following figure contains quotes related to authenticity. In the last two boxes are readings that can be used for this activity.

Authenticity Read-Rotate-Reflect	
"The purpose of life seems to be to acquaint man with himself." Ralph Waldo Emerson	"The secret [to success] is authenticity. The reason people fail is because they're pretending to be something they're not." Oprah Winfrey
" The person you imagine yourself to be in the very best and most powerful moments of your life, is the authentic you." Richie Norton	"You cannot travel within and stand still without." James Allen
"My life is an indivisible whole, and all my activities run into one another . . . My life is my message." Mahatma Gandhi	"Authentic influence is not simply refining our presentation style—it's deeper than that. Some of the most authentic leaders I know stumble around a bit in their delivery, but the words come right from their hearts and experiences. You can feel it." Kevin Cashman
"I want you to be everything that's you, deep at the center of your being." Confucius	"This above all: To thine own self be true, And it must follow, as the night the day, Thou canst not then be false to any man." - *Hamlet*, Shakespeare
The Velveteen Rabbit by Margery Williams *The Emperor's New Clothes* by Hans Christian Anderson *If* by Rudyard Kipling *Do It Anyway* attributed to Mother Teresa	*The True Professional* by Margaret Wheatley *The Lesser Man* by Mike Murburg *Authentic Leadership Model* by Rebecca Frazier *Growing Pains* by Melissa True *The Boy Who Cried Wolf* by Aesop

Authentic Self-Assessment

1. Take this self-assessment before you set an intention to consciously find ways to become more authentic.

2. Implement some of the practical application ideas, resources, and/or authentic S.O.A.K. supports found below (or use some of your own ideas).

3. In a month or so, see whether you have been able to improve your thoughts, motivations, and behaviors surrounding the important coaching characteristic of being authentic. Think upon the six attributes of an authentic leader noted in this chapter, and determine how to make them a more conscious part of your daily life. Synonyms of "authentic": *real, genuine, credible, pure, true.*

Spirituality influences the development of values ("Look Up"). Values provide a framework for integrity. Integrity is strengthened through personal mastery ("Look In"). Striving for personal mastery can expose vulnerability. Vulnerability allows for "real" relationships ("Look Out").

	Strongly Disagree	Disagree	Neutral Not Sure	Agree	Strongly Agree
	1	2	3	4	5
I have taken time to search my heart, look for helpful resources, and reach for inspiration to determine my core values. (Support for this can be found in Chapter 6.)					
My core values guide my work and life in a meaningful and productive direction. (I am a more effective parent/teacher/coach/leader because I have identified my core values.)					
I sincerely strive to live with harmony and integrity to my core values.					
I know I do not do everything perfectly and am willing to own and repair my mistakes.					
I realize being "real" in my relationships can create connections that will enrich my life and help me accomplish my work more effectively.					
I like myself and know that the support I give and the contributions I make are valuable.					
Column Totals:					

Grand Total: _____

What totals mean: 26–30 = Authentic Rock Star, 21–25 = Very Authentic, 16–20 = Sort of Authentic, 11–15 = Some Authenticity Is Happening, 6–10 = Better Step It Up, 0–5 = Would Setting a Goal to Be More Authentic Be Useful?

Practical Application Ideas for Authentic

The Seven Habits of Highly Effective People: Restoring the Character Ethic, by Stephen R. Covey

My search for authenticity began in earnest many years ago, after reading the book *Seven Habits of Highly Effective People*, by Stephen Covey. In the 1990s, I was the mother of three young sons, and I deeply desired (and still do) to be the best mother I could possibly be. I wanted this partly because I was fortunate to have a wonderful, loving, angelic mother and wanted the same for my children (our heritage can powerfully influence our authentic selves). When I started feeling completely depleted and overwhelmed with the demands of raising young children, my considerate husband would cover for me and I would take some occasional mini-vacations to the mountains. These respites were designed for me to experience the rare joy of a couple of uninterrupted nights' sleep, eating some quiet meals that someone else cleaned up, and organizing my life and parenting thoughts.

During these times of reflection, I found that there is great power in:

1) determining (with "Look Up" guidance) what you want to accomplish in life and

2) writing those thoughts/goals down, so that you can refer to them later.

Covey's Principles, along with his "personal mission statement" idea (pp. 96–143) and my sincere desire to connect with God and ask Him to help me understand and write down what I was about and what I was going to do in this life, were central to everything I have spent (and not spent) my time on since. I developed other types of goals and mission statements as the years progressed, but it's the original that my heart remembers easily. One of the specific parts of the mission statement was "Be a haven of happiness and a harbor of hope and healing." Perhaps overdone alliteration, but the words have stuck with me over many decades. I received the following email from one of my students just a couple of years ago, many years after she attended my class:

From: Gray, Darian
To: FRAZIER, REBECCA A.
Inbox
Tuesday, July 29, 2014 - 12:55 PM

Our decisions are powerful.

Mrs. Frazier,

My name is Darian Gray. I was in your 4/5th grade combo class in 2004 at Madison Elementary School. Your classroom was a **haven** for me at a time when I truly needed it. Today I am entering my senior year at the University of Northern Colorado majoring in history with an emphasis in secondary education. It is partly because of you and your encouragement that I made it through school and it is mostly because of you that I am going into teaching. I pray that my classroom will someday be the **haven** for my students that yours was for me. Thank you so much!

Best,

Darian Gray
History Education Major

This sweet girl—whom I remembered as a beautiful child of color, with a variety of difficult struggles and trials—could have been another discouraging statistic. But she had conquered them, or succeeded in spite of them, and I was and am immensely proud of her!

Darian had no idea I was specifically trying to create a haven for her or encourage her with hope and healing. Her note has been so reassuring to me (we all need encouragement)! I wanted to create a haven, and she thinks I did. Tears are in my eyes as I write this . . . *it worked*! I believe we all often feel sparks of this same type of excitement when we hear from teachers that our coaching and leadership efforts have helped them (and their students) be successful.

I am grateful for the time to reflect, the spiritual help, the meaningful resources found in Covey's book, and the family support that were provided to help me know myself better. It was a beautiful opportunity to have a bit of a glimpse up front of what I could accomplish if I could understand and focus on unique contributions I could make to benefit others. I think it is even more difficult now, in this technology-infused life of ours, to set aside time and listen for the wisdom within us, but it will always be worth the effort. Intentionally creating a purposeful life is an incredible reward in and of itself, because then we can see that every day is an opportunity to live our purpose in our own creative way.

Rewarding interactions like the one I experienced with Darian have likely happened at home, at school, or in other situations for you too! They happen when we are sincere about putting forth our best efforts and are engaged in work that matters. They are usually service-oriented. Having chosen education as part of our life's work, we can get up every day knowing that our unique efforts, encouragement, and support can make life-changing differences for others.

Leadership From the Inside Out, by Kevin Cashman

I refer to this book often. It is a wonderful resource for finding motivation to improve ourselves and, by so doing, improve our leadership and coaching. I find Cashman's "six points for authentic interpersonal mastery" (pp. 96–102) intriguing.

1. Know Yourself Authentically—"Practice being what you wish others to become." (p. 96)

2. Listen Authentically—"Place another person's self-expression as primary at that moment." (p. 97)

3. Influence Authentically—"Expressing yourself authentically is sharing your real thoughts and feelings in a manner that opens up possibilities." (p. 99)

4. Appreciate Authentically—"Criticism may get some short-term results, but a constant dosage tends to be toxic. Judging others critically doesn't define them anyway, it defines us." (p. 99)

5. Share Stories Authentically—"Craft authentic stories to bring your values to life and to build deeper connections with people." (p. 100)

6. Serve Authentically—"Let us ask ourselves, 'How do I want to be of service to others?'" (p. 100)

(Continued)

(Continued)

Authentic or Not?

An Authentic Person . . .	A Person Who Is Not Authentic . . .
speaks the truth in ways that do not intentionally injure others.	lies when it's convenient to do so or to cover up faults or flaws.
sees that personal beliefs and values consistently guide choices, at work and home.	changes beliefs and values to try to please others, even when what they want may be unethical.
experiences internal peace frequently, and others often feel peaceful when in his or her presence.	feels stress trying to find people and situations that might provide quick access to superficial goals and pursuits. Peacefulness is rarely felt or projected.
acts consistently with personal beliefs and values even when nobody is holding him or her accountable and no matter what circumstances he or she may be in. What you see is what you get.	exhibits few stable or reliable behaviors, because there is no conscious core of values to guide good decision making.
does not feel a need to push his or her agenda on others but is strong within himself or herself; does not give up important values just because others do not agree.	is fearful others' ideas may not support hidden, possibly self-serving agendas and, as a result, can be dismissive, forceful, and paranoid.
is honest and comfortable with himself or herself, knows he or she doesn't know everything, and is willing to listen.	filters input from others through changing values and beliefs, so consistency in responses or decisions is not possible.
often experiences joy and satisfaction, because his or her life is consistent with personal values and life purposes.	experiences emotional, social, and mental roller coasters when not being able to decipher what is important.
effectively builds trust and lasting relationships.	has trouble building trust and maintaining relationships.
creates a life that is always expanding and moving forward positively, meaningfully influencing others along the way.	creates a life that may not make sense to him or her and limits the opportunities to serve and make life better for others because of internal conflicts.

AUTHENTIC ~S.O.A.K.~

Sometimes learning penetrates best when we are relaxed and not trying too hard to make it happen. (Like an "Authentic" bath bomb infused with personalized nutrients)

Stress-free Opportunities to Absorb Knowledge

Choose what works for you.

Quotes	Music	Statements affirmations	Books poetry stories	Art & More	Videos movies	Movement other ideas
"The purpose of life seems to be to acquaint man with himself." —Ralph Waldo Emerson	"Who You Are" Jessie J	**For coaches:** The words I choose to use are truthful and inspire possibility.	**The Velveteen Rabbit** Margery Williams	**Authentic Works of the Masters:**	**Tall Girl** (2019) Netflix	**Savasana**
"My life is an indivisible whole, and all my activities run into one another.... My life is my message." —Mahatma Gandhi	"Brave" Sara Bareilles	I have internalized the importance of service and consider it an honor to spend time supporting teachers.	**The Shallows: What the Internet Is Doing to Our Brains** Nicholas Carr	**The Order of Release 1746** Sir John Everett Millais, Bt	**Beauty and the Beast** (1991, 2017) Walt Disney Pictures	**Child's Pose**
"I want you to be everything that's you, deep at the center of your being." —Confucius	"I Am a Child of God" Naomi Ward Randall & Mildred Tanner Pettit "Who I Am" Jessica Andrews	The way I spend my professional time aligns with my personal beliefs and goals.	**The Emperor's New Clothes** Hans Christian Anderson	**More Quotes:** "Because true belonging only happens when we present our authentic, imperfect selves to the world, our sense of belonging can never be greater than our level of self-acceptance." —Brené Brown	**I Have a Dream Speech on Video—Dr. Martin Luther King** YouTube	
"Our birth is but a sleep and a forgetting: The Soul that rises with us, our life's Star, hath elsewhere its setting and cometh from afar; not in entire forgetfulness, and not in utter nakedness, but trailing clouds of glory do we come from God, who is our home." —William Wordsworth, "Ode on Intimations of Immortality"	"Place in This World" Michael W. Smith "Try" Colbie Caillat (focusing on being fake perfect physically to make others like us undermines our personal growth because the focus is superficial, not about being connected to our real, internal, authentic self	**For teachers:** My students can tell the caring I express for them is real. Supporting students to achieve academic and personal success aligns with my core beliefs and purpose.	**"If"** Rudyard Kipling **The Paradoxical Commandments** Kent M. Keith **"The Boy Who Cried Wolf"** Aesop	"In order to love who you are, you cannot hate the experiences that shaped you." —Andrea Dykstra	**American Express TV Commercial, "Right Behind You"** Many authentic moments are caught in this commercial.	**Oils:** bergamot **Stones:** vivianite **Color:** yellow gold

During the finest or worst moments of life, within our authentic selves, there is no place for arrogance or discouragement. Connected to a greater source of light than we can completely internalize or emanate at the moment, we peacefully continue forward on our paths, and the world is brighter because of it.

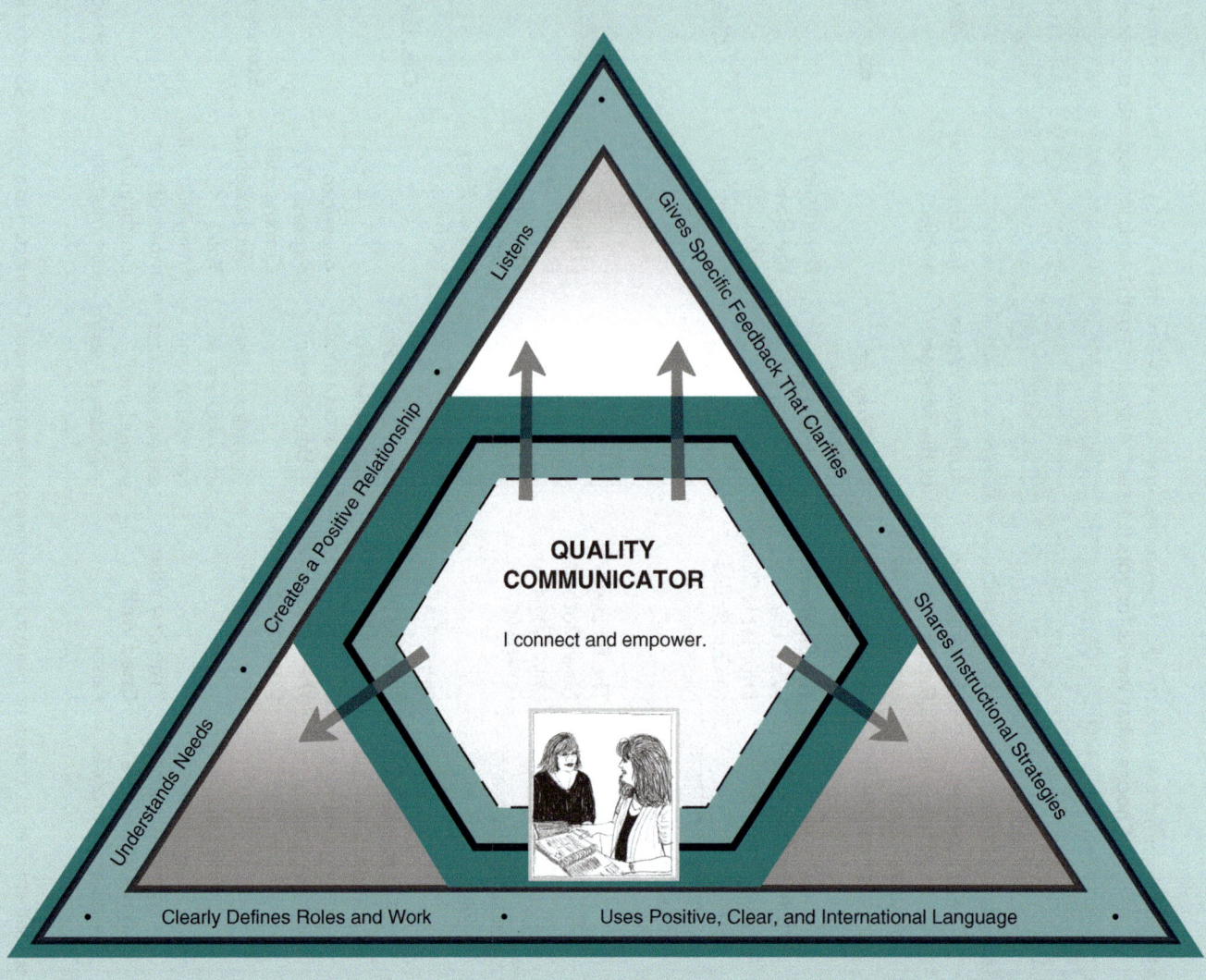

QUALITY COMMUNICATOR

I connect and empower.

Listens

Gives Specific Feedback That Clarifies

Creates a Positive Relationship

Shares Instructional Strategies

Understands Needs

Clearly Defines Roles and Work

Uses Positive, Clear, and International Language

The teachers I coach are empowered by: The words I speak; my knowledge and preparation; my sincere desire to understand and help; and the consistent support I provide.

Quality Communicator

5

My words and presence create understanding, peace, and power.

Being a quality communicator is the second of two filters we can use to deliver our coaching effectively. We effectively coach by radiating a joyful influence outward from the core of merged caring and competence, through the filters of authenticity and quality communication.

Columns of Communication

The necessity of being a skilled communicator in coaching/teaching/leading roles is obvious. But how do we organize our skill development? There are so many parts and pieces to becoming an effective communicator! The diagram below categorizes communication skills in a way that supports the central idea of this book: the importance of finding an operative balance of heart and mind when we coach.

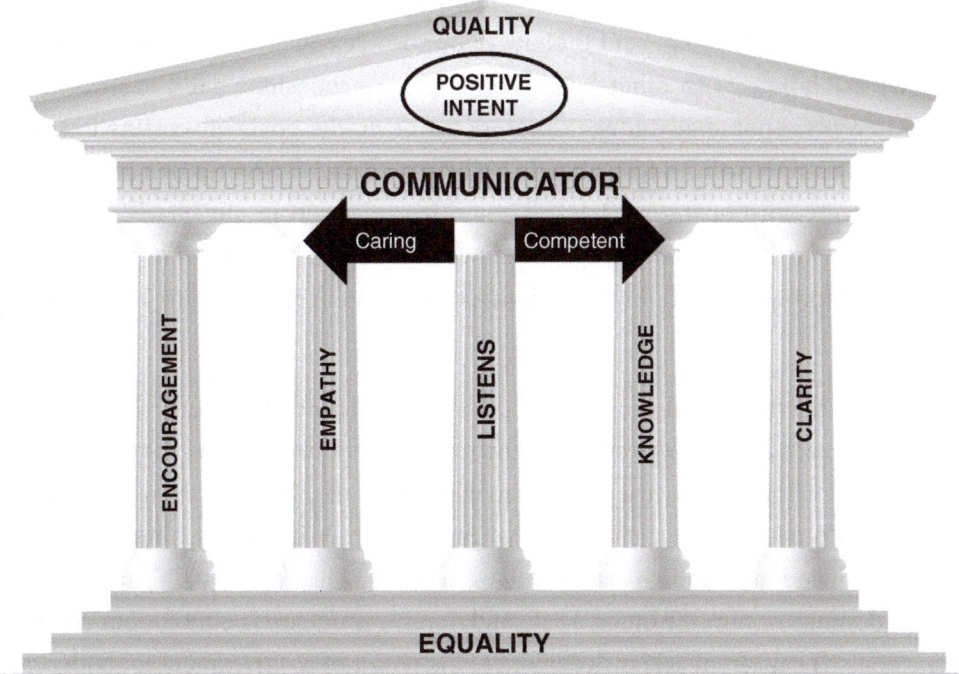

image by https://www.istockphoto.com/portfolio/vectorartnow

At the base of these "columns of communication" is the foundational principle of equality, the first of Jim Knight's Partnership Principles (2007). This principle means that both the coach and the person being coached are of equal value in the relationship, and each person has important thoughts and information to share.

How do we consider everyone equal when hierarchies may exist or are assumed in our roles? One way might be to think about how many talented people there are who haven't had the opportunity to develop their talents fully. We all know the administrative assistant who could be running the whole school but never had the opportunity to go to college; the musician who can play every tune by ear but wasn't able to take lessons to further his or her talent; the woman who successfully completes complicated projects with heavy workloads but is never given appropriate credit for her work or the opportunity to crack the glass ceiling of the "old boys' club"; or talented people who are marginalized or discounted because of their race, lifestyles, or physical manifestations of their poverty (e.g., dental work; clothing; college-level speaking and writing skills).

Acknowledging that everyone has something to offer and that our hierarchies are at times subjective and are, in part, a product of opportunity helps us not count anyone out. There's also a bigger-picture morality to this type of thinking. Is any one person more important than another, really? If you believe in equality, the answer is no, no matter your personal experiences with or biases toward certain people or situations.

Sometimes, however, we unintentionally make people feel "less than." There are many ways we can do this, but an example is when we shut off our computers and phones and give our undivided attention to someone who could do something for us or to us (such as the superintendent) but then leave our devices on and let them interrupt us when we are talking with others. This sometimes unconscious habit of prioritizing people to our supposed advantage can undermine nobler goals of wanting everyone we come in contact with to feel valued. Authentic caring dissipates disrespect. If we go back to the core of the model and commit to delivering our coaching (or any interactions) with authentic caring, we can communicate in a way that will be better understood and welcomed. Love for all those we come in contact with is the essence of equality.

The "roof" of the diagram above signifies the overarching protection and grace available for both the coach and the person being coached when positive intent is assumed by both parties. We don't always say everything thoughtfully or clearly—though we try—and we don't always know everything either, but when both people in the coaching relationship assume positive intent and choose to believe the coach/teacher wouldn't purposefully try to undermine or hurt the other, a safe and durable residence is built for our coaching interactions. The up-front acknowledgment of the power of positive intent for both coach and teacher bolsters the opportunity for trust to be developed over time (see Chapter 8). Assuming positive intent also creates a type of safety net for our unintended blunders and human imperfections.

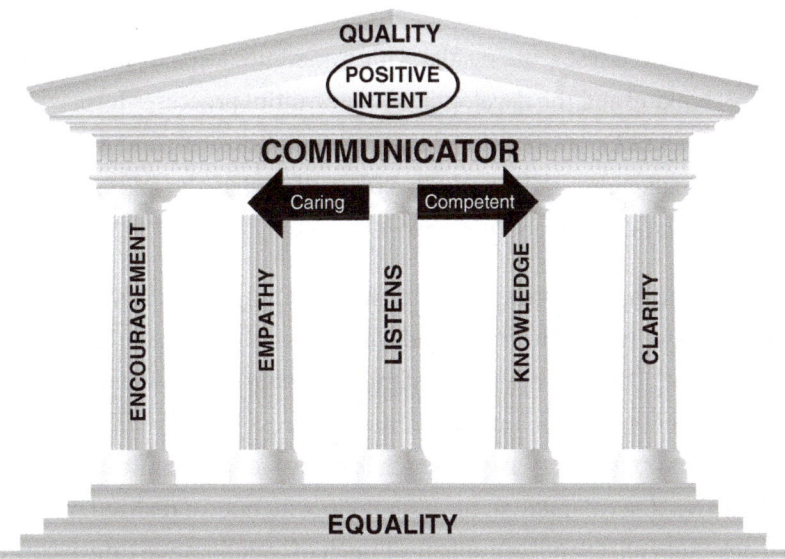

image by https://www.istockphoto.com/portfolio/vectorartnow

The Central Pillar: Listens

Why is this so hard? We have been reminded of the need to really listen to others many, many times. It is addressed in almost every resource on effective communication, but it's still a problem for most of us; guess we didn't listen? Noted in the diagram above as the central column, "listening" was mentioned by the respondents in my research study (Frazier, 2014; see the introduction) more than any other communication skill. How well we listen determines whether we will be able to provide competent and caring support, resulting in a happy and productive coaching relationship. We can't use and clearly share our knowledge to support a teacher if we don't know what is going on; neither can we empathize or provide encouragement if our understanding is limited.

Listed below are some of the things that can get in our way when we are trying to deeply listen:

1. *Limited time.* Most of us lead very busy lives, and, with so many things to do, any chance we have to access a spare mental minute to figure out details to accomplish our tasks is welcomed. This may mean that during coaching conversations, we could be mentally flying in and out of both the conversation and the possible connection we could be making. One of the worst things about this is that people can tell when we aren't really "into" them or their situation.

2. *A desire to immediately respond.* We have ideas and want to get them on the table quickly to support the teacher (and student growth). Sometimes we do this without listening enough to fully understand the teacher's situation or desires. This tendency may indicate a need to check our egos or slow down the pace of the coaching conversation. However, it is also likely that both the coach and the

teacher are under some pressure to produce results, meaning student assessment and standardized test score results. This sometimes leads to stressed, less-than-helpful thinking and the development of unfruitful processes focused on speed rather than building instructional and emotional strength and capacity. For instance, challenging and stress-filled discussions like the following one are happening in many schools nationwide:

"Our students have to score better, or we are going to need to have the state come in, so we have to hurry up and solve the problem of our lagging student achievement! The tests are on the standards, right? So how can our students do well when there are so many standards to address in one year's time (actually 6–8 months)? Okay, let's try to schedule those standards into our calendars. Well, we tried to calendar all those standards in, but we realized it's not possible to teach them all. Okay, let's spend a bunch of collaborative time prioritizing the standards, then work as fast as possible to make sure they all get taught on a schedule, so that we can compare data. But what if our plans don't work for close to half of our students who aren't ready for these standards because they are two to three grade levels behind? And if we could plan for at least two to three different levels, do we have access to the curriculum resources and materials for all those levels? And what about the students who are at grade level but don't learn the concepts quickly enough and we run out of time and can't keep to our schedule—then what do we do . . . just cut our losses and leave students behind?"

This is not to say some schools, teachers, and coaches haven't figured out ways to work around and through these problems with coaching to help with planning and differentiation, interventions, peer tutors, study centers, creative scheduling, resource sharing, and parent involvement, but these are not easy problems to solve! Many teachers *and* coaches *and* leaders feel pressure to produce results as quickly as possible, so we rush not only coaching, but many other things as well.

3. *Outside influences.* We are constantly bombarded with interruptions—unending emails, texts, notifications from a myriad of apps and social media platforms, and so on. These realities also influence #2 above, our desire to respond immediately, because in many cases we feel we should and sometimes are expected to do so. Our brains are being changed, often not for the better, because of technology.

Nicholas Carr (2011) recorded his personal experience of becoming accustomed to and then almost addicted to technology. The initial exhilaration and, later, the associated concerns he experienced are shared below in the following excerpt from his book, *The Shallows: What the Internet Is Doing to Our Brains*:

"By the mid-nineties, I had become trapped, not unhappily, in the "upgrade cycle." I retired the aging Plus in 1994, replacing it with a Macintosh Performa 550 with a color screen. . . .

"You know the rest of the story because it's probably your story too. Ever-faster chips. Ever quicker modems. DVDs and DVD burners. Gigabyte-sized hard drives. Yahoo and Amazon and eBay. MP3s. Streaming video. Broadband. Napster and Google. BlackBerrys and iPods. Wi-Fi networks. YouTube and Wikipedia. Blogging and microblogging. Smartphones, thumb drives, netbooks. Who could resist? Certainly not I.

". . . One click on a link led to a dozen or a hundred more. New emails popped into my in-box every minute or two. I registered for accounts with MySpace and Facebook, Digg and Twitter. . . .

"Sometime in 2007, a serpent of doubt slithered into my info-paradise. I began to notice that the Net was exerting a much stronger and broader influence over me than my old stand-alone PC ever had. It wasn't just that I was spending so much time staring into a computer screen. It wasn't just that so many of my habits and routines were changing as I became more accustomed to and dependent on the sites and services of the Net. The very way my brain worked seemed to be changing. *It was then that I began worrying about my inability to pay attention to one thing for more than a couple of minutes.* At first I'd figured that the problem was a symptom of middle-age mind rot. But my brain, I realized, wasn't just drifting. It was hungry. It was demanding to be fed the way the Net fed it—and the more it was fed, the hungrier it became. Even when I was away from my computer, I yearned to check e-mail, click links, do some Googling. I wanted to be *connected.* Just as Microsoft Word had turned me into a flesh-and-blood word processor, the Internet, I sensed, was turning me into something like a high-speed data-processing machine, a human HAL.

"I missed my old brain."

(pp. 14–16, emphasis added)

Have you ever attended a professional development session, a leadership meeting, presentations, or staff meetings where people took the time to show up, sat down, opened their laptops, and then proceeded to engage in a pretended attempt to listen, assuming that the speaker would give them the benefit of the doubt that they were taking notes on their computers the whole time? But, when you went to the back of the room to get a drink of water and saw their screens, you knew the transfer of information hoped for during that professional development, leadership meeting, or staff meeting wasn't actually happening. People were engaged in their screens; that was what was really going on.

As instructional coaches, we help teachers learn how to manage students' technology use and suggest they know what is happening on students' screens, to help keep students focused on the learning goal. We are also wise enough to know students aren't paying attention when they minimize quickly when the teacher is walking by, or, as one high-school principal summarized when making an announcement, "We're not stupid; we notice when you're looking at your crotch" (checking your phone/texting).

We remind, redirect, and do our best to keep students on topic, because, as Carr suggested, technology can be addictive. It can keep us from having meaningful interactions with others and getting to deeper levels of thinking and reasoning. Both students and adults are affected by the omnipresent influence of technology.

So, what can we do to bypass these listening roadblocks?

We can revisit the core of the characteristics model and think about grounding our communication in caring and competence, expressed through the filter of authenticity. We can be curious and more interested in the other person rather than stressing about being interesting (Canfield, 2005). Giving others our full attention shows we truly value them and have a desire to learn from and about them. This increases the chance that reciprocal learning or reciprocity will take place (Knight, 2007). We will learn as we coach, and it is likely the teacher will learn too. In the words of Kevin Cashman (2008):

> How often are we truly present with someone? How often do we pause, set aside all our concerns—past, present, and future—and completely "be there" for someone else? How often do we really hear what the other person is saying and feeling vs. filtering it heavily through our own immediate concerns and time pressures? Authentic listening is not easy. We hear the words, but rarely do we really listen. We hear the words, but do we also "hear" the emotions, fears, underlying concerns? Authentic listening is not a technique. It is centered in presence and in a concern for the other person that goes beyond our self-centered needs. . . . Authentic listening is about being generous—listening with a giving attitude that seeks to bring forth the contributions in someone vs. listening with our limiting assessments, opinions, and judgments. Authentic listening is about being open to the purpose and learning coming to us through the other person.
>
> (pp. 96–97)

We can offer competent and caring support when we let go of every concern or possible distraction in that moment and wholeheartedly make the person we are with the center of our world for a time. When we do this, we are much more likely to hear and understand that person's academic/technical and emotional needs, desires, or dreams. As a result of this focused listening, we, as coaches and education leaders, are equipped to make a real and lasting difference in the life of this unique and important person.

 To make this simple, we can create the environment for quality listening to occur when we prioritize:

1. the person and

2. the present moment.

To summarize, when the question "What would be the most important advice you could give to someone striving to be an effective instructional coach?" was posed to Coach #10, her response was:

> ***"Be quiet and listen."***

Empathy

Moving to the left of the central column of "listening" within the diagram above, the focus turns to how we can experience and convey authentic caring by developing the ability to feel and show empathy.

Noted as the first habit in the reflection guide associated with the book *Better Conversations* (Knight, Knight, & Carlson, 2015), expressing empathy involves the sincere desire to provide place inside our hearts (affective empathy) and minds (cognitive empathy) for the other person, for a time (pp. 70–72).

Daniel Goleman (1995) described empathy as "the fundamental people skill" (p. 43). In his words:

> Failure to register another's feelings is a major deficit in emotional intelligence, and a tragic failing in what it means to be human. For all rapport, the root of caring, stems from emotional attunement, from the capacity for empathy. That capacity—the ability to know how another feels—comes into play in a vast array of life arenas.
>
> (p. 96)

What if we aren't very good at understanding how others are feeling; what if we have spent most of our life relying heavily on our IQ (intelligence quotient) and haven't learned to develop much of our EQ (emotion quotient)? This situation happens often in our knowledge-focused profession. Even if it's not as comfortable or natural to intentionally think about how someone else may be feeling, becoming empathetic is not beyond our reach.

As coaches, teachers, and educational leaders, our jobs are grounded in the concept that individuals have the capacity to change, to learn, to become more. When we are open and willing to share in what others are feeling, new insights become available to us. Our understanding and compassion are expanded, and even our actions can be changed when we empathize with the experiences and feelings of those we coach. When answering the question "What leadership traits do you feel are most beneficial for an instructional coach to possess?" Coach #10 shared:

> Okay, I think listening skills. Really being able to hear the other people and empathize and put yourself in their place, and so to be able to listen from their viewpoint. I think . . . I have some of that, and I've grown in it this year a lot, and I think it's

been a saving grace. It's being able to say, "Okay, why are they saying this? Why are they being like this?" and being able to listen and empathize and say, "Oh, I understand them, because I know where they're coming from, not where I'm coming from." I think that's important.

Goleman (1995) noted studies by National Institute of Mental Health researchers that found that children "were more empathetic when [their] discipline included calling strong attention to the distress their misbehavior caused someone else: [for example,] 'Look how sad you've made her feel' instead of 'That was naughty'" (p. 99). Luckily, we probably don't need intense empathy treatment, but if we want to become more empathetic, we can learn about the teachers we are coaching by truly hearing their words and also noticing their facial expressions, gestures, voice pitch and tone, posture, eye contact, and other nonverbal clues to how they may be feeling and what their needs might be.

In response to the question "What would be the most important advice you could give to someone striving to be an effective instructional coach?" Coach #1 shared some ideas about how to listen with empathy:

> I think practicing those listening skills. I think we all assume we have good listening skills, and until I went through Cognitive Coaching and did the scenarios where I had to practice and I had to play both sides, coach and mentee, I didn't realize how much time I spend thinking about something they said and what I'm going to say next about that and that I tune out everything else. I didn't realize just how effective some of those silly-sounding things—like the eye contact, the nodding, the mimicry that goes on in really active listening—how that helps us attune, and so I think that's where I'd tell someone to start. If you have an interest in coaching, first pursue whether or not you can be a truly genuinely active listener; and if you can and you aren't bothered by it, then go to the next step. Because if that's not in place, you won't be successful.

Here are Coach #15's thoughts when answering the same question:

> It's not about you, it's about them and what they need, because you have to have that kind of thinking, I believe, if you're going to make a difference for people . . . I didn't go in [to coaching] thinking that, but the more I do it, the more I'm like, "You know what . . . it's about what the people you are working with need and what you can do for them."

Encouragement

I really, really think having an encouraging personality is vital. Because I, you know, we talk. Well, at least the coaches talk. And, I can hear judgment—I mean I hear judgment from myself sometimes, you know, we're all human—but I think if you're not an encouraging person, people can't take what you have to say to them, because you're not putting them in a good frame of mind. You're putting them in that fight-or-flight frame of mind just by talking to them. So, I think being encouraging to people—and to yourself, too!—is really important!

(Coach #10)

We can be intentional about our word choices and try to minimize our use of words that could undermine encouragement, such as "I" (too often), "should," and "but" (see "Reflect and Connect" in this chapter for an activity to practice this).

Coach #3 shared the following thoughts when talking about important leadership traits to have as an instructional coach:

I think you need to have people skills. You need to be able to get along with everybody, and you have to like people, just [as] teachers have to like their kids. There is nothing worse than a teacher who doesn't like their kids!

Kind of basic: If we don't like people, it's going to be a challenge for us to encourage them.

One well-known example of the positive power of encouragement is the documented home-field advantage in sports. There are different reasons for this phenomenon, such as the amount of travel the visiting team makes, familiarity with local conditions, and, then, the crowd! The crowd makes a big difference! When we and fellow fans cheer for our team, we can actually increase the likelihood that our team will win. Fans can influence both the players and the referees (Nevill & Holder, 1999).

Coaching can provide teachers with feelings of comfort, support, and positive energy to do the work in front of them, similar to a home-field advantage, when they feel we are cheering for them. Encouragement is powerful! We want teachers to experience an increase of hope, confidence, and success as a result of our coaching.

Unfortunately, people in general remember negative experiences more easily than positive ones (Warner, 2007). Stephen Covey (1989) wrote about the importance of making many more "deposits" rather than "withdrawals" into others' "emotional bank accounts" so that they feel safe with us. Jack Zenger and Joseph Folkman (2013) shared business research that indicated high-performing teams shared about six positives for every one criticism. The lowest-performing teams had about three negative comments for every one positive comment. Does this make you as worried as it does me about how often students hear negative comments from teachers and peers?

The importance of developing our observational skills to notice more positive things than negative ones absolutely applies to coaching! Randy Sprick, when speaking at the 2018 Teaching | Learning | Coaching Conference in Las Vegas, shared that when we approach students with the intention to correct or redirect an action they need to change, they will perceive it as a negative interaction, even though we may verbalize our correction

nicely. As a result of learning this, we at TCT have decided to provide supports to improve teachers' positive observational skills and then to encourage them to approach and interact positively with students many times more than they make behavioral corrections. As coaches, if we can hone our awareness to notice mostly good things that are happening at least six times as often as we notice negative things (Zenger & Folkman, 2013), we can spread more joy in our coaching role. My mentor and former boss Judy Williams said it this way: "Praise what you want to see more of." When we communicate positive messages and accentuate the good happening around us, we will have better results, and people will want to be around us! If we are looking for problems or inadequacies all the time, we will surely find them all the time. My takeaway from this research is that we've all probably experienced way more negatives than positives in our lives. We've got to catch up! Pour on the happy! We can help teachers overcome life's jeers, fears, and tears with our joyful cheers!

We all need fans. This morning, I coached two wonderful high-school teachers who suffer with chronic, severe physical challenges. They are dedicated heroes working in the most challenging of urban environments, and they get up and go, even when they don't feel well, because what they do matters. Though my coaching purposes today included supporting quality instruction with lesson-plan ideas and classroom-management details, what meant the most to those teachers was that I somehow connected with the pain they were experiencing by taking the time to see it in their eyes and notice minimized mobility (probably because I had just researched empathy yesterday and sadly realized I'm not very good at it).

I had been coaching them for a while but hadn't registered their struggles at a deep level, though intellectually I knew what they were going through. We openly talked about how they really weren't feeling well. I felt awed by their nobility and dedication to the teaching profession and to their students. My words flowed authentically and easily as I acknowledged the importance of their contributions and encouraged them to continue on, despite their challenging paths. They truly deserve hero status. I naturally became a completely genuine fan today as I found a way to allow their pain to become mine, and I think today was the day we became "real" to each other, similar to the story of the Velveteen Rabbit (Bianco, 2003).

I'm usually a happy person and can find good things to focus on and be positive about, but today was different. The encouragement I offered came from a more substantial empathetic foundation of relationship. I do think the people I coached felt authentically seen and loved today, and I had explored an unexpected new inroad leading to joy. It didn't feel bubbly, sunny, and excited as it does sometimes; it included tearing up in the car because I felt their struggles, and it inspired me to immediately act on thoughts about how to make their lives easier. The joy of our connection was magnified when I found encouraging things to say to give them strength even though we both knew significant physical pain was currently part of their journey.

Today, I didn't interrupt them or try too hard to get my points across. True connection cemented our relationship, because it was grounded in shared struggle, and it was powerful because it magnified the indomitable power of their human spirits. Researching listening and empathy has been hard on me, as I have had to acknowledge that my dogged determination has sometimes gotten in the way of things that matter more than the task at hand. Writing about—and, in the process, learning at a deeper level about—the importance of listening, empathy, and encouragement in order to be a quality communicator has been incredibly important for my continued growth as a person. I'm beginning to realize that almost every person I know (and likely those I don't know) has had or is now experiencing an excess of negative and critical interactions. We can change this. Coaching allows us the perfect opportunity. May we pause ("Be quiet, and listen"—Coach #10) and then allow our presence and words to inspire hope and healing.

> *Shards of sadness surfacing in memory's misty waters smooth and heal in*
> *your presence, becoming colorful lessons learned. Clarity and hope are mine*
> *through your life-giving words.*

Knowledge

Let's move to the competent/right side of the center "listening" column in the diagram and discuss the importance of knowledge when striving to be a quality communicator. Instructional coaches need to know how to teach, and they need to know how to do it well! This is not the profession for someone who just wants to get out of the classroom. An instructional coach will not be respected if he or she doesn't know how to help teachers. In the words of Coach #3 when answering the question "What leadership traits do you feel are most beneficial for an instructional coach to possess?":

> Competency. I think you have to be knowledgeable about your craft. . . . I couldn't
> go out in a military situation and lead soldiers, 'cause I wouldn't know what the
> hell I'm doing . . . [the leader/coach] has to know where you're going and have
> knowledge about how to get people there.

Coach #13 said, in response to the question "What does being an effective instructional coach mean to you? What does effective mean?":

> It means knowing what the classroom environment is, what clientele that teacher
> has, what difficulties, behavior or academic modifications that are going on in that
> room. It's really knowing the classroom and the teacher and their instructional
> strategies and the way they're teaching—oh, what do you call it? Approach . . .
> we all have our own individual approaches in teaching. I think you have to know
> [teachers] and have to be respectful of where they're coming from and what they
> do before you ever open your mouth to do or say anything with them. And when
> you take that step to really know who they are, I think that gentleness comes from
> that . . . you can actually guide somebody in their own steps—you know, so you're

not trying to change somebody. So I think really getting to know the clientele [students] and the teacher, their academics, everything, and their grade level [is what it takes to be an effective coach].

Effective instructional coaches are dedicated to:

- learning about and working alongside individuals to support their growth;

have an almost insatiable desire to:

- continue learning and becoming better at both teaching and coaching; and

won't stop until:

- as many quality teachers as humanly possible are with students every day.

Effective coaches learn as much as possible about the teacher and students they are serving, and they regularly take advantage of learning opportunities. They are not satisfied with sharing only what they did back when that worked; they continue to stay updated, aware, and curious. They read and study professional books, journals, and online resources to increase their understanding of local and national educational trends and movements. They go to professional development offerings, discuss best practices, and make time to learn about what the teachers they are working with are facing and what they need. Specific information related to becoming a competent and knowledgeable coach are communicated in Chapter 3 and in Appendix A.

When answering the question "What does being an effective instructional coach mean to you? What does effective mean?" Coach #5 shared:

> So, I think the most important thing is you have to have rapport, and you also have to have the background knowledge. You have to understand the strategies. I think it's important that you've tried them yourself, and that when you are sitting down with [the teacher] you don't try to sugarcoat everything. You know [you might say to the teacher], "I hated this strategy; it wasn't good. Maybe it will work for you, and, if it does, then let me know and I can come in and observe you." But I think those two things go hand in hand, and you have to have rapport to be open and honest, and you have to have the skills to come in and work effectively with the teachers.

Instructional coaches need to (1) be knowledgeable about best instructional practices, (2) be able to model or provide models and supports for teachers that will move them in a positive direction, and (3) understand and follow a solid structure for delivering coaching effectively. However, they do not have to know everything about everything. That's impossible anyway, so coaches would do well to not pretend they are the be-all and end-all when it comes to instructional practice. If we don't know something, we can do research, we can look for models, we can ask for help, or we can phone a friend.

An example of this concept from my family life comes to mind when I don't have the expertise to handle something. Our youngest son, Jon, when he was about 5 years old, was up early on a Saturday morning and wanted to eat pancakes. Since my husband and I were not awake yet, he decided to go ahead and try to make pancakes by referring to the recipe on the back of the Bisquick box. When he ran into a problem with understanding the word "blended," he didn't come in and wake us up—he called the 1-800 number on the back of the box and asked the lady what "blended" meant. We woke up to the smell of pancakes and were so impressed with his resourcefulness. If we don't know, we can find out. The most important thing is to not pretend that we do know to make ourselves look good and then end up with a mess to clean up.

Clarity

1. Spend time getting to know the teacher and try to understand how she or he sees the world.

Stephen R. Covey (1982) explained the importance of understanding that our perceptions are the lenses through which we see the world and they influence our ability to see how things really are.

> Prior experiences have great impact on present perceptions, and these perceptions significantly affect or even determine our feelings, our communication, and our behavior. . . . How, then, do we see? Most of us think we see the world as it is, but I believe this is not the case. We each see not with the eye but with the soul. Each person sees the world not as it is but as *he* or *she* is. When he opens his mouth to describe what he sees, he in effect describes himself, that is, his perceptions.

(p. 3)

When we take the time to find out about the teacher we are working with, we have more insight into how that person is interpreting his or her experiences. This gives us greater awareness as we work to personalize the coaching experience for that person. At TCT, we have added a Human Connection form to our coaching processes (see Chapter 9) to help us understand where the people we coach are coming from and what they would like to achieve.

2. Use simple, clear processes.

The power of simplicity cannot be overstated. We, as humans, are typically willing to do only what we feel we can do (this goes for students as well). If we overload teachers with complicated processes or too many goals, they can shut down. Straightforward processes and a simple Action Plan template that includes guiding questions and components of a SMART goal are shared in Chapter 9. At TCT, we have used a similar straightforward template for peer coaching—a program in which teachers work together on common goals. Teachers report that the process helps them structure their collaborative work efficiently and effectively. Other coaching models have helpful processes as well. I like the easy-to-understand organization of The Impact Cycle (Knight, 2018), a three-step (Identify → Learn → Improve) color-coded process. When we use simple processes that both coaches and teachers can understand and implement without feeling like it's all too much, goals will more likely be accomplished.

3. Summarize each coaching session and review actions and timelines for both teacher and coach before completing the coaching session.

While working to develop the peer-coaching program, I spent a lot of time with Jennifer Gonzales, a first-grade teacher and colleague on the development team. We authored online modules together, reviewed forms teachers uploaded, and had many thorough discussions about how to make sure all necessary details were addressed. One thing Jennifer would do (which at first seemed redundant to me) was ask questions similar to these at the end of our meetings: "Can we run through everything that needs to be done, just to make sure I have it all down?" "Let's review what our plans are," and "Would it work to revisit the list of what needs to be done?"

Her consistent, but pleasant, insistence on being clear about what actions needed to be taken at the close of each of our meetings made me realize I could and should incorporate this level of clarity into my coaching and leadership roles more fully. We did not forget important details or suffer much disorganization or lack of follow-through, in part because of her focus on clarity; as a result, the program is flourishing.

Humor

Something I always appreciate when people are trying to communicate with me (whether in writing or in person) is when they make an effort to be funny or see the lighter side of things. For the past five years, I have sent out a weekly email to our coaches and leaders on a variety of topics. The subject line reads "MnMnJ," for Motivating Moments and Jokes (MnM, because the idea started with my handing out M&M's to encourage focusing on Motivating Moments).

Though I receive some comments on the research and instructional topics I share, most of the comments are on the jokes. Coaches say they keep them and tell them to their students; leaders and coaches share jokes with me to put in the email, and the jokes are what they scroll down to first before they dive into some of the more weighty content. Here is a recent favorite:

Q: "What sound is generated when you cross a cow with a bell?

A: "DUNG!"

It is so easy to become overfocused on all the serious problems we are dealing with in education, but there's a lot of funny stuff we deal with too—we just have to notice it and remember to share it.

Reflect and Connect

The following game can be used in a coach training or as a PD activity. It is designed to get us talking about coaching scenarios and then let someone give us feedback when we are focusing on ourselves too much (e.g., using too many "I"s), minimizing others' thoughts by saying "but," or sounding like a parent when we tell people they "should" do something. There is also an opportunity to identify or flag any other words that might limit credibility or connection.

"Stop Saying That!"
(from *The Princess Bride*)

Time: 20 minutes; 5 minutes of practice coaching session with 5-minute discussion following, then switch roles and repeat

Materials Needed:

- Coaching scenarios located on the back of this card. Choose 2 scenarios for each pair of coaches
- But, I, Should, and Other stick pack – 1 for each pair of coaches

Directions:

- Coaches divide into pairs, decide who is Coach 1 and who is Coach 2, *agree to rise above being offended*
- Coach 1 picks up the sticks, Coach 2 reads the coaching scenario, then verbalizes a coaching session (just do what you normally do, or what you think a good coach does) trying not to use the words I, should, but, or any other word that would limit connection or credibility. Coach 1 engages in conversation (answers questions, etc.) with Coach 2 and holds up the matching stick of Coach 2 says but, should, I, or a word that doesn't work for Coach 1. Coach 1 could take data on how often the ineffective words are used (or not used).
- Coaches discuss the results and brainstorm how to improve word choice if needed
- Coaches repeat the process with Coach 1 reading the scenario and verbalizing a coaching session, and Coach 2 holding up the sticks

Modification Idea: Use a coaching/teaching video or a script and analyze it together. Hold up sticks as appropriate and discuss how the coach/teacher could improve

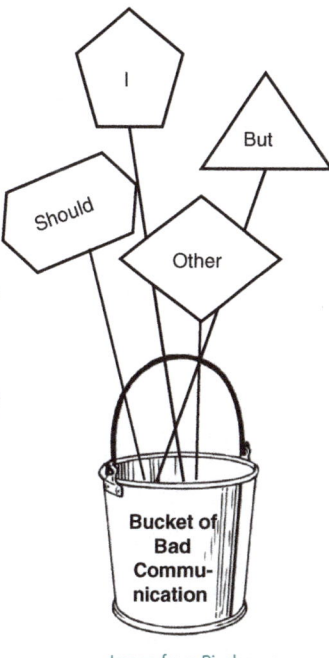

Image from Pixabay.com

QUALITY COMMUNICATOR

- **Summary:** Choose a scenario, then coach a partner through the situation for 3-5 minutes **without using the words but, should, I, or any other words that might limit connections or credibility; discuss results for 5 minutes.**

- **Objective:** Coaches will become aware of their tendencies to use ineffective language and will brainstorm with a partner how to improve word choice.

Coaching Scenarios

A new/veteran teacher is struggling with classroom management.	A teacher would like coaching support to learn how to set up engaging reading centers.
A teacher would like some help understanding how to change his/her instructional delivery to encourage students to think about using a variety of processes to find answers to questions.	A teacher has requested coaching to improve her/his small group instruction skills.
A teacher is not sure how to schedule her/his day to most effectively include both whole and small group opportunities for students. The teacher is unclear about how to organize rotations and accommodate interventions by support personnel.	A teacher, who teaches in a computer lab using specific software, is being allowed some flexibility in instructional delivery. The teacher wants to know how to organize and present short bursts of different types of instruction to meet the needs of students with different learning preferences.
A teacher would like help organizing his/her physical classroom environment.	A teacher would like support planning standards-based lessons.
A teacher notices that the same students answer her/his questions all the time. The teacher would like some help figuring out ways to have more students actively participate during the lessons.	A veteran teacher is having trouble keeping up with technology and new initiatives. She feels that most of these changes are unnecessary.
A teacher would like some help developing rubrics and knowing how to effectively analyze student work.	A teacher would like to know how to design and implement formative assessments.
A teacher is feeling overwhelmed and wants to know how to prioritize and manage all the requests being made of him/her.	A teacher would like coaching support to better implement new "Next Generation" teaching structures. The teacher would like to incorporate 21st Century Skills more effectively, including the 4 C's (Collaboration, Creativity, Communication, and Critical Thinking).

Quality Communicator Self-Assessment

1. Take this self-assessment before you set an intention to consciously find ways to become a better quality communicator.

2. Implement some of the practical application ideas and/or quality communicator S.O.A.K. supports found below (or use some of your own ideas).

3. In a month or so, see whether you have been able to improve your thoughts, motivations, and behaviors surrounding the important coaching characteristic of becoming a quality communicator. Reference the following synonyms/specifics, offered by coaches like you, as you personally determine what being a quality communicator is and determine how to make it a more conscious part of your daily life: *listens; creates a positive relationship; understands needs; clearly defines roles and work; uses positive, clear, and intentional language; gives specific feedback that clarifies; shares instructional strategies to refine or reinforce* (Frazier, 2014).

	Strongly Disagree	Disagree	Neutral/ Not Sure	Agree	Strongly Agree
	1	2	3	4	5
I value and treat the person I am coaching/leading as an equal.					
I intentionally use clear, positive, and empowering language.					
I am committed to listening with empathy and building awareness of important things that may be unspoken. I stop myself from mentally going off task, interrupting, or feeling compelled to immediately respond.					
I am continually learning and practicing my coaching and teaching skills.					
I coach with knowledge and clarity in the following ways: • I research and provide a variety of vetted instructional strategies as options for teachers. • I provide specific feedback to reinforce positive teaching strategies and to refine others. • The processes I use can be easily understood.					
When I complete a coaching session, both the teacher and the coach are clear about the goal and what actions will be taken by whom by when.					
BONUS: Give yourself extra credit points for finding ways to add humor to your coaching work.					
Column Totals:					

Grand Total: _____

What totals mean: 26–30 = Quality Communicator Rock Star, 21–25 = Very Good at Being a Quality Communicator, 16–20 = Sort of a Quality Communicator, 11–15 = Some Quality Communication Is Happening, 6–10 = Better Step It Up, 0–5 = Maybe Becoming a Quality Communicator Would Be a Great Goal?

Practical Application Ideas for Quality Communicator

Communication problems can begin with distorted ways of thinking. A favorite resource I use to help with this common problem was compiled by Caralee Frederic, LCSW, CGT (2014). She uses it in her practice to help people recognize when their thinking isn't making sense. It includes her takeaways from the works of David Burns (*Feeling Good*, 1981), Martin Seligman (*Learned Optimism*, 1998), Christine Padesky, and Dennis Greenberger. This resource has been well-received by both coaches and teachers, because it helps us recognize how our distorted thinking may be stealing our joy and causing problems, both internally and within our home and work relationships. One teacher used it to help her teenage stepdaughter understand how her thinking was undermining her self-confidence and relationships.

Following is a list of some of the more common kinds of thinking distortions. It is important to remember that everyone falls into these cognitive traps some of the time. Many of them are similar to each other. It's more important to be able to "spot" them in your thinking (and your speaking) than to distinguish them one from another.

1. *Overgeneralization*: You believe that because you've had one bad experience, the bad experience will always repeat itself in similar situations. Words like "never," "always," "all," "every," "none," "nobody," and "everyone" in your thoughts and speech are tip-offs.

2. *Either/or thinking* (also known as *polarized thinking*): Situations are either terrible or wonderful. You are either perfect or worthless. In depressed thinking, you often see yourself as "bad" and those you admire, or like, as "good."

3. *Rejecting the positive*: You focus on the negative and find reasons to devalue or reject positive experiences or compliments.

   Example: Your mother-in-law compliments you on your cooking, and you think: *She's just being nice. The potatoes weren't even hot.*

4. *Focusing on the negative*: You selectively pay attention to the negative in a situation and disregard the positive.

   Example: You give a presentation to 50 people. All of the evaluations are positive, with one exception. You focus all your attention on the one critical comment and feel like a failure.

5. *Thinking feelings are facts*: You believe that what you feel about life, situations, and people must be true.

   Examples: *I feel inferior, so I must not be as good as others.*

   I feel hopeless. My depression will never get better.

6. *Expecting perfection*: You make inflexible demands of yourself or others about how you "should"/"must"/"ought to" act. There is no allowance for variations in situations or changing conditions.

   Examples: "He shouldn't be so self-centered and thoughtless."

   "She should be more prompt."

   "I shouldn't be angry or jealous."

7. *Name calling*: You label yourself or others with a negative name or stereotype.

   Examples: "loser"/"dork"/"idiot"

   "I'm boring."

(Continued)

(Continued)

8. *Feeling controlled*: You believe that you can't influence the most important things in your life. This belief can lead you to blame situations or others for your unhappiness.

> Examples: "Nothing I say or do makes a difference anyway; why bother speaking up?"
>
> "If it weren't for my ex's selfishness, I could have gotten my degree by now."

9. *Feeling all-responsible*: You believe you have control and responsibility for everything and everyone. You must fill every need and comfort every hurt; if you don't, you feel guilty. This thinking results in blaming yourself.

> Examples: "I can't take vacation. The office/my clients would fall apart if I leave."
>
> *If I had been a better mother, my daughter wouldn't have gotten in trouble at school.*

10. *Hoping for Heaven's reward*: You expect that personal sacrifice and self-denial will "pay off" in appreciation or returned favors. When this doesn't work, you feel resentful, hurt, or disappointed.

> Example: "I spent all day cleaning this house, and no one even notices."

11. *Comparing worth*: You think you are not good enough unless you are "as good as" someone else in all areas.

> Example: "He keeps his office space so clean! Mine is just a mess. I'm no good at anything."

12. *Always expecting disaster* (aka *catastrophizing*): You notice or hear about a problem or situation and anticipate the worst possible outcome.

> Example: "I can't believe I made that mistake! Everyone will find out! My reputation and future are ruined!"

13. *Predicting the future*: You make a negative prediction about how something will turn out or how someone will act.

> Example: "I know I'll never be able to stay on a diet. I'll never lose weight."
>
> "We'll never be able to afford to buy a house."

14. *Believing you can read minds*: This involves thinking you know what someone else is thinking or feeling, without checking it out.

> Examples: You decide not to ask a friend for help, because he or she will say no anyway.
>
> You see a friend at the supermarket and she doesn't say hello, so you decide she doesn't like you.

Avoid being pulled into galaxies of gloom and gossip. Many of the most happy and effective teachers I know have made a conscious choice to be kind but to stay away (as much as possible) from people and situations that drain their positive energy. It seems that, in almost every school (or almost any working environment, for that matter), we can feel the dark pull coming from the occasional black hole of negativity. Maybe this happens in the teacher's lounge, where some teachers feel it's okay to speak negatively about students, other teachers, or leadership, even to the point of breaking confidences or sharing personal information that is inappropriate. Maybe it happens in the back of the room at staff meetings, where words of resistance or unkindness are whispered in low tones. Maybe a force of negativity is found in the front office or within specialized groups. In these places, and within the people that create these dim places, others are judged and torn down in a twisted effort to make the speakers feel better by expressing toxic emotions and damaging words. Of course, this doesn't work, they don't feel better, and the negative pull continues, unless there is no one left to commiserate with them in their black hole, gloomy galaxy, or asteroid of awfulizing.

This is not to say that we avoid listening to legitimate negative feedback that could be helpful or that we don't try to encourage and include in positive ways people who often feel negative (there is probably something else going on that we don't know about). It is to say that we should not buy acreage and begin building in the subdivision of Shaming Others on the planet of Perpetual Problems.

New teachers are especially vulnerable to being pulled into these negative situations, and they can be unhealthily influenced early on as they try to fit into a new school culture. New teachers may not understand that a few extra-friendly teachers may be hoping (often unconsciously) to sell them real estate in their negative worlds. If you need to show new teachers these paragraphs, please do. Note that none of us is perfect; sometimes frustration or a difficult situation gets the better of us, and we may say some things we later wish we hadn't. Yet we will get better at controlling our speech over time if we notice when we could have done better. This is not like that—what I'm talking about is a chronic, pervasive need among certain people to be negative for whatever reason. If it has invaded the environment your new teacher is in, steer her or him clear of its destructive influence.

Conclusion

It is unlikely we will make unrecoverable communication mistakes if we deeply desire to listen and learn about others and our craft, are grounded in the foundational principle of equality, and allow ourselves to be gentled and guided by love.

QUALITY COMMUNICATOR ~S.O.A.K.~

Sometimes learning penetrates best when we are relaxed and not trying too hard to make it happen. (Like a "Quality Communicator" Bath Bomb infused with personalized nutrients.)

Choose what works for you.

Quotes	Music	Statements affirmations	Books poetry stories	Art	Videos movies	Movement other ideas
"To effectively communicate, we must realize that we are all different in the way we perceive the world and use this understanding as a guide to our communication with others." —Tony Robbins	"Bridge Over Troubled Water" Simon and Garfunkel	**For coaches and teachers:** I connect and empower.	*Deliberate Optimism: Reclaiming the Joy in Education* D. Silver, J. Berckemeyer, & J. Baenen	*Two Women Putting the World to Rights* (Sculpture) Dublin's Talking Statues	*How to Speak So That People Want to Listen* (TED Talk) Julian Treasure	**Tree Pose**
"The most important thing in communication is hearing what isn't said." —Peter Drucker	"When You Say Nothin' at All" Alison Krauss	I attune to how others may be feeling as I listen and look for nonverbal cues.	*Healing Conversations: What to Say When You Don't Know What to Say* Nance Guilmartin	*Friends Under the Rain* Leonid Afremov	*How to Tame Your Wandering Mind* (TEDx Talk) Amishi Jha	
"Listen with the intent to understand, not with the intent to reply." —Stephen R. Covey	"You've Got a Friend in Me" Randy Newman	The encouraging words I use leave a legacy of light and love.			*Navy Ship vs. Lighthouse* YouTube	
	"Careless Talk" Billy Joel	I give the gift of my undivided attention and am fully present when I coach/teach.	*Fierce Conversations: Achieving Success in Work & in Life, One Conversation at a Time* Susan Scott	*Two Friends and Rooster* Leonid Afremov		**Oil:** rosemary
"All great speakers were bad speakers first." —Ralph Waldo Emerson	"I Want to Talk About Me" Toby Keith	I recognize and correct thinking distortions that undermine my relationships and my well-being.		*Patrick Henry Speaking* Peter Rothermel	*How miscommunication happens (and how to avoid it)* (TED-Ed Feb. 22, 2016) Katherine Hampsten	
"People may hear your words, but they feel your attitude." —John C. Maxwell	"Rumor Has It" Adele	I am learning to filter my thoughts and words to support myself and others. I can envision a time when I will allow only my best, most helpful thoughts to be spoken.	*Emotional Intelligence: Why It Can Matter More Than IQ* Daniel Goleman	*Book: Nonverbal Communication in Everyday Life*, 4th ed. Martin Remland	*Monty Python Quest for the Holy Grails Poor Communication* YouTube	**Stones:** blue angelite; lapis lazuli
	"Whatever You Say" Martina McBride		"Communication" (story) Bruce King			**Color:** royal blue

Connection flows freely as I listen, learn, and love.

NOTES

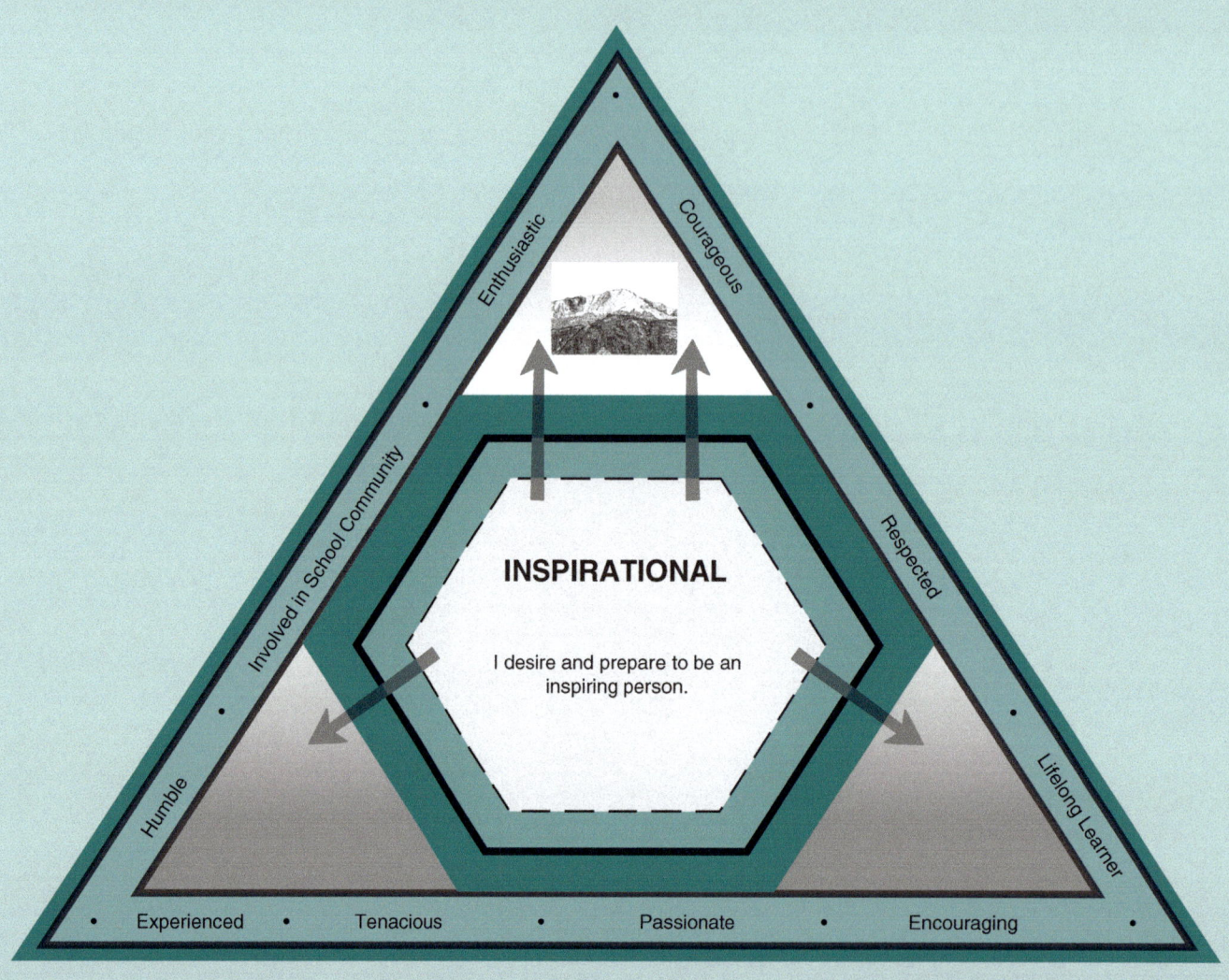

I am dedicated to personal and professional growth and enjoy learning with and encouraging others. I spend time caring for my body, mind, and spirit so I can function at my best. I smile, learn new things, and passionately and courageously go about my work. I strive to deliver joyful, inspired coaching by being: humble; quick to laugh and celebrate; and by modeling enthusiasm. I tenaciously stand in service to and authentically believe in those I coach until the goal set is the goal met!

Inspirational

6

When looking at the central characteristics of "caring" and "competent" in the model, we notice that directly above the words are two arrows pointing upward, making their way through the filters of authenticity and being a quality communicator, ending in the top triangle of the model, at the characteristic of "inspirational." People are inspired by those who are invested in them and show they truly care in a variety of ways. People are also inspired by those who are incredibly talented at what they do. Being inspirational incorporates some elements of all the other characteristics. In this chapter, discussion and processes for "bringing home" some of the other concepts shared in the book—including the H.O.P.E. elements described in Chapter 3, the "touchstone" process mentioned in the introduction, and the determination of values mentioned in Chapter 4—will be provided, along with inspirational resources.

This chapter is meant to focus on the positive, on what we can do, and on how incredible each individual is! Sometimes in the world of education, we focus too much on deficiencies and, in the process, undermine the energy and positivity that is necessary to fuel forward movement.

Many of our educational processes miss the boat by focusing so heavily on deficits. We try to improve teacher competency through evaluation by identifying areas in which teachers could improve, even though there is little research to suggest that teacher evaluations positively affect teacher growth (Peterson, n.d.) or that critical feedback leads to better performance (Buckingham & Goodall, 2019). We blame the lack of supportive student home lives, the lack of aligned and helpful resources, the lack of quality teachers and leadership, the lack of . . . just about everything. And though these situations may be legitimate and need to be addressed, the average teacher can't really change them on a large scale, and if we're always talking about the same depressing things, guess what happens? The energy needed to do anything positive is sucked right down the drain with all the sadness, hopelessness, criticism, and focus on things we can't control. This often results in teachers and leaders erecting defensive walls, desperately trying to save any semblance of their self-worth because student learning results are not where they would like them to be.

Human energy is not boundless. Our ability to work with efficiency is limited. At some point we have to stop, rest, and sleep. At times, we run low on or completely deplete our physical and mental energy. Teachers are especially challenged to keep fueled with positivity, because they interact with many students per day and spend much of their energy trying to find creative ways to work through and around the individual circumstances and challenges each student brings to school. Teachers often have multiple subjects to plan for, team responsibilities, parent communication, data analysis, data entry, and technology pieces, resulting in the need to work extra hours beyond their contract day. Managing all this, along with personal and family responsibilities, can significantly drain their energy levels.

Coaches are really in the business of energy management.

I have not seen great growth in teacher competency over the long term when teachers are identified as weak in certain areas and coaching centers on the teacher's deficits. Without incorporating into coaching specific evidence of good things the teacher has done and identifying where things *are* working, the get-up-and-go to produce long-term change can be limited. Fear can be an unpleasant short-term motivator, but top-down coaching (often interpreted and sometimes delivered as criticism) breeds resentment. As shared previously, Jim Knight often shares W. Timothy Gallwey's (2001) words, "When you insist, they will resist" (Knight, Knight, & Carlson, 2015, p. 34). As soon as the pressure is off, teachers may abandon new teaching strategies because someone forced the issue, or the new ideas (whether they are good or not) become buried in the "if I have time" pile, because it is natural to not prioritize something that brings up negative emotions.

Fear can also cause paralysis. Teachers can become frozen in their practice, because they are afraid whatever they do won't be "right." When teachers are afraid and don't think they do anything well, they can implode on themselves, unable to believe in anything they do. As a result, their teaching in every situation can suffer. I have seen teachers afraid to follow through on behavioral expectations or scared to face or communicate less than stellar results because they might look bad to administrators or colleagues or because students might get upset. I have seen or heard of instances of teachers hiding in bathrooms, barricading themselves under computers (seriously), and taking "sick" days repeatedly—along with instances of "pretending not to know" like those described by Susan Scott (2011, p. 17), when a teacher might "get that look on his face like a cat occupied in the litter box—sort of far away as if to indicate that he is not really here and neither are you." This quote made me laugh, but I have seen that exact same look when teachers are trying to ignore uncomfortable situations—for example, when a coach shares difficult data and asks the teacher, "What do you think could be causing the low engagement numbers?" or when a teacher is sitting at his or her desk pretending not to notice that students are completely off task, talking, swearing, or walking on their desks.

Professional development of any sort needs to have at its core the specific intention of not only supporting instructional competence, but also bringing caring, hope, encouragement, and positive energy into the daily, often hectic, challenging lives of teachers. One way we can do this is to identify teacher strengths, as will be noted in Chapter 9. But there is a preliminary step, one we sometimes forget to take. Before we can produce a powerful positive presence that leads to increased energy and instructional success for teachers, we need to be intentional about knowing ourselves, identifying our strengths, and deciding what we as coaches and educational leaders can positively bring to the table. By doing this, we can cultivate fertile environments that will inspire those we coach to move in a positive direction. This intentional landscaping can then inspire teachers to, in turn, create positive environments for students.

Finding Home

The name of the process to be shared in this chapter is *Finding Home*. Four basic components, involving both personal and practical pieces, are included in this process, which is designed to help the reader become more inspirational. The visual analogy is a simple baseball field, with forward-moving paths between bases providing space for us to identify what we need to move to the next step or base on our way to becoming more inspirational. This analogy is also meant to help us understand that in a way we will be "coming home" to ourselves, finding ways to identify and bring into reality the most authentic and inspirational version of ourselves.

One important thing to understand when beginning this process is that you start from a position of strength. When you step up to the plate, you bring yourself: who you are, where you come from, and all the skills and talents you have developed over time. You are already important and of great worth. As a teacher, a coach, or an educational leader, it is likely that you are already inspirational in many ways, and your willingness to go through a process to refine yourself even further speaks to your inspiring nature.

I will not attempt to go into detail about everything we could possibly include when organizing ourselves and our lives to be more inspiring, but I will guide you through a process and integrate pieces that have helped teachers coached by the wonderful coaches in the TCT program. This plan is, in part, a slightly modified version of the "touchstone" process shared elsewhere in this book, with the concepts of H.O.P.E. (Health, Organization, Positivity, and Encouragement) found in Chapter 3 and the S.O.A.K. (Stress-free Opportunities to Absorb Knowledge) ideas found at the end of each chapter.

You could organize these pieces into any type of analogy and/or visual image that works for you. You could think of anything with four components: a bird's head, tail, and two wings; the cornerstones of a home; anything that would be an inspiring support for your thinking. The organizational structure for the *Finding Home* process will be a simple baseball analogy taking place on your personal "field of inspiration," providing a structure for identifying and recording specifics that will produce forward movement in your quest to become an inspirational player in the lives of others. Here are the four main pieces:

1. *Define YOU.* (Identify your strengths, who you are, what your core values are, and what your individuality can bring to the table; step up to the plate.)

2. *Identify Resources.* (Search for, connect with, and spend time immersing yourself in inspiring resources and spending time with people who reflect your values, bring you strength, and fill you with positive energy.)

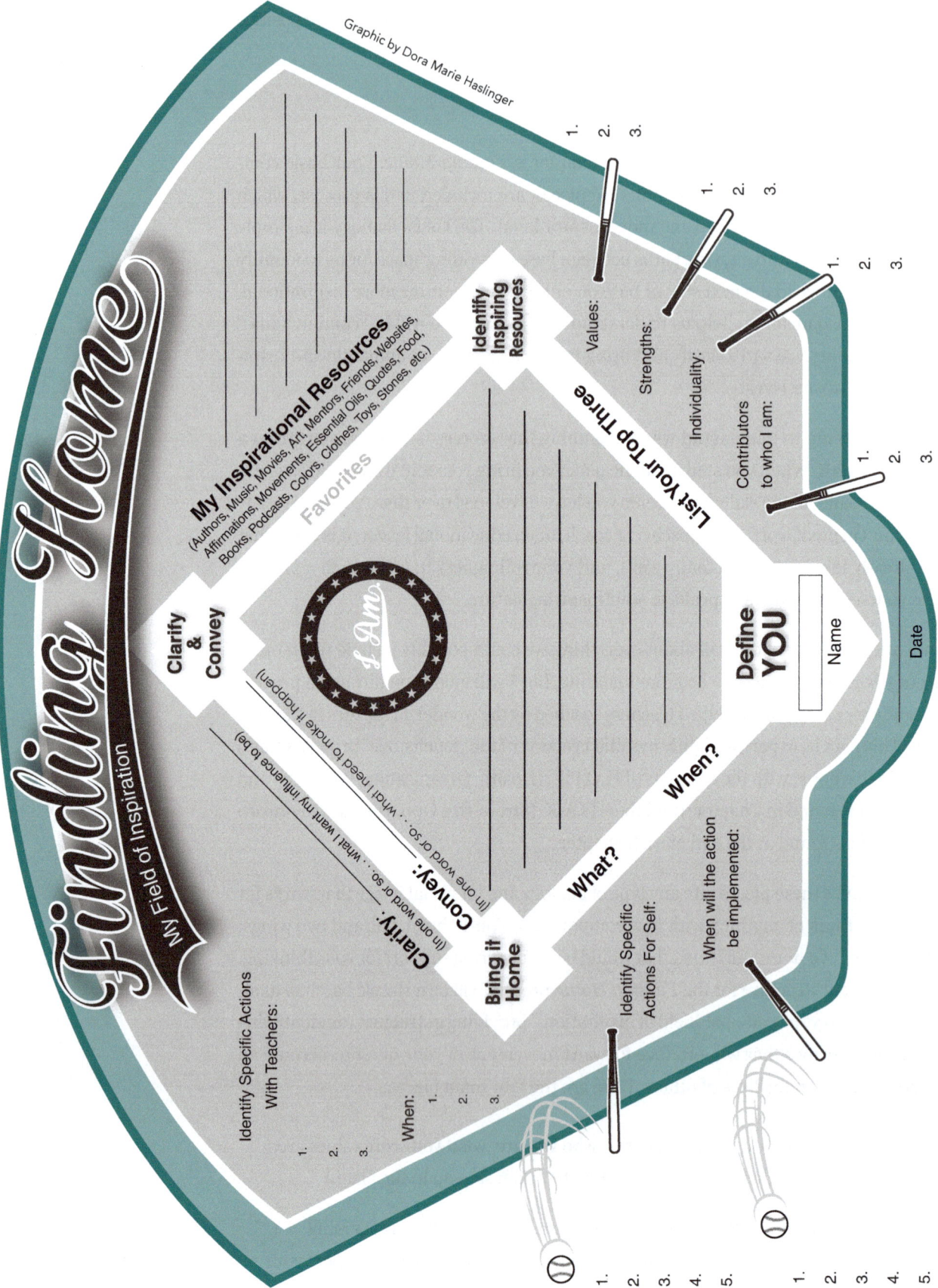

Graphic by Dora Marie Haslinger

Finding Home

My Field of Inspiration

My Inspirational Resources
(Authors, Music, Movies, Art, Mentors, Friends, Websites, Affirmations, Movements, Essential Oils, Quotes, Food, Books, Podcasts, Colors, Clothes, Toys, Stones, etc.)

Favorites

Identify Inspiring Resources

Values:
1.
2.
3.

Strengths:
1.
2.
3.

Individuality:
1.
2.
3.

Contributors to who I am:
1.
2.
3.

List your Top Three

Define YOU

Name

Date

I Am

Clarify & Convey

Clarify:
(in one word or so... what I want my influence to be)

Convey:
(in one word or so... what I need to make it happen)

Bring it Home

What?

When?

Identify Specific Actions For Self:
1.
2.
3.
4.
5.

When will the action be implemented:
1.
2.
3.
4.
5.

Identify Specific Actions With Teachers:
1.
2.
3.

When:
1.
2.
3.

3. *Clarify and Convey.* Clarify what you want your influence to be with teachers. What do you want them to feel or experience as a result of your influence and interactions with them? Then identify what you need to help you Convey what you have clarified.

4. *Bring It Home.* (Organize your day-to-day life and activities to support yourself as you intentionally create an inspirational life.)

The *Finding Home* graphic above provides an overview of the process you will be going through during the remainder of this chapter. As you take time (and it may take days, weeks, or months) to read through the narrative and thoughtfully go through the activities associated with the four pieces listed above, you will be able to create your own "field of inspiration."

Define YOU

To begin this process, there is really just one thing you need to do to become more inspirational, and that is to decide to make it happen. Set aside some quiet time, step up to the plate, start from where you are, take some swings—show up.

How do we figure out who we are? This is likely a lifelong process, one that is ever-expanding as we continue to grow, learn, and have more experiences. Let go of any fear or worry as you allow yourself to think and feel deeply. Here you will unearth treasures that may be hidden within and bring them to light so that your sources of strength, your core desires, and your unique gifts are made known to you and can then be intentionally used to benefit others.

Do you know who you are? Maybe you feel a strong connection to family and your heritage, and that connection helps ground you and define who you are (as in the song "Who I Am" by Jessica Andrews); maybe you feel a strong connection to God, and your priorities and values are influenced by faith; maybe you have come to know more about who you are through activities you are passionate about, talents you possess, things you love to do, goals you have accomplished, or dreams you look forward to achieving. Maybe you deeply connect with certain people, writings, poems, artworks, physical activities, animals, or places. Freely think and feel through what makes you who you are, and record your thoughts below (no judgment or criticism allowed by you or others), then circle the three things you think contribute the most.

What Contributes to Who I Am?

_____

_____

_____

_____

_____

_____

_____

_____

What Does My Individuality Bring to the Table?

What skills, talents, education, experience, wisdom, encouragement, and personality traits do I have to offer that are especially powerful, helpful, dynamic, useful, or insightful? (Circle your top three.)

_____

_____

_____

_____

_____

_____

_____

_____

My Strengths Include:

List as many strengths as you can think of, then circle the three you feel are your greatest. Here are some words to get you thinking about inspirational qualities; they could be categorized as strengths or values: _courageous, tenacious, passionate, encouraging, enthusiastic, humble, involved, engaged, experienced, respected, lifelong learner._

_____

_____

_____

_____

_____

_____

_____

_____

Values That Are Important to Me

You may already know the values that are important to you and have organized your life around them. If so, please list them below. If you would like some help identifying values, a list of different values and a short process that can help you identify five core values can be found on Carnegie Mellon University's website at https://www.cmu.edu/career/documents/my-career-path-activities/values-exercise.pdf.

(List as many as you would like, then determine your top three and circle them.)

_____

_____

_____

_____

_____

_____

_____

Personal Statement(s)

Check the boxes below when you complete the following steps:

❑ Take some time to think through your previous responses, refer back to your top choices in each section, and note or highlight key words and/or phrases that strike you as exceptionally meaningful.

❑ Create a statement, affirmation, or phrase (or join a few together, create more than one—whatever works for you; there are no punctuation or formatting rules) that will guide your work and/or life and inspire you every time you speak or think through it (them). Write your thoughts on the lines below. Starting each statement using the words "I am ..." will keep your inspiring words in the present moment and can help you through difficult days when you speak or think them.

Here are some examples:

- I am a courageous and passionate educator filled with a collaborative and encouraging spirit. My enthusiasm, tenacity, and communication skills result in greater teacher competency and high levels of student learning.

- I am wise, consistent, and strong. I inspire with humility, grace, and good humor, and, as I light the way for others, hope is my guiding star.

- I am a caring, competent, and committed friend who moves instructional practice forward and conveys the joy and nobility of the teaching profession during every coaching conversation.

- I am an adventurous, risk-taking, joyful educator who is dedicated to continuously learning, sharing best practices, and radiating positivity.

- I am an experienced, competent coach and a thoughtful person of substance. What I share with others is well-researched and personalized to meet individual teacher needs, resulting in quality teaching.

_____

_____

_____

_____

_____

_____

_____

_____

_____

Doodles; Drawings; Free-Form Notes:

Identify Inspiring Resources

Similar to the S.O.A.K. page (Stress-free Opportunities to Absorb Knowledge) found at the end of each chapter, this table is designed to provide a place to record the most inspiring resources you have come across. These resources are where you might go when you want to gain perspective, when you need strength and insight. "We are the product of all we read, all we view, all we hear, and all we think" (Monson, 2015). What we fill our minds and senses with significantly impacts the quality of what we can offer others. Wisely arranging our time to immerse ourselves in life-giving, positive resources and activities expands our ability to positively influence and inspire others. If, as you are filling out this grid, you find you haven't intentionally identified many inspiring resources, or you find yourself limited to a few categories, consider adding to your collection. After you have gathered this information, consider sharing some or all of it to provide others with ideas about where to go to find inspiring resources.

Inspiring Resources

Books/ Authors				
Quotes				
Music				
Poetry/ Fables/ Short Stories				
Movies/ Videos/ Websites/ Blogs				
Art				
Positive Statements or Affirmations				
Movement				
Mentors/ Colleagues/ Leaders/ Friends				
Others (Your Thoughts, Foods, Oils, Stones, etc.)				

Clarify and Convey

In this section, you'll *clarify* what you want your influence to be with teachers this school year or within a certain time frame, then you will identify what you need in your own life to help you best *convey* what you have clarified.

Let's work through a modified coaches/leaders version of the "touchstone" process, explained in the introduction, to clearly decide what you want to accomplish in your coaching/leadership role at this particular time.

First, choose a word written on the stones below (or use real stones), and/or write a word of your own that best captures what you would like the teachers you work with to take away from, gain, feel, or incorporate into their lives as a result of your coaching/leadership, influence, or interactions with them this year. Please do not limit yourself to only the words presented, unless they work for you; more ideas are found below, just to spark your thinking. This process will not work unless the word you choose comes from your own heart and mind. *What is it you want people to take away from their interactions with you? This is important—this is you deciding what your influence in general will be. It may help to refer back to your "I am" statement.*

TOUCHSTONE PROCESS FOR COACH OR EDUCATION LEADER

INSPIRATIONAL

More Word Ideas:

We have had amazing results with this process. It quickly <u>grounds</u> individuals to what is important to them and allows us to use that information to coach more effectively.

ROCK ON!

CLARIFY: What Do You Want Your Influence to Be? Write chosen word here: _____

Next, choose or think of a word (or one idea expressed with a few words) that would increase your ability to *convey* the desired influence to teachers or staff. Coaches and educational leaders benefit from identifying what they personally need to assist themselves as they act to make their core desires for those they coach or lead come to life. On the following line (or on the "Convey" line of the graphic), write the word or an idea expressed with a few words you have chosen.

CONVEY: What Do You Need to Make It Happen? (one word or so): _____

Does choosing just one word or phrase mean you are committing to that focus forever? Probably not; however, I am still trying to create "havens of happiness and harbors of hope and healing" (as mentioned in Chapter 4) everywhere I can. Thinking of my student Darian and her note to me many years later about how our classroom had been a "haven" (see Chapter 4) gives me courage to continue to be intentional, hopeful, and excited about new possibilities. Some things do stick with us when we go deep. The focus words you will be choosing are for where you are now, what you think or feel is needed for you and the people you are surrounded by and influencing at this moment in time. Maybe they will be your focus for a year, for a quarter, or for the duration of a difficult period in a school district or in your life. Maybe they will stick with you for decades or even a lifetime.

This process is meant to help you determine with clarity what you want your influence to be, decide how that will look with students/teachers/staff, and then identify supports to assist you as you strive to effectively convey that influence. For the past four years, we at TCT have been using this process with teachers we coach. We have not organized a serious study of the results, but we have found that teachers are often looking to inspire confidence in their students both personally and with academic content, and they want their influence to result in happiness for their students. Personally, teachers are often hoping to find more peace, strength, and serenity for themselves. As mentioned in the introduction and noted on the diagram of the characteristics model (see the introduction), our coaching program has incorporated more human connection pieces as we strive to find ways to address both the technical and the emotional components of teaching, coaching, and leading.

Following are two possible coaching scenarios. One example for each of the two central components (caring and competent) of the characteristics model are shared. These examples show how coaches could use the *Finding Home* process to intentionally increase their inspirational influence with teachers. It might be helpful for you to refer back to the *Finding Home* graphic as we go along (feel free to photocopy it).

How Joe Decided to Clarify and Convey

Let's see how Joe, a young, energetic, newly hired instructional coach who was formerly an excellent teacher, used the *Finding Home* process. Joe wanted to find ways to provide effective, personalized support for teachers and to help them and other coaches see him as capable and competent. He felt this way because many of the teachers he had been working with were very experienced and were much older than him. Joe wanted to be able to connect with and support everyone he coached. Sometimes it seemed teachers assumed he didn't know much, resulting in Joe feeling disrespected and the work progressing slowly. After working through the components of "Define YOU" (home plate) and listing his top three contributors to his sense of self, his individuality, strengths, and values (on the way to first base), then creating his "I Am" statement (center of *Finding Home* graphic) and identifying his inspirational resources (first base), Joe moved on to second base (Clarify & Convey) and then to third base—Bring It Home (Actions and Timelines).

On the left side of the *Finding Home* graphic, there are two areas to list specific actions and timelines. The first section, closer to the top of the graphic, is for identifying actions that will happen *directly with teachers*. The other is a place for identifying *Specific Actions for Self* that would be helpful. These two areas may overlap, and that is okay. The main thing is to drill down to the details of what needs to happen to ***Clarify*** what you want your influence to be as a coach, and figure out what you need in order to effectively ***Convey*** that influence.

Joe wrote "respected resource" (he couldn't quite fit it into one word—that's okay) on the **"Clarify"** line of the *Finding Home* graphic. He thought that if he could provide well-researched, personalized resources including models and exemplars for the teachers he coached, they would take him seriously and he would learn in the process. So, on the *what I need to* **"Convey"** (*that I'm a respected resource*) line, he wrote that he needed "quality resources and time to research and practice." Then Joe identified what his *Specific Actions With Teachers* were going to be and *When* he was going to accomplish those actions. Then, he identified more *Specific Actions for Himself*, also with timelines, to ensure he would be able to bring into his daily life (*Bring It Home)* the actions that were needed to become a respected resource for teachers, providing personalized support that would most benefit them and their students.

Here's how Joe's actions were recorded on the corresponding sections of the graphic:

> **Clarify** (what I want my influence to be): **Respected Resource** (that can provide personalized support to meet the needs of teachers and students)

> **Convey** (what do I need to become a respected resource for the teachers I serve?): **Quality Resources and Time to Research and Practice**

How Joe Decided to Bring It Home

Listed below are the actions and timelines Joe chose to implement with teachers and then the personal actions he chose (see corresponding sections on the graphic).

Identify Specific Actions *With* Teachers (*What*) and *When*:

1. What (Identify Specific Actions With Teachers): Provide well-researched, personalized resources for teachers, including models and exemplars. When: At least twice a month for each teacher coached. Ideas for abbreviating on the graphic—[What: Bring H.Q. pers. resources; When: 2X per month 4 each tchr]. What: List goals and resource needs of teachers; stay current. When: Note this information each time I coach a teacher. [Keep list of tchr goals/resource needs; When: Update list after each visit]

Identify Specific Actions for Self: *What* and *When*:

> 1. What (Identify Specific Actions for Self): Research district professional development offerings and conference brochures. Attend relevant classes when

possible, view websites and educational videos, listen to podcasts, read books, and ask experienced colleagues which resources would be best to address topics that would meet identified teacher needs. When: Set aside 45 minutes every other day to look for resources. [What: Research/Classes; When: 45 min. every other day or EOD]

2.   What: Practice modeling strategies, then video myself practicing the new strategies and ask coaches and teachers to provide feedback. When: Set aside 45 minutes every other day to practice, organize, and determine how to best share the resources found with teachers. [What: Practice w/video & feedback; When: 45 min. every other day or EOD]

3.   What: Shadow three experienced coaches and ask to video them. Debrief with them after the shadowing sessions, and ask about their go-to quality coaching resources. When: Set aside time to shadow and debrief with one experienced coach two Fridays per month for three months, October—December. [What: Shadow 3 coaches, their fav. resources? When: 2 Fri./month for 3 months]

How Megan Decides to Clarify and Convey

Megan is an experienced, respected coach who also trains other coaches and helps support the professional development department in her school district. Megan works in an urban school district with low student achievement. Teacher morale is often not very high, as teachers struggle with how to do better when many students are just beginning to learn English, and there are limited resources to help them address student needs at a variety of levels within a reasonable amount of time.

Megan cares about the teachers she works with, but she wants to up her game in this area and believes that one of the best things she could do would be to use her influence to inspire hope, something she feels is greatly needed for teachers to have the energy to conquer challenging situations. She decides to reference the H.O.P.E. information shared in this book to get some ideas to support teachers who find themselves in difficult circumstances. So, she fills in the word **"Hope"** on the **"Clarify"** line. Then, she thinks of a few ideas for specific actions she could take *with teachers* (the top left set of actions and timelines on the graphic are the actions to be taken *with teachers*) to make hope be what her influence inspires. She chooses (1) Smile often (during coaching visits), (2) Verbalize positive strengths of teachers (3 per coaching visit), and (3) Share inspiring quotes/videos with teachers during coaching sessions (at least once per month).

As Megan thinks about what her "hope" actions might look like with teachers, she starts feeling worried. She realizes she has trouble conveying hope because she is tired a lot of the time. She is not happy about gaining weight since she began her coaching role, which has included more driving in the car, communicating by email, and observing rather than being up and teaching. Because of this, she has been feeling kind of frumpy. She is also finding that she feels scattered and disorganized trying to meet the needs of her two chil-dren (a 3-year-old son who often wakes up in the middle of the night, and a bright, energetic 10-year-old daughter).

Since leaving the classroom, Megan has been tasked not only with coaching teachers, but also with a variety of extra duties as assigned, and she needs clarification and support regarding her job description. Some inaccurate assumptions have been made that since she is not in the classroom anymore, she has extra time. She also recently found out she is hypoglycemic and needs to be careful of what she eats, to help prevent diabetes. She comes to the realization that a focus on self-care might really help her and the teachers she works with. She writes the word **"Health"** on the *what I need to* **"Convey"** (*hope*) line of the graphic.

How Megan Decides to Bring It Home

Megan decides to use (with a few tweaks, so that they work for her as a coach) four compo-nents intended to help teachers create more hope in their daily lives. These four components are explained in the acronym H.O.P.E., below. They were initially shared in Chapter 3 as the first of the "Frequent Five" requests/needs teachers have when accessing coaching.

- Health: good nutrition, sleep, exercise, and the use of stress-management techniques

- Organization: tools to take control of the physical classroom environment, files (both paper and electronic), desk, student materials, calendars, prioritizing, time-management/planning-time structures, student notebooks, materials, etc.

- Positivity: Model and provide supports to help teachers intentionally choose positive thoughts and words, identify purpose and motivation, laugh, cultivate joyful awareness and gratitude, connect to core beliefs, use empowering words to self and students, and gather resources that build professionalism, capacity, longevity, resilience, and happiness in both teacher and students.

- Encouragement: Help teachers surround themselves with good influences and rally support by cultivating relationships and communicating regularly with supportive family members, friends, mentors, teammates, coaches, parents, leaders, community members, take advantage of stress-free opportunities to absorb knowledge (S.O.A.K.).

Megan has the technical expertise to help teachers differentiate their lessons, and she is an expert at implementing strategies to support English language learners. Her com-petence is not an issue. Megan realizes she can't inspire hope if she doesn't feel it, yet she has a heartfelt desire to bring it with her to her coaching conversations and into her family life. She knows she will be much more effective doing that if she can model, demonstrate, and embody hope. She references the four components of H.O.P.E.:

Health, Organization, Positivity, and Encouragement, and then lists a variety of ways they could come alive for her.

> After considering a number of options for bringing "Hope" home (see below), Megan chose the five starred actions that were reasonable for her and listed them on her Finding Home graphic. However, many ideas related to the H.O.P.E. acronym are shared below, to provide a variety of support options to help teachers, coaches, and educational leaders experience more hope. When we feel healthy, organized, positive, and have encouraging people/supports (H.O.P.E.), we have more strength to weather any challenging storms that may come our way.

1. * She (Megan) will collaboratively determine a set bedtime with her husband and children. She will ask her husband to trade off getting up with their son during the night and fixing breakfast in the morning. That way, at least every other night, one of them will likely get enough sleep. [What: Set a bedtime and trade off getting up with son. When: Today]

2. * She will meet with her boss to discuss her coaching role and where to prioritize her time. [What: Meet with boss and determine priorities. When: By Friday]

3. * She will fit in one 30-minute walk or two 15-minute walks each day by showing up early or staying late after coaching appointments and briskly walking on trails in nearby parks on tracks or around sidewalks at schools, scheduling walking coaching appointments, or using her lunch time to walk while eating finger foods. [What: Walk 30 minutes per day. When: Begin next Monday.]

4. She will search for an adjustable standing desk at the district warehouse so that she won't be sitting all the time at work and will walk around more during observations, stopping while standing to write. [What: Locate or purchase a standing desk. When: 10/6]

5. * She will hire her 10-year-old daughter to pack healthy lunches that can be eaten while walking or driving.

6. She will create a playlist of songs that help her feel hopeful. She will wake up to them every morning and play them while preparing for the day.

7. She will check out joke books from the local library and have her family read jokes to her each day to help her (and them) smile more, then record the best ones and send them to the coaches she trains and the teachers she coaches.

8. She will research and post quotes related to hope around her home and in her office, then share them with the teachers she coaches. She will surround herself

with H.O.P.E. resources in the form of video clips, affirmations, and books, and share them with teachers and other coaches when it might be helpful.

9. She will purchase a funny wooden box that, when opened, cheers for her. She will listen to it when she implements her H.O.P.E. plans or when she is feeling discouraged.

10. * As often as possible, she will immerse herself in her favorite inspiring resources organized in the personal S.O.A.K. table she has created (containing authors, affirmations, movies, video clips, music, books, art, movements, quotes, mentors, leaders, and other inspirational resources).

11. She will create a daily checklist, to remind her of her plans, and organize her daily planner to include some of the checklist items.

12. She will ask her family and colleagues to encourage and help her in her quest to make Health and Hope happen!

As Megan begins to implement these changes, she begins to feel physically stronger and less tired. As a result of the meeting with her boss, in which they both agreed to prioritize one-on-one coaching, a time-consuming responsibility not related to coaching was eliminated from her job, and another responsibility was significantly lightened. With her renewed health, Megan is able to bring a smile and positive presence to her coaching sessions, share the resources she has compiled on the topic of hope and just enjoy her job and life more. She is *embodying* hope, and that is inspiring!

Though Megan is a fictional character created from a mix of my own experiences and experiences of coaches I have worked with, many of the ideas shared above have been implemented successfully with coaches and/or teachers. Maybe your situations are more challenging than Megan's. It would likely be overwhelming to contemplate implementing all 12 ideas listed above. Many ideas were listed, to provide the reader with examples for all four H.O.P.E. components. Maybe you don't have a partner who can help you out or a boss who can lighten your load, but coaches and educational leaders are creative and tenacious—we can figure out how to make what we want and need happen. You wouldn't be in a coaching or leadership position if you couldn't solve problems. Sometimes the small and simple things produce the best results. Maybe you only need to do a couple of things listed above to feel more hopeful. Isn't it incredible how much better and more hopeful everything seems after a good night's sleep?

Health is a need, a priority for us all, and the more we can cultivate it, the better our performance in all areas of our lives will be. This goes for teachers as well and is why there is a self-care section included on the "Human Connection" planning page in Chapter 9 and why the H.O.P.E. acronym was noted as the first of the "Frequent Five" coaching topics in Chapter 3.

Reflect and Connect

Hopefully, reading through the examples of Joe and Megan has provided you with enough information to feel comfortable and clear about completing the *Finding Home* process yourself. At this time (or when it is convenient for you), record your four components: (1) define YOU, (2) identify resources, (3) clarify and convey, and (4) bring it home on your own personal "field of inspiration" shared previously. The *Finding Home* graphic was designed to be a one-stop resource for you to capture the most pertinent pieces of each component and make it easy for you to remember and reference your thoughtful work.

The *Finding Home* process can be adapted to be useful in a variety of situations. Recently, students of a teacher I was coaching in an alternative high school used the process to expand what they knew of themselves and determine what values were important to them. Then, the students were grouped with like-minded students, and presentations were prepared to persuade the student body to move in positive directions. I was fortunate to be able to hear quite a few of the presentations and was impressed with the depth of thought and intention to do good that came from their taking the time to search within themselves. Their teacher also modeled the process as they went through it, and that was incredible to see! Please feel free to adapt and use the *Finding Home* process with groups you are involved in, with family members, or in whatever situation you think it may be helpful.

The opportunity to spend our time in service to children, teens, and teachers who look to us and trust us to have their best interests at heart is an honor, and a noble and compelling reason to go to work every day. We know of their importance and how one person can make such a difference for many. Because of this and because we care, we, as coaches and leaders, look for ways to be the most inspiring people we can possibly be.

How we coach matters. Putting forth focused and intentional effort to deliver coaching in an inspiring way has paid, and will pay, great dividends.

Inspiring People I Think of Often

I often reflect with fondness and loving gratitude on two inspiring people from my childhood who modeled for me what it means to be inspiring: my mother, Jean Williams, and my fifth- and sixth-grade teacher and softball coach, Mr. Bush. The story of Mr. Bush is recorded in Chapter 2. His memory always inspires me to do better, to do more, to individualize my support for students and teachers, and to let them know I am with them on this journey.

My wonderful mother passed away 13 years ago. She was the ultimate teacher and coach. A teacher by trade before I was born, she devoted her life and considerable talents to being a plucky, intentional, and loving mother to 10 children. Her family was her school. We were organized; we did chores; we played; we cooked; we learned to play the piano, sing, and conduct music; we learned to teach, to be disciplined, to value education, to have faith and be faithful, and to be consistently on top of our schoolwork; and, most important, we learned to love everyone. Her willingness to sacrifice for the good of her children and husband and for those less fortunate, her gift of storytelling to make a point, her integrity and unwavering commitment to faith and goodness, and her uncanny ability to make you feel loved even when you were being corrected was nothing short of miraculous.

I hope there are inspiring people like this in your life, people you can look up to and follow after to help you make the difference you wish to make in the lives of others. If you can't pinpoint anyone in particular, or if you are running low on inspiring people in your life, you must be exceptionally strong to be able to fulfill your life goals/mission without a lot of support. Being an inspirational educator may be harder for you at times than it is for those who have experienced at least some loving and inspiring support throughout their lives and have seen "inspirational" up close and personal. But no matter where you are in receiving the support you need, you can bolster your mood and enrich your support options by looking for incredible people to be inspiring role models, reading books to find beautiful words to strengthen your soul, listening to encouraging song lyrics, watching documentaries about inspiring people, referencing uplifting quotes, participating in groups that do good in the world, or even writing your own words in the form of confidence building personal statements such as the "I Am" statement in the center of the *Finding Home* graphic. Working in the field of education can be very difficult. No matter your background, challenges, or difficult past experiences, I stand with you in your dedication to children and teachers and honor your goodness and tenacity. I am grateful you are willing to face the challenges of our day in the field of education. Our kids need you; our teachers need you. You matter. Thank you.

Conclusion

Inspirational people experience and express joy (passion, enthusiasm, encouragement, belief).

The possibility of authentically and profoundly inspiring positive characteristics in others, especially joy, is enhanced when we engage in focused efforts to develop, internalize, and experience those characteristics within ourselves. The S.O.A.K. sections at the end of each chapter are meant to help us:

1) understand the power of intentionally surrounding ourselves with positive and inspiring resources (The sources and people we choose to let influence us make their mark on our characters!) and

2) realize that it is the essence of effective modeling and authenticity to do the work to become what we wish to inspire.

Inspirational Self-Assessment

1. Take this self-assessment before you set an intention to consciously find ways to become more inspirational.

2. Implement some of the practical application ideas, coaching ideas, and/or inspirational S.O.A.K. supports found below (or use some of your own ideas).

3. In a month or so, see whether you have been able to improve your thoughts, motivations, and behaviors surrounding the important coaching characteristic of becoming more inspirational. Remember the synonyms/phrases associated with "inspirational," identified by coaching authors and by coaches like you, as you define what being inspirational is and determine how to make it a more conscious part of your daily life: courageous, tenacious, passionate, encouraging, enthusiastic, humble, involved in school community, experienced, respected, lifelong learner (Frazier, 2014).

	Strongly Disagree	Disagree	Neutral/ Not Sure	Agree	Strongly Agree
	1	2	3	4	5
I know who I am and what makes me unique. I recognize that my support is important to those I serve. I have identified my strengths, values, and what my individuality can provide.					
I know what I want my overarching influence to be with those I coach/lead and have identified what I need to convey that influence. My daily plans include specifics that will help make my inspirational intentions a reality.					
I am courageous. I act consistently on my values and am willing to say what I think and feel, even when it's uncomfortable. I go with my instincts and trust that my highest thoughts and feelings will be of benefit to others when shared graciously.					
I am tenacious. I regularly check in with teachers and support them until they achieve their meaningful goals. I know that when goals are met, teachers' confidence levels will increase, giving them strength to take on new challenges.					
I experience and express joy in my coaching/ leadership interactions. I do this by taking care of my physical health, immersing myself in inspiring, encouraging resources, and sharing what I learn with those I coach/lead.					
I strive to be humble and acknowledge those I work with as equal partners while we identify relevant best teaching practices and solve challenging situations together.					
Column Totals:					

Grand Total: _____

What totals mean: 26–30 = Inspirational Rock Star, 21–25 = Very Inspirational, 16–20 = Sort of Inspirational, 11–15 = Some Inspiration Is Happening, 6–10 = Better Step It Up, 0–5 = Would Working to Become More Inspirational Be a Worthwhile Goal?

Practical Application Ideas for Inspirational

Be Courageous

We can't be courageous if we don't know what to be courageous about! This is why it is so important to take the time to define ourselves, identify our values, strengths, and resources, clarify what we want our influence to be and what we need to effectively convey it, and then "bring it home" by organizing our daily lives so that what we have determined to be most important actually happens. In my research study (Frazier, 2014), "courageous" was the most frequently mentioned word linked to the characteristic "inspirational."

For me, the hardest times to summon personal courage have not been only when big things were happening—like finding the courage to forgo the corporate nod and add thoughts I knew would not be welcomed by all during meetings (sometimes with lots of people in attendance). What was even more difficult was to remember and stick to personal commitments, such as "Be a haven of happiness" with students and teachers. This was especially difficult as a teacher when Sarai had interrupted me again for the 39th time that day, or I had to repeat the page number six times, or if there had been indoor recess for a week straight and I was on my last nerve! Similarly, it was difficult to create havens of happiness after I moved into a coaching role when teachers had to cancel after I had spent a long time preparing my action items identified at our previous meeting, or struggling to keep a good, joyful attitude for the next teacher I was going to meet after ruining my clothes again because I had to cram food down my throat while driving, or trying to summon the strength to gracefully share difficult data with a teacher who was already feeling upset and find ways to positively encourage him or her to make a challenging change to his or her instructional practice. Determining what is important to us and then courageously doing what we say we are going to do by keeping personal commitments is a challenge worth taking on. Courage is such an inside job!

Be Tenacious

When you get into a tight place and everything goes against you, till it seems as though you could not hang on a minute longer, never give up then, for that is just the place and time that the tide will turn.

—Mr. Avery, in Harriet Beecher Stowe's *Oldtown Folks* (1869)

It is critical that we do not give up on a goal that is important to a teacher just because the timeline had to be adjusted or some of the action steps or strategies didn't work. If we can find ways to keep going—to be persistent without being annoying, to support teachers to set new action steps/strategies if needed, but keep our eyes on the prize until *the goal set is the goal met*—we will be modeling the grit and determination it takes to be successful in the teaching profession and in life generally. When teachers experience success, there is an influx of positive energy that can inspire them to take on another challenging goal. We want to grow teachers' confidence and energy levels and provide evidence of their success, so that when new challenges arise, they can refer back to their successful results and not be afraid to keep moving forward. Our reputations as coaches will grow as we inspire teachers to stay on course and stay with them/stand by them until they have achieved what they have determined to be their measurable and emotionally important goal.

Fast-Track Ways to *Not Be Inspiring*

- Trying to convince others of your ideas or opinions in a pompous and annoying way

- Talking incessantly about your personal experiences and opinions and not even being curious about what the other person thinks, feels, or might have to contribute to the conversation

- Authoritatively insisting you have a sure and complete knowledge of best instructional choices for a certain situation when you actually have no recent experience being successful with that problem in that environment (Don't pretend to have all the answers to all questions.)

- Neglecting to shower, wear clean clothes, freshen your breath, or take care of basic personal hygiene

- Using language that is crude, gossipy, unkind, thoughtless, depressing, or grammatically incorrect

- Asking for feedback and then shutting people down when they share it

- Using an irritated, dismissive, or rushed tone of voice

- Using overly aggressive, overly submissive, disconnected, and/or uninterested body language

- Sending written communications (e.g., emails, texts, and coaching resources) that are full of mistakes

- Using extremely outdated resources (Purple mimeograph ink)

- Neglecting to maintain a reasonably organized, uncluttered, and sanitary work or home environment (including vehicles)

We can help ourselves gain effective coaching/teaching/leadership characteristics by absorbing, infusing, hearing, reflecting, seeing, moving, practicing, and connecting with positive resources and people that will help us become better. As we do this, we will be able to inspire better ways and better days for others. This is one of the most ironic things about being inspirational—a lot of it is about taking care of ourselves (physically, emotionally, spiritually, socially, mentally), so that we have the strength, energy, and depth of character to lift others.

Inspiring people bring energy, passion, and enthusiasm to their work, spontaneously igniting excitement and renewal within the hearts and souls of those they come in contact with. They are happy doing the work they are helping others with. When they talk about the work, they share that happiness; they are not trying to sell or force anything. Their passion and excitement for the work is real.

Inspiring people believe in those they are supporting. They listen and value others' thoughts, feelings, and experiences. There is a feeling of confidence, of safety, of trust—an unspoken voice that is perceived loud and clear. This voice is transmitted on a foundational frequency, speaking with encouraging power to the heart of the person being coached: "I believe in you"; "I know you can do this"; "We can do this together"; "Don't worry, I believe in you and in me"; "We've got this!"

INSPIRATIONAL ~S.O.A.K. ~

Sometimes learning penetrates best when we are relaxed and not trying too hard to make it happen. (Like an "Inspirational" bath bomb infused with personalized nutrients)

Stress-free Opportunities to Absorb Knowledge   Choose what works for you.

Quotes	Music	Statements affirmations	Books poetry stories	Art	Videos movies	Movement other ideas
"No one is useless in this world who lightens the burdens of others." —Charles Dickens	"Eye of the Tiger" (Rocky) Survivor	**For coaches:** My influence and energy build greatness in teachers and kids!	"Don't Quit" Edgar Guest	The Ninth Wave Ivan Aivazovsky	Great Leadership Comes Down to Only Two Rules (TEDx Talk) Peter Anderton	**Hero Pose**
"Remember this. Hold on to this. This is the only perfection there is, the perfection of helping others. This is the only thing we can do that has any lasting meaning. This is why we're here. To make each other feel safe." —Andre Agassi	"I Believe I Can Fly" R. Kelly	My gentleness and expertise inspire excellence.	Finding Your True North Bill George	The Five Eldest Children of Charles I Anthony Van Dyck	First Follower: Leadership Lessons From Dancing Guy Derek Sivers (YouTube)	**Handstand**
	"Hero" Mariah Carey	Teachers are attracted to and inspired by the way I coach. My knowledge coupled with my pure intentions equals success for teachers.	The Six Secrets of Change: What the Best Leaders Do … Michael Fullan	Two Sisters (On the Terrace) Pierre-Auguste Renoir	Everest (2015) Hidden Figures (2016)	
"Real women fight for something other than their own emotions." —Shannon L. Alder	"Stronger" Kelly Clarkson "When We Were Kings" Bryan McKnight and Diana King	I coach with clarity and joy! I offer encouragement that will endure.	The Power of Moments Chip and Dan Heath	Whistlejacket George Stubbs The Starry Night Vincent Van Gogh	Rudy (1993) It's a Wonderful Life (1946)	**Oils:** spruce; cedarwood; pine
	"Firework" Katy Perry	I am capable, insightful, and compassionate. **Coaches to teachers:** Your power is immeasurable, your purpose undeniable, your heart…. incredible!	Better Conversations: Coaching Ourselves and Each Other … Jim Knight	Water Lilies Claude Monet Happy Birthday, Miss Jones Norman Rockwell	Cast Away (2000) The Help (2011) Gandhi (1982) The Diary of Anne Frank (1959)	
"Joy not shared is joy wasted." —Abhijit Naskar	"A New Day Has Come" Celine Dion "The Greatest" SIA	You find and fuel fires of talent within children/teens! You are paving the way for students' dreams to become their realities.	The Seven Habits of Highly Effective People: Restoring the Character Ethic Stephen R. Covey	The Thinker (Sculpture) Auguste Rodin	Cool Runnings (1993) To Sir With Love (1967) Seven Pounds (2008)	**Stones:** tiger's eye; citrine
"There is nothing noble in being superior to your fellow man; true nobility is being superior to your former self." —Ernest Hemingway	The Four Seasons Antonio Vivaldi	**For teachers:** I am an inspiring force for good in the lives of my students. My students will fondly remember how they felt in my class.	Leadership From the Inside Out: Becoming a Leader for Life Kevin Cashman	Morning Breakfast William Bouguereau	Patch Adams (1998) Million Dollar Baby (2004) The Karate Kid (1984)	**Color:** sparkling white
	"Invincible" Kelly Clarkson	I ignore discouragement and inspire success.	Outliers: The Story of Success Malcolm Gladwell	Wanderer Above the Sea of Fog Caspar David Friedrich	Akeelah and the Bee (2006)	**Visual Symbol:** mountain

The influence I radiate is powerful, positive, and memorable.

NOTES

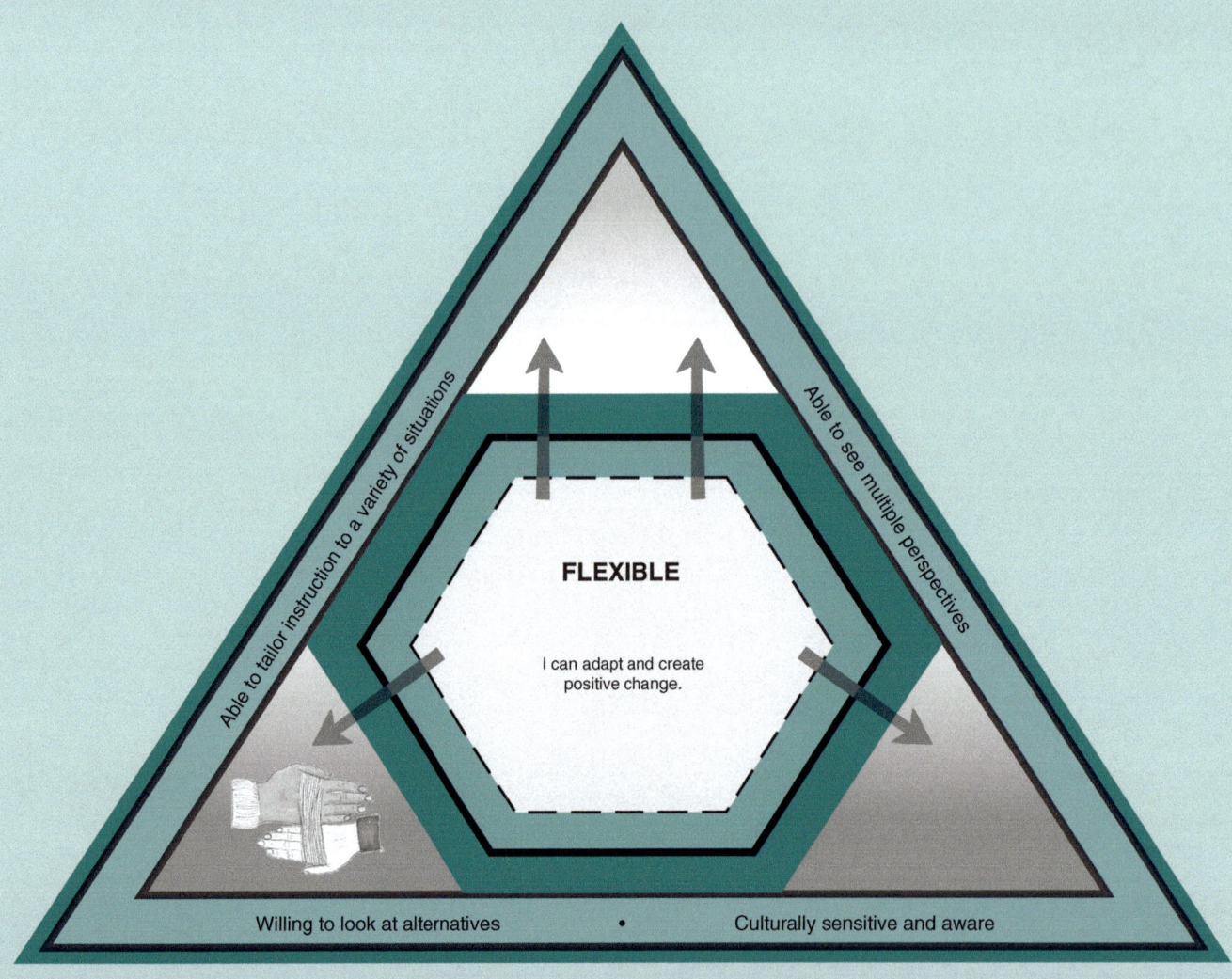

The teachers I coach and the colleagues I work with know that they don't have to look, act, or think exactly like me to be accepted and respected. I tailor my coaching to individual teacher needs and do not assume my past experiences will always be the right solution for their situation.

Flexible

The measure of intelligence is the ability to change.

—Albert Einstein

Developing Cultural Flexibility

My husband is half Japanese. Early in our marriage, his mother gave us a very large, beautifully illustrated book she had read to her children, entitled *Japanese Fairy Tales* (1960). We enjoyed reading the stories to our three sons as they were growing up. Similar to Aesop's fables, the fairy tales always had a moral. One of the stories, entitled "The Sparrow Whose Tongue Was Cut Out," was about an ill-mannered wife who didn't like that her husband had saved a little sparrow with a broken wing and was jealous the husband and sparrow had become close friends. One day, after the sparrow spilled some of her starch, she cut out its tongue (kind of morbid, but no worse than Grimm's), and it flew back home to its bird family many miles away. When the husband came home, he was devastated to find the sparrow had flown away. The old man went searching for the sparrow for many days and nights. When he found his friend with its bird family, they welcomed him warmly, fed him well, and gave him a party. When it was time for him to go home, they gave him a little box to take back with him and open when he arrived home. When the old man arrived home, he opened the box. Inside were many diamonds and precious golden objects. The wife was furious and started yelling about how she deserved some too—for all she had put up with. So, she took off for the sparrow's house, being rude to everyone along the way. When she arrived at the home of the sparrow family, she went on and on about how many sacrifices she had made to feed such an ungrateful bird. The sparrows apologized repeatedly and thanked her. When it was time for the woman to return home, the sparrow family offered the woman her choice of one of two boxes and told her not to open the box until she reached her home. One box was small and ugly, and the other was much bigger and brightly colored. Of course, the woman chose the larger, more attractive box. She was so excited she left for home without even thanking the sparrows. "I wonder what beautiful, expensive things are in this box? Soon I will be wealthy and everyone will respect me," said the woman to herself as she was walking home. She forgot the warning and opened the box. The rest of the story reads like this:

> She had hardly lifted the cover when ugly little imps jumped up before her eyes and began dancing around her and making thousands of terrible faces. Disappointed and frightened, she fled as fast as her legs could carry her, like a madwoman. . . . She is still running.

Her husband, on the contrary, gave all his fortune to the poor people of the village and built himself a little house beside the sparrow's. He possessed a wonderful treasure; a treasure which all the gold in the world could not buy: a sincere and devoted friend.

(p. 46)

As discussed in Chapter 4, and as illustrated in the preceding story, there are universal values often considered to be spiritual values that can benefit every life when they are employed. Shalom Schwartz (2006) conducted a number of research studies about values. By analyzing data from the European Social Survey, in which 35,000 people were surveyed in 67 countries (representing many cultures), he identified 10 types of universal values. Included within the 10 types were *benevolence*, defined as "preserving and enhancing the welfare of those with whom one is in frequent, personal contact"; *universalism*, "understanding, appreciation, tolerance, and protection for the welfare of all people and for nature"; and *self-direction*, "independent thought and action; choosing, creating, exploring (Schwartz, 2006, pp. 1–2).

However, in Schwartz's study, these values often ran in direct opposition to other values the survey respondents determined to be universally important as well, such as *power*, defined as "social status and prestige, control or dominance over people and resources" (p. 1), *achievement*, and *hedonism or pleasure*. So, the struggle is on: When do we take care of ourselves and what we may individually want, and when are others' needs more important than our own? Can we always be like the good husband, or do we sometimes feel like taking the bigger, gaily wrapped box? I would guess most of us can think of times when we have felt the emotions of both characters in the story. In our coaching and leadership roles, with our families, and in all interactions with others, we benefit from understanding universal values and choosing to inspire change using the values that honor the intrinsic worth of both individuals and groups/cultures. Aside from the family jokes about being careful not to choose big presents over little ones, we did gain many insights from those stories and from Japanese culture.

Understanding cultural backgrounds enriches our coaching practice. We can start by focusing on learning more about the cultures of people we interact with closely, the cultures of students in teachers' classes, and the cultures of the teachers we coach. One coach shared the following story about the challenges a woman from India faced when she began teaching in the United States. She also shared what she did to understand more about the Indian culture and help the teacher have a positive urban American middle-school experience.

A veteran teacher named Dachsa (name changed) moved from India to the United States and began teaching history in an urban middle-school environment. She called for coaching support when, as she put it, "The kids are totally out of control." During her initial observation, the coach confirmed it: Students were showing blatant disregard for anything Dachsa said, getting up and moving around so that they could talk with their friends while she attempted to teach, throwing things across the room, not doing the work assigned, and talking back to Dachsa using mean tones and sarcasm.

In Dachsa's situation in India, teachers and the teaching profession were highly regarded and her students had been eager to learn. She said (about India), "I could stand up there, and I could lecture the whole time, and students would take notes and soak it up with no behavior issues." Teaching middle school in America was an enormous culture shock for Dachsa. To help Dachsa make such a huge life transition along with a professional transition, her coach learned as much as she could about Indian culture by reading the Indian section in the book *Kiss, Bow, or Shake Hands: The Bestselling Guide to Doing Business in More Than 60 Countries* (Morrison & Conaway, 2006), and *Multicultural Manners* (Dresser, 2005). The coach spent a lot of time asking questions and intently listening to Dachsa's explanations about the differences between her teaching experiences in India and her current experience. The coach was open to new learning and tried to figure out how to honor and use Dachsa's previous experiences as a veteran teacher and mesh them with the American culture to make Dachsa's students successful. Dachsa and her coach designed a classroom-management plan using the processes shared in Chapter 3. A slideshow was developed to explain the process to students and to be easily referenced as needed. The coach shared her thoughts in the following quote:

> We were very particular about the words we used as we prepared and practiced the plan. We built her confidence in order to effectively communicate the plan to her kids. She didn't really have to set expectations in India, so that part was a little challenging; she had never had to think about all the minute details we have to think about. She felt very strongly about no food, drink, or gum in the classroom. Well, a lot of teachers in America let students have snacks in class. Some of her students would not be able to eat until 1:00 p.m., so she decided to be a little more flexible with them and allowed those students two minutes outside of class to eat before they came in. I tried to help her understand that "If you want it, you have to teach it." Dachsa was in a new country, new city, new house, new district, new school, [and] new classroom, and [she] was using a new curriculum and materials. Everything was new and foreign to her, she didn't know what she could do and couldn't do and what was expected of her, she didn't know basically anything. She was stunned by the disrespect from her students and the disregard [for] and disrespect of teachers in general. When she contacted parents, some were receptive, but a lot of them were dismissive toward her about their child's behavior, and she didn't know what to do about that. So we:

> 1. Developed a classroom management system that created clarity through expectations, what will happen when boundaries are broken, and then built in fun, celebratory incentives
>
> 2. Developed a rewards system for PBIS tickets

In America, you have to explicitly state expectations, processes, and procedures clearly, [whereas] in India it is more culturally implied and expected by all that students will just behave. The teaching profession is seen differently in different countries. In India it is highly respected; here [United States] it is not, and that filters down to our kids [if parents and society disrespect teachers, why should students respect teachers?]. It has crossed my mind how great it would be to teach in India!

This coaching situation was a wonderful success! Dachsa quickly got on top of basic classroom-management pieces and began to build relationships with students. The coach's dedication to being flexible and willing to learn about Indian culture enhanced the power of the coaching process, and Dachsa's willingness to trust the coach and consistently implement ideas the coach shared made the classroom-management plan work.

Unfortunately, it's not always easy to be completely open and accepting of other races or cultures. Maybe we have had bad experiences, or maybe those close to us have suffered at the hands of people of a particular race or culture. My mother, who had always been loving and accepting of everyone (and had taught that to me through her example as a parent), at first had a hard time with my deciding to marry a man who was half Japanese. This was because her brothers had fought the Japanese in World War II and she had constantly feared for their lives. She related to me that as a child, she had nightmares of Japanese men surrounding their house at night. She knew she had a bias, she knew why, and she decided to not let it keep her from loving my husband. Thinking through our biases as objectively as possible and then coming to the realization that it would be inaccurate and unfair to let negative judgments about one or a few people of a certain race apply to all people of that race is a great step toward being flexible in how we see others and being open and fair with everyone.

I've been struggling for a while with what the buzzword "cultural competence" really means. I've had leadership classes on it, agree with the idea of white privilege (I'm white), and intellectually understand and feel I am becoming more aware of how minority cultures in certain countries are often unconsciously treated as "less than" by the dominant culture and/or other cultures within a country. There is also gender privilege, as evidenced by more men being given leadership opportunities than women. And the sad truth is that discrimination regularly happens to those who are considered different, classified as lacking, or deemed less than inherently equal in some minds for a variety of reasons: old people, poor people, gay people, people with disabilities, rich people, black people, white people, people from a variety of cultures that are a variety of colors, and so on. I don't think the core of what it takes to become culturally competent has to be backed up by scholarly research for us to get it, or that anyone should have to make an argument for it. For me, it's just about equality and love.

A foundational belief that everyone is valuable, an awareness of biases we may have developed as a result of our experiences or the experiences of those close to us, and a heartfelt interest in understanding and learning as much as we can about other cultures will go a long way toward bringing more kindness and civility into our areas of influence. We can start by focusing on learning more about the cultures of people we interact with closely, the cultures of the teachers we coach, and the cultures of the students in their classes.

Stephen R. Covey's reminder that everyone sees the world "how they are" (1989, p. 28) can help us recognize the need to make a thoughtful effort to really get to know people, where they come from, and what is important to them, so that we can be flexible as we strive to understand how to meet their individual needs.

One of my biggest coaching fails was when I was trying to help a high-school teacher with classroom management. We decided he needed an attention-getter, some type of physical signal students could see, so that they would know to stop what they were doing and turn their attention to him. He chose an odd kind of gesture, but I wanted to support him, so I let it go. The students laughed when he made the gesture, but I didn't think much about it. Later, I found out it was an obscene gesture in another culture. I should have done my homework or at least asked a student why it was funny!

Flexibility in Coaching

Coaches can show flexibility by offering those they coach choices to address specific, collaboratively determined instructional goals. For example, let's say a middle-school science teacher wants to improve how students take notes, so that the process can be more powerful, engaging, and useful for students. Measures to achieve this goal could include analyzing pre/mid/post-strategy implementation data surrounding (1) how often students took notes, (2) how often they referred back to them during quizzes, and (3) a comparison of average assessment data scores between those who took notes and those who didn't. At the teacher's request, the coach could provide three note-taking strategies, such as the following:

1. Science Journal

    Teacher and coach collaboratively develop, or students and teacher develop, a science journal rubric outlining types of entries and how they will be scored. Students organize the journal, including a table of contents, page numbers, and resource pages, with exemplar entries for regular student reference. Teacher models daily by displaying his or her own journal under the document camera. All meaningful handouts and resources are stapled or glued into the journal, for easy reference and organization.

2. Two-Column Notes, With Summary Line of Learning

    Students write the learning-period goal as the title for their notes at the top of the paper, along with the date and their name. Students fold the paper in half vertically. Students note the main ideas on the left side of the paper/fold. Students note details about each main idea on the right side of the paper/fold. Students draw a horizontal line of learning close to where the notes end, leaving about 1.5 inches from the bottom of the paper. Students summarize their learning under the line each day, and notes are scored using a posted rubric (also shared electronically or on paper), with student exemplars at each level. Teacher models the note-taking process at some point during each learning period. Students record their notes on three-hole-punched paper and keep them in chronological order in a notebook.

3. Power Bytes (a novel way to inspire students to create short summaries of important content)

   Teacher and coach develop a quick skeleton summarization strategy, to be recorded by students either in a small notebook or in an electronic document. Teacher videotapes the teaching or lecture part of the lesson ahead of time, and students watch it at home or individually with headphones at the start of the lesson on computers, either alone or in small groups. Students record what they think the Power Bytes of the lesson are, in either a small (bite-sized) notebook or a Power Byte electronic document. Students share their Power Bytes with other students when appropriate. Teacher organizes his or her Power Bytes for each day/learning period, then shares them with students to record in their notebooks if they did not internalize the main points, or—and even more powerfully— teacher asks students to share their Power Bytes that include main points he or she wanted made clear. Students are allowed to use their Power Bytes resources on their quizzes. An incentive for the best Power Byte of the day/week is awarded (maybe a Power Bar?).

When coaches offer options, teachers feel empowered and are more willing to implement the chosen strategy or tweak it for their needs with the coach, partially because the strategy has been explained well and because they were able to think through a few ideas and choose the best one for their students. Being flexible also inspires the coach to be resourceful and creative and fills both the coach's and the teacher's toolboxes with many viable strategies.

Flexibility Creates Peace

There is a certain peace that can be found when we value and understand how to implement flexibility into our coaching and into our lives. Many of us are goal-setting people—we have achieved success because of our ability to be persistent and, sometimes, maybe a little rigid. If we set a goal, then come heck or high water, we're going to do it. This is a good quality, but we have to tone it down a notch when reality intervenes. As Susan Scott wrote, "No plan survives its collision with reality" (2011, p. xv).

For instance, let's say you have set two goals: (1) to go to bed on time and (2) to exercise every day. At the end of one very busy day, in which you were responsive to others' needs and had a lot of meaningful interactions, you find you're out of time to make both goals happen. You realize you have to choose one goal over another: you could go to bed on time and bag the exercise; you could do half the exercise and go to bed just a little later; or you could stay up even later, to get the full amount of exercise in. It is unproductive to beat yourself up when so many daily life situations are beyond your control. So, you decide to get in bed on time at the expense of the exercise, but then you get a phone call from one of your grown children who needs you in that moment. You decide the goal of being a good parent trumps the goal of getting to bed on time. So, you failed twice, right?

You didn't complete either of your goals, so you might as well not even try—maybe those goals are just too hard. *Not true!* Do not give in to this downward-spiral thinking. You are still committed to your goals, but you can make peace with life *as it came to you that day* and not forget to think on what you *did* accomplish. Flexibility with yourself, coupled with kindness and an understanding that certain goals may lose the priority status they had at the beginning of the day based on what came at you during the day, creates a more peaceful internal world that will likely help you get to sleep more quickly! The important thing is not to give up on your goals altogether. You can get that exercise in and get to bed at least close to your planned bedtime on many days—which is better than no days—if you structure your schedules to meet your goals.

We can help teachers meet their goals and also internalize the peaceful power of flexibility as we teach, model, and coach it. *Persistence without prickly pacing* is more important than time-stamping every action step exactly when we scheduled it to happen. This is why, as part of the TCT action plan, we have one set of dates for when action steps are *planned* to be implemented and one set of dates to fill in when the action step actually happened. As we know, what is really going to present itself in the classroom each day is not completely predictable. This is what we love and fear about teaching. There was never a lack of things to discuss at the dinner table during my tenure as a teacher. Amazing, crazy, and funny things happened all the time, and sometimes those things were not aligned with or supportive of what I had scheduled to happen that day. Teachers will sometimes say: "Why plan? I never get to implement my plans the way I envisioned, or something always happens to mess things up." Every day is different with kids—and so, every day is different with teachers.

Planning gives us our structures and guidelines and helps us organize, so that teachers can make sure they address the content they need to in ways that meet the needs of their students. But, teachers are right: Often the implementation of lesson plans doesn't turn out exactly as expected. Maybe a kid starts the school day by pulling up his shirt and showing a bunch of other boys some big, red, raised circles on his back that look like welts or bruises, so you report child abuse, but then you find out the bruises are an Asian home remedy called "cupping." True story. I wish I had known more about that boy's culture before overreacting! Didn't quite get right on my lesson plans that morning.

The process of developing and thinking through lesson plans—identifying the learning goals, figuring out how to deliver the information in ways students can best understand, finding ways to determine whether they did understand, and thinking through ways to help those who didn't understand or to enrich the learning for those who did—is not wasted time. It can be a lot to think through, but even if teachers don't do it perfectly, or the day blows up into something they never expected, it is likely they will do a much better job addressing the things they need to because they have gone over it mentally, have the materials ready, and are confident because they do have a plan. Nothing gave me a stomachache more than hearing the squealing sound of the bus wheels at the beginning of a school day and knowing I hadn't planned very well. Thirty kids with not much meaningful to do equaled mega stress and anxiety for all 31 of us, all day. It's worth the peace of mind to plan. Similarly, coaching that incorporates setting specific, measurable goals with deliberate action steps and timelines is very powerful, but don't let the realities of life steal your peace of mind if sometimes teaching and coaching goals take a little longer than expected.

Surprising work requirements are often dropped on teachers at less than ideal times. Let's say the principal of a teacher you are coaching just found out she has to have a report with data from every teacher in the school, and it has to be turned in to the assistant superintendent within two days. The teacher you are coaching will need to support the principal, and you, as the coach, will need to figure out how to help the teacher get through that as efficiently as possible. Better to be flexible and to model flexibility rather than get upset and begin complaining (along with the teacher): "I can't believe they would do that to you. We had important plans; why do they expect you to just jump when they say how high, for no meaningful reason? This district always does crap like this; didn't the principal want you to make our coaching goals a priority?" Stop. STOP. Help the teacher get through it, maybe even offer extra support to other teachers and/or the principal, then get back to the coaching goals at a later, less stressful time.

Increasing our knowledge about coaching and leadership style options, languages, cultures, religions, the effects of affluence and poverty, and so on, can help inform us generally and allow us to respond with less rigidity in our teaching, coaching, and leadership roles. We show flexibility when the decisions we make and the support we provide are not solely based on our own thinking and experiences. Plus, that lack of flexibility is just lazy. If we, as coaches, are thinking we know exactly what to do, maybe our thoughts go something like this: *Looks like this is just another classroom-management situation. I've got this. I'll just share what I did over at the last school and help the teacher get on top of this, pronto,* but we haven't even been curious enough to learn about the person, the situation, and the students . . . well, we've just limited our effectiveness. We can't flexibly meet the needs of individual teachers if we don't take the time to listen and learn about the unique person and situation.

A common concern among teachers is that they are not really in control of what they are teaching or how to manage student behavior, yet they are held responsible for the outcomes. Some teachers might not feel they have authority or are unsure it is okay to take the initiative or the responsibility to be the leader in the classroom. Or maybe it's as Coach #10 said, "Teachers don't feel they are 'smart enough' to make decisions." The end goal of coaching is not to create dependence on the coach's support, but to develop teachers who feel powerful and productive, capable of being strong and confident in their decisions and in their ability to positively impact student learning.

Coach #10 continued to express her thinking on this topic in response to the question "What specific actions did you take as an instructional coach that you felt were most effective?"

> I think the thing that I did that maybe made the most difference was I encouraged people to know how good they are as teachers, and I encouraged them to do what they thought was best for their kids. . . . I said, "Well, what do you think *you* could do?" What would be better for your kids?" . . . and so I saw that with teachers, you know, saying, "Oh, I want to do a novel! Or I want to do this" [rather than] "I will just do what I'm told" . . . to a little more of "I need to think for myself . . . I am the expert, and I need to do what's best for my kids." . . . I just kept telling them those things, and I'm going to continue even more, 'cause I think that's where we are in education: where too many teachers are in a state of learned helplessness—where they just do what they're told, because they have been yelled at too much when they try to think for themselves. And by golly, we're [teachers and coaches] the experts! And we need to take charge of that. So, I think that's probably the best thing I've done this year.

For many reasons, teachers are feeling limited in their opportunities to be flexible and creative, even when they see student needs and want to address them in unique ways. Possibly the pendulum is swinging too much toward collaboration, with not enough attention being given to empowering individual teachers, or maybe many teachers are feeling inadequate and scared.

Teachers need to feel some level of freedom and support as they work to create memorable, instructionally powerful, and happy experiences for kids. Multisensory, relevant, and surprising experiences make lasting impressions (Heath & Heath, 2017), but how do teachers intentionally create those amazing teaching moments if they don't feel they have the authority to run their classrooms, the latitude to include strategic opportunities to involve multiple senses or intelligences (through art, music, movement, demonstrations, props, games, drama, etc.), or the resources and support to do things differently? Our joy as educators—at the coaching and leadership levels, at the teacher level, and even down to the student level—can be dimmed if we do not have opportunities to be self-directed (Schwartz, 2006, p. 1), creative, and adaptive.

I recently spoke with my niece and nephew, who are very good students in another state. I tried in many ways to search for any joy they were feeling during their school experiences. I asked the following questions: "What did you do this past week in school? What is your favorite subject? Are there any classes you really like or are excited about? Do you have any favorite teachers who make the class exciting and the content fun?"

In response to all these questions, I received a blank stare—no emotion, just a kind of deadness, and a few stilted answers: "I just did a bunch of tests and stuff," "No, they [the classes] are all just okay; there's not any I really like that much," "I'm not really into it; I just do what I have to do—you know, like the bare minimum to get by," "My friends make it fun, but the classes aren't fun," "I just come home and do homework all the time."

I wish this were an isolated situation, but I see many emotionless, joyless faces every day, and I'm thinking you probably do too.

I would venture to agree with Qin Zhang (2014) that when we see those blank, emotionless student faces, they are just reflections of the blank, emotionless faces of their teachers.

> Emotional convergence and collective affect generally occur in groups, and in the classroom, students typically model, mimic, and thus acquire teachers' emotions displayed in their teaching. Enthusiastic teachers can "rub off" their enthusiasm on students, fostering an increased incidence of prosocial, supportive, and cooperative behavior. Conversely, teachers' negative emotions may provoke an increased presence of anti-social, disruptive, and deviant behavior.
>
> (p. 1)

The lack of opportunity for teachers to be flexible and creative may be killing joy and motivation all the way down the line. Systems focused on fidelity to curriculums and governed by fear (overfocused on how students will perform on standardized tests) to the point that it's more important for teammates to be literally on the same page than to meet the needs of students, who may be at a variety of grade levels or who have completely different needs than those in a teammate's class, can cause teachers to feel undervalued and de-motivated.

Supporting Flexible Coaching and Teaching

It is my belief that coaching is at its best when it is organized as a voluntary, self-selected, confidential PD option. Principals should be able to suggest coaching if they feel it would be of benefit to move an effective or high-performing teacher to the next level or to help a struggling teacher more effectively meet the needs of students. The intentional creation of a positive coaching culture and the understanding of what "coaching" is relies heavily on how it is offered to teachers. It is of great importance that the energy surrounding coaching be positive, not punitive. Sometimes principals will say: "But what about those teachers who won't ask for support when they need it? How can we make sure they get what they need to become better teachers?" This is a good question, and it represents an ongoing philosophical battle being waged pretty much everywhere, in numerous environments.

Is making things (achievement/money/goals) happen, no matter the human cost (as long as it gets quick results) better than creating cultures of love and support for the people involved in the work? The answer is no. And it's emphatically no, if we want sustainable long-term positive results. Not long ago, many people thought educators would be able to help students make significant achievement gains through forced compliance with assessments. The idea was that better teaching and student learning would be achieved over time, as a result of increased pressure and accountability. This did not work (Strauss, 2015). A similar focus hasn't worked that well in other fields either. The following excerpt from the book *Firms of Endearment* (previously mentioned in Chapter 2), by Raj Sisodia, David Wolfe, and Jag Sheth (2014), explains a comparison of companies identified in the book *Good to Great: Why Some Companies Make the Leap . . . and Others Don't* (Collins, 2001). These companies were successful financially, but their focus was typically on the bottom line, which was money, not people. Sisodia, Sheth, and Wolfe compared the *Good to Great* companies' financial results to the results of companies these authors classified as Firms of Endearment (FoEs), which were deemed successful because people loved them—in part because they valued not only financial returns, but also making their companies great for employees, customers, suppliers, and society in general. The results were as follows:

> Jim Collins's bestselling *Good to Great* identified 11 companies that it described as going from "good" to "great" by virtue of their having delivered superior returns to investors over an extended period of time. We compared our set of publicly traded FoEs [Firms of Endearment] with the 11 *Good to Great* companies. This is what we discovered:
>
> - Over a 10-year horizon, the 13 FoEs outperformed the *Good to Great* companies by 1,026 percent to 331 percent (a 3 to 1 ratio).
>
> - Over five years, the 17 FoEs outperformed the *Good to Great* companies by 128 percent to 77 percent.
>
> - Over three years, the 18 FoEs performed on par with the *Good to Great* companies: 73 percent to 75 percent. . . .
>
> Great companies sustain their superior performance over time for investors, but equally important in our view, for their employees, customers, suppliers, and society in general. . . . If you are looking for a meaningful and deeply satisfying career, take a look at the opportunities these companies offer.
>
> (pp. 14–16)

Valuing people more than money helped FoEs create environments where people were happy—*and*, as a result, they produced incredible financial success that bested even the most successful corporations over time. We can and need to be intentional about creating environments of support, and coaching is the ideal place to make that happen. It may take a few years for teachers to trust the sincerity of this different approach, especially if, in their experience, coaching has been used only as a forced intervention for teachers who are struggling.

We are now experiencing the results of test scores (like money, for the corporations: the "bottom line") being touted as more important than students or teachers. We are experiencing teacher shortages and record levels of low teacher job satisfaction (MetLife, 2012). Families are moving their children to charter schools, homeschooling, or eschooling to escape discouraging environments. We need to catch up—we can create schools of endearment! Let's focus on what is good—on strengths, on how to build success through creating "peak" experiences for teachers and students—rather than looking for and focusing on problems, wasting our lives and energy in daily drudgery by "filling potholes" (Heath & Heath, 2017). It's not about gaps; it's about gifts! What can we give our students and teachers to help them successfully tackle the challenges in front of them? We want our kids and teachers to love school, and one way to promote that love is to offer coaching in supportive and caring ways so that teachers will want to participate and enjoy being involved.

When coaching is offered as helpful support without risk, teachers are more apt to seek it early if they are really interested in remaining in the teaching profession. The amount of trust in coaching also depends on the quality of the coaches. Neither teachers or principals will ask for or suggest coaching if coaches are not instructionally competent. As one middle-school principal told me, "We wouldn't use you if you sucked!" It can be difficult for principals to be coaches. It may have been a long time since they were teachers themselves (or maybe they have never been), and principals are evaluators, which often adds an element of fear for the teachers they try to coach.

Though some principals keep their teaching skills sharp through practice, many may be coming from a place of rusty competence, trying to coach from a position in which they are not completely trusted because they may be (and may need to be) considering letting a teacher go. This sounds uncomfortable for everyone involved, unless the principal has learned to embody many of the characteristics of an effective coach that are discussed in this book. But even then, if a teacher continues to receive substandard evaluations and turns down suggestions to engage in voluntary coaching that would help him or her be successful, it is not likely that any type of "forced" coaching would have better results in the long term, since the teacher doesn't seem interested in improving. Unless a coach or principal has the time to be in the coached teacher's classroom for quite some time every day, checking on implementation of strategies a teacher is feeling forced to do, it's going to take way too much time and money to make sure commitment to coaching goals is happening. And, who's to say that as soon as the coach or principal stops making the "rounds," the teacher won't just stop implementing the strategies? Who wants to be the police? Not any principals or coaches I know.

When teachers at all levels of experience and expertise are given the flexibility to ask for coaching, they are more likely to see it as something to run *to* rather than something to run *from*. Also, it is human nature to put more energy into something we have *chosen* to do. This positive attitude about coaching helps teachers follow through with collaboratively determined coaching actions. Data results for percentage of teachers' *action steps met* for teachers who were coached by the TCT program (which is a district-level voluntary, nonevaluative, and confidential coaching program) over three years are as follows: 2015–16, 97%; 2016–17, 97%; and 2017–18, 98%. During these same three years, the TCT instructional coaching program *overall* received a 99% customer satisfaction rating from teachers and a 97% satisfaction rating from principals. Let's create coaching programs and protocols that teachers want to be involved with!

Coach #11 shared this insight about learning to work with adults:

> I think once you make the transition that when you're coaching people and teaching adult learnings, it's not like teaching high-school students, and you have to approach them in a different manner. You have to approach them more empathetically; you have to approach them more scientifically or in a data-driven statistical manner.... Once you accept that kids are by and large a captive audience where you're concerned, but for adult learners, you always want to be offering them something that is useful to them the minute they walk away from the meeting with you or the professional development, then you put yourself in their shoes and remember how much you wanted to take something away that worked.

Sharan B. Merriam (2001) explained Malcolm Knowles's basics of the theory of adult learning, or andragogy:

> The five assumptions underlying andragogy describe the adult learner as someone who (1) has an independent self-concept and who can direct his or her own learning, (2) has accumulated a reservoir of life experiences that is a rich resource for learning, (3) has learning needs closely related to changing social roles, (4) is problem-centered and interested in immediate application of knowledge, and (5) is motivated to learn by internal rather than external factors. From these assumptions, Knowles proposed a program planning model for designing, implementing, and evaluating educational experiences with adults. For example, with regard to the first assumption that as adults mature they become more independent and self-directing, Knowles suggested that the classroom climate should be one of "adultness," both physically and psychologically. In an "adult" classroom, adults "feel accepted, respected, and supported"; further, there exists "a spirit of mutuality between teachers and students as joint inquirers" (1980, p. 47). And because adults manage other aspects of their lives, they are capable of directing, or at least assisting in planning, their own learning.

> (p. 5)

Summarized by Cyril Houle (1996), the theory of andragogy explains the need to "involve [adult] learners in as many aspects of their education as possible and in the creation of a climate in which they can most fruitfully learn" (p. 30). Setting up coaching that allows teacher choice and honors teacher voice incorporates best practices for adult learning into coaching and is critical for coaching effectiveness (Knight, 2018):

> When coaches act in ways that are consistent with the Partnership Principles [Equality, Choice, Voice, Dialogue, Reflection, Praxis, Reciprocity] as opposed to a top-down approach, teachers do most of the thinking, and coaches and teachers work as equals with the goal of making a powerful, positive difference in children's lives.
>
> (p. 5)

Results of the TCT coaching practice—which aligns with these partnership principles and the basics of appropriate adult learning, both in the organization of the program and in the implementation of coaching practices—showed higher levels of growth in teacher competency and more positive experiences for teachers, as evidenced by (1) the growth in perceived competency of coached teachers in 22 instructional areas being four to five times as much the growth in perceived competency of the control group of non-coached teachers and (2) growth in job satisfaction among coached teachers being an incredible 57 times as much as growth in job satisfaction among the control group (Frazier, 2018).

Also, when coaching is voluntary, it is not limited to just those who are struggling. In the TCT coaching practice, high-performing teachers choose to work with coaches to be able to move their instructional practice forward at a faster pace. This is similar to an Olympic athlete or professional tennis player employing a coach. Opening coaching to all teachers who would like support, rather than just those who are deeply struggling, helps coaching be recognized as a legitimate PD strategy and support, not a punishment for poor performance. Why set coaching up so that teachers feel a need to resist it in order to keep themselves from feeling shamed? "When we insist, they will resist" (Knight, 2015). A similar application of this thought can be found in Newton's third law of motion, which states that for every action, there is an equal and opposite reaction, or, as massage therapist Shelley Helfegger related, "The harder I push, the harder the muscle tightens or pushes back, so sometimes I can't get anything done by pushing in too deep" (personal communication, November 9, 2018).

The existence of coaching assumes the belief that people can change. An important question is "How do we set up the environment and the work of coaching to most effectively meet the needs of a variety of people and situations? And, how do we make sure coaching is something people want to participate in?" Fear and force can motivate, in the short term. But creating an inviting situation where coaching is seen as an opportunity to work alongside someone, cultivating instructional growth together that could be implemented for years to come, would not involve either of these two F-words.

In my experience, teachers in a situation where an administrator has basically demanded they get a coach, or they have been assigned one, are running scared and are more interested in a quick fix to please the principal than in deeply examining their instructional practice. These teachers are not as able to process the honest, reflective thinking required to make and retain meaningful changes to their practice over the long term, because they are operating in "fight or flight" mode. Coaches also feel stress when they are expected to be the "long arm of the law" and have someone "fixed" in a short amount of time. Inviting teachers kindly (and honoring their right to say no) long before any negative actions need to be taken spares them from that "under the gun" feeling that can undermine authentically motivated collaborative work. It is difficult for anyone to do their best work when they experience the stress of being called out as "less than" and their livelihood is threatened (Medina, 2014). Some teachers do need to find a different profession, but making coaching a forced intervention (or a box to check off to prove some kind of help was given, when the intent was never to support the teacher's success) severely damages the reputation of coaching and sends teachers running rather than reaching for it.

Flexibility and Leadership

It would make sense that leaders who have put in a lot of time and effort to obtain leadership positions would be motivated to retain their social status and/or the situation or position they feel allows them, in some ways, to have control or dominance. Unfortunately, this internal value of working hard to attain power, which has helped leaders be successful, can put them in a difficult position and even at odds with themselves if they decide not to let power—again, as defined by Schwartz, "social status and prestige, control or dominance over people and resources" (2006, p. 1)—reign in their leadership approach. It may be counterintuitive for some leaders that prioritizing the values of benevolence, universalism, and self-direction would benefit their employees. Schwartz communicates that benevolence values are generated from internal motivation to promote supportive and cooperative social relationships (p. 1). How, without internal motivation (possibly found through introspection and connection—see Chapter 6), can we organize our coaching and leadership in ways that support others' growth and not be overly focused on our own ambitions or the development of rigid systems that may limit others' opportunities for freedom, creativity, and growth?

It may help us to be able to prioritize those conflicting values when we think of those people or leaders who have most positively influenced our lives or who are admired universally for the good they do or have done throughout the world. It is likely that many, if not all, of those inspirational people were authentically full of love and concern for others (caring), had studied and learned enough to know at a very high level what they were teaching or talking about (competent), and were flexible in the ways they addressed the individual needs of others. It is likely those types of people have been the ones who have made a lasting difference in our lives and in many lives, because they were/are not overly consumed with their own pleasures or obtaining power over others.

We need wonderful leaders. We want good people in power. They are so important! I have been fortunate to have brilliant and caring principals, supervisors, and colleagues throughout my career who have supported and trusted me by encouraging my collaborative endeavors yet giving me space to grow in creativity, individuality, and resourcefulness. This book would never have been written without their wisdom and the many opportunities they provided me to learn and grow. I honor, appreciate, and strive to be like them. Their dedication to building others' capacity through the power of teaching, coaching, and leading has lit my soul with similar desires and helped me internalize how powerful and personally satisfying facilitating the growth of students, teachers, and coaches can be.

Unfortunately, I have also experienced situations where individual leaders and groups of leaders block forward progress.

Barriers to Flexible and Supportive School and District Cultures

In Chapter 1, we learned that a wide spread of satellite inputs are necessary for a GPS system to generate an accurate destination. I remember a discussion with a highly educated and popular legislator who represented a large area of a city that included people at many different income levels. I thought he would understand the need to support the students and their families who were living in poverty. When I asked him about what we could do to provide great educational experiences for all kids, his answer was that if they didn't like the neighborhood school they could just go to a private school, like he did and like his own kids did. This answer left me stunned, because it was so shallow and uninformed. He had never personally experienced the trauma and difficulties that families in poverty face; he had never noticed the physical hunger, desperation, and sometimes hopelessness I was seeing every day in the eyes of children and teens I loved. And then there was just the basic piece of how could a person with so much education not understand that families in poverty wouldn't be able to afford to transport their children or pay for private school? How could he effectively lead and represent the people in his care when he did not know them and obviously had no understanding of what life looked like for them on a daily basis?

Unfortunately, many leaders, like him, are out of touch with what the people they are leading go through, yet they profess to care. I have heard it defined as "benevolent arrogance." In other words, a leader might think or say: "I care and am trying to help you, but I'm the one who is smart enough to figure out what to do, and what I decide will be what is best for you. I do not need to take the time to listen to you or learn about what you are dealing with every day, particularly if you are not at my same pay grade, do not have sufficient education, or haven't somehow earned the right to take up some of my time." These types of leaders tend to surround themselves with those who think like them and end up taking schools, districts, states, and countries in directions that do not create supportive and growth-filled futures for those they are entrusted to lead.

When leaders act in these ways, they create barriers to forward movement and minimize the importance of the basic foundations of positive interactions with people, which include courtesy, kindness, and respect for all. There are leaders and groups of people similar to the legislator above, who do not have a real understanding of a basic tenet of this book: the importance of caring. I have experienced the clashing of coaching cultures where force and fear (rather than warmth and competent support) were touted as effective motivators. I have also experienced firsthand an arrogance by leadership that included a general lack of respect for others. This toxic attitude was verbalized by one of the leaders as "Teachers are stupid." When I was talking with a custodian at one of the buildings where leadership meetings were sometimes held, he shared: "I have worked in this building for many, many years, and I often set up and take down the tables and chairs for the leadership meetings, and not one of those people who are supposed to be leaders have ever said hello to me. It's like I'm not worth talking to, like I'm a piece of dog shit."

It is philosophically against the core values of those who try to teach the higher ways of caring, equality, kindness, and respect for all to force them on anyone, so sometimes these softer voices are ignored or treated with disrespect. And sometimes, there's just not an opportunity for those voices to be heard. I believe many leaders would listen to what the custodian had to say if there was a culture that valued and allowed his voice to be heard. As much as it is in our power as leaders and coaches, may we hear and teach the ways of the heart. These ways mark the path that will lead to the lasting confidence, motivation, competency, unity, enjoyment, and success that we all seek in the workplace.

Forgiveness, Flexibility's Final Frontier

One last thought—and it can be a tough one. A central component of being flexible is developing the ability to forgive. This does not mean letting people take advantage of or be abusive toward us. It means letting go of ill feelings that hold us back and waste our time and energy when we angrily and rigidly focus on how we were poorly treated. Letting go of mistakes others have made toward us does not excuse their behavior, but it allows us to modify our internal filter of automatically classifying those people as horrible in every aspect because of what they did to us. Sometimes we even need to forgive ourselves for things we wish we hadn't done.

This forgiveness process can be difficult and sometimes seems unnatural (in very rare cases, some people really are mentally ill or scary evil, so we've just got to get away from them), but if we can free ourselves from focusing on things that have hurt us, and move forward with less baggage, we will have more positive flow and energy in our lives. Giving people another chance whenever possible (when it is reasonably safe to do so), or peacefully disconnecting (if we need to protect ourselves from toxic people) without malice, is a light and happy way to go about life. It's going to happen—we're going to be treated horribly sometimes, and we will probably treat people horribly sometimes. But we don't have to stay in a negative frame of mind because of it. This is not to say we should automatically go back to bad situations that weren't healthy for us or do something dumb, like rehire someone who stole money from our company. It is to say that we shouldn't let our minds run around in circles to the point that we can't think outside those well-worn, discouraging ruts. Forgiving others (and ourselves) frees our minds and hearts, and it creates space for us to recognize and internalize productive and wonderful thoughts and experiences. It also offers grace and kindness to others, improving the chances that they will come back to us when we ourselves make mistakes. Forgiveness allows us to flow flexibly and freely into and through our lives.

Reflect and Connect

Flexible

- Choose a new partner.

- Pick up at least 10 rubber bands each.

- Sit in a dyad (in chairs facing each other, with knees almost touching) at least 10 feet away from the bucket on the table.

- Take the Cultural Bias Self-assessment.

- Take turns reading to each other the general culture trend excerpts from the book *Kiss, Bow, or Shake Hands*, by Terri Morrison & Wayne A. Conaway (2006).

- Share ideas with your partner about how the results of the self-assessment and the cultural trends information could change the way you coach. Be specific: What will you say, what will you do, or what different questions will you ask based on what you have learned?

- For each idea you come up with, try to shoot a rubber band into the bucket on the table.

- Activity Analogy:

  - Making permanent personal and program changes takes practice as we replace old thoughts and behaviors.

  - Changing for the better can be painful (rubber bands flying ☺), but we can handle it!

~Talk together about the process of change and why cultural bias is sometimes especially hard to address. ~

Don't forget to have some fun!

The Personal Assessment of Anti-Bias Behavior is available online from the Anti-Defamation League (ADL's) Education Division (www.adl.org/education) at:

https://www.adl.org/sites/default/files/documents/assets/pdf/education-outreach/Personal-Self-Assessment-of-Anti-Bias-Behavior.pdf

During workshops or conferences, I typically have participants fill out the questions on the self-assessment that I feel would work for the group and that would fit well on one page front to back. After members of the group discuss their thoughts, I have them refer to the Cultural Trend information (below) from the book *Kiss, Bow, or Shake Hands* (Morrison & Conaway, 2006), and proceed through the activity as explained above.

CULTURAL TREND INFORMATION

—From KISS, BOW, or SHAKE HANDS (2006) by Terri Morrison and Wayne A. Conaway—

Country/ Dominant Language	Dominant Religion/ Values	Personal-Space/ Eye-Contact wNorms/ Greetings	Social Norms	More Social Norms	Dos and Don'ts
Mexico Spanish	• Catholic • Family is the most important institution.	• Closer physical distance when conversing than typical in USA or Europe—more touching • Intermittent eye contact—not continuous or intense	• Elaborate courtesy • Unhurried attitudes • Family roles are important—lifelong support is expected.	• Mother as central family figure • Men: Machismo—strong masculine pride; tough • Punctuality—not strictly adhered to	**Do:** • Respect the dignity of the individual • Be courteous and friendly **Don't:** • Publicly criticize • Pull rank
Japan Japanese	• Shintoism • Buddhism • Age is revered.	• Japanese remain farther apart in conversation than North Americans. • Eye contact—prolonged direct eye contact is not the norm. • Bowing—if bowed to, if by an equal, bow the same depth; if it is someone of higher rank, bow lower. As you bow, quickly lower your eyes. Keep palms flat against thighs	• Always be on time—tardiness is rude. • Poker face—excessive displays of emotions are disliked. • Groups are rewarded, not individuals.	• Apologies are important. • Competitive • Consensus is strived for. • Strong work ethic	**Do:** • Say, "I'm sorry" • Be on time and be polite • Respect older people **Don't:** • Point or touch people • Use extreme or dramatic gestures/ facial expressions • Give a gift from China
India Hindi	• Buddhism, Hinduism, Islam • Caste system • Personal decisions must be in harmony with the family, group, and social structure.	• Comfortable standing distance between people varies among Indian cultures but is typically 3 to 3-½ feet. • Eye contact—typically direct during conversation • Side-to-side toss of the head indicates agreement.	• Friendships and kinships are more important than expertise. • Tipping is often the way to ensure things get done. • Rigid structure of inequality	• Punctuality is appreciated but not always adhered to. • Indians consider the head to be the seat of the soul. • Do not touch someone else's head or even pat the hair of a child. • Success and failure in India are often attributed to environmental factors.	**Do:** • Eat only with right hand (left hand is traditionally used for hygiene) • Wash your hands before and after a meal **Don't:** • Serve or order beef for Hindus or pork for Muslims • Just say no; be vague rather than refuse an invitation • Point or whistle

Flexible Self-Assessment

1. Take this self-assessment before you set an intention to consciously find ways to become more flexible.

2. Implement some of the practical application ideas and/or flexible S.O.A.K. supports found below (or use some of your own ideas).

3. In a month or so, see whether you have been able to improve your thoughts, motivations, and behaviors surrounding the important coaching characteristic of becoming more flexible. Reference the following synonyms/specifics as you personally determine what being flexible is and how to make it a more conscious part of your daily life: *willing to look at alternatives; able to tailor instruction to a variety of situations; able to see multiple perspectives; culturally sensitive and aware* (Frazier, 2014).

	Strongly Disagree	Disagree	Neutral/ Not Sure	Agree	Strongly Agree
	1	2	3	4	5
I believe the people I coach/lead are equal to me, even though we are different.					
I am careful to learn as much as I can about the people I coach and the situations they are facing. I try to see what they see from their perspective.					
It is not in my nature to think rigidly or unkindly about (stereotype/categorize/see only the worst in) others or put them down (and if it is, I am working to eliminate that tendency).					
I can adapt and change my coaching strategies and priorities when a teacher is facing a situation that calls for a different approach.					
I try to understand my biases and can temper my responses appropriately, even when I don't agree with someone. I can forgive mistakes.					
I work toward organizing coaching interactions and systems that support flexibility (teacher and coach have voice and choice), fairness (equality), flow (offer choices and inspire peaceful interactions), and fun ("peak" moments, multisensory strategies, surprises, etc.).					
Column Totals:					

Grand Total: _____

What totals mean: 26–30 = Flexible Rock Star, 21–25 = Very Flexible, 16–20 = Sort of Flexible, 11–15 = Some Flexibility Is Happening, 6–10 = Better Step It Up, 0–5 = Would Setting a Goal to Be More Flexible Be Helpful?

Practical Application Ideas for Flexible

Creating "Peak" Moments and "Breaking the Script"

In their book *The Power of Moments* (Heath & Heath, 2017), the Heath brothers encouraged us to be flexible by changing things up and intentionally creating meaningful and unexpected bursts of joy in our teaching and our lives in general. They shared powerful stories about educators who created unforgettable moments for their students ("Signing Day" and "The Trial of Human Nature") while addressing school goals and content standards.

We can be flexible by breaking the script of monotony in our schedules and surprising people with different reactions than they would normally expect from us. We can create "elevation" or "peak" moments that infuse incredible amounts of positive energy into our work and home lives. According to the Heath brothers, moments of elevation can be created when we include elements of sensory appeal, emotion, and surprise; also, we would do well to focus on creating positive "peaks" rather than just "filling potholes." We can be strategic about when we create those "peaks" by implementing them at times when the human mind and heart will most likely remember them. These times include beginnings, endings, transitions, and milestones. How often do we or teachers squander the chance to organize powerful closures to coaching sessions or lessons? There is so much we can do to enjoy our lives and work more, and the Heath brothers' stories and specific insights can help us make joy happen!

Adopt an Explorer Attitude

Take some risks; look for new ideas; search for insights and fun to share, even if you might have to pass through some wild (and frightening) territory. To give you an example from my personal life, I used to be reluctant to try healthy alternatives to cow's milk, such as coconut, cashew, and almond milk. For a long time, these things just sounded wrong to me. But the allure of fewer calories and "good" fats finally enticed me. Now I use them in smoothies all the time and feel good about trying to be healthier, even though I have to think of the nuts or coconuts being squeezed by a machine to kind of get it and not be weirded out by it.

If we aren't willing to be flexible enough to try new things, we could miss out on some great experiences, strategies, or useful things that could bring us happiness and be shared with others. Having an explorer attitude makes us more interesting to talk with and more energized, and it helps us fill our toolbox with a variety of unique and exciting tools to use in our relationships, both at work and at home.

It is rare to find treasures or tools immediately or without effort—we usually have to explore for a while. I often give the teachers I coach Halls Breezers Creamy Strawberry Pectin Drops to help with sore or overworked throats. I found this gem of a product only by trying a bunch of cough drops over time, some of which were not very tasty or helpful. Other discoveries I often share include Lily's caramelized and salted chocolate bars sweetened with stevia (it's hard to find good chocolate sweetened with healthy sugar substitutes). Then there's Mavalus tape, also a great gift for teachers because it sticks to and holds up almost anything without damaging things like whiteboards.

Some favorite ideas/strategies I've found as a result of exploring include these:

- Jim Knight's "playbook" idea (2018): This is a great way to organize the determination of and coach/teacher implementation of high-yield strategies into one-page chunks. Coaches collaboratively discuss and determine their top picks of high-yield strategies to facilitate coach clarity, then organize the choices into a one-page table of contents, then prepare one-page checklists outlining the implementation pieces necessary for teachers to use the strategies. This process addresses the need for a common understanding of best practices within coaching programs, simplifies the training of coaches when hired, and addresses the common problem of edu-overload for teachers.

(Continued)

(Continued)

Educators are notorious for providing lots of resources and page after page of instructions, with every detail noted and referenced. Unfortunately, at times our thoroughness (usually prepared by seasoned and knowledgeable coaches/leaders) can scare teachers, particularly new ones. We want to organize our coaching work in ways that keep teachers wanting more support, not make them feel the need to hide from our full-on fire hoses. Not that we shouldn't understand specific details or be thorough; but, just like a teacher, how we deliver great teaching/coaching depends on our ability to understand and address the needs and knowledge levels of our audience. Coaching support delivered in bite-sized pieces, such as this playbook idea, keeps teachers from choking on too much meaty or maybe gristly (indigestible and unnecessary) information at one time.

- Dinah Zike's Foldables (mentioned in Chapter 3): After seeing the results of over a thousand student surveys, I have concluded that the majority of students we serve enjoy their learning most when it's presented in kinesthetic and visual ways. Helping teachers deliver instruction kinesthetically makes learning interesting and easier to understand for many students. Foldables are an odd find; they've been around for a while, but they're incredibly useful. They can be used as 3-D graphic organizers to support students as they gather information and practice skills.

Using a variety of Foldables to help students organize their thinking and learning is easy. Some people think Foldables are just for the elementary-school crowd. Not so. I've seen middle- and high-school teachers use Foldables successfully. One I particularly remember was a middle-school math teacher trying to help students remember the order of operations (PEMDAS). I've even seen Foldables used in a middle school in Iizuka, Japan. Origami is very popular over there, fun for all ages, so the Foldables were a hit! Students in both America and Japan were able to successfully organize their work in an enjoyable and effective way using this wonderful tool. Some of my favorites are The Layered Book Foldable; Shutter Foldable; Four-Door Foldable; Folded Tables and Charts; and the Matchbook Foldable and Portfolio. Dinah Zike has quite a few books showing how to use Foldables in different subjects at numerous grade levels. For a great example, visit http://www.k12.wa.us/IndianEd/TribalSovereignty/High/CWP-HS/Unit4/Level1-Materials/foldables.pdf.

Conclusion

In a nutshell, being flexible is about making a conscious effort to create fairness, flow, and fun!

Images by https://www.istockphoto.com/portfolio/fizkes

FLEXIBLE ~S.O.A.K. ~   Sometimes learning penetrates best when we are relaxed and not trying too hard to make it happen. (Like a "Flexible" bath bomb infused with personalized nutrients)

Stress-free Opportunities to Absorb Knowledge   **Choose what works for you.**

Quotes	Music	Statements affirmations	Books poetry stories	Art	Videos movies	Movement other ideas
"Creativity has always depended on openness and flexibility, so let us hope for more of both in the future." —Siri Hustvedt	**"The Man in the Mirror"** Michael Jackson	**For coaches:** My ability to be flexible and forgiving inspires peaceful interactions.	**"The Oak and the Reeds"** Aesop	**Special Olympics Nagano Japan** (Paintings) Leroy Neiman (2005)	**Finding Opportunities in Unexpected Events** Avish Parashar—DingHappens.com	**Utkata Konasana**
"There is no greater force of amiability, or ability, than to have strength combined with flexibility. —Ana Claudia Antunes	**"Getting to Know You"** (From *The King and I*) Julie Andrews	Welcoming new people and experiences into my life expands my understanding and capabilities.	**"Advice From a River"** Ilan Shamir			**Fire Log Pose**
	"Breakaway" Kelly Clarkson	I can quickly catch and eliminate unkind or judgmental thinking or speaking that marginalizes others.	**Who Moved My Cheese? An Amazing Way to Deal With Change in Your Work and in Your Life** Spencer Johnson	**The Peace Negotiations Between Claudius Civilis and Cerealis** Ferdinand Bol	**Wonder** (2017)	
"Blessed are the flexible for they will not allow themselves to become bent out of shape!" —Robert Ludlum	**"We Can Work It Out"** The Beatles	I intentionally create surprises, multisensory experiences, and "peak" moments for others.			**Rocky III** (1982)	
	"You Can't Always Get What You Want" The Rolling Stones	I find ways to create fairness, freedom, and fun when coaching, leading, and interacting with my family.		**Balance Beam** (Bronze sculpture) Rebecca J. Crob	**Remember the Titans** (2000)	**Oils:** orange, rose
	"The Room Where It Happens" (From the musical *Hamilton*) Odom Jr., Miranda, Diggs & Onaodowan	**For teachers:**	**"The Last Dinosaurs"** Pedro Pablo Sacristán			
	"For Good" (From the musical *Wicked*) Kristen Chenowith and Idina Menzel	My students know I like, accept, and care for each of them, even though they are all different.		**Dancers at the Barre** Edgar Degas	**Moneyball** (2011)	**Stones:** bloodstone, muscovite
"When you forgive, you in no way change the past—but you sure do change the future." —Bernard Meltzer	**"Strong Enough to Bend"** Tanya Tucker **"I Dreamed a Dream"** (From the musical *Les Misérables*) Ruthie Henshall	I intentionally create surprises, multisensory experiences, and "peak" moments for students.	**Out of Our Minds: Learning to Be Creative** Ken Robinson	**Pioneer Woman** Jim Clements	**Honey, I Shrunk the Kids** (1989)	**Color:** light blue

Capable of bending without breaking (Oxford English Dictionary, s.v. "flexible").

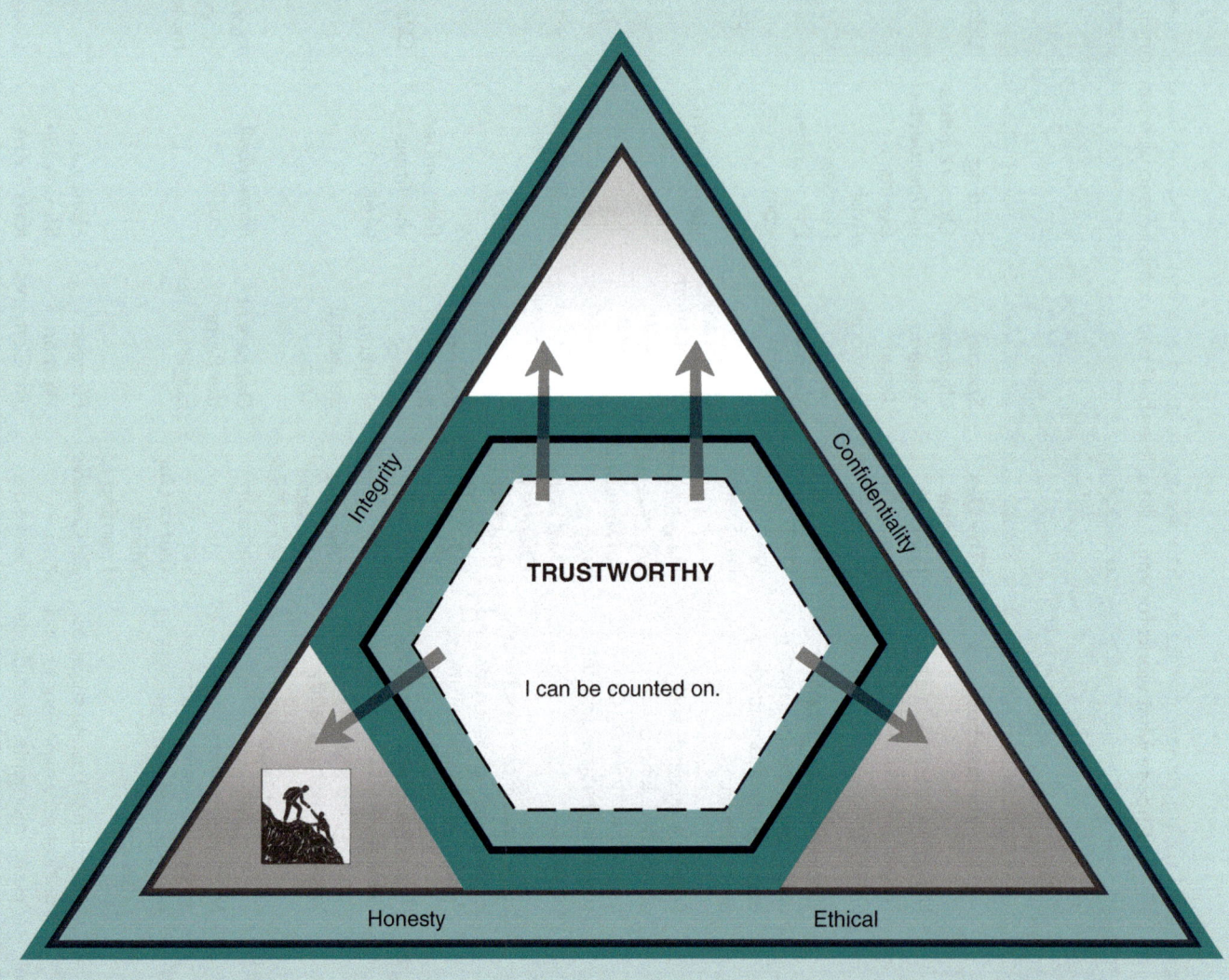

The teachers I coach know their reputations and their hearts are safe with me.
I do what I say I am going to do.

Trustworthy

8

Trust brings out the best in people and literally changes the dynamics of the situation.

—Stephen Covey (2006, p. 319)

As we continue moving from the central aspect of "caring," outward to the left of the diagram, through the filters of "authenticity" and being a "quality communicator," we see the characteristic listed underneath "flexible" is "trustworthy." When interview scripts of coaches were both manually and electronically analyzed, the word "trust" surfaced numerous times within a variety of categories (Frazier, 2014). When reviewing the text of the interviews with coaches, I noted that the word "trust" was recurrently mentioned and could be organized under many categories, including "ethical," "caring," "inspirational," and "quality communicator." Because of this, "trustworthy" was then included as a key characteristic on the "caring" side of the model, incorporating the words "ethical," "honesty," "integrity," and "confidentiality."

If we want to be trusted, we must strive to be trustworthy. On the subject of trustworthiness, Jim Knight (2016) wrote, "We know we can trust someone when they have our best interests at heart—that is, that they genuinely care about our well-being. . . . When we listen and demonstrate empathy, when we really want to hear what others have to say, we show that we care" (p. 201). "When trust exists, there is learning, joy, and love. When trust does not exist, there is caution, inertia, and fear. Trust is just that important" (p. 188).

In response to the question "What leadership traits do you feel are most beneficial for an instructional coach to possess?" Coach #1 shared these thoughts:

> I think because we are always going to encounter dissatisfaction, fear, anxiety, among a staff, that's just life. I think a true leader has to be able to set those aside, not judge too harshly, and if we goof up, and I know I have, be able to come back to the person or people and say, "Here is what I would like to take back and do differently," so that we can maintain that trust that, you know, hopefully we've already established. I think once trust is gone—once someone hears us feeding into negativity, talking about someone behind their back, criticizing them, or blaming another person—then that trust isn't coming back unless we fix it right away, like that day. So, maintaining trust. I think sometimes leaders think they do enough to establish trust initially and then they're golden, and that isn't true. I think every single day, every action, people decide whether we can be trusted or not.

Coach #2 answered the question "What does being an effective instructional coach mean to you?" in the following way:

> I think the top part of it is the trust-building with teachers, where they understand that you're not here in the "gotcha mode," you're here to help and support them. Building that trust is really important and can be very difficult to get.

Why Is Trust So Difficult to Get?

One reason why trust is often difficult to obtain involves previous negative experiences. People can like a coach or leader and want to give him or her the benefit of the doubt, but they may have had difficult life experiences when people they trusted let them down. As Coach #10 said: "every single day, every action, people decide whether we can be trusted or not. Teachers, or anyone who has been let down—whether in their personal lives or professional lives—are watching carefully to ascertain whether others can be trusted and can be very hesitant to risk trusting again."

Another reason is that many of us are still a work in progress. We are all in the process of learning how to inspire more trust as we strive to align our actions with our best intentions, and we may not be very good at it yet. As William Bennett (1993) wrote:

> Human beings need both practice and study over time to become persons of integrity and effective goodwill. And until they have achieved such a state, they may do all sorts of things that prudence tells them had better be concealed. Lying is an "easy" tool of concealment, and when often employed, all too easily hardens into a malignant vice. . . . Parents often say, "Don't let me catch you doing that again!" and that is all right, but a good, honest life is more than that. Moral development is not a game of "Catch me if you can." It is better to focus clearly on what really matters: *the kind of person one is.*

> (pp. 599–600)

We can all move toward being more trusted by nurturing positive, trustworthy traits and eliminating untrustworthy ones in ourselves. Below are some of the traits, identified by participants in a global communication study, that we should work on either developing or avoiding if we want to be considered trustworthy (Knight, 2016, pp. 192–193):

There is a lot we can do to inspire trust and a lot we can do to wreck it. As Stephen Covey (2006) related: "As you work on behaving in ways that build trust, one helpful way to visualize and quantify your efforts is by thinking in terms of 'Trust Accounts.' . . . By behaving in ways that destroy trust, you make withdrawals. The 'balance' in the account reflects the amount of trust in the relationship at any given time" (p. 135). Covey also warned that all deposits and withdrawals are not equal and that withdrawals are often larger than deposits. There are things we can do that would be so bad, the whole account would be wiped out in

Trustworthy Traits BECOME	Untrustworthy Traits ELIMINATE
Loyal	Disloyal
Able to admit when wrong	Unable to admit when wrong
Owns their own stuff; responsible	Blames, cannot own their stuff; irresponsible
Tells the truth, even at personal cost	Hides the truth; lies
Others-focused	Self-focused and self-pitying
Open-minded	Closed-minded
Good listener	Doesn't listen well
Habitually compassionate	Lacks compassion
Shows integrity; leads by example	Lacks integrity, both verbally and physically
Kind	Kind in order to get something, otherwise generally unkind
Honest, genuine, transparent	Dishonest, ingenuous, sly, sneaky
Refuses to manipulate	Manipulative
Doesn't gossip	Gossips
Giver, generous without strings attached	Taker
Respectful of others	Bossy
Focused on solutions	Focused on problems
Whines	Doesn't whine
Non-judgmental	Judgmental
Isn't afraid to be vulnerable	Never shows vulnerability
Avoids being late	Is careless of others' time
Puts forth clear, solid effort	Puts forth minimal effort
Doesn't seek glory	Seeks glory
Takes oneself lightly	Cannot laugh at oneself
Protective of others' dignity and person	Does not care about others' dignity and person; makes fun at others' expense
Encourages	Discourages
Allowing for others' choice	Controlling
Speaks appropriately; isn't the loudest person in the conversation	Talks too much, too loudly
Speaks with clarity	Speaks vaguely
Engages others	Engages others to get their way

Jim Knight, *Better Conversations* (2016), Corwin Press

one stroke. "You're going to make mistakes—everybody does—but try not to make the ones that completely destroy trust, and work hard to build trust and to restore whatever trust has been lost" (p. 136). Maybe when we understand there really is a lot involved in building and maintaining trust, we can be more forgiving when people mess it up. There are many challenging coaching situations that can undermine trust.

What Can Undermine Trust in a Coaching Relationship?

The invitation to coaching may have scared the teacher. It may have come off as "There's something wrong with you, and so we are going to have to get someone to come in and help you fix it or else [you'll get a bad evaluation/you'll lose your job/we'll move you to another grade level, one that isn't tested/we'll put another teacher in there with you, to make sure the kids learn what they need to/etc.]. When a teacher interprets the offer of coaching assistance as a thinly veiled threat, it becomes very difficult for that teacher to trust that the coaching is sincerely for his or her benefit.

Time limitations sometimes make it difficult for coaches to be immediately responsive or see teachers as often as they would like. This may lead to teachers not feeling the coach can be there to support them when difficult situations arise. This feeling of being low on the coach's priority list can also happen when coaches have to readjust their schedules with teachers when tasked with roles on top of their coaching responsibilities.

We don't usually like or trust people who talk down to us. If the coach comes off as less of a partner and more of an overzealous preacher, noting everything that's wrong with us in detail, then trust has no opportunity to grow, because the person being coached is minimized from the start of the relationship.

In addition, when coaches don't follow through on what they say they are going to do, trust is undermined.

How to Build Trust in a Coaching Relationship

Coach #7 shared how to build trust when answering the question "What was your most memorable success story as an instructional coach?"

> There was a teacher at the beginning of the year who was resistant . . . and very dubious about anything. [She] questioned any suggestions . . . that were offered to her . . . so I kind of came in . . . and started with that foundation of trust, just highlighting the positive that I saw with that teacher, and just [leaving] notes, you know, this is what I noticed. "I noticed that you had your standards and objectives posted. I noticed your higher-level questioning really targeted your group of students that you were working with today." Through just supporting her and highlighting the positive, we began to build a level of trust, and by the end of the year she was filming herself teaching and then was able to see what [the previous]

mentor had suggested during the very first observation . . . but she was able to say, "Now I get what you guys were talking about." But it took a year, and had we not built that relationship and that foundation of trust, I think there still would have been resistance; and then her own teaching would not have grown and the kids wouldn't have benefited, because she wouldn't have seen what she was doing that was strong and be able to continue that. So that would probably be my biggest success story.

Integrity, Confidentiality, Honesty, Ethical

In answer to the question "What would be the most important advice you could give to someone striving to be an effective instructional coach?" Coach #3 replied:

> I think the most important thing is to walk your talk . . . whatever you're asking of them, you'd better be doing. So you'd better be kind to them when they're sick, because you want them to be kind to the kids when they're sick, right? If you want them to confront bullies in the classroom, then you have to be willing to confront the bullies on your staff, and if you want your kids to have excellence and you want your teachers to be well-planned, then as a coach, you'd better be well-planned, and you don't get to hang out and have a cup of coffee just because you don't have a class. You're working the whole time, you know. . . . So, anyway, I guess that would be it. To walk your talk. Practice what you preach!

Coach #3 responded to the question "What leadership traits do you feel are most beneficial for an instructional coach to possess?"

> Integrity. Which would include the honesty, the confidentiality. Being sincere . . . lump it in.

Coach #3 continued, in response to the question "What specific actions did you take as an instructional coach that you felt were most effective?"

> Just kind of reassuring them that I'm not going to judge them or talk about them. A lot of it's trust-building, you know. And being sincere in it. Not like talking out my mouth and going over there and bad-mouthing them. . . . So, confidentiality. [The specific actions I took that I felt were most effective were] building relationships, being trustworthy, being honest, and being confidential.

William Bennett (1993) shared the following thoughts on honesty:

> To be honest is to be real, genuine, authentic, and bona fide. To be dishonest is to be partly feigned, forged, fake, or fictitious. Honesty expresses both self-respect and respect for others. Dishonesty fully respects neither oneself nor others. Honesty imbues lives with openness, reliability, and candor; it expresses a disposition

to live in the light. Dishonesty seeks shade, cover, or concealment. It is a disposition to live partly in the dark.

(p. 599)

Integrity is evidenced in the little things we do, as mentioned by Coach #9 in response to the question "What leadership traits do you feel are most beneficial for an instructional coach to possess?"

> Something else I think is important is follow-through. I think several of the . . . teachers that I've mentored have told me they've really appreciated that I've followed through. You know, because you have these pass-by-in-the-hallway conversations of "How's it going?" "Oh, great, but I've really wanted to do this and try this." And I'd say, "Oh, I can get that for you; I'll bring you that book so you can try that." And in the pass-by, you never know if it's going to happen or not. And, so, I just made a point to carry a little notepad with me, and when we had one of those fly-by conversations, I wrote it down so that I'd follow through on everything that I said I would do. And teachers told me they really appreciated that.

Trust is rooted on the "caring" side of the characteristics model, similar to the findings and writings of other authors. Gayle Gregory and Martha Kaufeldt (2015) listed trusting as one of seven "Caring Habits," and Stephen M. R. Covey (2006), in his book *The Speed of Trust*, listed four "Cores of Credibility," with the first two relating to the character of the individual, similar to the findings of my study (Frazier, 2014). Core 1 is integrity, which Covey explained in this way: "While integrity includes honesty, it's much more. It's integratedness. It's walking your talk. It's being congruent, inside and out. It's having the courage to act in accordance with your values and beliefs. Interestingly, most massive violations of trust are violations of integrity" (p. 56).

Knowing our values and beliefs is critical to being congruent. Part of the *Finding Home* process described in Chapter 6 is designed to help us clarify our internal world so that we can more intentionally align both our internal and external worlds, allowing us to become more fully integrated and congruent, as Covey (2006) explained.

Covey's Core of Credibility 2 has to do with our "motives, our agendas. . . . Trust grows when our motives are straightforward and based on mutual benefit—in other words, when we genuinely care not only for ourselves, but also for the people we interact with, lead, or serve. When we suspect a hidden agenda from someone or we don't believe they are acting in our best interests, we are suspicious about everything they say and do" (pp. 56–57).

Covey's Core 3 has to do with capabilities—or, as referred to in my study (Frazier, 2014), competency. Core 4, also related to competency, has to do with the results we produce, "our track record, our performance, our getting the right things done . . . our reputation" (Covey, 2006, p. 57). Knight (2016) wrote, "If we want to be trusted, we need to be people of character, who live in ways that others consider ethical. If you act in untrustworthy ways, you can't expect others to trust you. . . . We trust people who know what they are talking about and who deliver on what they promise" (pp. 194, 198).

The authors of the book *RESULTS Coaching* (Kee, Anderson, Dearing, Harris, & Shuster, 2010) reminded us there is a code of ethics for coaches: Coaches should know of and adhere to the International Coach Federation (ICF) Code of Ethics. Trust and confidentiality, then honesty and professionalism, are key pieces of effective coaching (Kee et al., 2010).

Character pieces come first when we are trying to build trust. This includes having integrity, which means living true to our values, walking our talk, doing what we say we are going to do, and in general being ethical, which includes being honest and confidential. Another necessity of building trust is learning to be a caring person, a person who serves others with pure intention, having their best interests at heart. When we come from a place of wishing only good for the teacher and aligning our communications and actions with that authentic caring, teachers can feel safe with us and can grow more quickly without debilitating fear.

We can build another layer of trust through increasing our competency as coaches. Not much good will come out of coaching interactions if the teacher can't trust the coach knows what he or she is talking about. In Chapter 7, when the TCT coach was working with Dachsa, the veteran teacher from India, the coach spent a lot of time learning about India, Dachsa's skill set, and the students from both countries before sharing any instructional support options. The coach's desire to listen and learn was centered in how much she cared for Dachsa and how much she wanted coaching support to result in success for Dachsa and her students.

Because of the coach's sincere desire to help Dachsa, she put in the extra work to be prepared and brought meaningful resources to this new and challenging situation. Our growth in competency as coaches is often dependent on how much we care about those we coach, which then translates into how motivated we are and how much work we are willing to do to best support each teacher. When we develop our empathy and caring to the point that it motivates us to reach higher and work harder, we can provide each teacher with the best coaching we are capable of.

Self-Trust

Have you ever had a gut instinct, or a little voice, or a thought that you should do something as you coach? *Trust it.* A while back, I was trying to figure out how to best support two young male teachers fairly new to teaching in a challenging environment. One was a relatively new teacher and a new dad who was up with babies at night and often felt exhausted, and the other was just beginning his career at a new school. They were young, exciting teammates working hard to develop systems and plans that would work for their students. Their students loved them, but some days teaching felt crazy hard!

One day, a strange thought popped into my head out of nowhere. It was to go buy them a pizza and take it to their school. I didn't have an appointment, and I knew if I acted on that thought right then, I would probably miss their lunch time, so it didn't make any sense. However, I decided to go with it. I went and bought the pizza, and when I arrived at the school, they had just returned from a field trip with their students. They were exhausted, and one of them hadn't brought a lunch. I don't think I have ever seen two happier young men!

A huge amount of trust was built that day between me and those wonderful teachers I had the privilege of coaching. I also increased my trust in myself as I acted on that surprising internal message. And do you think that, afterward, those teachers thought I was inspired? They seemed to care even more about listening to me, even though I'm sure I was "way old" in their books. This was especially exciting to me, because the thought hadn't arisen as the result of a rational process; it came out of the blue, and I had never taken a pizza to anyone I'd coached before. So, I trusted that it came from a higher source outside of me that was working within me. I had been working on trying to "Look Up," "Look In," and then "Look Out," as explained in Chapter 4. It was a little miracle.

Sometimes there are things we just know. Sometimes you just know you should do certain things for others—you know what feels right. Trust yourself, even if what you are thinking or feeling doesn't seem to make sense. Your unique gifts and insights matter and could positively impact others' lives and let them know they are being looked after. The best advice I've heard about acting on thoughts or feelings is that if it involves doing something good for someone, go with it, even if it seems out of the ordinary or inconvenient.

Reflect and Connect

GO FISH...COACH!

The following is a card game similar to "Go Fish," with scenarios coaches may face. The purpose of the game is to identify coaching interactions that inspire or discourage trust. First the instructions will be listed, and then the game cards will be shared. Feel free to copy the game cards (you can download the full-sized version from the book's companion website, https://resources.corwin.com/JoyofCoaching) and play the game during coach trainings.

1. Materials: Prepare card decks, and label three baskets for each group, with the words "I trust you," "I'm not so sure I trust you," and "I don't trust you."

2. Form groups of three to five people, and choose a dealer.

3. The dealer deals five cards face-down to each person and puts the rest face-down in a "Go Coach" pile.

   a. Each person looks at their cards and determines pairs. If group members have a match before the game begins, they discuss the match with the group and decide together into which basket the matching pair should be placed. (For example, a matching pair of "The Coach Shares So Much

Information That the Teacher Feels Overwhelmed" might go into the "I don't trust you" or the "I'm not so sure . . ." basket.) If some "Keep Calm and Listen to Your Coach" cards are matched, wait to address them later (see #4).

b. The game begins with the person to the dealer's left and proceeds clockwise.

c. The first person asks any player if he/she has a _____ (first player describes the picture on the card). If the person does have the card, that player gives the first player the matching card, and, after discussion, the group decides into which basket the match should be placed. (For example, a matching pair of "The Coach Notices the Teacher's Strengths" would likely go in the "I trust you" basket.) If the person who was asked if he/she had a certain card does not have the card, he or she says, "Go Coach!" The first person then draws the top card from the pile. If a match is then found, discussion ensues, and the match is placed into the appropriate basket. If a match is not found when the person draws from the card pile, the game continues, and the next person to the left takes a turn.

d. When a player runs out of cards, the game can be stopped and a discussion about all players' remaining cards can be had, or the group can continue until all cards are matched.

4. "Keep Calm and Listen to Your Coach" card: When this card is matched, the player who has the match leads a discussion to think of a coaching situation that either inspires or discourages trust, then the match is placed into the basket determined most appropriate by the group.

5. If your group decides to determine a winner, keep track of how many matching pairs were acquired by each player, and then pronounce the person with the most matches the Go Coach Champion!

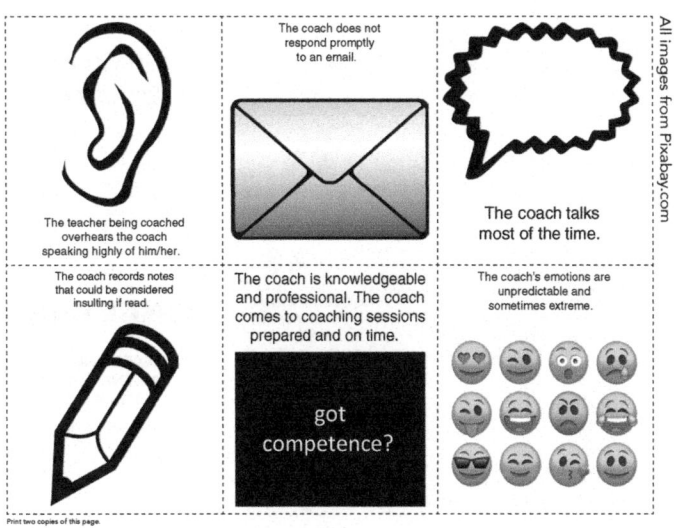

The coach takes the teacher's side when the teacher expresses a difference of opinion with another colleague or the principal during a coaching session, but doesn't support the teacher in the presence of the principal or colleague (two-faced).

The coach gossips or shares confidential information with the principal and/or colleagues following a coaching appointment.

The coach takes time to learn about the teacher and understand what motivates the teacher. Coaching is tailored accordingly.

The coach conveys confidence in the teacher's ability to be successful. The coach is committed to supporting the teacher's professional growth.

I believe in you

The coach focuses solely on the details of instructional practices and getting the job done. The coach does do not care about building a caring relationship with the teacher.

The coach focuses solely on relationships and does not see the value of doing the professional homework required to be competent.

I am uninformed and I am HAPPY

Print two copies of this page.

All images from Pixabay.com

The coach is organized. The coach has a plan for coaching processes and can find resources quickly.

ORGANIZED

The coach jumps from one idea to another and offers confusing and sometimes conflicting opinions and ideas.

WARNING

INDECISIVE

The coach regularly uses outdated resources and refers to personal experiences that may not be relevant to the teacher.

The coach interrupts, argues, blurts out information, or engages in side conversations when the teacher is speaking.

RUDE

The coach remains positive and can often provide timely wisdom, hope, and humor during challenging situations.

The teacher figures out the coach's aunt or uncle was sick one too many times (coach lies to avoid embarrassment at not following through, being late, forgetting an appointment, etc.).

Print two copies of this page.

All images from Pixabay.com

The coach recognizes and communicates the teacher's strengths.

The coach recognizes and communicates the teacher's strengths.

Go Coach! Directions

- Purpose: To identify coaching interactions that inspire or discourage trust
- General process: Acquire as many pairs of trusting/distrusting coaching scenarios as possible and after the group discussion, discard them into the "I trust you," "I'm not sure I trust you," or "I don't trust you," baskets

The coach shares so much information that the teacher feels overwhelmed.

The coach shares so much information that the teacher feels overwhelmed.

FINAL CARD

PLEASE READ THIS AT THE END OF THE GAME:

Because of you, teachers feel valued, confident, and successful. GO, you *incredible* COACH!

Print only one copy of this page.

All images from Pixabay.com

Make two copies of the Keep Calm cards (above) so three of your own coaching scenarios can be discussed. The Go Coach! torch cards are designed to be used as the back of all other cards, if desired.

 Available for download at **https://resources.corwin.com/JoyofCoaching**

Trustworthy Self-Assessment

1. Take this self-assessment before you set an intention to consciously find ways to become more trustworthy.

2. Implement some of the practical application ideas and/or trustworthy S.O.A.K. supports found below (or use some of your own ideas).

3. In a month or so, see whether you have been able to improve your thoughts, motivations, and behaviors surrounding the important coaching characteristic of becoming more trustworthy. Reference the following synonyms/specifics as you personally determine what trustworthiness is and determine how to make it a more conscious part of your daily life: integrity, confidentiality, honesty, ethical (Frazier, 2014).

	Strongly Disagree	Disagree	Neutral Not Sure	Agree	Strongly Agree
	1	2	3	4	5
I do what I say I am going to do.					
The life I live is ethical and congruent with my highest values. I do not lie, cheat, steal, gossip, or break confidences.					
I am the same person no matter where I am, what I'm doing, who is with me, or whether anyone is watching. I am not fake or two-faced.					
I am willing to be truthful and vulnerable, even if it might make me look less than perfect.					
I am service-oriented and wish the best for others. The caring and empathy I have for teachers I coach is evidenced in my willingness to listen and is a key motivator in my willingness to work hard and grow in my coaching capabilities.					
I am always looking for ways to authentically recognize and praise the positive things others do. I am not self-absorbed.					
Column Totals:					

Grand Total: _____

What totals mean: 26–30 = Trustworthy Rock Star, 21–25 = Very Trustworthy, 16–20 = Sort of Trustworthy, 11–15 = Some Trustworthy Pieces Are Happening, 6–10 = Better Step It Up, 0–5 = Would Being More Trustworthy Be a Helpful Goal to Set?

Practical Application Ideas for Trustworthy

Show Up

So basic. So necessary. If we say we will do something, be somewhere, or support something or someone, we must do it if we want to be trusted. This is where it becomes important to not overschedule ourselves or make promises we cannot act on. This can even be a thing with email. People start to wonder whether they can trust that we are interested in them or care about them when we don't seem to be showing up on the other end of the communications. But how can we keep up with all that? Maybe we can just send a note back to people saying something like "Thanks for your email. I just wanted you to know I care about what you have to say and will get back to you as soon as possible." I am trying to do something like this myself, so that people don't think I'm totally blowing them off if I can't respond immediately. Sometimes we just have to say, "I don't think I can get that done within that timeline," or note a scheduling conflict, or in some way try to let people know that not being able to do something they want us to do has nothing to do with us not caring about them or their needs. This is hard, because we all prioritize our lives and work, but it's better to say, "I'm so sorry, I won't be able to do that," rather than to say, "Yes, I would love to," and then not show up. Covey (2006) described this idea of "showing up" this way in his list of 13 behaviors that are needed to build trust: "Keep Commitments is the 'Big Kahuna' of all behaviors. It's the quickest way to build trust in any relationship . . . [and] its *opposite* . . . is, without question, the quickest way to destroy trust. . . . When you make a commitment, you build hope; when you keep it, you build trust" (p. 222).

Be Ethical

Technology has made its way into almost every nook and cranny of our lives. It speeds up and allows us more variety in our communication, expands our ability to access information, and in some ways demands authenticity and transparency. In the past, I have tried to make sure to have my makeup on and hair done when I go out or am on the computer video camera, but I can't keep up with it all the time anymore. If I worried about having my hair done every time I wanted to talk with my kids on Google Hangouts or Marco Polo, I would be a crazy person. Our "realness" these days is often undeniable, and the knowledge that our bad-hair days (and many other things) will likely be documented on camera can make us feel vulnerable.

If people are unethical, it is likely at some point they will be caught. There is no guarantee that moments of dishonesty, breaches of integrity or confidentiality, or situations when people lack common sense will be kept secret. This may be a good side effect of technology, because people can't get away with much these days. It seems there's always a camera, a viewing history, or some device that could easily record our least impressive moments—then those moments could be shared on Facebook, with a variety of agencies, or on some other platform.

As a flight attendant said on a recent flight I took to Las Vegas, "What happens in Vegas . . . [normally the end of this phrase would be 'stays in Vegas'] ends up on Facebook, Instagram, or Twitter and is recorded forever for all to see!" Credibility can be damaged in an instant, and fewer people will trust us if we have posted or done questionable things that are electronically documented. We all want to avoid doing stupid things; we can learn to be the kind of people whose lives would be able to withstand and even welcome transparency.

Conclusion

Coaching is a demanding job, because it requires us to become the kind of people who can be trusted in order to be effective. We aren't going to be able to skate by and be *sort of* ethical; we really do have to be ethical—we must be honest, have integrity, and keep confidences in order to be great coaches. We can do so much, so quickly, in this role once trust has been established and when we continually act in ways that keep trust alive with each person we coach. When we act in ways that show we can be trusted, teachers can be at peace with our support, because they know their hearts and reputations are being held safe with us and that we are going to do what we say we'll do. Thank you for being willing to take on the role of coach, a role that encourages and offers opportunities for internal refinement, inspiring us to become better people as we work to more effectively support and serve teachers and students.

TRUSTWORTHY ~S.O.A.K.~ — Sometimes learning penetrates best when we are relaxed and not trying too hard to make it happen.

Stress-free Opportunities to Absorb Knowledge   Choose what works for you. (Like a "Trustworthy" bath bomb infused with personalized nutrients)

Quotes	Music	Statements affirmations	Books poetry stories	Art	Videos movies	Movement other ideas
"To thine own self be true, and it must follow, as the night the day, thou canst not then be false to any man." —Polonius, in Hamlet (act I, scene 3)	"Get Together" The Youngbloods	For coaches: Because of the things I do, the people I coach have evidence that I care and have their best interests at heart.	"The Boy Who Cried Wolf" Aesop	Give and Take (Bronze sculpture) Lorenzo Quinn	How to Build (and Rebuild) Trust (TED Talk) Frances Frei	Plank Pose
"Trust yourself, you know more than you think you do." —Benjamin Spock	"His Eye Is on the Sparrow" (Gospel hymn) Civilla Martin and Charles H. Gabriel	I spend time thinking about the teachers I work with and how to best support them. I trust myself and act on service-oriented thoughts and feelings.	"The Honest Woodman" Jean de La Fontaine	Sweet Thunder Peter Chilelli	Liberty Horse Training: Heartland Amy and Spartan on YouTube	5 Ways to Build Trust With Your Body Language: Rhett Power
"Trust is earned when actions meet words." —Chris Butler	"I'll Be There" Jackson 5	I am dedicated to becoming more ethical, honest, and full of integrity.	The Speed of Trust Stephen M. R. Covey	Sunset Climbers Posters and Art Prints barewalls.com		• Hold eye contact. • Keep good posture: Stand up or sit up straight and lean in to listen, arms in an open position.
"The glue that holds all relationships together—including the relationship between the leader and the led—is trust, and trust is based on integrity." —Brian Tracy	"I'm Already There" Lonestar	I keep my word. I follow through on what I say I will do.	Pinocchio Carlo Lorenzini	First Steps Vincent van Gogh	Frozen (2013)	• Smile: Show some teeth, let your smile fade slowly. • Mind your hands: Give firm handshakes, avoid excessive movements or pockets, keep your hands where people can see them.
	"I'll Stand by You" The Pretenders	For teachers:	"The Indian Cinderella" Cyrus Macmillan		Gandhi (1982)	• Be a mirror: Show empathy; reflect the same emotions to show you're listening and you care, but don't copy exactly.
	"Consider the Lilies" Roger Hoffman	When I tell my students I will do something, they can trust it will happen.	"The Story of Regulus" James Baldwin	Siblings Marisa Gabetta	Homeward Bound: The Incredible Journey (1993)	
"If you sense that I am being authentic, that I have real rigor in my logic, and if you believe that my empathy is directed towards you, you are far more likely to trust me." —Frances Frei	"Before He Cheats" Carrie Underwood	I regularly do little things for students, to ensure they know I care and am thinking about them.	"Honest Abe" Horatio Alger	Rowing Sparkles Kip Decker		Oil: German chamomile
	"Trust in Me" Etta James		"The Pied Piper of Hamelin" Joseph Jacobs	Cirque du Soleil's Trapeze Artists Catching Google Search/ Images	Up (2009)	Stone: sodalite
	"Best Friend" Queen	I listen to and trust my heart and mind, then act in ways I feel would be best for students and others.	The Thousandth Man Rudyard Kipling		A Man for All Seasons (1966)	Color: purple

When trust exists, there is learning, joy, and love. (Knight, 2016, p. 188)

215

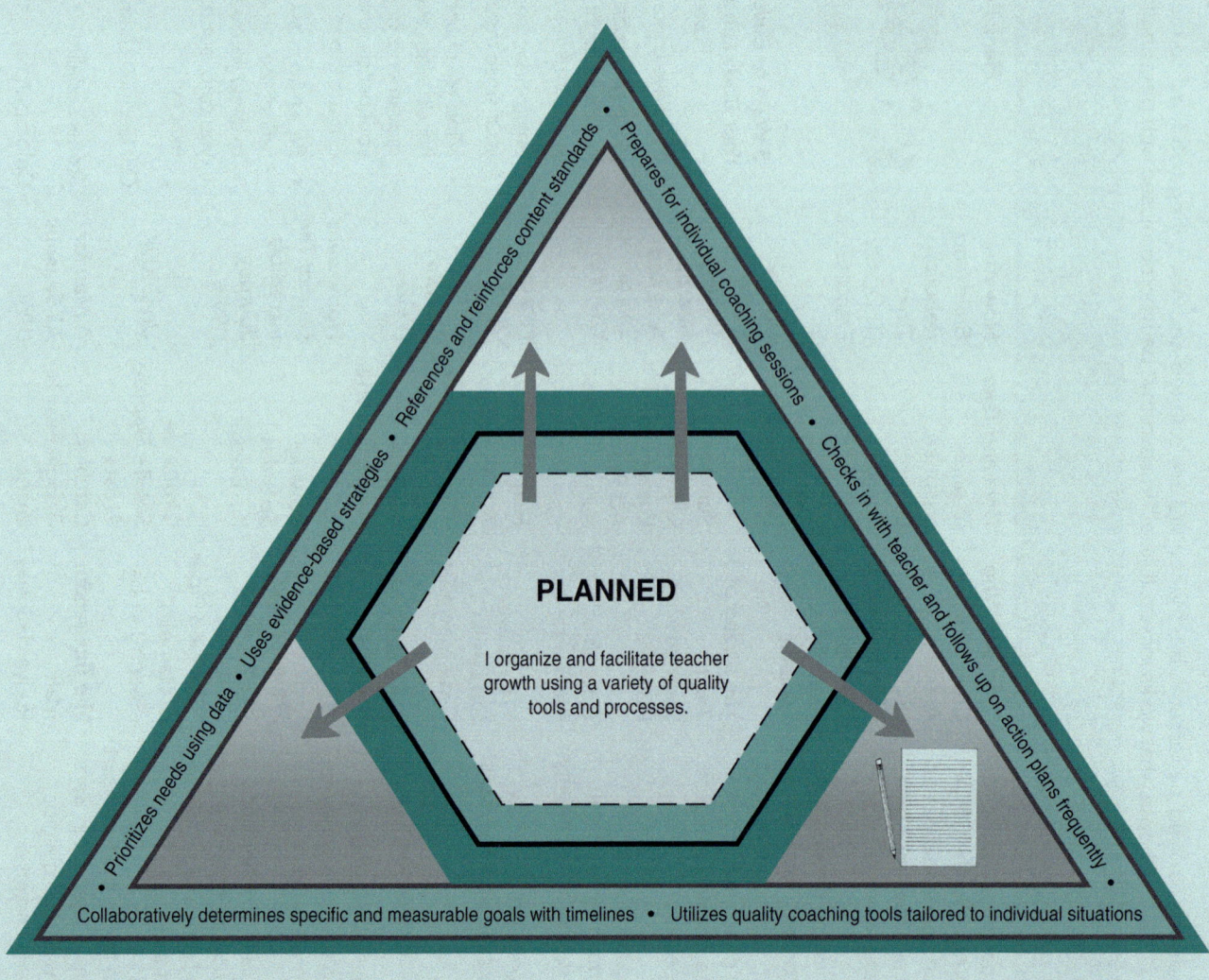

PLANNED

I organize and facilitate teacher growth using a variety of quality tools and processes.

References and reinforces content standards • Prepares for individual coaching sessions • Checks in with teacher and follows up on action plans frequently •

• Prioritizes needs using data • Uses evidence-based strategies •

Collaboratively determines specific and measurable goals with timelines • Utilizes quality coaching tools tailored to individual situations

The teachers I coach are confident I will come to each coaching session with personalized resources and coaching structures that are relevant and meaningful. I use targeted data collection to inform individual coaching goals and to provide reportable feedback on coaching effectiveness.

Planned

Thoughtful, personalized preparation honors those we coach, organizes our thoughts and resources, and maximizes collaborative time.

The sections in this chapter are explanations of a four-page planner created for coaches. There are also a few other support tools included later in the chapter. I developed this coaching planner to organize coaching interactions during the summer of 2014. Though I organized and created this process, the former coaching program coordinator Judy Williams's planning ideas were interwoven into its organization and structure, and it has been refined over the years through collaboration with current coaches Nancy Shanklin, Kate Shannon, and Jennifer Gonzales. Some of Jim Knight's coaching questions were also included (with permission), along with a conscious choice to include the components of the S.M.A.R.T. goal process (Doran, 1981; Meyer, 2003), which encourages setting goals that are specific, measurable, attainable, relevant, and time-bound.

The processes shared in this chapter have been vetted and improved over time and were recently found to have contributed to a significant increase in growth in teacher competency and job satisfaction compared to control groups (Frazier, 2018). The forms can be organized in an electronic format so that there is more space to answer the questions, or they can be filled in by hand. I prefer filling them in by hand, because it seems to create less of a barrier when juggling listening to the teacher and documenting information during coaching sessions. The forms are organized to conserve space and yet access as much information as possible, so there are places where the coach just circles or checks items. Responses may need to be simplified by using key words or phrases, since space is limited, but in actual practice this has worked out. It does help to use a mechanical pencil or fine-point pen. I also prefer variety in the organization and in how the forms look (different types of boxes, lists, lines, check boxes, circling, places to record), but they could be redesigned to fit the content and preferences of other users.

The four pages for basic coach planning can be easily and efficiently accessed when printed on an 11 × 17 piece of cardstock folded in half so that each page can be flipped to easily, and extra action plans with different goals can be kept inside the folded cardstock on top of the initial action plan and goal. Here is the page order that has worked for us:

1) Teacher Information | Coach Planning

2) Human Connection

3) Action Plan

4) Tracking

First there will be an explanation of the page, then an exemplar page showing how that page could be filled out. Blank planner pages can be seen at the end of the chapter and are available for download as full-sized, single pages at https://resources.corwin.com/JoyofCoaching. Example planner pages are filled out for a fictitious teacher named Jo Cotton. Her situation, and the information recorded about her, are a mixture of the situations of many middle-school teachers I have worked with over the past 10 years and represent some of their challenges and successes.

Jo was an experienced middle-school teacher with eight years under her belt. Her classroom management was reasonable, but lately she had been feeling a little off her game. Students didn't seem to be interested in math concepts with the level of enthusiasm she would have liked them to have, and their confidence regarding their ability to understand mathematical concepts was fragile. Her lessons didn't seem very engaging, as evidenced by the lack of instructional variety and relatively low student engagement found in the observation data recorded on the Time Distribution Tool (TDT). She decided to work with a coach to help her plan more engaging lessons, with the hope that student engagement would increase.

To complicate the situation, Jo had recently suffered a head injury that was slightly impacting her ability to process information quickly without becoming overwhelmed. She needed help organizing her teaching in a more structured and straightforward way that would allow her to insert high-engagement strategies in an intentional, organized manner. You will be able to see Jo's process while reading through the forms.

Not every action necessary to complete planning and implementing a highly engaging unit is recorded on the Action Plan, but the skeleton structure is there, and the rest happens as a matter of course during the coaching sessions. Note: If you decide to use this process, don't feel as though everything has to be perfect. If you do, you could find yourself stuck in "Analysis Paralyis." The main thing is that you have a plan that makes sense, is measurable, and has most steps identified, with timelines for completion.

Page 1: Teacher Information and Coach Planning

Each heading below refers to a specific section of Page 1 of the planner.

Professional Info | Contact Info

As coaching begins, it is helpful to gather basic professional information about the teacher. This section is for the coach to record basic information about the teacher, the teacher's job situation, where and when coaching sessions could occur, the preferred frequency of the coaching, and what the teacher would like to work on. Before the initial coaching conference, if possible, the coach should observe a class taught by the teacher. This may give the coach a better understanding of the situation and provide useful student data to refer to when the teacher and coach determine the area of assistance and identify a specific goal. The initial discussion provides general information and is mostly about listening intently to figure out what the teacher feels the real need is and where he or she would like support.

During the first coaching meeting, the coach will administer an Instructional Survey with 22 questions in five areas of teaching practice (Planning, Assessment, Instruction, Classroom Environment, and Professional Growth; the survey is included in this chapter). This survey serves as a pre/post self-assessment tool and provides data to capture perceived teacher growth over time. It includes a 0–10 scale for 22 areas of teaching practice, indicating current levels of evidence of implementation for each topic. On the right side of the survey is an area for the coach and the teacher to note goal areas to target if certain areas showed lower amounts of evidence than others. Item 23 is a 0–10 rating of job satisfaction. This item will provide coaches with valuable information and can be considered as more data to supplement the Human Connection page, which is Page 2 of the planner.

As we get further into the details of human connection, review student-level data, discuss the results of the Instructional Survey, and implement the specifics of goal-setting, the details of what needs to be accomplished and how it will be accomplished through the coaching process will be made clear.

Assistance Menu | Coaching Focus

During the discussion about what the teacher would like to work on, it might be helpful for the coach to share an assistance menu of what other teachers have requested. This menu could include topics the coach or coaching program has successfully addressed in the past, or perhaps they could be the "instructional playbook" topics determined with accompanying checklists developed by the coaching team, as Jim Knight (2013) suggested. You can find a model playbook with checklists at https://www.instructionalcoaching.com/wp-content/uploads/2016/03/Instructional-Playbook.v4.pdf.

In Jo's case, she wanted to work on improving her daily and unit lesson planning to increase student engagement. You will notice on the exemplar that "Standards-based Lesson Planning" is checked, under which "Daily" and "Unit Development" are marked.

Coach Planning

This is a checklist of coaching paperwork and processes to help the coach remember to follow the process, record what has been completed, and collect relevant information and data.

Coaching Resources

This section is organized to facilitate coach planning. Meaningful resources are listed, and the coach can check the boxes next to any of them that might be helpful for this teacher.

Instructional Survey

Date: _____ | Pre: _____ Post: _____ | Teacher Name: _____ | Content Area(s): _____

Grade Level(s): _____ Education Level: BS MA MA2 PhD   Years of Teaching Experience: _____

Categories — For each numbered topic, place an X in the appropriate column (0–10). 0 indicates **No Evidence** of implementation, and 10 indicates **Strong Evidence** of implementation.	0 No Evidence	1	2	3	4	5 Limited Evidence	6	7	8	9	10 Consistent Strong Evidence	Goal Areas to Target
Planning												
1. Long-range planning with sequencing												
2. Alignment with state standards and district curriculum												
3. Learning targets clearly defined and supported with learning activities												
Instruction												
4. Context of the lesson (where individual lessons fit within a unit of study)												
5. Content knowledge and presentation												
6. Appropriateness of the lesson (ability levels/pacing/child development)												
7. Use of technology												
8. Effectiveness of instructional strategies												
9. Strategies for differentiation of instruction												
10. Questioning techniques												
Assessment												
11. Development of appropriate assessment (Formative/Interim/Summative)												
12. Meaningful student work assignments												
13. Quality of feedback to students												
14. Analysis of assessment results												
15. Readjustment of instruction based on feedback												

Teacher Name: _____

Pre: _____ **Post:** _____

Categories For each numbered topic, place an **X** in the appropriate column (0–10). 0 indicates **No Evidence** of implementation, and 10 indicates **Strong Evidence** of implementation.	0 No Evidence	1	2	3	4	5 Limited Evidence	6	7	8	9	10 Consistent Strong Evidence	Goal Areas to Target
Classroom Environment												
16. Expectations and procedures in place/consistently implemented												
17. Expectations and belief for student success												
18. Student interest and participation												
19. Positive classroom climate												
Professional Growth												
20. Acquirement and alignment of professional development												
21. Implementation of professional development												
22. Reflection on teaching practice for improvement												
TOTALS												

Instructional Survey Results: (Total number of points divided by 220 = %) Pre-Support: _____ % **Post-Support:** _____ %

	0 I want to quit.	1	2	3	4	5	6	7	8	9	10 I love my job; I wouldn't want to do anything else.
Job Satisfaction											
23. Place an **X** in this row underneath the number that most accurately reflects your current level of overall job satisfaction.											

Job Satisfaction Results: Pre-Support: _____ **Post-Support:** _____

Instructional Coaching 4 Page Planner

1. Teacher Information | Coaching Planning

Date: 3-8-19   Name: Jo Cotton   School: Washington Middle   Grade Level(s): 7th   Content: Math   Coach: Rebecca

Professional Info | Contact Info

Number of Years Teaching in/out of District: 6 / 2

Teacher Certification: License Type (circle): Initial [Professional] Master

Induction this year? Y (N)   Probationary (1, 2, 3): _____ Non-Probationary: X

E-mail: jcotton@d60.org | Phone: Classroom/Office: 619-765-4321

Home/Cell: 619-624-1631 | Room #(s): 36; 121

Planning Time(s): 10:25-11:15; 3:05-3:55 | Coaching Frequency: 2X per week

Observation Time(s): 9:30-10:20; 2:10-3:00

Assistance Menu | Coaching Focus

□ Analyzing Student Work-Processes/Rubrics
□ Assessment: Checks for Understanding, Formative, Interim, Summative
□ Classroom Management-Presence/Planning/Procedures
□ Content Support for Specific Programs
□ Data Analysis
□ Differentiation/Modifications for-SPED/GT/ELL/Other: _____
□ Effective Questioning/Rigor/Depth of Knowledge (DOK)
□ PLC Support
□ Professionalism-Basics/Affect/Building Relationships
✓ Standards-based Lesson Planning:
   [Daily: Standards | Learning Targets | Instructional Delivery Choices with Rationale | Formative Assessment]
   [Unit Development: Sequencing | Assessments] Yearly Sequencing - Curriculum Mapping
□ Student Engagement/Motivation
□ Teacher Evaluation: Professional Preparation-Teacher Quality Standards/Measures of Student Learning
□ Workshop Format with Team: Topic _____

Other Area(s) of Assistance Requested: _____

Coach Planning

✓ Professional Agreement reviewed and signed

✓ Teacher Information [p. 1-this page] completed

✓ Pre-Instructional Survey completed by teacher

✓ Human Connection [p. 2] most applicable sections completed over time

✓ Action Plan [p. 3] *Working Document*

□ Keep up with tracking Goals/Action Steps progress, Instructional Time, Student Engagement, and Positive Support or "Lift" Idea actions on the Tracking page [p.4]

□ Use Time Distribution Tool during observations for individual teacher and program data collection

□ Post-Instructional Survey completed by teacher

Coaching Resources

□ Analyzing Student Work Processes
□ Classroom Management Self-Assessment and Checklists Forms
□ Classroom Management System Exemplars
□ Collegial Observation Form □ Conference Documentation Form □ Cultural Understanding & Bias Process □ Data Collection Tools & Checklists □ Developing Rubrics Tool □ Unpacking Standards Process & Form □ DOK Flip Folder □ Educator Effectiveness Video □ Effective Questioning Analysis and Creation Processes □ Next Generation Learning resources □ Professional Portfolio □ Socratic Seminar ✓ Standards-based Lesson Planning Color-coded Process ✓ Student Engagement resources □ Student Survey Form □ Teacher/Coach Observations Over Time Form □ Video Analysis Observation Form □ Video Notification Forms □ Workshop Format Template

□ Instructional Videos and Websites:
_____
_____

□ Other Resources, Checklists, Strategies:
Review previews plans - discuss what worked and what didn't; Choose 1 unit of study to begin with
_____

Assemble a standards notebook; Provide to with exemplars of different planning processes to inform planning choices along with student interest and learning modality surveys; Schedule a half day session if possible to get a solid start; Review 7th grade math curriculum with applicable assessments.

Included in this section is a place for the coach to identify useful videos, websites, checklists, or instructional strategies that might benefit the teacher.

Notice that in the example for Page 1, the coach (Rebecca) identified the need to review previous plans and choose one unit of study.

Notes

The Notes section is a continuation of coach planning and allows some space for the coach to add notes that might be helpful while personalizing support for this teacher.

In the example, the coach recorded notes to remind her to collaboratively assemble a standards notebook; provide exemplars of different planning processes; schedule a half-day coaching session, if possible, to get a solid start; survey students to determine their interests and learning modality preferences; and review the seventh-grade math curriculum with applicable assessments.

Page 2: Human Connection

While researching coaching authors, looking at the evaluations of coaches, and scripting and analyzing qualitative interviews, I realized that TCT (which was mostly focused on analyzing observational data and setting measurable goals to meet student and teacher needs) was lacking a way to address and support the needs of the whole person: not just the data and the processes, but the human and emotional components that really drive whether a person is going to be successful in the long term (Goleman, 2006).

The intangibles (e.g., the willingness to persevere, the level of emotional resilience, the depth of dedication to students and the profession, and the self-knowledge of what teachers really want to accomplish with students and what they want their long-term influence to be) were not included in our typical coaching protocols. As a result of the research this book was based upon (see the introduction), an emphasis on human connection, including specific protocols, was added to our coaching processes. Many of these additions are found on this Human Connection planning page or form. Each category on the form is discussed in the following paragraphs.

Identifying Teacher Motivation and Purpose: The Touchstone Process

This process was designed to help teachers identify and connect with their core purpose and motivation(s) for teaching. Through this process, a heartfelt emotion, desire, or feeling they want to share with students is made clear. To define and share with a coach the personally significant reason a teacher gets up every morning and takes on the task of teaching is powerful for both the teacher and the coach.

In many ways, we can decide what students take away from our interactions with them by aligning our behavior and actions to our best intentions and heartfelt desires. As mentioned in the introduction, when I was a teacher I created a personal creed to "be a haven of happiness and a harbor of hope and healing" for my students. When Darian (a former student of mine) sent me an email many years later saying that our class had been a haven for her, I was reminded of the power of personal clarity and intention.

If teachers are deliberate about what they want to create and what messages they want to send to their students, students can be influenced in ways that will build both academic and emotional strength to move forward and keep trying, even during difficult times. We are currently facing a deepening crisis in the United States: Our children are struggling emotionally; the suicide and attempted suicide rates are devastating. A recent article in the *New York Times* (Klass, 2018) reported a marked increase (almost triple) in the number of suicide-related hospital visits between 2008 and 2015. Central to our cause as coaches should be helping teachers intentionally create the best possible emotionally healthy *and* academically engaging experiences for students.

It is also much easier for us as teachers and coaches to handle stressful and frustrating situations, exhaustion, unexpected and hard-to-understand behaviors, and at times seemingly meaningless demands on our time when we are coming from a place of purposefully living each moment of our day to produce a meaningful outcome. This idea was explored in depth in Chapter 6.

Coaching is also about helping teachers with what they need most, so that they can be their best for students. If we can identify and support core individual teacher needs, other issues will take care of themselves. Finding out what teachers would like to have in their lives to help support them as they work to realize their highest hopes for students helps coaches know how meaningful support can be offered. Having teachers identify a current need, want, or desire that will help them achieve their purpose with students can supply coaches with information that will allow them to be of service in ways they may not have considered. If a teacher is open about difficult concerns that are beyond the scope of the coaching role (we are not certified counselors, medical doctors, matchmakers, or referees), the coach should listen; show empathy; let the teacher know that it is the human condition to struggle at times with difficult situations that come into our lives; and share knowledge of appropriate resources.

Learning Modality Preferences

A simple learning modality preference survey can provide the coach with useful information about how to organize, create, or structure coaching resources for teachers. For instance, working on lesson planning with a teacher who shares a preference for visual and kinesthetic learning would mean making coaching choices consistent with that preference (e.g., choosing a color-coded planning process with posters and sticky notes rather than an electronic planning template).

Personality Information

Recording the results of personality tests the teacher has already taken or any survey information you might like to use can provide helpful insights. Jane Kise's book *Differentiated Coaching* (both editions; 2006, 2017), is organized using the Myers-Briggs four-letter personality type as a trusted framework to provide useful insights for both the teacher and the coach. Kise masterfully shares specific ways for coaches to effectively interact with teachers when taking into consideration the personality type of the teacher and the coach. Sometimes districts will have personality identification supports (Leadership Blueprint, Emergenetics, Teach With Your Strengths, What Color is Your Parachute, Hexaco, The Enneagram, etc.) intended to provide a common language or understanding, to encourage positive collaborative interactions.

"Getting to Know You" Questions and Information

Next on the Human Connection form, you will see four small rectangular boxes with questions/categories. Within these boxes, the coach may record brief notes, a quick summary, or key words to address the following questions and categories:

- Where do you see yourself in five years?

- What was your favorite childhood dream?

- Hobbies/Interests | Likes/Dislikes

- Personal/Family Info

Ideas

This section serves to provide support if the coach can't think of specifics to ask and/or if teachers are stumped and don't have any ideas to share about themselves. It's not always easy to come up with questions or topics on the fly that will provide interesting information about the teacher that a coach might find helpful. Hence, these hints!

Self-Care

We all know we feel better and function better in any situation when we are taking care of ourselves. The importance of eating nutritious foods, drinking lots of water, getting enough sleep, exercising, and having good family and social relationships cannot be overestimated. Self-care is our first line of defense when we feel overwhelmed or incredibly challenged. However, it is often overlooked or not viewed as central to our ability to function well at work. This area can be tricky to address, but for some teachers, getting a handle on taking care of themselves can greatly enhance their success in the classroom.

Is there anything else you think I ought to know as your coach?

This question has proven to be a very easy way to "check in to see if I've missed anything important" when coaches are about to finish collecting Human Connection information.

Teachers will sometimes share things the coach would never have thought to ask about. Incredible insight into challenging circumstances or out-of-the-box concerns may be shared when this question is asked. Here are a few real-life examples:

- "When I was a kid, I had trouble with relationships, like I didn't fit in or kids didn't like me or something [and it seems this is happening now as well]."

- "I was recently diagnosed with cancer."

- "I am in the middle of a divorce and am having trouble functioning."

- "I have a special-needs child who is very ill, and I am having to miss a lot of work."

When teachers are willing to share important parts of their lives that may be affecting their teaching, coaches can access resources and structure coaching that is tailored to individual needs.

Coach Reflection

This is an opportunity for the coach to pause and consider the human connection information collected, then think through how to use the information to best meet the individual teacher's needs.

If there isn't sufficient time to fill out every section of the Human Connection page during the initial coaching session, suggested priorities would be (1) the "touchstone" process, (2) learning preferences, (3) two questions: "Where do you see yourself in five years?" and "Is there anything else you think I ought to know as your coach?," and (4) coach reflection. The Human Connection page could also be filled out a section at a time, over a few coaching sessions, rather than all at once during the initial meeting.

Jo picked "confidence" as her core desire for students to gain from her interactions with them, and her desire for herself to support her students gaining more confidence was to have more patience. Other useful information gleaned from the Human Connection form included the insight that Jo wanted to become an administrator, she preferred information presented in kinesthetic and visual ways, did not like people being late, and was having some trouble processing quickly, as noted above.

While reflecting on what she had learned from Jo's responses, Jo's coach wrote some notes to help guide her coaching. These notes included suggesting the use of a color-coded planning process with sticky notes to address Jo's learning modality preferences, her compass personality type (detail oriented) and to provide a simple planning structure to help with processing challenges due to Jo's head injury (which was caused by a car accident). Other notes included researching ways to help students feel confident in both math and life and preparing a Hawaiian "patience" quote for her desk. The coach also made a note not to be late and to look up the characteristics of Jo's Myers-Briggs personality type.

2. Human Connection

Date: **3-8-19** Teacher Name: **Jo Cotton** School: **Washington** Grade Level(s): **7th** Content: **Math** Coach: **Rebecca**
School (cont.): **Middle**

Identifying Teacher Motivation and Purpose: *The Touchstone Process*

☑ **#1. For Teacher's Students:** Ask teacher to, "Choose a word written on the stones below (or use real stones), and/or write a word of your own that best captures what you would like your students to take away from, gain, feel, or incorporate into their lives as a result of your teaching, influence, or interactions with them this year." **Teacher's core emotion/desire/feeling to share with students: confidence**

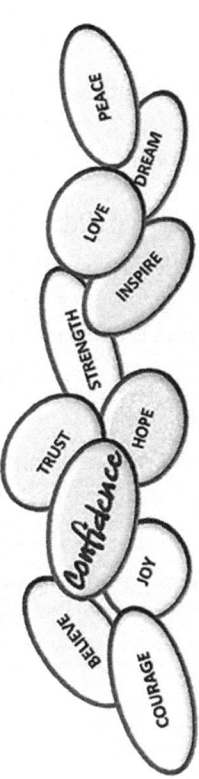

BELIEVE · COURAGE · JOY · Confidence · TRUST · HOPE · STRENGTH · LOVE · INSPIRE · DREAM · PEACE

Other Word Ideas: Humor, Organization, Creativity, Trust, Connection, Gentleness, Passion, Caring, Flexible, Serenity, Plan, Health, Kindness, Communication, Faith, Competency, Happiness, Gratitude, Knowledge, Confidence, Content Mastery, Authenticity

☑ **# 2. For Teacher:** "Choose a word on the stones (or think of one) that best describes something you would like to have in your life right now that could help increase your ability to convey choice/stone #1 to your students: **Patience**
Teacher's Support Choice to make her/his core desire for these students happen: **Kinesthetic & Visual**

☑ **Learning Modality Preferences:** **Kinesthetic & Visual**

☑ **Personality Information:** Record results of surveys already taken or administer one and record results in the table below: *Ideas:* ☐ Myers-Briggs; ☐ Multiple Intelligences; ☐ Emergenetics; ☐ North, South, East, West-Compass Personality Test; ☐ Other

Compass	Myers-Briggs
West (detail oriented)	ISTJ

☐ **Is there anything else you think I ought to know as your coach?**
Recent car accident, concussion, slower processing than normal

☐ **Coach Reflection:** Knowing this information, how could you tailor your coaching to meet this teacher's individual needs?
Suggest using a color-coded planning process with sticky notes to address Jo's learning modality preferences, compass type and provide a simple structure to help with processing challenges. Research ways to help students feel confident in both math and life. Prepare a Hawaiian "Patience" quote for her desk. Don't be late! Look up ISTJ in Kise's book. Differentiated Coaching.

Self-Care:

What works, what would you like to do?

- Exercise
- Eat Healthy
- (Be In Nature)
- Listen to Music
- Spend Time with Family and Friends
- (Read)
- Other Ideas:
  Spend time w/sister
  Drink More Water!

Ideas:

Personal/Family: Birth order, siblings, husband/wife, children, grandchildren, places lived, places visited, favorite memories, etc.

Hobbies/Interests: Music, sports, drama, games-board/video, collections, nature, reading traveling, computers, motorcycles, etc.

Likes/Dislikes: Food, what people do, houses, books, landscaping, clothes, gifts, leaders, stores, restaurants, etc.

Where do you see yourself in 5 years?
Being a Principal

What was your favorite childhood dream?
To become an astronaut and build own spaceship

Hobbies/Interests/Likes/Dislikes:
+ Biking | Piano | Food
− People being late

Personal/Family Info:
3 children
Grew up in Hawaii;
misses it

Page 3: Action Plan

As mentioned, if possible, before the initial coaching session, the coach and teacher would benefit from the coach observing a class the teacher would appreciate information about. Doing this gives the coach a better understanding of the situation and provides useful data to refer to when collaboratively determining a measurable goal.

As the coach begins collaboratively setting goals with the teacher, a blank copy of the Action Plan is provided to the teacher so that he or she can write goals and action steps alongside the coach while the plan is being developed. This helps teachers participate directly in the goal-setting process and leaves them with a record of the plan in their own words. Providing or suggesting the use of a notebook to help teachers organize action plans, notes, coaching information, and resources provided has been a good addition to TCT's coaching practice.

Goal

This box is for numbering the goals (1, 2, 3 . . .). There are also two words above the goal box, with small boxes to check, to help remind the coach and the teacher to write specific and measurable goals.

Questions to Consider

- What have you already tried?

- What student needs can be addressed by setting this goal?

- How do you want to grow as an educator?

- What teacher quality standards will this goal address (this section would align with your state/district teacher-evaluation structures)?

- On a scale of 1 (low) to 5 (high), how much would it matter if you met this goal? (Knight et al., 2015)

Goal Attainment Measure: How will I know I have achieved this goal?

Ideas to Consider:

- Teacher choice of data collected and compared over time

- Pre/Post video analyses

- Observation data

- Pre/Post student assessments

- Pre/Post pictures

- Pre/Post surveys

- Other Ideas

Basic to quality coaching are relevant goals organized and monitored so that levels of growth and completion can be determined. Determining goals with a predetermined plan of how implementation of the goal will be measured and how and when completion will be determined establishes the necessary parameters for coaching to be a documented successful professional growth experience.

Jo's goal was to plan and implement an engaging unit that would increase student engagement by at least 10%.

Her measure was to compare a student-engagement percentage previous to the implementation of the planned unit to the average percentage of engagement during three random observations by her coach during unit implementation.

Action Steps/Strategies to Implement

In this section, the coach first enters the step in the shaded area. Then the coach enters the date on which this step is planned to be completed in the box on the left. Later, when the step is completed, the coach dates and checks the box on the right.

The action steps are organized A–F. If Goal 1 had three action steps, they would be noted and tracked on Page 4 as 1A, 1B, and 1C. If Goal 2 (on another copy of the Action Plan kept inside the four-page planner) had four action steps, they would be noted and tracked as 2A, 2B, 2C, and 2D. Some goals require more action steps, some less. The coach can help the teacher organize the goal into a reasonable number of steps. Some teachers like bigger goals, with lots of action steps; others prefer smaller goals, with just a few action steps. A teacher might have one big goal organized with a lot of action steps and then another goal with just a few steps. The goal itself and how the measure of successful completion will be determined often drives the number of action steps needed. Working with a coach to collaboratively decide on the specific action steps needed to reach a goal is one of the main reasons teachers ask for coaching. The Action Plan is where the *how* comes alive!

Jo had one goal with six action steps. The action steps were recorded, and planned dates for implementation of action steps were scheduled. However, sometimes it took longer than originally planned to complete the step (note that action step 1A was scheduled to be completed on 3/18 but was not completed until 3/21).

Sometimes our plans for completion dates get interrupted, but keeping track of when we are planning to accomplish something and sticking with the action step until it happens—whether on time or a bit later—encourages both coaches and teachers to keep working toward completion, even if unforeseen circumstances get in the way. With all the details and unexpected things teachers are tasked/asked/required to make happen, too many goals important to the teacher can be given up on and forgotten. When the teacher and the coach regularly review the collaboratively determined action steps, and address them with both tenacity and helpful flexibility when needed, action steps and goals will be accomplished! The initial planned date for completion is recorded in the box to the left of the action step; then, when the action step is completed, the date is recorded and the action step checked off the list in the two-part box on the right of the action step. Evidence of completion is also considered.

Notes

This section is for the coach to write any notes that might be helpful. It includes (as do the other pages in the planner) a disclaimer that coaching notes are not to be used as evidence for teacher evaluations. When a coaching program is nonevaluative and confidential, notes are not shared with administrators unless the teacher requests it, in which case the coach, the administrator, and the teacher would meet to share teacher data and progress. Structuring coaching in this way helps teachers feel safe and supported while adjusting their instructional practice in a risk-free environment.

Completion Evidence of Action Steps

This section contains space for the coach to write how he or she checked in on completion of action steps A–F. This section helps the coach remember to check in with the teacher on action-step details leading to goal completion, so that evidence of progress can be noted and small successes celebrated. Most of us are terrible about celebrating small successes in education, probably because many of them are not documented, so we are on to the next thing and forget that something good happened. Documenting progress at least helps us pause for a second and be happy we are moving in a positive direction.

Goal Attainment Measurement Results

This section is where the coach records results of the original goal. For example, if a teacher decided to implement a classroom-management system with the goal being "Student engagement will increase 15% from the pre-observation measure to the post-observation measure," the pre-observation engagement percentage would be subtracted from the post-observation engagement percentage; the difference would be recorded in the box, to determine whether the 15% goal was met.

Jo's initial engagement measure before changing her planning to more effectively engage students was 86%. The average of three observations during the time she was teaching the new unit was 96.66%. This meant that Jo had met her goal of increasing student engagement by at least 10% through intentional planning.

Next Steps

This section follows the data-analysis section and helps the coach and the teacher determine what is going to happen next with coaching. Perhaps the goal was not quite met, or perhaps it was met with great success—do we keep moving forward with it, choose a different goal, or take a break? The wording found in the bullets below is from Jim Knight et al. (2015); it is so to the point and helpful! There is also a little space left for a few notes.

- Continue with this goal.

- Choose a different goal.

- Take some time off.

Two exemplar action plans are found below. The first plan was written for our fictitious middle-school teacher Jo Cotton, and her results are noted above. As mentioned previously, Jo wanted to work on the huge goal of planning an engaging unit, so there needed to be quite a few action steps. The coach could have written three pages of action steps or broken the whole thing into two or three separate goals, but this might have been overwhelming for Jo, so she just tried to fit as much detail into each action-step box as she could. Since some of the details could be completed in one coaching session, she wrote more than one detail in some action-step boxes.

The second Action Plan is more of a short-cycle, quick-turnaround goal. Jack Rayon was an elementary-school teacher whose students couldn't seem to get out the door at the end of the day. As mentioned before, don't worry about perfection when filling out the plans; the main thing is that the goal be specific and measurable, action steps be defined with timelines, and the teacher knows the coach is there to provide support until the goal is achieved. Personally, I don't always write Action Plans with my best handwriting, or worry about every single detail being documented until it becomes nauseating. Sometimes I just like to make sure I have the main pieces and then add some fun to the process!

3. Action Plan

Date: **3-15-19** Teacher Name: **Jo Cotton** School: **Washington Middle** Grade Level(s): **7th** Content: **Math** Coach: **Rebecca**

GOAL # [ ]	Process to Goal Completion: ACTION STEPS/STRATEGIES TO IMPLEMENT:	Completion Evidence of Action Steps:
☑Specific ☑Measurable	*What steps do I need to take to achieve this goal? What are my timelines for completion?*	A. **PRE** Observation Data Taken by coach

GOAL (Specific ☑ Measurable ☑):
Plan and implement an engaging unit that will increase student engagement by at least 10%

ACTION STEPS/STRATEGIES TO IMPLEMENT:
What steps do I need to take to achieve this goal? What are my timelines for completion?
- Enter step in shaded area
- Enter the date when you plan to complete this step in the box on the left
- Date and check the box on the right when step is completed

Coach collects pre student engagement data

A. 3/18	• Jo & Reb compile standards; assemble SB notebook; collect materials for color-coded planning process; locate curricular supports; Prepare student surveys - interests & learning modalities. data: 3/8 - Initial % = 86%	☑ 3/1
B. 3/22	First Planning Session: Determine overall Unit structure; Names of lessons in sequence with associated standards; Reb provides some engaging strategies to review; Review student surveys	☑ 3/21
C. 3/29	Second Planning Session: Complete daily planning for the first four lessons in the first section of the unit; Reb models process; Fill out daily learning targets, instructional delivery choices and formative assessments	☑ 3/29
D. by 4/5	Jo completes unit plan with phone support as needed. Reb reviews and final unit plan is completed by 4/5.	☑ 4/4
E. 4/15	Unit dates of implementation: 4/15 - 5/3 Coach stops by randomly 3x's and records student engagement	☑ 5/3
F. 5/10	Jo & Reb analyze data and discuss next steps	☑

Completion Evidence of Action Steps:
A. PRE Observation Data Taken by coach
B. Color-coded sticky notes and materials/notebooks
C. Pictures taken organized of progress
D. Completion delayed - illness Coach reviewed plan 4/4
E. Coach observed randomly 3x's and collected data on Time Dist. Tool
F. Data analysis review - Results below - *Goal Attainment Measurement?*

Results:
Pre on 3/8 = 86%
Average of 3 random observations during unit
4/17: 95%
4/23: 98%
5/2: 97%
Average: 96.6%
Engagement Goal **MET**!

Next Steps:
☑ Continue with this goal
☐ Choose a different goal
☐ Take some time off
Knight, J. (2010).
Jo would like to plan another engaging unit with coaching support.

Goal Attainment Measure:
How will I know I have achieved this goal?

1) Unit Plan is completed
2) Comparison of PRE Student Engagement Data to average of 3 random observations during unit implementation

Ideas to Consider:
-Pre/Post Video Analyses
-(Observation Data)
-Pre/Post Student Assessments
-Pre/Post Pictures
-Pre/Post Surveys
-Other: Unit plan is completed

(Teacher choice of data collected & compared over time)

Questions to consider: What have you already tried?
Small Groups
Power Points

What student needs can be addressed by setting this goal?
students will be more interested and willing to put in effort to be confident/skilled

How do you want to grow as an educator?
I wish students would be excited to be in my class

What Teacher Quality Standards will this goal address? I, II, III, IV, V, VI

On a scale of 1(low)-5(high), how much would it matter to you if you met this goal? 1 2 3 4 ⑤
Knight, J. (2010)

Notes: Jo's students showed patterns of interest in music, technology and art as recorded on the interest survey data during observations. 76% of Jo's students were made. Use this info when looking for engaging strategies to share.

Coaching paperwork not to be used as a part of a teacher's evaluation. All comments written by the coach are non-evaluative and not to be interpreted as an indication of success or lack of success of the teacher being coached.

3. Action Plan

Date: **10-7-19** Teacher Name: **Jack Rayon** School: **Jefferson Elementary** Grade Level(s): **5th** Content: **All** Coach: **Rebecca**

GOAL # 1	Goal Attainment	Process to Goal Completion: ACTION STEPS/STRATEGIES TO IMPLEMENT:	Completion Evidence of Action Steps:

☑ Specific ☑ Measurable

Measure: How will I know I have achieved this goal?

Decrease the amount of time it takes for students to prepare to leave at the end of the day.

Goal: 3 min. or less

If students are out the door in 3 minutes or less for 7 out of 10 days

Process to Goal Completion: ACTION STEPS/STRATEGIES TO IMPLEMENT:
What steps do I need to take to achieve this goal? What are my timelines for completion?

- Enter step in shaded area
- Enter the date when you plan to complete this step in the box on the left
- Date and check the box on the right when step is completed

A. **10/7** Teacher and coach - Jack & Reb design a checklist of what students need to do before leaving. Jack runs it by students to get their ideas. → 10/7 ✓

B. **10/8** Coach takes pre video and student engagement data. Jack & Reb brainstorm ideas to help students be more efficient. → 10/8 ✓

C. **10/11** Jack shows video to students and gets their thoughts on how to list and asks for student volunteers to time the class each day for 10 days. → 10/11 ✓

D. **10/15** Jack asks students to create a 10 day poster to record how long it takes the class to get ready to go each day. Students help determine incentive. Perhaps some of the time saved goes to something students enjoy → 10/15 ✓

E. **10/21** The challenge begins! Checklist items need to be completed in 3 min. or less. (Done 1st, line up) Students fill in poster each day w/ times. → 10/21 ✓

F. **11/1** Post video & time is recorded by Reb. Time is recorded also by students. This is the 10th day. Review data and determine next steps. → 11/1 ✓

Completion Evidence of Action Steps:

A. Check list designed together

B. Coach records how long it takes for students to get ready to go.

C. Checklist posted - took pic

D. Poster created & posted

E. Poster is being filled in each day. Students are enjoying the process.

F. Data review and celebration with students. Goal Attainment Measurement

Results:

Initial/PRE Data: 9 minutes
PRE Video: 28 seconds for students to get ready to go.

After implementing goal/action steps: 6 days at 3 min. or under out of 10; average time 3 min. 30 sec.

Next Steps:

☑ Continue with this goal
☐ Choose a different goal
☐ Take some time off

Knight, J. (2010).

Though the goal was not quite met, the plan totally worked! Lots of instructional time was saved.

Questions to consider:

What have you already tried?
- Bribes
- Getting Angry

What student needs can be addressed by setting this goal?
- More instruction
- Less disorganization

How do you want to grow as an educator?
- Be more organized

What Teacher Quality Standards will this goal address? I, II, III, IV, V, VI

On a scale of 1(low)–5(high), how much would it matter to you if you met this goal? 1 2 3 4 5

Knight, J. (2010).

Ideas to Consider:
- Teacher choice of data collected & compared over time
- Pre/Post Video Analyses
- Observation Data
- Pre/Post Student Assessments
- Pre/Post Pictures
- Pre/Post Surveys
- Other:

Notes: Research resources including videos to show students about how important it is to manage time well. Maybe some thing about how much can be accomplished in 10 minutes.

Coaching paperwork not to be used as a part of a teacher's evaluation. All comments within or by the coach are non-evaluative and not to be interpreted as an indication of success or lack of success of the teacher being coached.

Page 4: Tracking

This is a place to record dates when the coach shares something with the teacher that is specifically designed to address social-emotional needs. When we at TCT first started realizing it was important to balance our coaching by adding more of the relational "softer skills" into our coaching work, we began with giving out the stones as part of the "touchstone" process and provided a "BELIEVE" bookmark for the teachers we were coaching. It is amazing how many teachers appreciated those two attempts to encourage them and remind them of their purpose. We have found those little motivators still on teachers' desks or computers many years later. Chapter 2 offered some specific ideas about how to provide emotional support. In reality, the "how" ideas are innumerable, as long as coaches are sincere in their efforts to make life better for the people they coach. Encouragement is so needed!

When I take teachers I coach to visit other teachers who can effectively model for them, I organize observational feedback for the teacher being observed and include everything positive I can think of that the teacher demonstrated. It's just something nice to do for him or her. I will often write my feedback mostly in education-ese, with specific examples, like this:

- Evidence of significant preparation

- Differentiation noted with leveled graphic organizers

- Clarity in presentation—students were not confused about they needed to do

- Opportunities provided for students to share their ideas and create alternate solutions

- Mutual respect exhibited, positive relationship building evidenced by greeting students at the door, talking with students about their activities, noticing a new hairstyle, kindly redirecting, etc.

You would not believe how grateful teachers are to just hear some good news about their teaching! There is an incredible amount of power in acknowledging what is going well. As my mentor Judy Williams so succinctly said, "Praise what you want to see more of" (personal communication, April 17, 2008).

Goal/Action Steps Progress Tracking

In this section, the coach records the date of the meeting. The coach records the overall goal number first, then the action-step letter being worked on at this point in the coaching process (e.g., 1A, 1B, and 2A). "Met (M)" or "In Process (IP)" to the right of the goal indicates progress toward the goal on that date.

As action steps are met (M), they do not need to be recorded again. An average of the average percentage of action steps completed for all teachers could be recorded and reported as general program data.

4. Tracking

Date: 3-8-19 Teacher Name: Jo Cotton School: Washington Grade Level(s): 7th Content: Math Coach: Rebecca
Middle

Encouragement | Celebrations | Creative Positive Support | Ways to "Lift" Teachers We Coach

☑ Patience quote ☑ Building confidence
☑ saved with ☑ Water Bottle ☑ in teeks bookmark
☑ Hawaiian Flowers

Goal/Action Steps Progress Tracking

-A process for regularly checking on goal progress with teacher being coached-

☑ Record Date of Meeting ☑ Record Overall Goal # First, Then Action Step Letter ☑ Note In Progress (IP) or Met (M) to record progress toward goal

Date	Goal # Action Steps Letter	In Process or Met	Date	Goal # Action Steps Letter	In Process or Met	Date	Goal # Action Steps Letter	In Process or Met
1. 3-15-19	1A;1B;1C	M;IP;IP	7. 5-10-19	1F;2A	M;IP	13.		
2. 3-22-19	1B;1C;1D	M;M;IP	8. 5-15-19	2A;2B	M;M	14.		
3. 3-29-19	1D;1E	IP;IP	9.			15.		
4. 4-9-19	1D;1E	M;IP	10.			16.		
5. 4-15-19	1E;1F	IP;IP	11.			17.		
6. 4-19-19	1E;1F	M;IP	12.			18.		
						19.		
						20.		
						21.		
						22.		
						23.		
						24.		

Total number of Action Steps Completed: __8__ Total # of Action Steps Planned: __8__
Divide total number of action steps completed by total # of action steps planned = Percentage of Action Steps Completed: __100%__

Instructional Time and Student Engagement Data

Track % of Time Spent on Instruction and % Student Engagement During Observations-Track this data using the Time Distribution Tool
This individual teacher data provides feedback for teachers. The average of the average %'s of all teachers will be recorded as general program data.

Date	% Teacher Instruction	% Student Engagement	Date	% Teacher Instruction	% Student Engagement
1. 3-8-19	82%	86%	5.		
2. 4-17-19	91%	95%	6.		
3. 4-23-19	94%	98%	7.		
4. 5-2-19	96%	97%	8.		
			9.		
			10.		
			11.		
			12.		

Total Averages: % Instructional Time: __91%__ %Student Engagement: __94%__

Instructional Time and Student Engagement Data

- Record Date of Observation

- Track % of Time Spent on Instruction and % Student Engagement During Observations—Track this data using the Time Distribution Tool (TDT) offered in this chapter. This tool will be explained in detail after the example Tracking page.

- This individual teacher data provides feedback for teachers. Averaged data of the percentage of time spent on instruction and the percentage of student engagement for all teachers coached before coaching began and at the end of coaching could be used as program data. On the Tracking form, data collected for action steps completed, percentage of time spent on instruction and student engagement are averaged for each teacher.

Time Distribution Tool (TDT)

This tool allows the coach to record a variety of data pieces on one concise tool:

- A visual and numeric distribution of how time was spent during an observation is prepared by recording minutes within categories, with one tally mark signifying one minute.

- A comments column, for summarizing what is happening during each five-minute segment

- A column to record scans for student engagement every five minutes is found on the right side of the form. Students are considered engaged if they are doing what the teacher has asked them to do—we can't tell exactly what is in a student's mind, whether they are totally engaged or not, using this form, but we can tell whether students are participating, following instructions, and completing work. During each five-minute segment, the observer records the number of students engaged (numerator) over the total number of students in the room during that five-minute segment (denominator). Sometimes students leave the room or students come in late, so the denominator can change.

- The last activity column is for noting any non-instructional activities that take place, such as learning digressions, interruptions, routine checking of homework, preparing for recess, lunch, end of day, end of class, announcements, classroom visitors, and videos not connected to student learning.

How to Fill Out the TDT

1) Place one tally mark in the appropriate column for each minute of instruction (five tallies or minutes per row). See column categories information at the bottom

of the form to determine where to place the tally mark. When the observation is over, record the total time and number of minutes spent in each column. Subtract the number of minutes spent on non-instructional pieces from the total amount of time, and divide that number by the total time to provide a percentage of time spent on instruction.

2) Briefly record what is happening during each five-minute segment/row in the Comments column.

3) Record number of engaged students for each five-minute segment over the total number of students in the room at that time in the Student Engagement column, then determine a total average for student engagement by adding up the denominators and dividing by the number of five-minute segments recorded, then doing the same for the numerators, then placing the averaged numerator over the averaged denominator and dividing to provide a student-engagement percentage.

Ideas for Sharing Data With the Teacher

The TDT provides the following information that could be collaboratively reviewed and discussed with the teacher:

- Time spent on different types of instructional delivery methods

- Student engagement numbers at different points throughout lesson

- Percentage of time spent on instruction

- Comments about each five-minute segment of time during the lesson

Multiple observations with this tool provide depth to the data.

Questions That Could Be Discussed When Reviewing Data Collected

What are your thoughts about this data? Are we seeing any patterns? Was one type of instruction preferred or used more/less than others? Where in the lesson was student engagement the highest, the lowest? What was happening at that point in the lesson? What was the total percentage of time spent on instruction? Is there anything we can learn from this information? Is the use of time as efficient as we would like it to be? Are there disruptions or transitions that could be minimized?

Providing this analysis for teachers and collaboratively unpacking it is powerful, because it shows teachers where things were going well during a lesson and where they could be improved in a very straightforward and timely manner. For more specific feedback, the Comments section could be split into what the teacher is doing and what students are doing during each five-minute period. Another way to use this tool is to video the lesson,

Time Distribution Tool (TDT)

Mark 1 tally in the appropriate category for each minute of instruction (5 tallies or minutes per row)

Briefly record what is happening during each 5-minute segment/row in the Comments column and record # of engaged students for each 5 minute segment over total number of students in the Student Engagement column

Date: **3-8-19** School: **Washington** Teacher: **Jo Cotton** Grade: **8th** Content: **Math** # of Students: **29** Observer: **Rebecca**

Coaching paperwork not to be used as a part of a teacher's evaluation. All comments written by the coach are non-evaluative and not to be interpreted as an indication of success or lack of success of the teacher being coached.

Minutes	5-Minute Intervals	Teacher Lecture	Teacher-led Discussion	Student-Engaged Discussion *Whole Class*	Small Group-Engaged Activities	Student-Engaged Activities	Student Engaged Seat Work	Assessment	Video	Individual Student Help	Non-Instructional Activities	Comments — Teacher	Comments — Students	Student Engagement
15	5	II							w/graphic organizer		III	Announcements/Attendance/Begins Lesson	Setting in talking/listening	21/26
	10	HH	HH									Explaining Topic	students counting in late/some listening	29/28
	15	I	I									Explaining topic and asking for responses	some students regarding late at time	19/28
	20	IIII	I									Displaying/explaining graphic organizer	some students looking & listening	24/28
30	25								III		II	Graphic organizer distributed	some students listening	27/29
	30							HH				Moving around room filling in organizer	video starting watching video	28/29
35	35							IIII			I	Leads discussion about video	students participating using notes	29/29
45	40		HH									Lecture about Topic	students listen, talk put heads on	27/29
	45	IIII									I	Reprimands for off-task students	students listening, some working	24/29
	50							III			II	Reprimands/gave ticket out/end of day getting ready to go	ticket out	24/28
60	55													24/28
	60													
Total Time	**50**	**16**	**10**					**3**	**12**		**9**	Total Time – Time Spent on Non-Instructional Activities Divided By Total Time = % Time Spent on Instruction: 50–9 = 41 41/50 = 82%	SE Average: **86%**

Most time spent were

Teacher-Lecture *Whole Class*	Teacher-Led Discussions *Whole Class*	Student-Engaged Discussions *Whole Class*	Small Group Engaged Activities *Small Group*	Student-Engaged Activities *Individual*	Student-Engaged Seat Work *Individual*	Assessment	Video	Individual Student Help	Non-Instructional Activities
One-way communication: Teacher speaks, no student responses requested	Teacher leads discussion & requests responses from students	Two-way sharing of information among students: students initiate questions & answers, presentations	Groups are actively engaged in activities promoting problem solving, higher level thinking skills	Individual students actively engaged in activities: projects, experiments, writing, sustained silent reading - that promote problem solving, higher level thinking	Repetitive, low level seat work: drills or practice	Formative Assessments: Quizzes, tickets out, plickers, peer reviews, self-assessments, summaries, reflections, etc. Interim/Summative Assessments	Video connected to student learning goals	Teacher supporting individual students one on one	Learning digressions; interruptions; routine checking of homework; preparing for recess, lunch, end of day, end of class, announcements; classroom visitors; video not connected to student learning, etc.

w/graphic organizer — students used graphic organizer for notes then fill out the tool together, or fill out the tool separately and then compare the results. In our experience at TCT, teachers are typically willing to look at data recorded by a coach on this form and use it to help them clearly understand what is happening during the time they are teaching. There are times, however (e.g., if the data looks really terrible and the teacher already feels the observation was a disaster), that it may be best to share the data at a different time (not during the first coaching visit). Usually the TDT data is helpful to use when teachers are getting ready to set measurable goals. The data could also be used as evidence of goals achieved if the teacher and the coach want to collect data over time regarding instructional variety, student engagement, or instructional time as appropriate measures for goals they have set. When a coaching program is set up to be nonevaluative and confidential, a safe environment is created, in which teachers don't have to worry that, if they decide to face and address some challenging data, the data and risk-taking to improve will be used against them.

Strengths | Questions | Ideas (SQI)

As mentioned previously, I like to intentionally focus on specific strengths exhibited when I observe teachers. I have found it incredibly helpful to list what teachers are doing well, so that they want to continue doing those things! Teachers might try to find the extra time they need to incorporate new strategies and address new goals by giving up things that are working for them. We definitely don't want coaching to eliminate what is going well! The Time Distribution Tool (TDT) and the Strengths | Questions | Ideas (SQI) tool can be filled out at the same time. The SQI tool can be drawn or copied on the back of the TDT. After an observation, the coach can share the strengths of the teacher and the data on the TDT, to make the coaching session both encouraging and informative (caring and competent). Using both forms during a post-observation conference also allows the coach to ask questions and share ideas as part of a coaching protocol.

Ideas

Questions

Strengths

Strengths Reference—Coaching Hack!

This is a reference sheet to provide examples of how coaches can identify what teachers are doing well (using some education-ese ☺). Coaches will be able to think of many more ideas, but brain freeze happens. I hope this helps!

General Delivery	Relationships	Content	Student Work	Student Interactions	Presence	Planning	Procedures
-Directions were clear and concise (no rambling or confusing off-topic comments). -The number of steps students were asked to remember when you gave directions was appropriate for their developmental level. -Pacing of the lesson was quick enough to hold students' interest, and differentiation strategies for students who needed more time for processing and completing work were provided.	-Specific interactions showing evidence of your care and concern for students were noted: 1) When Joey came in late, you checked in with him to see if everything was okay. 2) You greeted students at the door with a smile and asked them questions specific to their lives and interests. 3) You enthusiastically called Sara's parents when she won the review game.	-Significant preparation of content was evident: 1) Use of technology to address topic, with previously prepared student-created slides 2) Leveled notes provided support for EL students 3) Engaging and easy-to-follow demonstration, with previously prepared kinesthetic materials 4) Math lesson on solving equations showed effective use of and alignment with district math curriculum.	-Your modeling of how to complete the work assigned was excellent; students knew exactly what to do and how to do it. -Student assignments and assessments were aligned with your learning goals. -Both you and your students knew exactly how and when their work was going to be assessed, so you were able to do it quickly and provide timely feedback. -Student assignments were interesting and relevant. It was obvious you had tailored the assignment to address student interests.	-Group work was well organized! Each student had a responsibility, and all students were accountable for work completion. -When students were allowed time to discuss the topic with a partner, you had them first write their ideas down for a few minutes and then discuss their thoughts. This allowed more processing time for students and helped keep the conversations on target. -Students were not afraid to share their thoughts; they asked clarifying questions and persevered during productive struggles.	-You have a contagious smile! -Your professional attire showed respect for yourself, the students, and the teaching profession. -You have an organized, clutter-free classroom. -You appropriately referenced and consistently implemented previously determined expectations and procedures. -You intentionally and appropriately used humor. -You made it a point to listen to students and tried to find ways to say yes to any request you could.	-Learning goals and purposes for learning the content were made clear to students verbally, and the learning goal was visible throughout the lesson. -How students could achieve the learning goals, and how they would show what they learned, was not a mystery to you or your students. -Your lessons fit strategically into a logical sequence aligned with content standards. -You effectively designed a formative assessment that provided student data to inform tomorrow's instruction.	-Behavioral expectations, including what happens when expectations are followed or not followed, were clear, visible, to the point, reasonable, and consistently implemented. -Students knew and followed procedures for asking questions, getting notebooks, sharpening pencils, working with partners, going to the bathroom, managing transitions such as the beginning and end of class, moving around the room, etc.

(Continued)

(Continued)

-You used a variety of powerful learning strategies: music, visual images, stories, exemplars, manipulatives, foldables, student notebooks, analogies, etc. -Your presence was positive and confident; preparation was evident. Students could trust you knew what you were talking about and were happy you were their teacher!	-Positive and inspiring messages for and about students, including their academic work, are visible in your classroom. -Mutual respect between students and teacher was regularly exhibited. -One of your students had a note you had written to him glued into the front of his notebook.	5) Content support stations and resources for common challenging grade-level misconceptions were made available to students. 6) Students created an order of operations flipbook resource to organize and reference to support important math content.	-The length of the assignment was appropriate for students' developmental level. -Students had been taught how to organize notes and work and knew where to turn work in—no papers were lost.	-Opportunities were provided for students to lead their learning. Students were able to choose how to show mastery of content project, research paper, visual display, electronic presentations, speeches, etc.	-Your students understand they are important and have a voice in their learning. -You allowed time for student questions and comments. -You expertly blend a confident and strong presence with novelty and kindness creating order, trust, and fun!	-Your understanding of brain research was evident in your planning, as you included brain breaks when necessary, movement, games, music, storytelling, and manipulatives.	-Your procedures included time set aside for positive interactions, such as your "joke of the day," and time for students to share positive experiences. -You use a variety of strategies to regularly check for student understanding throughout the lesson: response cards, hand signals, monitoring, whiteboards.

1. Teacher Information | Coach Planning

Date: _____ Name: _____ School: _____ Grade Level(s): _____ Content: _____

Coach: _____

Professional Info | Contact Info

Number of Years Teaching in/out of District: _____

Teacher Certification: License Type (circle): Initial | Professional | Master

Induction this year? Y N   Probationary (1, 2, 3): _____   Non-Probationary: _____

E-mail: _____ | Phone: Classroom/Office: _____

Home/Cell: _____ | Room #(s): _____

Planning Time(s): _____ | Coaching Frequency: _____

Observation Time(s): _____

Coach Planning

☐ Professional Agreement reviewed and signed
☐ Teacher Information [p. 1-this page] completed
☐ Pre-Instructional Survey completed by teacher
☐ Human Connection [p. 2] most applicable sections completed over time

Coaching Resources

☐ Analyzing Student Work Processes
☐ Classroom Management Self-Assessment and Checklists Forms
☐ Classroom Management System Exemplars
☐ Collegial Observation Form Conference Documentation Form ☐ Cultural Understanding & Bias Process ☐ Data Collection Tools & Checklists ☐ Developing

Assistance Menu | Coaching Focus

☐ Analyzing Student Work—Processes/Rubrics

☐ Assessment: Checks for Understanding, Formative, Interim, Summative

☐ Classroom Management—Presence/Planning/Procedures

☐ Content Support for Specific Programs

☐ Data Analysis

☐ Differentiation/Modifications for SPED/GT/ELL/Other: _____

☐ Effective Questioning/Rigor/Depth of Knowledge (DOK)

☐ PLC Support

☐ Professionalism—Basics/Affect/Building Relationships

☐ Standards-Based Lesson Planning:

Daily: Standards | Learning Targets | Instructional Delivery Choices with Rationale | Formative Assessment

Unit Development: Sequencing | Assessments | Yearly Sequencing—Curriculum Mapping

☐ Student Engagement/Motivation

☐ Teacher Evaluation: Professional Preparation—Teacher Quality Standards/Measures of Student Learning

☐ Workshop Format with Team: Topic _____

Other Area(s) of Assistance Requested: _____

☐ Action Plan [p. 3] Working Document

☐ Keep up with tracking Goals/Action Steps progress, Instructional Time, Student Engagement, and Positive Support or "Lift" idea actions on the Tracking page [p.4]

☐ Use Time Distribution Tool during observations for individual teacher and program data collection

☐ Post-Instructional Survey completed by teacher

Rubrics Tool ☐ Unpacking Standards Process & Form ☐ DOK Flip Folder ☐ Educator Effectiveness Video

☐ Effective Questioning Analysis and Creation Processes ☐ Next Generation Learning resources ☐ Professional Portfolio ☐ Socratic Seminar

☐ Standards-based Lesson Planning Color-coded Process ☐ Student Engagement resources ☐ Student Survey Form ☐ Teacher/Coach Observations Over Time Form ☐ Video Analysis Observation Form ☐ Video Notification Forms ☐ Workshop Format Template

☐ Instructional Videos and Websites: _____

☐ Other Resources, Checklists, Strategies: _____

Notes:

2. Human Connection

Date: _____ Teacher Name: _____ School: _____ Grade Level(s): _____ Content: _____ Coach: _____

Identifying Teacher Motivation and Purpose: *The Touchstone Process*

☐ **#1. For Teacher's Students:** Ask teacher to "Choose a word written on the stones below (or use real stones), and/or write a word of your own that best captures what you would like your students to take away from, gain, feel, or incorporate into their lives as a result of your teaching, influence, or interactions with them this year." **Teacher's core emotion/desire/feeling to share with students:** _____

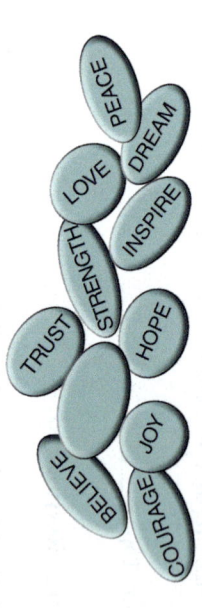

Stones: PEACE, DREAM, LOVE, INSPIRE, STRENGTH, TRUST, HOPE, JOY, BELIEVE, COURAGE

Other Word Ideas: *Humor, Organization, Creativity, Trust, Connection, Gentleness, Passion, Caring, Flexible, Serenity, Plan, Health, Kindness, Communication, Faith, Competency, Happiness, Gratitude, Knowledge, Confidence, Content Mastery, Authenticity*

☐ **# 2. For Teacher:** Choose a word on the stones (or think of one) that best describes something you would like to have in your life right now that could help increase your ability to convey choice/stone #1 to your students: _____

Teacher's Support Choice to make her/his core desire for these students happen: _____

☐ **Learning Modality Preferences:** _____

☐ **Personality Information:** Record results of surveys already taken, or administer one and record results in the table below: Ideas: ☐ Myers-Briggs ☐ Multiple Intelligences ☐ Emergenetics ☐ North, South, East, West—Compass Personality Test ☐ Other

☐ **Is there anything else you think I ought to know as your coach?** _____

☐ **Coach Reflection:** Knowing this information, how could you tailor your coaching to meet this teacher's individual needs?

Where do you see yourself in 5 years?

What was your favorite childhood dream?

Hobbies/Interests/Likes/Dislikes:

Personal/Family Info:

Ideas:

Personal/Family: Birth order, siblings, husband/wife, children, grandchildren, places lived, places visited, favorite memories, etc.

Hobbies/Interests: Music, sports, drama, games-board/video, collections, nature, reading traveling, computers, motorcycles, etc.

Likes/Dislikes: Food, what people do, houses, books, landscaping, clothes, gifts, leaders, stores, restaurants, etc.

Self-Care:

What works, what would you like to do?

- Exercise
- Eat Healthy
- Be in Nature
- Listen to Music
- Spend Time with Family and Friends
- Read
- Other Ideas:

3. Action Plan

Date: _____ Teacher Name: _____ School: _____ Grade Level(s): _____ Content: _____ Coach: _____

GOAL # ☐

☐ Specific ☐ Measurable

Goal Attainment Measure: How will I know I have achieved this goal?

Questions to consider: What have you already tried?

What student needs can be addressed by setting this goal?

How do you want to grow as an educator?

What Teacher Quality Standards will this goal address? I, II, III, IV, V, VI

On a scale of 1 (low) to 5 (high), how much would it matter to you if you met this goal? 1 2 3 4 5 Knight (2010)

Ideas to Consider:

-Teacher choice of data collected & compared over time

-Pre/Post Video Analyses

-Observation Data

-Pre/Post Student Assessments

-Pre/Post Pictures

-Pre/Post Surveys

-Other:

Process to Goal Completion: ACTION STEPS/STRATEGIES TO IMPLEMENT:

What steps do I need to take to achieve this goal? What are my timelines for completion?

- Enter step in shaded area.
- Enter the date when you plan to complete this step in the box on the left.
- Date and check the box on the right when step is completed.

A.

B.

C.

D.

E.

F.

Notes:

Coaching paperwork not to be used as a part of a teacher's evaluation. All comments written by the coach are nonevaluative and not to be interpreted as an indication of success or lack of success of the teacher being coached.

Completion Evidence of Action Steps:

A.

B.

C.

D.

E.

F.

Goal Attainment Measurement Results:

Next Steps:

☐ Continue with this goal
☐ Choose a different goal
☐ Take some time off

Knight, J. (2010).

4. Tracking

Date: ________ Teacher Name: ____________ School: ____________ Grade Level(s): _______ Content: ____________ Coach: ________________

Encouragement | Celebrations | Creative Positive Support | Ways to "Lift" Teachers We Coach

☐ __________ ☐ __________ ☐ __________ ☐ __________ ☐ __________

Goal/Action Steps Progress Tracking

-A process for regularly checking on goal progress with teacher being coached-

□ Record date of meeting □ Record overall Goal # first, then Action Step Letter

□ Note In Progress (IP) or Met (M) to record progress toward goal

Date	Goal # Action Steps Letter	In Process or Met	Date	Goal # Action Steps Letter	In Process or Met	Date	Goal # Action Steps Letter	In Process or Met	Date	Goal # Action Steps Letter	In Process or Met
1.			7.			13.			19.		
2.			8.			14.			20.		
3.			9.			15.			21.		
4.			10.			16.			22.		
5.			11.			17.			23.		
6.			12.			18.			24.		

Total number of Action Steps Completed: ______ **Total # of Action Steps Planned:** ______

Divide total number of action steps completed by total # of action steps planned = **Percentage of Action Steps Completed:** ________

Instructional Time and Student Engagement Data

Track percentage of time spent on instruction and percentage student engagement during observations—Track this data using the Time Distribution Tool.

This individual teacher data provides feedback for teachers. The average of the average percentage for all teachers will be recorded as general program data.

Date	% Teacher Instruction	% Student Engagement	Date	% Teacher Instruction	% Student Engagement	Date	% Teacher Instruction	% Student Engagement
1.			5.			9.		
2.			6.			10.		
3.			7.			11.		
4.			8.			12.		

Total Averages: % Instructional Time: _____ % Student Engagement: _____

Coaching paperwork not to be used as a part of a teacher's evaluation. All comments written by the coach are nonevaluative and not to be interpreted as an indication of success or lack of success of the teacher being coached.

Time Distribution Tool (TDT)

Mark 1 tally in the appropriate category for each minute of instruction (5 tallies or minutes per row).

Briefly record what is happening during each five-minute segment/row in the Comments column and record # of engaged students for each five-minute segment over total number of students in the Student Engagement column.

Date: _____ School: _____ Teacher: _____ Grade: _____ Content: _____ # of Students: _____

Observer: _____

Coaching paperwork not to be used as a part of a teacher's evaluation. All comments written by the coach are nonevaluative and not to be interpreted as an indication of success or lack of success of the teacher being coached.

Minutes	5-Minute Intervals	Teacher Lecture	Teacher-Led Discussion	Student-Engaged Discussion	Small Group–Engaged Activities	Student-Engaged Activities	Student-Engaged Seat Work	Assessment	Video	Individual Student Help	Non-Instructional Activities	Comments	Student Engagement
15	5												
	10												
	15												
30	20												
	25												
	30												
45	35												
	40												
	45												
60	50												
	55												
	60												
Total Time											Total Time – Time Spent on Non-Instructional Activities Divided by Total Time = % Time Spent on Instruction:	SE Average:

Teacher Lecture *Whole Class*	Teacher-Led Discussions *Whole Class*	Student-Engaged Discussions *Whole Class*	Small Group-Engaged Activities *Small Group*	Student-Engaged Activities *Individual*	Student-Engaged Seat Work *Individual*	Assessment	Video	Individual Student Help	Non-Instructional Activities
One-way communication: Teacher speaks, no student responses requested	Teacher leads discussion & requests responses from students	Two-way sharing of information among students: students initiate questions & answers, presentations	Groups are actively engaged in activities promoting problem solving, higher-level thinking skills	Individual students actively engaged in activities—projects, experiments, writing, sustained silent reading—that promote problem solving, higher-level thinking	Repetitive, low-level seat work: drills or practice	Formative Assessments: Quizzes, tickets out, plickers, peer reviews, self-assessments, summaries, reflections, etc. Interim/Summative Assessments	Video connected to student learning goals	Teacher supporting individual students one-on-one	Learning digressions; interruptions; routine checking of homework; preparing for recess, lunch, end of day, end of class; announcements; classroom visitors; video not connected to student learning, etc.

Ideas

Questions

Strengths

Reflect and Connect

The following questions are designed to get coaches or educational leaders thinking about their planning and coaching. The questions could be answered and kept for personal review; they could also be shared with others in dyads, or triads, then discussed. Or, to put a twist into the activity, other coaches/leaders (or possibly teachers) who know the coach/ educational leader well could fill in some of the answers for him or her and then discuss the results.

1. What are you already doing, or what ideas can you think of, to regularly and intentionally share with teachers what they are doing well?

   _____
   _____
   _____
   _____

2. Record one of your most successful planning experiences that led to increased teacher success:

   _____
   _____
   _____
   _____

3. What are some of your motivations and purposes for being a coach or educational leader (why this job)?

   _____
   _____
   _____
   _____

4. What do you do well as a coach or educational leader?

   _____
   _____
   _____
   _____

5. Are there ideas from this chapter that could help you plan your coaching more effectively? If so, list them here:

   _____
   _____
   _____
   _____

Planned Self-Assessment

1. Take this self-assessment before you set an intention to consciously find ways to become more planned.

2. Implement some of the practical application ideas and/or planned S.O.A.K. supports found below (or use some of your own ideas).

3. In a month or so, see whether you have been able to improve your thoughts, motivations, and behaviors surrounding the important coaching characteristic of being planned. Remember the synonyms/phrases associated with being planned, identified by coaching authors and by coaches like you, as you define what being planned is and determine how to make it a more conscious part of your daily life: collaboratively determines goals, plans, prioritizes needs using data, uses evidence-based strategies, utilizes meaningful coaching tools, references and reinforces content standards, checks in and follows up on plans frequently (Frazier, 2014).

	Strongly Disagree	Disagree	Neutral Not Sure	Agree	Strongly Agree
	1	2	3	4	5
When I meet with a teacher, I am prepared with a systematic way to capture information and organize our work together.					
Teachers I work with are involved in the creation of goals and action steps and have a desire to complete the goal—or, in other words, the goal matters to them.					
Teachers I work with clearly understand how goals will be measured and what the timelines for completion are, for both the goal and the action steps.					
I regularly follow up with teachers and creatively encourage them to reach their goals. I enjoy cheering them on!					
I believe coaching can be enhanced when I am sincerely interested in each teacher and genuinely want to learn about him or her.					
I gather relevant information, including student data, and thoughtfully review it to provide the best possible individualized coaching support.					
Column Totals:					

Grand Total: _____

What totals mean: 26–30 = Planned Rock Star, 21–25 = Very Planned, 16–20 = Sort of Planned, 11–15 = Some Planning Is Happening, 6–10 = Better Step It Up, 0–5 = Would Setting a Goal to Be More Planned Be Helpful?

Practical Application Ideas for Planned

This entire chapter is basically a Practical Application. Listed here are a couple of my favorite tools explained previously.

1. The Time Distribution Tool (TDT) provides so much information during an observation that it is a definite favorite for data collection. I can go to more specific student assessments or observation protocols by standards as needed, but this tool gives me a good overall picture of the amount of variety a teacher uses during his or her instruction. The student engagement and instructional time percentages are useful for discussion and could be collected by all coaches and averaged for reportable overall program data. The use of the TDT with the addition of the Strengths | Questions | Ideas (SQI) tool organizes observational data to be well-documented, easily explained, and useful for determining and measuring goals, along with recognizing teacher strengths.

2. Instructional Survey: Before coaching begins and after coaching is completed, an instructional survey that includes basic components of quality teaching is completed by teachers being coached. The categories are Planning, Instruction, Assessment, Classroom Environment, Professional Growth, and Job Satisfaction. The results of this survey were discussed with teachers being coached in the TCT program both before and after coaching and were also used to inform goal-setting. The survey has been included previously in this chapter. The Instructional Survey results were reported as overall program data pre and post each year to show how much perceived growth teachers were experiencing in the previously mentioned categories. The survey was developed using many of the components Charlotte Danielson (1996) used to create a framework that "identifies those aspects of a teacher's responsibilities that have been documented through empirical studies and theoretical research as promoting improved student learning" (p. 1). Updates and alignment with district areas of focus were ongoing by coaching program leaders throughout the years. This survey was used during the years student growth was measured in a statistical study (Frazier, 2018). Students of teachers who were coached outperformed students of teachers who were not coached by almost half a year of student growth, as measured by differences in student growth using the NWEA Measures of Academic Progress (MAP) assessment.

Conclusion

In the words of Zig Ziglar: "You were born to be a winner, you must plan to win and prepare to win. Then, and only then, can you legitimately expect to win" (2017). While watching one of Ziglar's videos on YouTube, I heard him say that he had presented the same content yesterday and many times before that, but what he did when he finished presenting yesterday was prepare for six hours for today's presentation. To summarize his words about planning from the video, he said it is arrogant to think we can perform well without planning and preparing. I hadn't ever thought of it that way, but if we are just going about our coaching (or any type of work, for that matter), figuring we know enough and not preparing for individual people and their situations—I can see how that is arrogance, in a way. We can't possibly know how to help, know what to do, or provide inspiring support without continually asking questions to gain information, learning new techniques, and searching for the best possible way to address individual needs. We must consider both the technical and the emotional (the heart and the mind), stay humble, and put in the work required to achieve exceptional results.

PLANNED ~S.O.A.K. ~

Sometimes learning penetrates best when we are relaxed and not trying too hard to make it happen.

Stress-free Opportunities to Absorb Knowledge   **Choose what works for you.** (Like a "Planned" bath bomb infused with personalized nutrients)

Quotes	Music	Statements affirmations	Books poetry stories	Art & More	Videos movies	Movement other ideas
"You were born to be a winner, you must plan to win and prepare to win. Then, and only then can you legitimately expect to win." —Zig Ziglar	**"Big Plans"** Why Don't We	**For coaches:** My ability to plan and organize my coaching work sets teachers up for success!	**"The Ant and the Grasshopper"** Aesop	**Blueprints by Frank Lloyd Wright**	*NASA Planning Trip Around Mars in 2033?* Fox Business (YouTube)	Downward Dog
"Proper Planning Prevents Poor Performance" —short version of British Army 7 P's	**"Takin' Care of Business"** Bachman-Turner Overdrive	The teachers I coach know I appreciate and respect their individuality. Through my coaching, teachers' support needs and personal dreams are brought to light. Then, through intentional planning, we partner together to make their most effective and heartfelt teaching become a daily reality.	***The Impact Cycle: What Instructional Coaches Should Do . . . .*** Jim Knight	Success What people think it looks like	*Importance of Planning—Why Planning Is Important? (Funny Story)* BeOnTrack (YouTube)	Tripod Headstand
"A goal without a plan is just a wish." —Anonymous	**"The Climb"** Miley Cyrus		***RESULTS Coaching: The New Essential for School Leaders*** Kathryn Kee et al.	Success What it really Looks like	*Why Planning Matters* barneyellevsen (YouTube)	**Oils:** ginger, eucalyptus
"Plan your work and work your plan." —Napoleon Hill			***Coaching Matters*** Joellen Killion et al.		*Stephen Covey's 4 Quadrants Time Management Strategies | Time Management Matrix | Ep. 9* Mr Smart (YouTube)	
"An hour of planning can save you 10 hours of doing." —Dale Carnegie	**"Teach Your Children Well"** Crosby, Stills, Nash & Young	**For teachers:** When I intentionally plan to meet the needs of students, I position myself to make a lasting, positive difference in their lives.	***Student-Centered Coaching: A Guide for K-8 Coaches and Principals*** Diane Sweeney	**The notebooks of Leonardo da Vinci**	*Plan the Work, Work the Plan—Motivational Video Will Smith* Video Advice (YouTube)	**Stones:** dumortierite, datolite
"Spectacular achievement is always preceded by unspectacular preparation." —Robert H. Schuller –			***Differentiated Coaching: A Framework for Helping Teachers Change*** Jane Kise	Great recipes for your favorite comfort foods!		
"Persevere until the goal set is the goal met!" —Rebecca Frazier	**"Car Wash"** Rose Royce	My willingness to put forth the effort to plan well is evidence of my dedication to and love for my students.	***Cognitive Coaching: A Foundation for Renaissance Schools*** Arthur Costa and Robert Garmston	Exemplary lesson plans of excellent teachers you know!		**Color:** orange

The ability to plan, prioritize, and strategically organize our complex workloads is an undervalued, but necessary and powerful skill! Planning paves the road to success!

NOTES

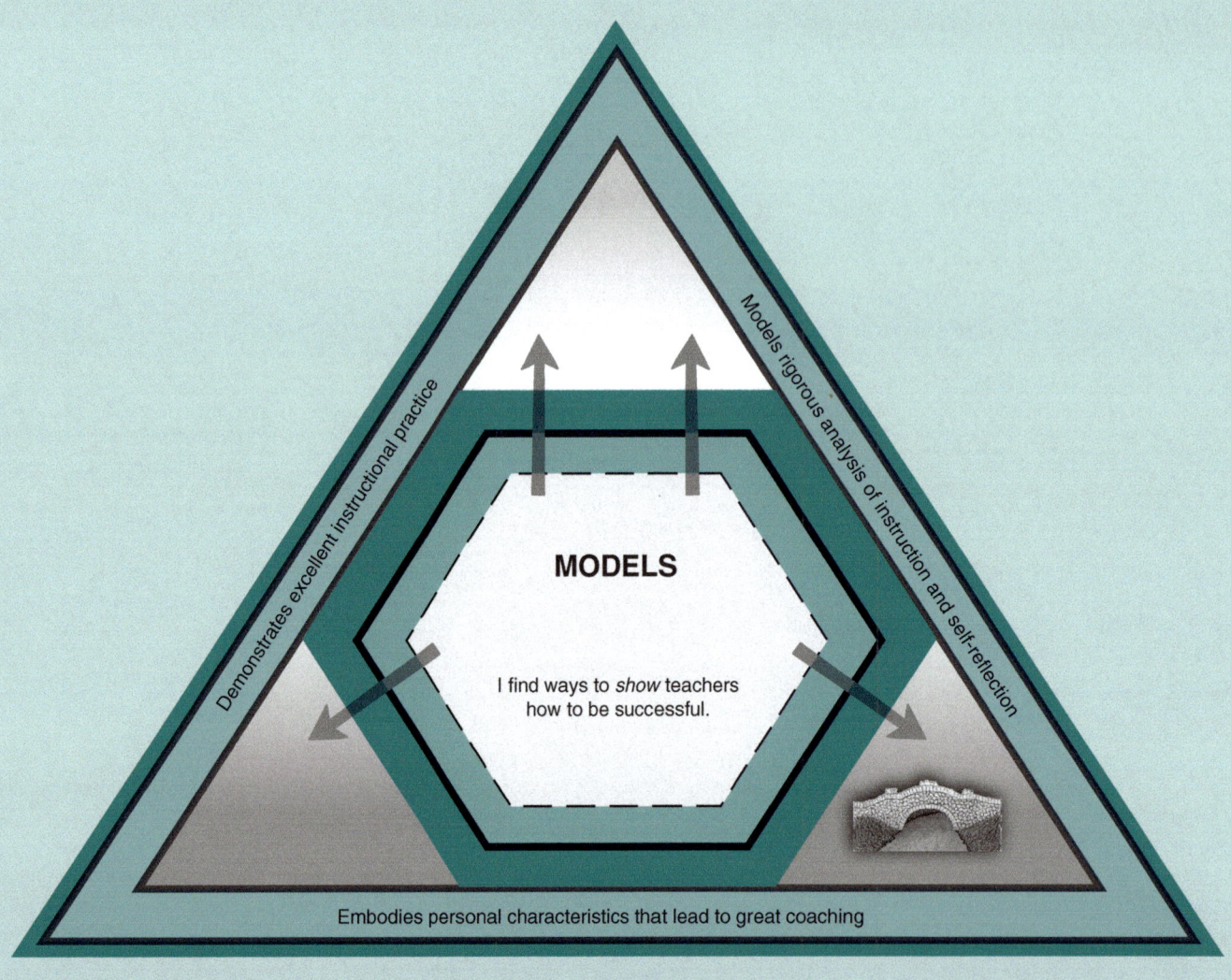

As a coach, I am continually learning and looking for opportunities to refine my own teaching. I can and do provide modeling personally, through videos, co-teaching, observations of other teachers, and in other ways to show the teachers I coach what quality instruction looks like.

Models

10

///

Be the change you want to see happen.

—Arleen Lorrance (1974), inspired by Mahatma Gandhi

Being authentically competent and able to embody that competence by demonstrating how to implement strategies or using other means to "show" teachers how to achieve success with students is where the rubber hits the road for instructional coaches. How do we help teachers bridge the gap between where they currently are and where they would like to be? The answer is, "We teach it!"

As we know, some of the most effective teaching strategies for supporting student learning include modeling for students exactly what needs to be done and how, and also providing exemplars of work successfully completed. Effective coaching includes these components as well. Adults also benefit from the use of best teaching practices when they are learning how to do something. For instance, I have had the amazing opportunity to facilitate a team in the development of a hybrid (face-to-face and online) peer-coaching model for the past six years. During the first year of implementation, we realized some teachers did not understand the detail and rigor they needed to include as they worked through the peer-coaching process. Quite a few teachers turned in work that was too simplistic, and their attention to detail was not what we had hoped. For these teachers, we were not able to ascertain whether the collaborative work had been meaningful or the instructional goals addressed successfully.

The peer-coaching team wanted high-quality submissions (and many teachers did do this naturally, but others did not). So, at first, we had to watch that we didn't go straight to blaming lazy teachers; we had to be willing to look at ourselves and ask, "Did we really do a good job of teaching how to fill out the forms?" When we asked ourselves that question, the answer was no. As a result of this reflection, we decided to model how to fill out the forms. Two members of the team, with district media help, created a video showing two teachers working through the peer-coaching process and filling out the Goal Process Form. The video explained in detail the process, referring to shots of the form throughout the video when appropriate. Since the time we modeled this process and added the video and exemplar forms to every online module, the quality of form submissions has improved dramatically.

We can't just assume adults will get it. It is not humanly possible to understand everything the first time, so, once a strategy has been collaboratively chosen, let's find ways to "Show until they know!"

Great Coaches Provide Models of Excellent Instructional Practice Personally and in Other Ways

"Over the past 10 years, we have found that Instructional Coaches (ICs) must be excellent teachers, particularly because they will likely provide model lessons in other teachers' classrooms" (Corwin Press, 2008, p. 160).

In response to the question "What specific actions did you take as an instructional coach that you felt were most effective?" Coach #2 explained:

> Well, I think the modeling. I spent a week going into the teacher's classroom and kind of, you know, demonstrating "I do, we do, you do," with the teacher, where I teach one class, then we'd co-teach the next class, and then I'd watch her teach that last class, so that she could see what her kids are really capable of doing . . . when allowed to think critically and do different things . . . so going in and co-teaching with the teacher is really effective.

In response to the question "What was the most frequently occurring problem that you addressed as an instructional coach?" Coach #3 related:

> I think that people [teachers] didn't really understand how to model. I think that was a huge "Aha" for staff. They didn't understand the power of "I do" a couple times, [and not doing] "We do" until they're ready for it, and then "you do" when they're ready for it . . . and understanding the power of rolling it out in that way [modeling for students] . . . if you still think you need to teach [a learning objective] cause they haven't mastered it, then why wouldn't you model it? If you don't think they need the model, then why is it your objective? Right? If they understand it well enough, then you should be moving on to something else. If they don't understand it, then they need to see you again and again until they get it. So I would say, [the lack of modeling] was the biggest thing I saw that I was kind of surprised at.

Have you noticed that teachers often forget to model? Do we as coaches or educational leaders forget to model or provide models for what we want to see happen? We can get such a positive rush of energy when our modeling for teachers goes well! Check out this story from Coach #6 in answer to the question "What was your most memorable success story as an instructional coach?"

> I was an instructional coach for teachers who teach English language learners, I was able to intervene in a Math department at a middle school in such a way that they really stepped back and changed everything they were doing. . . . What happened is, they served their monolingual kids better, and that's what changed their minds. When I was able to make that connection that you're not serving the few, even though there's federal laws that say we're to serve the few, please. But, that's okay . . . when I showed them, like, "Look, when you explain it this way, the

monolingual kids get it better too!" and then they were in. They totally revamped what they were doing: they started with vocab; they started with pre-loading; they did everything with their bodies; they made sense of it in real life before they did it on paper; they had different expectations of what products the kids should produce; they checked for understanding every lesson, but also multiple times [during the lesson]. And it was just tweaking a couple things like that and kind of seeing . . . just showing them . . . it was great. And their scores went up, and the kids were not falling off the math cliff. All of them. Especially in junior high.

Coach #9 shared a couple of great experiences she had with modeling:

[The teacher I was coaching] had a classroom of kindergarteners that were very difficult, very high need, and she just was struggling with how to deal with them. So I went in and we team-taught a lot, so that she could kind of see things that she could try or I could see things that weren't working well for her, because she was just having trouble picking them out. . . . So we did a lot of team teaching, and when it was all said and done, we sat down and we came up with a wonderful plan, and we took pictures of the kids doing the right thing and the kids not doing the right thing, and we made this big bulletin board of here's how a [school mascot name] Wildcat really looks; here's how a Wildcat really doesn't look. And then just referred to that all the time. And she said it just worked magic . . . and that was just awesome, because that worked great for her kids. Every time I would go in, [the students would say], "Look, I look like that kid. I'm doing what a Wildcat does. . . ."

I also would go in and model [for interventionists], and once we found the right strategy through that modeling and coaching them on how to deliver it and how to maintain their groups, we saw a lot of growth with our interventions with our tier 2 and tier 3 kids. We only had 13 kids that stayed flatlined out of the 312 that we provided interventions for.

Video

Another way to provide models for teachers is to use video.

Video can be used to help teachers understand what is happening when they are teaching, how they are delivering the instruction, and what it looks like when they are interacting with students. It also helps the coach and teacher have a common piece of evidence, so that they can reflect together and come to a mutual understanding of what was happening, what went well, and what could be worked on to facilitate greater student growth. With the intention of learning what coaching strategies teachers felt were most effective, we (TCT coaches) surveyed the teachers we coached. Using a Likert scale, teachers rated the strategies they had implemented from 1 to 5. The number-one strategy teachers listed overall as having the greatest positive impact was video analysis.

We often used a video analysis form to identify general components of quality instruction during lessons and to provide a common understanding between the coach and teacher of what was happening in teachers' classes. Some of the information found in the video analysis form is based on elements of effective instructional practice noted in a document entitled *The Architecture of Accomplished Teaching* by the National Board for Professional Teaching Standards (n.d.a).

The video analysis form that follows is organized to show elements of effective instructional practice on the left and evidence of the effective practices being demonstrated listed on the right. The form is filled out by the coach while the coach takes the video; then the video is given to the teacher on a disc, or the video is recorded on the teacher's phone, then returned to the teacher. After both the coach and the teacher have filled out the form, the teacher and coach meet and review the form results, going back to the video if/as needed. Evidence recorded is cause for celebration, and empty boxes facilitate reflective discussions and determination of new goals or next steps. Teachers have liked how straightforward this process is, and it provides evidence of many things that they do well, which then makes the empty spaces seem less daunting.

There are many good videos online that coaches can use to show teachers how to implement instructional strategies. It takes time to go through them, and usually this is best processed through with a team, so that everyone agrees the video provides a quality model for teachers. I have found the use of instructional videos to be very powerful.

One particular time when a video was helpful was when a second-grade teacher I was working with wanted a better vocabulary strategy that would help her students be more engaged when she was introducing the words to them. I pulled up an Anita Archer vocabulary video and scripted it out using the teacher's vocabulary words instead of the ones in the video. Then the teacher and I watched the video a couple times, practiced the hand movements and Anita's quick pacing, went over it a few times together using the teacher's vocabulary words, and finally added the use of the document camera to display the words. Anita's kinesthetic movements showed students when to chorally respond and how to indicate with their thumb on their stomach whether they knew the answer. (Anita is amazing; it's like she's conducting an orchestra with her hand movements when she teaches.) There weren't many words on the teacher's vocabulary list, so she almost had the whole thing memorized (words—actions—document camera use) after we practiced it a few times. I stayed and observed while her second-graders participated in an interactive and successful vocabulary lesson, with high levels of engagement.

This same teacher also wanted to create a kinesthetic component to her behavioral expectations and have students lead the presentation of those expectations with the associated actions each morning. We figured out some fun actions to go with her expectations and practiced them together. When she felt comfortable, I took videos of her with her phone as she enthusiastically modeled the behavioral expectations with the actions. We did this a few

Date: _____

Teacher: _____
Coach: _____

Video Analysis

Category of Effective Instructional Practice	Evidence of Effective Instructional Practice Found During Lesson
Significant preparation showing knowledge of students	
High, attainable, worthwhile goals	
Connection to prior learning and future content	
Real-world connections	
Activities and assignments connected to goals	
Teacher monitors student learning	
Teacher adjusts teaching strategies to meet student needs, if needed	
Appropriate use of "wait time"	
Open-ended questions	
Questions that reach higher levels (Bloom's; DOK)	
Teacher encourages student responses	
Opportunities for students to ask questions	
Attentive listening by teacher and students	
Checks for understanding and formative assessment	
Students interact with teacher	
Students interact with each other	
Students are engaged & interested	
Teacher redirects inactive students, to promote their participation	
Cooperation and respect exhibited	

times until she liked one of the takes. Then, she kept the video she liked best and played it while she was getting ready in the morning, to ensure she would present behavioral expectations with the associated actions in an enthusiastic and confident way. Video helped us tremendously to learn and practice good instruction together and to document and review things we wanted to remember.

Similarly, I had the opportunity to coach a young middle-school teacher who was having a hard time getting her students to take her seriously. When she tried to get their attention, she would often be ignored. I modeled, then she practiced a strategy for getting students' attention, then I videotaped her implementing the strategy a number of times until we felt she was coming across strong enough for students to know she meant business. This was done without students in the room, practicing a strategy with a coach until the teacher felt more comfortable owning her power. Video can give us confidence to step out of our comfort zones. We can practice until we look reasonable, or maybe even great, doing things we never thought we could!

Mentioned previously as an effective way to incorporate modeling by Coach #2, co-teaching can provide a structure for coaching support.

Co-Teaching

What is it?

> Co-teaching is not one teacher leading while the other grades essays. It's not both teachers doing the same thing at all times, a specialist pulling "her" students to the back corner while the main teacher instructs the rest of the class, or one teacher acting as the expert while the other is always the helper. It's not teaching the same way you always have.
>
> Rather, co-teaching is a partnering of two teachers with different areas of expertise to provide more comprehensive, effective instruction to students. Co-teaching most frequently occurs with a special education teacher and a classroom teacher, but it's becoming more common with all types of specialists. That's because educators recognize the inherent sense in bringing together individuals with different talents to produce the best instructional outcomes.
>
> (Beninghof, 2015/2016, p. 12)

Coaches can apply the concept of co-teaching in a variety of ways. A coach could work with two teachers at a time and help them set up processes for successful planning and implementation of co-teaching with students. Another idea would be for a coach and a teacher to go through the process of co-teaching together and incorporate some modeling by the coach of pieces the teacher would like to see. Then, the teacher could be given the opportunity to practice what was modeled and have the support of the coach as he or she incorporated components of effective lesson planning and delivery of instruction based on student needs. The main process pieces of co-teaching include co-planning, co-instruction; and co-assessing (Murawski & Lochner, 2017).

Marilyn Friend (2015/2016) offers six approaches to co-teaching that coaches can use to organize their own work with teachers. They are:

1. Station Teaching: Divide students into groups, and deliver lessons to each group independently. Both teachers work with each student as they pass from one station to the next.

2. Parallel Teaching: Students split into two groups, with one teacher supporting each. Instruction may be presented in two different ways (for example, providing alternative strategies for resolving math problems), or both teachers may present identical work (like test review).

3. Alternative Teaching: A small group of students is offered instruction for various purposes (like reteaching, enrichment, or pre-teaching), while the majority of the students continue their lessons with the other teacher.

4. Teaming: Two teachers work together with the same group, offering different contributions over the course of a lesson.

5. One Teach, One Assist: One teacher will lead instruction while the other interacts with individual students as needed. In this case, students remain in a single group, but the assisting teacher answers questions and focuses his or her attention on the students who need it most.

6. One Teach, One Observe: In this case, a single teacher presents the lesson while the other collects data as needed. This could mean focusing on one student for observation, observing a small group, or gathering data for the whole class.

Another way coaches can provide models for teachers is by setting up opportunities for teachers to visit colleagues who effectively demonstrate strategies the coached teacher is working to implement.

> **Teacher Observation Note Catcher**

Observations

Taking a teacher on a "field trip" to observe exemplary teachers is one of my favorite ways to provide models. For me, it has worked best to prepare for the visit with the teacher being coached using a template so that the teacher observing is clear about what

he or she is looking for, and the teacher being observed knows what to focus on during the observation. Have you ever taken a teacher to see another teacher, but nothing you wanted the coached teacher to see was demonstrated? Planning is powerful. If we want to see the teacher modeling something specific, we might want to let him or her know about it! I've facilitated meaningful observational experiences using the template/note catcher found below.

The teacher and I would discuss what he or she wanted to see modeled that aligned with the instructional goal we had collaboratively set. We would categorize our observation, and, if it was helpful, we would include the structure of the teacher evaluation rubric, refer to the rubric, and identify specific elements. Then we would identify any other resources we would like to have during the observation. For example, if we were working on writing essays and the school was using a particular organizational structure for essays, we would bring that with us for reference purposes. Then we would create a few general and related questions we wanted answered as we observed. After that, we would divide the note-taking space on the first page of the template (shown below) into the number of observational focus areas. Typically, we would have only two, maybe just one, but no more than three. The teacher would then be ready to organize his or her thinking and note-taking as he or she observed.

On the back page of the observation note catcher (shown below), the teacher observing could write more notes related to observational areas of focus if he or she had run out of room; list questions to ask the teacher after the observation; note any ideas not related to the observational focus areas that were impactful; and then begin listing ideas to implement and general ideas for timelines of implementation (often this last step was discussed collaboratively after the observation).

After the observation, the coached teacher, the coach (me), and the teacher who was observed would meet. The coached teacher would ask the teacher we had observed the questions listed, share any other thoughts, and then ask for help delineating implementation steps if needed.

One thing I do for teachers who are willing to be observed is, while they are teaching, I list every strength I can think of that I see them demonstrating (see Chapter 6 for a reference sheet of possible strengths to share). Then I share that list with them before the post-observation discussion. Coaches who are used to breaking down instruction into meaningful positive bites can bring joy into the lives of wonderful teachers by sharing specifically what those teachers do well. Teachers are very appreciative when they are provided with detailed, *positive* feedback about their teaching! I also sometimes use the video analysis form shared previously when I am in the presence of incredible teachers. I fill it out (whether I have a camera with me or not) and share it with them so that they can see recorded evidence of their wonderful instruction.

Teacher Observation Note Catcher

Observer:	Teacher:	Class:	Time:	Grade:	Date:

Teacher Quality Standards
Determine Observational Focus—circle choice(s):

I. Teachers demonstrate mastery of and pedagogical expertise in the content they teach.	II. Teachers establish a safe, inclusive and respectful learning environment for a diverse population of students.	III. Teachers plan and deliver effective instruction and create an environment that facilitates learning for their students.	IV. Teachers reflect on their practice.	V. Teachers demonstrate leadership.	VI. Teachers take responsibility for student academic growth.

Identify Elements of Teacher Quality Standard(s) for Observational Focus:

Reference Tool Ideas: Teacher Evaluation Rubric ■ District Reference Sheets

■ Other tools and/or resources specific to observational focus:

Observational Focus General Question(s):

Related Questions:

Record Focus-Area Notes Here (divide remaining space into number of focus areas chosen):

(Record more notes and questions to ask teacher being observed on the back of this form.)

Questions to Ask Teacher Being Observed:	When?
	Ideas to Implement:
Other Observational Notes Related to Focus Areas:	Observational Notes Not Related to Focus Areas:

Great Coaches Show Teachers How to Rigorously Analyze Instruction and Engage in Meaningful Reflection

Instruction is effective when students learn and are able to apply what was taught. So, we need to incorporate into our modeling some type of assessment designed to measure whether students can demonstrate an understanding of the learning objective or goal. Going back to the basics of *planning* and *assessment* as part of the "Frequent Five" in Chapter 3, we define a specific learning goal/objective/intention tied to a standard; then we determine how the instruction could best be delivered to the students involved (consider students' abilities; interests, etc.); then we choose a method of delivery and design an assessment and/or success criteria that work with the delivery choice and make sure each piece of instruction is aligned with the learning goal/objective/intention.

Sounds complicated, but really it's pretty straightforward: First, know what you want to teach and why (determine a clear goal incorporating standards); second, make the delivery of the learning meaningful for your kids; and, third, figure out a good way to know whether students understood and met the learning goal. From there, you'll be in a good position to decide what to do next (move on, reteach, etc.), because you'll have evidence to show who understood and who didn't. When a lesson plan includes these components, after the lesson is modeled and/or taught, the coach and teacher can review the original plan, possibly analyze a video of the modeling or teaching, and determine where things went well and where some adjustments need to be made. The Time Distribution Tool in Chapter 9 shows how instructional time during observations is used by the person teaching or modeling. The form could be filled in by a teacher while watching a coach model instruction or by a coach when observing a teacher. It could also be used when a coach and teacher are observing another teacher to provide useful data for discussion. Some reflective questions that could be discussed after a modeling session include:

What do you feel went well? Were there any surprises? Where in the lesson did we see the most engagement? The least? Do we have any evidence that the lesson was successful? What did you learn from this experience? Are there any changes you would make if you taught this lesson again?

In response to the question "What was your most memorable success story as an instructional coach?" Coach #3 answered:

> [S]omebody was embracing the rigor of self-assessment and not saying, "Oh, there's gonna be follow-up, and now I really do have to make a change, and it's gonna be a pain in the ass (excuse me), and it's gonna be hard, but I'm gonna do it . . ." [instead], she was telling me all of a sudden she had this, "Aha!" [regarding an opportunity to change and improve her practice].

Isn't it great when teachers being coached are okay with looking at what they need to change and are excited they noticed what they could do to improve their instruction?

We can help teachers be willing to reflect and plan for changes when things don't go well, if we do the same. It's helpful to teachers when coaches can voluntarily admit the modeling or something else they did wasn't that great. Teachers know there isn't anyone threatening us with a stick, forcing us to say we messed up. So, if we willingly admit it and don't make excuses or try to gloss over things to save face because we're supposed to be the experts, we can authentically model rigorous self-assessment through personal and collaborative reflection. And then both we and the teachers we coach can improve. It makes us more real (remember vulnerability, in Chapter 4) to others when we take risks and allow ourselves to be vulnerable. Modeling doesn't always go as planned—neither does teaching. But it's okay; we reflect, learn, and get better. Be proud of yourself for completely putting yourself out there.

Martha Sandstead (2015/2016) shared her thoughts on taking modeling risks:

> During my first year as a coach, I was thrilled when I received my first request to model a lesson, but I was nervous to have an adult audience. As I prepared, I tried to follow the curriculum, just as the teachers are expected to do, even though I thought it included too much for kindergartners to do in 30 minutes. Rather than a swan dive, I demonstrated a belly flop.
>
> When I met with the teacher the following day to debrief, I joked that it wasn't much of a model but that I hoped she got something out of it. Together we discussed what went well and what we would change the next time either of us tried to teach a similar lesson. I offered to return to try again, and the lesson went well the second time around.
>
> Model lessons are valuable coaching tools, even if they don't go well. It's powerful for teachers to watch you fail, reflect, and reteach successfully. And it's essential to maintain humility, honesty, and sincerity when working with teachers. They need to know that you too struggle to make the curriculum fit the students, that you understand the time involved in preparing lessons, that you value the support of colleagues, and that you are willing to take risks.
>
> (pp. 79–80)

We want teachers to experience joy in the relationship and in the results they experience through our coaching. To do this, we need to understand that coaching is basically a service industry. Our reputation is central to our success; the person we are, the person we have developed ourselves to be at that point in time when we are working with someone is essentially all we can bring to the table. So, all we can do to improve ourselves in as many ways as possible (by cultivating the 10 characteristics in this book) will help us be better with and for teachers. As Jim Knight (2011) related, "Without question, the most important factor relative to the effectiveness of a coaching program is, 'Who is the coach?'" (p. 122).

I thought it might be helpful to incorporate some of the elements of effective coaching and modeling into one story or scenario, something almost everyone could relate to. So, I chose a situation most of us have been through—sometimes successfully, sometimes not. I chose the often scary process of finding a person we can trust to cut our hair and/or do our nails. I am hoping this real-world example (elements of which we've probably all experienced) might illuminate differently and perhaps more clearly some points mentioned previously. The following model of good coaching practice, in another realm, is found in Mariah, the person who does my hair and nails. I don't cheat on her, I tip her well, and I feel renewed after spending time with her. I've had a lot of people do my hair and nails over the years, but Mariah is different in a really great way, so I started thinking about why she is basically "magical." Here's what I came up with:

1. *Mariah beautifully does her own hair and nails*, and she and the salon always look great! If I'm going to go to someone to try to look better and pay big money to get my hair and nails done, it is a major turnoff and a bit of a concern if the person looks disheveled with a bad haircut, little or no effort was given to washing or styling his or her hair, or I see that the person's nails are ratty, with polish peeling off and so on. Another thing that makes me want to run out the door of a salon is if it's dirty. It's like you're scared you're going to get some kind of disease by being in there. You get my point: Mariah models in her person and in the environment she creates that she's got this hair-and-nails stuff down and that she cares about it.

2. *Mariah attends to detail.* Throughout the haircut/pedicure/manicure, Mariah continuously checks to make sure the hair on each side of my head is even, my nails are filed symmetrically and similarly to each other, the polish goes on smoothly and covers completely, and so forth. I quit worrying that I might need to remind her of anything, because I knew she would do a thorough job. Mariah makes quality her responsibility, so I don't have that pressure of trying to remind her to not miss anything or tell her to step it up and do a better job in some nice way—which is stressful, because how do you say "Don't mess up my hair" kindly without upsetting the stylist? And you definitely do not want to offend someone with scissors, because what happens after that could go very badly for you. Trying to deal well with situations when we doubt competency is uncomfortable, as almost all of us know.

3. *Mariah is accomplished and respected.* She holds many certifications and is always learning and sharing her knowledge, new learnings, and creative applications of that learning with colleagues. The last time I was in her salon, she was using some technical vocabulary I was unfamiliar with in reference to the chemical makeup of hair products. She was talking with another colleague and offering helpful suggestions. It was obvious she had technical expertise galore. It reminded me of the education-ese we regularly use and sometimes assume everyone understands.

4. *Mariah is positive, passionate, and enthusiastic.* Not one negative word comes out of Mariah's mouth. She is too busy thinking about how to do the next thing better, noticing what her client may need, or sharing exciting news. Mariah smiles often and remarks on the beautiful mountains or on what is good in her life, in others' lives, and in the world. She is hopeful and happy. She also interacts at a pretty quick pace, definitely not dull or sluggish. I feel energized and uplifted after being with her.

5. *Mariah models.* I had to stop perming my hair, because it was getting too dry, especially after I moved to the mountains. So, for years, I had the ongoing problem of how to create "voluminous" curls on the top of my head without a perm. Mariah knew how to do this! She showed me how by taking me through a series of steps and modeling exactly what to do with my hair—she did it *on* my head; she didn't just tell me what to do. (I'm including the details here, because this is a seriously awesome hair hack.) She explained, "Put hair spray and gel in the hair while it is still wet, brush it through, then scrunch the hair, get some metal prong clips (she told me where to buy them) and clip the hair on the top and crown of the head up into little tufts all over, following any natural curls. Then blow dry the hair using a diffuser, and keep the diffuser on the tufts until they are dry, take the clips out, and voilà!" It actually worked, and now I have volume on top of my head without getting a root perm every few months!

6. *Mariah takes notes and reflects on her practice.* After every session, Mariah takes notes and reflects on what she can do better the next time she meets with a client. If there was anything she or the client weren't happy with, she is aware of it, records it, and is careful to adjust as needed the next time the client comes in. Mariah has processes in place to avoid making the same mistake twice.

7. *Mariah cares.* Mariah is incredibly competent, doesn't mess my hair up, knows her stuff, can model how to do wonderful things, attends to detail, has lots of school behind her, and is continually learning, but then there's this X factor. Here's why I think she's the most incredible cosmetologist I've ever had: when I'm in the salon, *I don't feel like I'm just a number* or a way for her to punch her daily lunch ticket. She doesn't seem rushed or in a hurry to finish with me just to get to the next customer, though she usually finishes on time. She is present with me, she remembers what I am up to, she asks questions, and then (and no other stylist has done much of this) she does extra little things for her clients. She does a neck massage before each haircut; she takes extra time doing the things her clients like—extends the foot rub, offers to carry things if the client's hands are full, and so forth. Both little and big courtesies seem to come to mind naturally for her. She thinks about how she can help when there is something on my mind

and offers suggestions showing she is mentally and emotionally interested in what I am doing and thinking. We are both interested in music and sing through parts of songs together here and there. She personalizes her support, and that's the feeling I leave with—I was supported, *and* I have great hair and nails. The way she integrates her caring and competence, the way she does business inspires me and models for me ways I could add more competent and caring personalized pieces to my instructional coaching practice and maybe be the most incredible coach ever for the teachers I work with.

Conclusion

Show until they know. We can do this in a variety of ways, through modeling personally, co-teaching, using video, and observing other teachers. The main thing is that we just do it. We make learning easier and more enjoyable when we incorporate modeling regularly into our coaching practice and encourage teachers to incorporate it into their teaching practice as well. In the characteristics study (Frazier, 2014), "models" was mostly mentioned as an integral part of being competent, but we know that how we deliver that competency is crucial, and if we do it in a way that makes teachers feel supported and valued—in a caring way—we can build joyful, balanced coaching relationships. Many of the people I have coached have become my dear friends, because if you authentically care about someone and have provided and gained meaningful support that has enriched both lives, that doesn't really end, even if they don't need a coach to help them with teaching anymore. Coaching continues to enrich my overall life satisfaction, because it provides an opportunity for me to get to know wonderful people and for them to get to know me. It is a beautiful and fulfilling role, one that challenges me to figure out how to do better and be better each day, and for that, I am truly grateful.

Reflect and Connect

Instructional Coaching Modeling Process Plan
- Overview Arrow
- Modeling Map

MODELS

Teacher & Coach Determine Modeling Topic

Teacher & Coach Determine Modeling Structure and Record Look For's, Measures, & Other Process Details (as they fill out the modeling graphic organizer —on back)

Teacher & Coach Determine Amount of Time for Modeling

Keep time short to allow for analysis of a specific topic and possible practice time for teacher immediately following modeling

Coach Plans Modeling
Typical plans include the standard(s) addressed, a learning target, a method of instructional delivery and a formative assessment. Coach chooses a plan that takes a reasonable amount of time and could be duplicated by the teacher. The coach shares the chosen planning process with the teacher and provides a rationale

Coach Models Instruction While Teacher Records Information

Teacher Practices

Teacher Implements Modeling Topic With Students While Coach Observes

Teacher & Coach Discuss Implementation and Analyze Both Qualitative and Quantitative Measures From Coach's Observation

Next Steps Are Determined

Choose a partner: Discuss modeling experiences you have had, seen, or one that you are in the process of planning. Identify issues or successes you have experienced. Review the Modeling Map and plan a modeling session with your partner.

PD

MODELING MAP
Showing the way!

Before Coach Models	During Coach Modeling:	After Modeling & When Teacher Implements
Name the Desire, Problem, or Topic of Interest:	1. **Standard(s) Addressed:**	**Discuss How Modeling Went/ Review Measures & Formative Assessment Results:**
Create Goal:	2. **Learning Target:**	
	3. **Instructional Delivery Method:**	**Teacher Practice:**
	4. **Formative Assessment:**	When?
Modeling Structure:		Where?
• Coach Models Only for Teacher	*1.	Questions after practicing?
• Coach Models for Teacher With Students	*2.	
• Co-teaching Including Modeling		**Coach Observes Teacher and Collects Data:**
• Modeling → Practice → Same-Day Implementation With Students		Quantitative:
• Coach & Teacher Analyze an Instructional Video Together	*3.	Qualitative:
What Does the Teacher Specifically Want to See?	*4.	
*1.		**Review Data & Formative Assessment Results:**
*2.		
*3.		
*4.		**Next Steps:**
Amount of Time Coach Will Spend Modeling:	**Modifications:** (Special Learning Needs/ Styles—SPED-GT-ELL, Visual-Kinesthetic, etc.)	Continue with this?
What Measures Could Be Added to the Coach's Planning to See If the Idea Worked With Students?		Try something else?
Quantitative Measure(s): (could be formative assessment)	**Formative Assessment Results:**	
	Process for Grading Formative Assessment:	
Qualitative Measure(s):		

→

(Continued)

(Continued)

Coach Planning:

Choice of Instructional Delivery Method: _____

Rationale: _____

☐ Appropriate Pacing & Student Behavior Expectations for Grade Level ☐ Professional Dress & Demeanor ☐ Positive, Warm, & Encouraging Words/Actions ☐ Address Multiple Learning Modalities ☐ Video for Future Use? ☐ Share Lesson Plan With Teacher ☐ Reasonable Plan Time

Formative Assessment Ideas: Quick 3-question quiz on Learning Target (ticket out, whiteboards, electronic response), students write a tweet (on paper or electronically) summarizing the learning for the day, students show understanding to teacher using manipulatives

Quantitative Measure Ideas: Student engagement level %s during lesson sections, # of student responses during lesson sections, questions categorized into DOK levels—determine % of total # of questions at each level, % distribution of time for parts of lesson

Qualitative Measure Ideas: Nonverbal cues (body language, smiles, student perceptions), flow of classroom (clarity in processes, directions and procedures, perceived confidence/interest/anxiety levels of students and teacher, group structures and dynamics, voice)

 Available for download at https://resources.corwin.com/JoyofCoaching

Models Self-Assessment

1. Take this self-assessment before you set an intention to consciously find ways to provide models.

2. Implement some of the practical application coaching ideas and/or models S.O.A.K. supports found below (or use some of your own ideas).

3. In a month or so, see whether you have been able to improve your thoughts, motivations, and behaviors surrounding the important coaching characteristic of modeling. Reference the following synonyms/specifics as you personally determine how to more effectively model and determine how to make it a more conscious part of your daily life: *demonstrates excellent instructional practice; models rigorous analysis of instruction and self-reflection; strives to internalize the 10 characteristics of effective instructional coaches and daily models balanced caring and competent coaching* (Frazier, 2014).

	Strongly Disagree	Disagree	Neutral/ Not Sure	Agree	Strongly Agree
	1	2	3	4	5
I can and do demonstrate quality instructional practice for teachers when it is appropriate.					
I regularly look for ways to "show" teachers how to be effective.					
I am comfortable with and have developed or located useful tools to help maximize the use of video, co-teaching, and collegial observations in my coaching practice.					
I am interested in the process of personal growth and refinement. I want to become the best person I can be.					
I value both the hearts and the minds of the people I coach and think of ways to show them I care while helping them build instructional competence.					
I value my own heart and mind and work to stay strong and sane. I recognize I am human and benefit from support. I take time to rest and renew myself both physically and emotionally. I am continually learning, practicing, and becoming better at caring and being instructionally competent, so that I can be a great model for teachers.					
Column Totals:					
Grand Total: _____					

What totals mean: 26–30 = Modeling Rock Star, 21–25 = I Model Well and Often! 16–20 = I Model Reasonably Well, 11–15 = Sometimes Modeling Happens in My Coaching Practice, 6–10 = Better Step Up My Modeling, 0–5 = Would Becoming Better at Modeling Be a Helpful Goal?

Practical Application Ideas for Models

Don't Overdo Modeling

When I was just beginning my coaching career, I was learning and wanted very badly to do a good job. I was thrilled when a teacher asked me to model a lesson for a fifth-grade class. I was crazy excited, I felt totally competent, it was paragraph writing (I could rock that), I was missing kids, and I *so* wanted to do my best for them and for the teacher. Twenty hours later, I had visuals for everything; a beautiful lesson plan, so that the teacher could see my processes; little games for the students to play; everything color-coded; incentives; prizes; and candy. I was stoked and couldn't wait for the chance to teach again!

The lesson went amazingly. Everyone was so impressed; the kids understood the concept and produced incredible paragraphs. I was feeling extremely successful, and then the teacher asked me to come back and do it again for her teammate—because, she said, "I would never have the time to do all that!"

Probably important to not model something a teacher can't reasonably do. Sadness.

Video Both Ways

Video is helpful for both the teacher and the coach. If you as a coach do have the chance to model for a teacher, why not have the teacher or someone else video you as you teach, then take apart the video using the video analysis form in this chapter or some other type of reflective process so that you can show your willingness to be vulnerable and real? By letting yourself be videotaped, you can show the teacher that video isn't that scary and model for the teacher how to determine whether learning goals were met, whether the instruction was focused on the learning goals and delivered in a way that was appropriate for the students in the room, whether you kept a good pace and students were engaged and interested, whether there was an assessment to ascertain students' level of mastery, and so on. Demonstrate how to get the most out of critically analyzing your performance, but don't forget to acknowledge your strengths. Be balanced about it, or the teacher may run the other way!

MODELS ~S.O.A.K. ~   Sometimes learning penetrates best when we are relaxed and not trying too hard to make it happen.

Stress-free Opportunities to Absorb Knowledge   **Choose what works for you.** (Like a "Models" Bath Bomb infused with personalized nutrients)

Quotes	Music	Statements affirmations	Books poetry stories	Art & More	Videos movies	Movement other ideas
"Can you show me how to do it?" —Most teachers	**"Count on Me"** Bruno Mars	**For coaches:** I strive to be the change I wish to see in the classroom. ☺	**"The Two Crabs"** Aesop	**Helping Hands** Toverwoudcreatief	**Why Teachers Teach and What They Need** http://29pieces.org/dallas-teachers-speak	**Standing Bow Pose**
"I actually think that the most efficacious way of making a difference is to lead by example and doing random acts of kindness is setting a very good example of how to behave in the world." —Misha Collins	**"Watching You"** Rodney Atkins **"Cat's in the Cradle"** Harry Chapin	When I find ways to show teachers what to do, the clarity and effectiveness of my coaching is magnified. I provide clear models of instructional content, so that the teachers I coach understand exactly how to proceed.	**The Art of Coaching: Effective Strategies for School Transformation** Elena Aguilar, pp. 220–222 **Focus on Teaching: Using Video for High-Impact Instruction** Jim Knight	**More Quotes:** "The greatest education in the world is watching the masters at work." —Michael Jackson "Important achievements require a clear focus, all-out effort, and a bottomless trunk full of strategies. Plus allies in learning."	**Patient Dog Teaches Puppy How to Get Down Stairs** The Dodo (YouTube) https://www.youtube.com/watch?v=J9pDAbpga_g	**Twin Tree Pose** **Oil:** lemon **Stone:** snowflake obsidian
"Example is not the main thing in influencing others, it is the only thing." —Albert Schweitzer	**"Hero"** Mariah Carey **"You've Got a Friend in Me"** Randy Newman **"Believe"** Shawn Mendes	I often express my belief in and best wishes for the teachers I coach.	**Mentoring, Coaching, and Collaboration** Corwin Press, pp. 150–157	—Carol Dweck		
"Educators [including coaches] should be chosen not merely for their special qualifications, but more for their personality and character because we teach [and lead] more by what we are than by what we teach." —Will Durant	**"Gift of a Friend"** Demi Lovato **"Stand by Me"** Ben E. King, 1961 **"Lean on Me"** Bill Withers	**For teachers:** I clearly model what I want students to do, so that they understand exactly what to do. I internalize and express to students the inherent joy associated with learning.	**Make Your Bed: Little Things That Can Change Your Life . . . And Maybe The World** William H. McRaven: "If you want to change the world . . . be your very best in the darkest moments" (p. 74).	"Unless you try to do something beyond what you have already mastered, you will never grow." —Ralph Waldo Emerson	**Jim Knight: Best Practices and Worst Mistakes for Video Instructional Coaching** https://blog.edthena.com/2018/09/26/best-practices-instructional-coachingvideo	**Color:** light green

(Continued)

Quotes	Music	Statements affirmations	Books poetry stories	Art & More	Videos movies	Movement other ideas
	"My Wish" Rascal Flatts **"This One's for the Girls"** Martina McBride **"Have It All"** Jason Mraz	I show my students with words and actions that I believe in them and wish them all the best things in life.			**Teaching Channel** https:// www.teaching-channel.org **Teaching Channel's mission is "to create an environment where teachers can watch, share, and learn new techniques to help every student grow."**	

Great modeling creates clarity.

Appendix A

Competent Cliff Notes

Common Core State Standards (CCSS)

In the spring of 2009, two groups, the National Governors Association and The Council of Chief State School Officers, began working on an initiative called the Common Core State Standards (CCSS). Internationally benchmarked academic standards in English language arts and mathematics were created, to more effectively prepare students for college, careers, and a global society by increasing exposure to and encouraging the application of more rigorous content.

Though they were developed and funded privately (for the most part), the U.S. Department of Education has promoted the standards by providing incentives for states that use them and has included them as part of a general goal to prepare high-school graduates to be better prepared for college and careers. Next-generation assessments aligned to CCSS are being developed at the state level with some federal support. (For background on CCSS, see www.nsba.org/advocayc/federal-legislative-priorities/academic-standards/background-common-core-state-standards and http://www.corestandards.org.)

Many states have adopted CCSS, and instructional coaches are learning how to support teachers as they address these new standards.

> Supporting students to learn requires more than presenting information to them. Learning occurs more often, and more deeply, when students understand, retain, and are able to apply and use what they are taught, not just routinely, but in new and novel ways. Getting students to these deeper levels of learning is a key goal of current educational reforms and one toward which most teachers strive, but the path to achieve that end may not always be clear.
>
> (Conley, 2014, p. 1)

CCSS have required pedagogical shifts in teaching priorities and instructional delivery methods to increase rigor and conceptual understanding. Some of the changes teachers are making to effectively address CCSS are found on the Common Core State Standards Initiative website (n.d.a, n.d.b). Shifts in language arts include (a) regular practice with complex texts and their academic language; (b) reading, writing, and speaking grounded in evidence from texts, both literary and informational; and (c) building knowledge through content-rich nonfiction. Suggested shifts in mathematics include (a) greater focus on fewer topics; (b) coherence: linking topics and thinking across grades; and (c) rigor: pursue conceptual understanding, procedural skills and fluency, and application with equal intensity.

The Changing Demographics of America's Schools

The majority of students in America's K–12 public schools will soon be children of color (Maxwell, 2014a). The Latino population is growing quickly, there are more Asian Americans, and the number of African American students is staying steady. The white population is declining (Maxwell, 2014b). Many changes to curriculum and professional development, including a focus on teaching English language learners (ELLs) and developing cultural competence, are being offered to address this change in demographics.

The Every Student Succeeds Act (ESSA)

The Every Student Succeeds Act (ESSA), a reauthorization of the Elementary and Secondary Education Act, was signed into law by President Obama on December 10, 2015. It replaced No Child Left Behind and is designed to reduce the power of the U.S. Department of Education and give more control to states and districts. Focus areas of ESSA include supporting equity by protecting and supporting high-need and disadvantaged students, increasing preschool access, requiring that all students receive instruction based on high academic standards, supporting and growing local innovations, and a continuation of annual statewide assessments to measure progress toward high standards (U.S. Department of Education, n.d.a).

Learning Forward Standards for Professional Learning

https://learningforward.org/standards/

These standards provide insight into what effective professional learning would need to include to effectively impact teacher development and student learning. Forty education associations and professional associations worked together to develop the new standards. These new standards incorporate findings from current educational research and include adaptations based on feedback from those who implemented the previous standards. The following notes are taken from a 2011 *Journal of Staff Development* article entitled "New Standards Put the Spotlight on Professional Learning," written by Mizell, Hord, Killion, and Hirsh, and a video by Stephanie Hirsh located at https://learningforward.org/standards.

Changes from the old Standards for Professional Development to the new Standards for Professional Learning include:

- A reduction in the number of standards from 12 to 7: Learning Communities, Leadership, Resources, Data, Learning Designs, Implementation, and Outcomes.

- Context, process, content organizer is less prominent, recognizing the need for a more holistic process and a realization that all standards are of equal importance.

- Reduced content standard expectations to one; the Outcomes standard relates to performance standards for teachers and students.

- The expectation is that the implementation of the standards will improve the quality of professional learning across the United States and across all countries.

- What is needed from educators and professional developers of all kinds:
  o Read and become familiar with the standards. Be an expert of and advocate for the standards and for professional learning that meets the standards.
  o Share the standards with those who have responsibilities for making decisions around professional learning.

The level of focus and the design of systems to support these standards is typically a state or district leadership decision, so coaches may not be daily immersed in or held to these standards. However, it would be good for coaches to know the consensus of 40 different associations and organizations regarding effective professional learning and be able to include components of this knowledge in instructional coaching processes.

National Board Certification and Five Core Propositions

Numerous studies have indicated that students of board-certified teachers learn more and that minority and low-income students are positively impacted at higher levels by teachers who have achieved national board certification (Charlotte-Mecklenburg Schools, 2010; Chingos & Peterson, 2011; CNA Corporation, 2004; Cowan & Goldhaber, 2016; Goldhaber & Anthony, 2007; NBPTS, 2015; Strategic Data Project, 2012).

National board certification is the highest credential in the teaching profession. Teachers with at least three years of experience who are interested in working toward becoming a National Board Certified Teacher can take a series of assessments to provide evidence that their teaching meets the highest professional standards. Twenty-five certificate areas are available for teachers to choose from as they work toward national board certification.

The standards for all certificate areas were developed based on five core propositions (Steeves & Browne, 2000). Whether or not teachers or coaches participate in the assessment process, instructional coaches will want to be aware of and help teachers understand and move toward incorporating the highest professional standards for teachers by integrating the foundational National Board Five Core Propositions for Teaching into their teaching practice.

The standards for national board certification were developed by teachers for teachers. When I went through the process, I could tell this was true. I didn't feel like the resources had been created by people who had never stepped into a classroom or dealt with teachers' everyday struggles and choices. The process was extremely effective in helping me improve my teaching practice in the following ways: (1) I learned to analyze data and use it to be intentional about my instructional choices, (2) I learned to be reflective in a productive way, not just feel badly and go home and eat ice cream if I had delivered a lousy lesson, and (3) I learned how to make students my central focus not only in my heart, but also in my daily "competent" professional choices.

I found a couple of really good resources and definitions that will help teachers or coaches who are considering this form of professional development. I will list the five Core Propositions below, but details about each one can be found in a visual entitled, "The Architecture of Accomplished Teaching," which shows the structure of accomplished teaching as defined by NBPTS. This visual can be found on the website, accomplishedteacher.org.

> The Five Core Propositions—comparable to medicine's Hippocratic Oath—set forth the profession's vision for accomplished teaching. Together, the propositions form the basis of all National Board Standards and the foundation for National Board Certification.
>
> **Proposition 1:** Teachers are committed to students and their learning.
>
> **Proposition 2:** Teachers know the subjects they teach and how to teach those subjects to students.
>
> **Proposition 3:** Teachers are responsible for managing and monitoring student learning.
>
> **Proposition 4:** Teachers think systematically about their practice and learn from experience.
>
> **Proposition 5:** Teachers are members of learning communities.
>
> (NBPTS, n.d.b)

It seems we are all searching for clarity as we set sail in the sometimes tumultuous sea of education reform. I have appreciated these clear definitions provided by NBPTS (Student Learning, Student Achievement Task Force, 2011, p. 28):

> **Student Achievement** is the status of subject-matter knowledge, understandings, and skills at one point in time.
>
> **Student Learning** is growth in subject-matter knowledge, understandings, and skill over time. In essence, a change in achievement constitutes learning. It is student learning—not achievement—that is most relevant to defining and assessing accomplished teaching.
>
> **Accomplished teaching** reflects skilled practice and contributes to student learning.

Next Generation Learning

According to the Bill & Melinda Gates Foundation (2010, p. 1), Next Generation Learning is "the intelligent use of technology to develop innovative learning models and personalized educational pathways."

"Over the past four years, the six-year old Next Generation Learning Challenges grant program has poured millions of dollars into K-12 school models that use technology, personalized learning, and new forms of assessment in an attempt to overhaul the traditional educational process" (Davis, 2016).

> It [Next Generation Learning] is part of a bigger opportunity to reimagine the entire experience students have in public schools. Personalized learning is a big part of it, but Next-Gen learning incorporates aspects of what is gradually coming to be thought of as personalized learning, as well as competency-based learning, blended or technology-enabled learning, and experiential learning.
>
> (Calkins, 2016, p. 16, quoted in Davis, 2016)

Finding ways to know students better—including learner profiles, along with flexible pacing and the identification of individualized learning pathways—are accomplished through a variety of learning modalities with Next Generation Learning. These may include peer-to-peer tutoring, small group direct instruction, individual diagnostic prescriptive software, or team-based project work (Calkins, 2016). "Next Generation Learning Challenges seeks to pinpoint technology solutions that can measurably improve the quality of learning experiences and improve students' college readiness and chances of completion" (Bill & Melinda Gates Foundation, 2010, p. 3).

Identifying ways to facilitate the effective implementation of 21st-century learning/skills and implementing many of the concepts of personalized learning are components of Next Generation Learning. With an emphasis on personalizing education to be motivating and relevant for individual students, supporting students to effectively engage in creating new learning, solve problems in team settings, and promote the use of current technologies as learning tools, the Next Generation Learning movement, with its many grant opportunities, has become a major player in education today.

Partnership for Assessment of Readiness for College and Careers (PARCC)

PARCC is an end-of-year computerized assessment for students in Grades 3–8, designed to measure student progress toward college and career readiness by assessing student levels of mastery of the new CCSS in English language arts and mathematics.

> The PARCC assessment system is an annual year-end test in English language arts/literacy, and mathematics in Grades 3-8 and high school.

Most states voluntarily adopted new, more rigorous academic standards in 2010 and 2011 and teachers have been using them since then in their daily instruction. As a result, states needed high-quality assessments aligned to those standards that would test students of all achievement levels on what they are learning.

Many of the old state tests measured only lower-level skills. The new assessments serve as an "educational GPS system," measure students' current performance, and point the way to what students need to learn by graduation so they are ready for college and/or a career.

(www.parcconline.org/about/the-parcc-tests)

Personalized Learning

Personalized learning (PL) is an educational movement that involves designing teaching and learning around the academic needs and personal interests of students. Digital tools are used to organize instruction and help students take ownership of their learning. These tools can also offer both students and teachers access to curriculum and assessments that are adaptive (Bushweller, 2016).

The use of multiple pathways for students to show mastery of identified competencies is also a key component of PL. There is sometimes confusion over the definition of PL. You will find through study that the philosophies and strategies of other initiatives, such as Next Generation Learning and 21st Century Skills, are part of the philosophical soup, as all of education tries to address less than exciting student progress (NCES, 2013; OECD, 2012) and incorporate the opportunities new technologies provide at the astonishingly fast pace they are being developed.

Try not to be confused with all this, and if you feel like you don't understand it all or don't know how to coach teachers to implement it, take heart from this statement by Benjamin Herold (2016) in *Education Week*: "One big problem: proponents [of personalized learning] have struggled to define personalized learning, let alone demonstrate its effectiveness [it is very new; not a lot of research exists]. The purpose, tools, and instructional techniques that make up the notion vary considerably, depending who you ask."

To try to understand and help teachers with this new concept, coaches could visit sites where it's working and talk with teachers and leaders who are successfully implementing the concept.

Professional Learning Communities (PLCs)

The concept of professional learning communities began to be communicated in earnest in 1998 with the publication of the book *Professional Learning Communities at Work: Best Practices for Enhancing Student Achievement* by Richard DuFour and Robert Eaker

(Solution Tree, n.d.). The general idea of this movement is that within districts, schools, and teams, educators can increase student learning through collaboration by participating in "an ongoing process in which educators work collaboratively in recurring cycles of collective inquiry and action research to achieve better results for the students they serve" (DuFour, DuFour, Eaker, & Many, 2010, p. 11).

PLC resources typically include thought-provoking questions to guide discussion and offer educational leaders, school staffs, and grade-level teams ways to process through and answer the questions as they work together to improve student results. Intentional, targeted, and regular data collection and analysis, through the use of collaboratively developed common assessments to inform and improve daily instruction, are central to this educational movement.

PLC's four essential questions are as follows:

1. What do we expect students to learn?

2. How will we know when they have learned it?

3. How will we respond when they don't learn it?

4. How will we respond when they already know it?

(DuFour, DuFour, Eaker, & Karhanek, 2004, pp. 21–27; DuFour, DuFour, Eaker, & Many, 2010, p. 28; Eaker, DuFour, & DuFour, 2002)

Sometimes districts will formulate their own models or planning tools based on the four questions. Check to see whether your school district has something developed; if so, you could use it as a guide and reference. Specific strategies that could be used by teachers are sometimes listed on the document.

Whether or not your school district uses a PLC model, asking the four questions as a coach could provide structure, clarity, and the inclusion of a data-collection plan to increase awareness of the effectiveness of instructional methods used. These results could then be analyzed and a non-biased discussion held that could include both celebrations and/or adjustments.

Rigor

One of the basic themes of the Common Core shifts is to increase "rigor" in both instructional delivery and student applications of content/concepts taught. Ways to help teachers understand what this might look like and how to incorporate better teaching practices that could prepare students more effectively for college and careers, and for the new PARCC assessments, are in high demand. Listed below are a few general philosophies/structures/resources for developing more rigorous teaching:

Revised Bloom's Taxonomy (2001)

Originally created in 1956 by Benjamin Bloom and colleagues and revised in 2001 by a group of psychologists, researchers, curriculum theorists, and assessment specialists, this series of categories is organized to explain different ways the mind can work with or process knowledge. The categories are Remember, Understand, Apply, Analyze, Evaluate, and Create (cft.vanderbilt.edu/guides-sub-pages/blooms-taxonomy). Understanding this structure encourages teachers to see the value of incorporating a variety of ways of thinking into all facets of their instructional practice.

Norman Webb's Depth of Knowledge (DOK) Levels

DOK levels can be used to determine the cognitive depth of academic tasks. Organizing academic tasks and instructional delivery designed to encourage and support students thinking deeply each day has become an expectation in the world of CCSS. Webb's Depth of Knowledge provides a structure and common language to help teachers evaluate and categorize questions, tasks, and learning objectives (Aungst, 2014).

The four levels are as follows:

Level 1: Recall and Reproduction

Level 2: Skills and Concepts

Level 3: Strategic Thinking

Level 4: Extended Thinking

Marzano's 13 Strategies to Achieve Rigor

[A]n analysis of more than 2 million data points collected from observer ratings on specific classroom instructional strategies, indicates that even today, with the increased focus on rigor, the great majority of teachers still devote the highest frequency of classroom instruction to introducing and practicing new knowledge, activities which are at the lower levels of Bloom's (1956), Webb's (2002), and Marzano's (2001) taxonomies of educational objectives. Students must develop the ability to test hypotheses, analyze and synthesize in order to be successful not just on the new assessments, but also in college and in future careers. Additionally, they must be able to work collaboratively, to take knowledge and utilize it in real-world situations. If we hope to move students to these higher levels of skills and cognition, it's imperative that we equip teachers with the "how," those essential teaching strategies that will scaffold students to problem-solve and make decisions in real-world scenarios with less teacher direction.

(Marzano & Toth, 2014, p. 17)

Marzano listed 13 strategies for achieving rigor:

1. Identifying critical content

2. Previewing new content

3. Organizing students to interact with content

4. Helping students process content

5. Helping students elaborate on content

6. Helping students record and represent knowledge

7. Managing response rates with tiered questioning techniques

8. Reviewing content

9. Helping students practice skills, strategies, and processes

10. Helping students examine similarities and differences

11. Helping students examine their reasoning

12. Helping students revise knowledge

13. Helping students engage in cognitively complex tasks

(Marzano & Toth, 2014, p. 17)

As Marzano said, resources that address the "how" to achieving rigorous instruction can be difficult for teachers to locate. Here are a couple of resources we have found useful:

Depth and Complexity

Using icons that represent a variety of ways of thinking and processing at rigorous levels, the Depth and Complexity program provides ways to specifically address higher-order thinking.

The Depth & Complexity Framework, . . .

. . . used originally within Gifted/Talented Education programs, . . . has [now] "spilled-over" as intended, into the heterogeneous classroom. With a renewed focus on college & career readiness and preparing the "21st-Century Learner," educators are turning to Depth & Complexity as the pedagogical engine that ensures students are prompted to think in a deeper manner about content.

The Depth & Complexity Framework's components:

- High-Level, Critical, Creative Thinking Skills

- Depth & Complexity Icons/Prompts

- Content Imperative Icons/Prompts

- Universal Concepts & Generalizations

- Disciplinarian Thinking and Scholarly Behaviors

(J Taylor Education, 2015)

Thinking Maps

Thinking Maps have been around for more than 25 years. They offer opportunities to help students organize and visualize their thinking, supporting students as they "create concrete images of abstract thoughts. These patterns help all students reach higher levels of critical and creative thinking—essential components of 21st Century education" (Thinkingmaps. com, 2018).

Science, Technology, Engineering, and Math: Education for Global Leadership (STEM)

In an ever-changing, increasingly complex world, it's more important than ever that our nation's youth be prepared to bring knowledge and skills to solve problems, make sense of information, and know how to gather and evaluate evidence to make decisions. These are the kinds of skills that students develop in science, technology, engineering, and math—disciplines collectively known as STEM. If we want a nation where our future leaders, neighbors, and workers have the ability to understand and solve some of the complex challenges of today and tomorrow, and to meet the demands of the dynamic and evolving workforce, then building students' skills, content knowledge, and fluency in STEM fields is essential.

U.S. Department of Education, n.d.b

STEM has become a major emphasis of the U.S. Department of Education. A focus on providing equitable support for all students to have a chance to engage in and hopefully enter into these less-populated disciplines was emphasized by President Obama, and a committee was formed that consisted of 13 agencies and the Department of Education. STEM resources allow more bridges to be built between current educational trends, philosophies, and funding sources such as personalized learning, Next Generation Learning, and the emphasis on increasing rigor.

Science, Technology, Engineering, Arts, and Math (STEAM)

The addition of the "A" is a movement to incorporate the arts into STEM subjects and lessons (Jolly, 2014).

The Smarter Balanced Assessment Consortium

Aligned with CCSS, the Smarter Balanced Assessment Consortium offers a digital library teachers can access, with a variety of resources created by educators. Interim assessments designed to be formative in nature cover specific concepts, and summative tests that can be used for accountability purposes are also available. For more information, see http://www.smarterbalanced.org.

State/District Teacher and Coach Evaluation Rubrics

A vital tool to determine what the components of competent teaching and coaching are, as defined by your state or district, can be found in evaluation documents. It is important for coaches to be very familiar with and understand these documents, to provide coaching that supports the components of quality instruction, as defined by the agencies that issue teacher licenses and credentials.

21st Century Skills/Learning

To address gaps in the traditional American education system, which was originally designed to prepare students for agrarian and manufacturing job opportunities, The Partnership for 21st Century Skills (P21), a group consisting of teachers, business leaders, and education experts, began creating a "Framework for 21st Century Learning" in 2002 that included 18 different skills students would need to learn to be successful in a global society. Recognizing that this framework was too long and complicated (NEA, n.d., p. 3), the skills were prioritized into the "four Cs":

1. Critical thinking

2. Communication

3. Collaboration

4. Creativity

Many states have incorporated 21st Century Skills into their standards, assessments, and professional development opportunities. The most recent framework (2007) includes student outcomes and support systems.

Appendix B

TCT Coaching Program Research Summary

To determine the effectiveness of the TCT program, doctorate-level statistical studies in a variety of areas were conducted. The results are as follows:

Sixty-nine coached teachers grew more than 70 non-coached teachers in perceived teacher competency (cumulative results in 22 areas of competency) by almost four times as much and in job satisfaction by 57 times as much. Individual survey sub-sections indicated that coached teachers grew more than non-coached teachers by significant amounts (typically four to five times as much) in the areas of planning, instruction, assessment, environment, and professional growth. Students in 30 third-, fourth-, and fifth-grade teachers' classes (half in the control group and half in the coached group) took the NWEA Reading MAP tests. Students of coached teachers showed almost half a year more growth than students of non-coached teachers (see Study 2).

For detailed information, please refer to the dissertation on Google Scholar entitled *The Impact of Instructional Coaching on Teacher Competency, Job Satisfaction, and Student Growth*, by Rebecca A. Frazier.

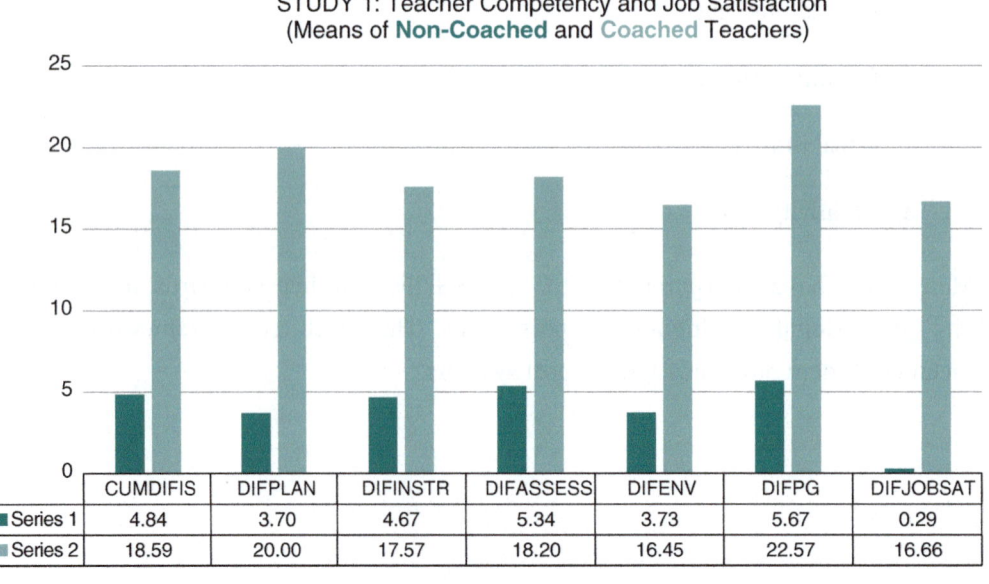

STUDY 1: Teacher Competency and Job Satisfaction
(Means of **Non-Coached** and **Coached** Teachers)

	CUMDIFIS	DIFPLAN	DIFINSTR	DIFASSESS	DIFENV	DIFPG	DIFJOBSAT
■ Series 1	4.84	3.70	4.67	5.34	3.73	5.67	0.29
■ Series 2	18.59	20.00	17.57	18.20	16.45	22.57	16.66

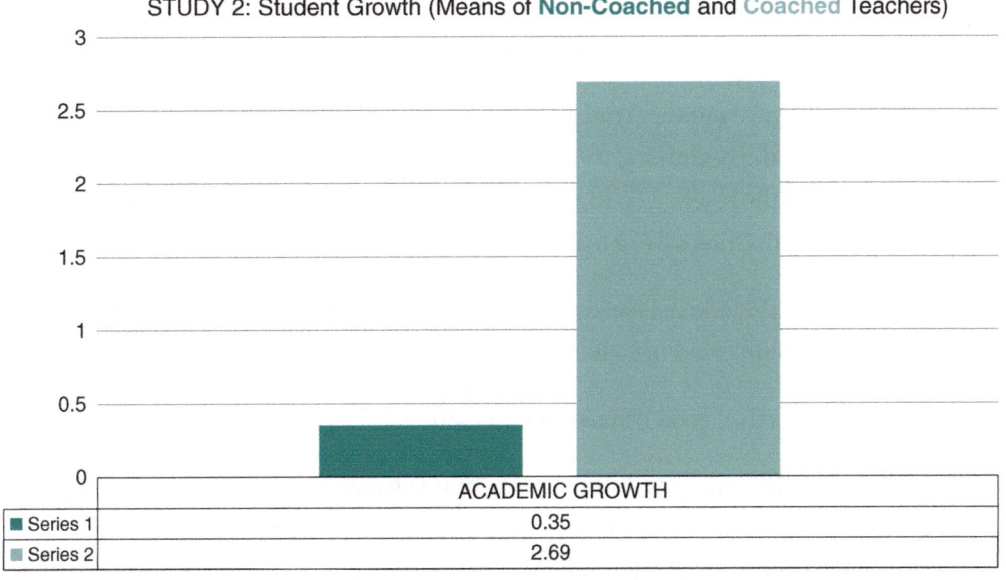

STUDY 2: Student Growth (Means of **Non-Coached** and Coached Teachers)

	ACADEMIC GROWTH
■ Series 1	0.35
■ Series 2	2.69

Significant Results		
Dependent Variables	GROUP VARIABLE Coached Compared to Not Coached $p \leq .05$	R^2_{adj}
Overall Teacher Competency	.000	.235
Job Satisfaction	.000	.236
Student Growth	.036	.423
All 5 Survey Sub-sections	.000	.134 – .280

Qualitative data on TCT coaching is shared below, to provide evidence of inspiring K–12 teacher experiences associated with *coaching delivered in the ways explained in this book*. The following quotes were found on anonymous customer-satisfaction surveys completed at the end of school year 2017–2018.

- "Coaching has impacted my students, because my coach helped me know more of what my students needed. I felt I could better attend to the needs of my students, which, in turn, helped them grow in the places they needed to."

- "My coach was a tremendous help to me in assessing phonemic awareness and identifying learning gaps in my students. She provided me with useful assessments, strategies, and recommendations for PD."

- "Covered in Awesome Sauce! Coach helped with planning and PLC; helped structure lessons, considering teaching and learning styles; and helped me change my style from lecturing to a constructivist approach. The coach also facilitated in-depth conversations with my content partner."

- "The coach gave me very concrete advice and support while I was implementing changes. At the beginning, trying out a new classroom-management strategy feels very new to the teacher, so the continuous encouragement provided by the coach was essential. Otherwise, a teacher might just feel like this will never work."

- "Great coach! Made me feel confident, shared resources, and was always there for questions. Supported me where I needed it the most."

- "Very supportive, good listeners, empathetic excellent mentors."

- "[As a result of coaching,] students are more engaged in the learning process, there is a positive learning environment in class, the refreshing change in teaching techniques made students eager to learn concepts, and behavioral issues with students are now handled effectively."

- "My coach was not only a great resource, but a truly inspirational coach and leader. Very explicit, friendly, and helpful!"

- "My coach was an ongoing wealth of skill, knowledge, and optimistic/ compassionate support. My effectiveness increased dramatically because of her support."

- "Very encouraging and provided many options and resources to become a better educator."

- "Thank you for being our peace, a place where we can go to ask questions and get clarification."

Anonymous survey quotes from administrators (2017–2018):

- "Very constructive feedback that's specific and directed at a need."

- "I am very grateful that Teachers Coaching Teachers (TCT) exists. There is no better program than this one to support teacher development and growth. Thank you!"

- "I love the coaches who work in this department. They are knowledgeable and approachable. I have seen results that are directly related to this work. Thank you!!"

References

Aguilar, E. (2013). *The art of coaching*. San Francisco, CA: Jossey-Bass.

Al Alhareth, Y., & Al Dighrir, I. (2014). The assessment process of pupils' learning in Saudi education system: A literature review. *American Journal of Educational Research, 2*(10), 883–891.

Alberti, S. (2012). Making the shifts. *Educational Leadership, 70*(4), 24–27.

Allen, T. J., & Sherman, J. W. (2011). Ego threat and intergroup bias: A test of motivated-activation versus self-regulatory accounts. *Psychological Science, 22*(3), 331–333. doi:10.1177/0956797611399291

Aragon, S. (2016, April). *Teacher shortages: What we know*. Retrieved from www.ecs.org

Archer, A. (n.d.). Vocabulary Instruction. Retrieved from https://explicitinstruction.org

Archer, A., & Hughes, C. A. (2011). *Explicit instruction: Effective and efficient teaching*. New York, NY: Guilford Press.

Aungst, G. (2014, September 4). Using Webb's Depth of Knowledge to increase rigor [Web log entry]. *Edutopia*. Retrieved from https://www.edutopia.org/blog/webbs-depth-knowledge-increase-rigor-gerald-aungst

BAD GPS Geometry: Bryce_Canyon_Hoodoos.jpg: "Jon Zander(digon3)"; Garmin_eTrex_Legend_C_in_hand.jpg: Paul Downey from Berkhamsted, UK; Navstar-2.jpg: NASA; Bad_gdop_screen.svg: Javiersanp; derivative work: Javiersanp - Bryce_Canyon_Hoodoos.jpg; Garmin_eTrex_Legend_C_in_hand.jpg; Navstar-2.jpg; Bad_gdop_screen.svg, CC BY-SA 3.0, https://commons.wikimedia.org/w/index.php?curid=9970306

Baumeister, R. F., Smart, L., & Boden, J. M. (1996). Relation of threatened egotism to violence and aggression: The dark side of high self-esteem. *Psychological Review, 103*(1), 5–33.

Beninghof, A. (2015/2016, December/January). To clone or not to clone? *Educational Leadership, 73*(4), 10–15.

Bennett, W. J. (Ed., with commentary). (1993). *The book of virtues: A treasury of great moral stories*. New York, NY: Simon & Schuster.

Bennett, W. J. (Ed., with commentary). (1995). *The moral compass: Stories for life's journey*. New York, NY: Simon & Schuster.

Bianco, M. W. (2003). *The velveteen rabbit: or how toys become real*. Leesburg, VA: GiGi Books.

Bill & Melinda Gates Foundation. (2010). *Next Generation Learning*. Retrieved from https://docs.gatesfoundation.org/documents/nextgenlearning.pdf

Bobek, B. L. (2002). Teacher resiliency: A key to career longevity. *The Clearing House, 75*(4), 202–205.

BrainyQuote. (n.d.). *65 Vince Lombardi quotes*. Retrieved from https://www.brainyquote.com/authors/vince-lombardi-quotes

Buckingham, M., & Goodall, A. (2019, March/April). The feedback fallacy. *Harvard Business Review*, pp. 92–101.

Burns, D. D. (1981). *Feeling good: The new mood therapy*. New York, NY: Penguin Books.

Burton, L. K. (2012, November). First observe, then serve. *Ensign, 78–80*.

Bush, R. N. (1984). *Effective staff development*. In *Making our schools more effective: Proceedings of three state conferences*. San Francisco, CA: Far West Laboratories.

Bushweller, K. (2016). Personalized twists, turns. *Education Week, 36*(9), 5.

Canfield, J. (with Switzer, J.). (2005). *The success principles: How to get from where you are to where you want to be*. New York, NY: HarperCollins.

Carr, N. (2011). *The shallows: What the internet is doing to our brains.* New York, NY: W. W. Norton & Company.

Carsciaro, T., & Sousa Lobo, M. (2005, June). Competent jerks, lovable fools, and the formation of social networks. *Harvard Business Review, 2–8.*

Cashman, K. (2008). *Leadership from the inside out: Becoming a leader for life* (2nd ed., rev. and expanded). San Francisco, CA: Berrett-Koehler Publishers.

Charlotte-Mecklenburg Schools. (2010, October). *National board certification report.* Retrieved from https://www .cms.k12.nc.us/cmsdepartments/accountability/REA/ Documents/National%20Board%20Certification%20Report.pdf

Chingos, M. M., & Peterson, P. E. (2011). It's easier to pick a good teacher than to train one: Familiar and new results on the correlates of teacher effectiveness. *Economics of Education Review, 30*(3), 449–465. doi:10.1016/j .econedurev.2010.12.010

Chopra, D. (1994). *The seven spiritual laws of success.* San Rafael, CA: Amber-Allen.

CNA Corporation. (2004). *Is national board certification an effective signal of teacher quality?* Retrieved from https:// files.eric.ed.gov/fulltext/ED485515.pdf

Cohen, D. K., & Moffit, S. L. (2009). *The ordeal of equality: Did federal regulation fix the schools?* Cambridge, MA: Harvard University Press.

Collins, J. (2001). *Good to great: Why some companies make the leap and others don't.* New York, NY: HarperCollins.

Common Core State Standards Initiative. (n.d.a). *Key shifts in English language arts.* Retrieved from http://www .corestandards.org/other-resources/key-shifts-in-english-language-arts

Common Core State Standards Initiative. (n.d.b). *Key shifts in mathematics.* Retrieved from http://www.corestandards .org/other-resources/key-shifts-in-mathematics

Conley, D. (2014). *Getting ready for college, careers, and the common core: What every educator needs to know.* San Francisco, CA: Jossey-Bass.

Corwin Press. (2008). *Mentoring, coaching, and collaboration.* Thousand Oaks, CA: Corwin.

Covey, S. M. R. (with Merrill, R. R.) (2006). *The speed of trust: The one thing that changes everything.* New York, NY: Free Press.

Covey, S. R. (1982). *The divine center.* Salt Lake City, UT: Bookcraft.

Covey, S. R. (1989). *The 7 habits of highly effective people: Restoring the character ethic.* New York, NY: Simon & Schuster.

Covey, S. R. (1992). *Principle-centered leadership.* New York, NY: Simon & Schuster.

Cowan, J., & Goldhaber, D. (2016). National board certification and teacher effectiveness: Evidence from Washington State. *Journal of Research on Educational Effectiveness, 9*(3), 233–258. doi:10.1080/19345747.2015.1099768

Da Vinci, L. (2016). *Leonardo da Vinci quotes...Vol. 16: Motivational & inspirational life quotes by Leonardo da Vinci.* The Secret Libraries: ISBN-13: 978-1540674043

Daft, R. L. (2011). First, lead yourself. *Leader to Leader, 60,* 28–33.

Danielson, C. (1996). *Enhancing professional practice: A framework for teaching.* Alexandria, VA: ASCD.

Davis, M. (2016). Q&A: Lessons learned from Next Generation Learning challenges; Q&A with Andrew Calkins. *Education Week, 36*(9), 16.

Dean, C. B., Hubbell, E. R., Pitler, H., & Stone, B. J. (2012). *Classroom instruction that works* (2nd ed.). Alexandria, VA: ASCD.

Denhardt, R. B. (2002). The new public service: Serving rather than steering. *Public Administration Review, 60*(6), 556.

Disney, W. (1992). *The great American bathroom book.* Salt Lake City, UT: Compact Classics 3-C2,1.

Doran, G. T. (1981). There's a S.M.A.R.T. way to write management's goals and objectives. *Management Review, 70*(11), 35–36.

Dresser, N. (2005). *Multicultural manners: Essential rules of etiquette for the 21st century.* Hoboken, NJ: John Wiley & Sons.

Driscoll, C., & McKee, M. (2007). Restorying a culture of ethical and spiritual values: A role for leader storytelling. *Journal of Business Ethics, 73*(2), 208.

DuFour, R., DuFour, R., Eaker, R., & Karhanek, G. (2004). *Whatever it Takes: How professional learning communities respond when kids don't learn.* Bloomington, IN: Solution Tree.

DuFour, R., DuFour, R., Eaker, R., & Many, T. (2010). *Learning by doing: A handbook for professional learning communities at work* (2nd ed.). Bloomington, IN: Solution Tree.

Dweck, C. (2014, December 17). *The power of believing you can improve* [Video file]. Retrieved from https://www.ted.com/talks/carol_dweck_the_power_of_believing_that_you_can_improve

Eaker, R., DuFour, R., DuFour, R. (2002). *Getting Started: Reculturing schools to become professional learning communities.* Bloomington, IN: National Educational Service.

Education Services Australia. (n.d.). *Learning intentions.* Retrieved from https://www.assessmentforlearning.edu.au/professional_learning/modules/learning_intentions/learning_intentions_landing_page.html

Elementary and Secondary Education Act. (2001). Retrieved from innovation.ed.gov/files/2016/07/NCLB-ESSA-Equitable-Services-Comparison-Chart-FINAL.pdf

English Oxford Living Dictionaries (n.d). Retrieved from: https://en.oxforddictionaries.com/definition/joy

Eriksen, M. (2009). Authentic leadership: Practical reflexivity, self-awareness, and self-authorship. *Journal of Management Education, 33*(6), 751–752.

Fein, S., & Spencer, S. J. (1997). Prejudice as self-image maintenance: Affirming the self through derogating others. *Journal of Personality and Social Psychology, 73*, 31–44.

Fillery-Travis, A., & Lane, D. (2007). Research: Does coaching work? In S. Palmer & A. Whybrow (Eds.), *Handbook of coaching psychology: A guide for practitioners* (pp. 57–70). New York, NY: Routledge.

Fisher, D., & Frey, N. (2014). *Better learning through structured teaching: A framework for the gradual release of responsibility* (2nd ed.). Alexandria, VA: ASCD.

Frazier, R. A. (2014). *Characteristics of effective instructional coaches.* Manuscript. Retrieved from https://rebeccafrazier.net/wp-content/uploads/2020/04/Characteristics-of-Effective-Instructional-Coaches-Final-Paper-February-8th-2014-.pdf

Frazier, R. A. (2018). *The impact of instructional coaching on teacher competency, job satisfaction, and student growth* (Doctoral dissertation, University of Colorado–Colorado Springs). Retrieved from https://mountainscholar.org/bitstream/handle/10976/166927/Frazier_uccs_0892D_10372.pdf

Frei, F. (2018). *How to build (and rebuild) trust* [Video file]. Retrieved from https://www.ted.com/talks/frances_frei_how_to_build_and_rebuild_trust?language=en#t-115817

Friend, M. (2015/2016, December/January). Welcome to Co-Teaching 2.0. *Educational Leadership, 73*(4), 16–22.

Fry, L. W. (2003). Toward a theory of spiritual leadership. *The Leadership Quarterly, 14,* 693–727.

Fullan, M. (2008). *The six secrets of change: What the best leaders do to help their organizations survive and thrive.* San Francisco, CA: Jossey-Bass.

Gallwey, W. (2001). *The inner game of work: Focus, learning, pleasure, and mobility in the workplace.* New York, NY: Random House.

Gardner, H. (1993). *Frames of mind: The theory of multiple intelligences* (10th anniversary ed., with a new introduction by the author). New York, NY: BasicBooks.

George, B. (2006). Truly authentic leadership. *U.S. News & World Report, 141*(16), 52–54.

George, B., McClain, A., & Craig, N. (2008). *Finding your true north: A personal guide.* San Francisco, CA: Jossey-Bass.

Goffee, R., & Jones, G. (2006). *Why should anyone be led by you? What it takes to be an authentic leader.* Boston, MA: Harvard Business Review Press.

Goldhaber, D., & Anthony, E. (2007). Can teacher quality be effectively assessed? National board certification as a signal of effective teaching. *Review of Economics and Statistics, 89*(1), 134.

Goleman, D. (1995). *Emotional intelligence: Why it can matter more than IQ.* New York, NY: Bantam Dell.

Goleman, D. (2006). *Emotional intelligence* (10th anniversary ed.). New York, NY: Bantam Dell.

GOOD GPS Geometry: Clear_sky.JPG: Suguru@Musashi/宮本すぐる; Garmin_eTrex_Legend_C_in_hand.jpg: Paul Downey from Berkhamsted, UK; Navstar-2.jpg: NASA; Good_gdop_screen.svg: Javiersanp; derivative work: Javiersanp - Clear_sky.JPG; Garmin_eTrex_Legend_C_in_hand.jpg;

Navstar-2.jpg; Good_gdop_screen.svg, CC BY-SA 3.0, https://commons.wikimedia.org/w/index.php?curid=9970220

Gray, L., & Taie, S. (2015). *Public school attrition and mobility in the first five years: Results from the first through fifth waves of the 2007–08 beginning teacher longitudinal study* (NCES 2015-337). U.S. Department of Education. Washington, DC: National Center for Education Statistics. Retrieved from https://nces.ed.gov/pubs2015/2015337.pdf

Gregory, G., & Kaufeldt, M. (2015). *The motivated brain: Improving student attention, engagement, and perseverance.* Alexandria, VA: ASCD.

Hackathorn, J., Garczynski, A. M., Blankmeyer, K., Tennial, R. D., & Solomon, E. D. (2011). All kidding aside: Humor increases learning at knowledge and comprehension levels. *Journal of the Scholarship of Teaching and Learning, 11*(4), 116–123.

Harmin, M., & Toth, M. (2006). *Inspiring active learning: A complete handbook for today's teachers.* Alexandria, VA: ASCD.

Hattie, J. A. C. (2009). *Visible learning: A synthesis of over 800 meta-analyses relating to achievement.* New York, NY: Routledge.

Heath, C., & Heath, D. (2017). *The power of moments: Why certain experiences have extraordinary impact.* London, England: Transworld Publishers.

Herman, J. L., & Choi, K. (2008). *Formative assessment and the improvement of middle school science learning: The role of teacher accuracy* (CRESST Report 740). Los Angeles, CA: National Center for Research on Evaluation, Standards, and Student Testing (CRESST).

Herold, B. (2016, October 18). Personalized Learning: What does the research say? *Education Week, 36*(9), 14–15. Retrieved from https://www.edweek.org/ew/articles/2016/10/19/personalized-learning-what-does-the-research-say.html

Houle, C. O. (1996). *The design of education* (2nd ed.) San Francisco, CA: Jossey-Bass.

Ingersoll, R. M., & Smith, T. M. (2003). The wrong solution to the teacher shortage. *Educational Leadership, 60*(8), 30–33.

J Taylor Education. (2015). *About.* Retrieved from https://www.jtayloreducation.com/about

Johnson, C. E. (2012). *Meeting the ethical challenges of leadership: Casting light or shadow.* Thousand Oaks, CA: SAGE.

Jolly, A. (2014, November 18). STEM vs. STEAM: Do the arts belong? *Education Week Teacher.* Retrieved from https://www.edweek.org/tm/articles/2014/11/18/ctq-jolly-stem-vs-steam.html

Jones, F. H. (2007). *Fred Jones tools for teaching: Discipline, instruction, motivation* (2nd ed.). Santa Cruz, CA: Fredric H. Jones & Associates.

Kahneman, D. (2011). *Thinking, fast and slow.* New York, NY: Farrar, Straus and Giroux.

Kanungo, R. N., & Mendonca, M. (1996*). Ethical dimensions of leadership.* Thousand Oaks, CA: SAGE.

Kee, K., Anderson, K., Dearing, V., Harris, E., & Shuster, F. (2010). *RESULTS coaching: The new essential for school leaders.* Thousand Oaks, CA: Corwin.

Kelly, F. S., McCain, T., & Jukes, I. (2009). *Teaching the digital generation: No more cookie-cutter high schools.* Thousand Oaks, CA: Corwin.

Kidder, R. M. (1994). *Shared values for a troubled world: Conversations with men and women of conscience.* San Francisco, CA: Jossey-Bass.

Killion, J., & Harrison, C. (2006). *Taking the lead: New roles for teachers and school-based coaches.* Oxford, OH: NSDC.

Killion, J., Harrison, C., Bryan, C., & Clifton, H. (2012). *Coaching matters.* Oxford, OH: Learning Forward.

Kise, J. A. G. (2006). *Differentiated coaching: A framework for helping teachers change.* Thousand Oaks, CA: Corwin.

Kise, J. A. G. (2017). *Differentiated Coaching: A framework for helping /teachers Change,* 2nd ed. Thousand Oaks, CA: Corwin.

Klass, P. (2018, May 16). Kid's suicide-related hospital visits rise sharply. *New York Times.* Retrieved from https://www.nytimes.com/2018/05/16/well/family/suicide-adolescents-hospital.html

Knight, J. (2007). *Instructional coaching: A partnership approach to improving instruction.* Thousand Oaks, CA: Corwin.

Knight, J. (2011). *Unmistakable impact: A partnership approach for dramatically improving instruction.* Thousand Oaks, CA: Corwin.

Knight, J. (2013). *High-impact instruction: A framework for great teaching.* Thousand Oaks, CA: Corwin.

Knight, J. (2014). *Focus on teaching: Using video for high-impact instruction.* Thousand Oaks, CA: Corwin.

Knight, J. (2015, October). Teaching | Learning | Coaching Conference, Denver, CO.

Knight, J. (2016). *Better conversations: Coaching ourselves and each other to be more credible, caring, and connected.* Thousand Oaks, CA: Corwin.

Knight, J. (2018). *The impact cycle: What instructional coaches should do to foster powerful improvements in teaching.* Thousand Oaks, CA: Corwin.

Knight, J., Elford, M., Hock, M., Dunekack, D., Bradley, B., Deshler, D. D., & Knight, D. (2015). 3 steps to great coaching: A simple but powerful coaching cycle nets results. *Journal of Staff Development: The Learning Forward Journal, 36*(1), 11–18.

Knight, J., Knight, J. R., & Carlson, C. (2015). *The reflection guide to better conversations: Coaching ourselves and each other to be more credible, caring, and connected.* Thousand Oaks, CA: Corwin.

Knowles, M. S. (1980). *The modern practice of adult education: From pedagogy to androgogy* (2nd ed.). New York, NY: Cambridge Books.

Kriger, M., & Seng, Y. (2005). Leadership with inner meaning: A contingency theory of leadership based on the worldviews of five religions. *The Leadership Quarterly, 16*(5), 771–806.

Leahy, S., Lyon, C., Thompson, M., & Wiliam, D. (2005). Classroom assessment: Minute by minute, day by day. *Educational Leadership, 63*(3), 19–24.

Lee, J. (2006). *Tracking achievement gaps and assessing the impact of NCLB on the gaps: An in-depth look into national and state reading and math outcome trends.* Cambridge, MA: The Civil Rights Project at Harvard University.

Locke, E. A., & Latham, G. P. (1990). *A theory of goal setting and task performance.* Englewood Cliffs, NJ: Prentice Hall.

Lorrance, A. (1974). The Love Project. In R. D. Kellough (Ed.), *Developing priorities and a style: Selected readings in education for teachers and parents* (2nd ed., pp. 85–97). New York, NY: MSS Information Corporation.

Love, N., Stiles, K. E., Mundry, S., & DiRanna, K. (2008). *The data coach's guide to improving learning for all students: Unleashing the power of collaborative inquiry.* Thousand Oaks, CA: Corwin.

Many, T. (2016, August 8). Presentation on Professional Learning Communities. Colorado Springs, CO.

Markow, D., Macia, L., Lee, H., and Harris Interactive. (2012). *The MetLife survey of the American teacher: Challenges for school leadership.* New York, NY: Metropolitan Life Insurance Company. Retrieved from www.metlife.com/assets/cao/foundation/MetLife-Teacher-Survey-2012.pdf

Marzano, R. J., & Simms, J. A. (2013). *Coaching classroom instruction.* Bloomington, IN: Marzano Research Laboratory.

Marzano, R. J., & Toth, M. D. (2014, March). *Teaching for rigor: A call for a critical instructional shift.* Retrieved from https://eohighschool.com/wp-content/uploads/MC05-01-Teaching-for-Rigor-Paper-05-20-14-Digital-1-1.pdf

Maslow, A. H. (1954). *Motivation and personality.* New York, NY: Harper & Row.

Maslow, A. H. (1987). *Motivation and personality* (3rd ed.). New York, NY: Harper & Row.

Maxwell, L. A. (2014a, August 21). ELLs to keep increasing as K-12 schools cross 'majority-minority' threshold [Web log post]. *Education Week.* Retrieved from https://blogs.edweek.org/edweek/learning-the-language/2014/08/english-learners_projected_to_.html

Maxwell, L. A. (2014b, August 19). U.S. school enrollment hits majority-minority milestone. *Education Week, 34*(1), 1, 12, 14–15. Retrieved from https://www.edweek.org/ew/articles/2014/08/20/01demographics.h34.html

Medina, J. J. (2014) *Brain rules: 12 principles for surviving and thriving at work, home, and school.* Seattle, WA: Pear Press.

Merriam, S. B. (2001, Spring). Andragogy and self-directed learning: Pillars of adult learning theory. *New Directions for Adult and Continuing Education, 89*, 3–14.

MetLife. (2012). *The MetLife survey of the American teacher: Teachers, parents and the economy.* Retrieved from files.eric.ed.gov/fulltext/ED530021.pdf

Meyer, P. J. (2003). *Attitude is everything: If you want to succeed above and beyond.* Waco, TX: Meyer Resource Group.

Mitroff, I. I. (2003). Do not promote religion under the guise of spirituality. *Organization, 10*(2), 375–382.

Mizell, H., Hord, S., Killion, J., & Hirsh, S. (2011). New standards put the spotlight on professional learning. *Journal of Staff Development, 32*(4), 10–12.

Monson, T. S. (2015). *A future as bright as your faith.* Salt Lake City, UT: Deseret Book Company.

Morrison, T., & Conaway, W. A. (2006). *Kiss, bow, or shake hands: The bestselling guide to doing business in more than 60 countries* (2nd ed.). Avon, MA: Adams Media.

Moss, C. M., & Brookhart, S. M. (2012). *Learning targets: Helping students aim for understanding in today's lesson.* Alexandria, VA: ASCD.

Moss, C. M., Brookhart, S. M., & Long, B. A. (2011). Knowing your learning target. *Educational Leadership, 68*(6), 66–69.

Munro, J. H. (2008). *Roundtable viewpoints: Organizational leadership.* Dubuque, IA: McGraw-Hill.

Murawski, W. W., & Lochner, W. W. (2017). *Beyond co-teaching basics: A data-driven, no-fail model for continuous improvement.* Alexandria, VA: ASCD.

National Board for Professional Teaching Standards. (n.d.a). *The architecture of accomplished teaching: What is underneath the surface?* Retrieved from http://accomplished-teacher.org/propositions-in-practice

National Board for Professional Teaching Standards. (n.d.b). *Standards for NBPTS | The Five Core Propositions.* Retrieved from http://www.nbpts.org/five-core-propositions

National Board for Professional Teaching Standards. (2015, March). *Board certification: A proven tool for identifying quality teaching.* Retrieved from http://www.nbpts.org/wp-content/uploads/policy_implications_of_new_research.pdf

National Center for Education Information. (2011). *Profile of teachers in the U.S. 2011.* Retrieved from http://www.edweek.org/media/pot2011final-blog.pdf

National Center for Education Statistics (NCES). (2013). *The nation's report card: Trends in academic progress 2012* (NCES 2013-456). Washington, DC: Institute of Education Sciences, U.S. Department of Education. Retrieved from http://nces.ed.gov/pubsearch/pubsinfo.asp?pubid=2013456

National Center for Injury Prevention and Control. (2018). *Ten leading causes of death and injury.* Centers for Disease Control and Prevention. Retrieved from https://www.cdc.gov/injury/wisqars/LeadingCauses.html

National Education Association. (n.d.). *Preparing 21st century students for a global society: An educator's guide to the "four Cs."* Retrieved from http://www.nea.org/assets/docs/A-Guide-to-Four-Cs.pdf

Nevill, A. M., & Holder, R. L. (1999). Home advantage in sport: An overview of studies on the advantage of playing at home. *Sports Medicine, 28*, 221–236. Retrieved from https://doi.org/10.2165/00007256-199928040-00001

Noddings, N. (2005). *The challenge to care in schools.* New York, NY: Teachers College Press.

Northouse, P. G. (2010). *Leadership: Theory and practice* (5th ed.). Thousand Oaks, CA: SAGE.

OECD. (2012). *Programme for International Student Assessment (PISA) results from PISA 2012.* Retrieved from https://www.oecd.org/unitedstates/PISA-2012-results-US.pdf

Palmer, P. (2007). *The courage to teach: Exploring the inner landscape of a teacher's life* (10th anniversary ed.). San Francisco, CA: Jossey-Bass.

Pells, R. (2017). One in ten teachers taking antidepressants to cope with work stresses. *Independent.* Retrieved from www.independent.co.uk/news/education/education-news/teachers-antidepressants-stress-workload-suicidal-one-in-ten-nasuwt-a7684466.html

Peterson, K. D. (n.d.). *Five myths of teacher evaluation.* Retrieved from http://www.teacherevaluation.net/Essay/fivemyth.html

Podolsky, A., Kini, T., Bishop, J., & Darling-Hammond, L. (2016). *Solving the teacher shortage: How to attract and retain excellent educators.* Retrieved from https://learning-policyinstitute.org/product/solving-teacher-shortage-brief

Post, S., & Neimark, J. (2007). *Why good things happen to good people: The exciting new research that proves the link between doing good and living a longer, healthier, happier life.* New York, NY: Broadway Books.

Post, S. G. (2011). *The hidden gifts of helping: How the power of giving, compassion, and hope can get us through hard times*. San Francisco, CA: Jossey-Bass.

Psalms 61:2. KJV (1979). *The holy bible*. Salt Lake City, UT: The Church of Jesus Christ of Latter-Day Saints.

Ridd, R. L. (2015, January 11). *Living with purpose: The importance of "real intent."* Retrieved from https://www.churchofjesuschrist.org/study/broadcasts/article/worldwide-devotionals/2015/01/living-with-purpose-the-importance-of-real-intent

Roberts, L. M. (2007). Bringing your whole self to work: Lessons in authentic engagement from women leaders. In B. Kellerman & D. L. Rhode (Eds.), *Women and leadership: The state of play and strategies for change* (pp. 329–360). San Francisco, CA: Jossey-Bass.

Robinson, D., Gibbs, J., Parks, B., Rea, V., White, K., & Willis, D. (2010). True north: Discover your authentic leadership by Bill George with Peter Sims [Book review]. *Administration in Social Work, 34*(3), 307–308.

Rogers, S. (2011). *Teaching for excellence*. Conifer, CO: Peak Learning Systems.

Rogers, S. (with the PEAK Team). (2013). *Teaching for excellence: Essential concepts, strategies, techniques, and processes for ensuring performance excellence for all kids* (5th ed.). Conifer, CO: PEAK Learning Systems.

Rosenthal, R., et al. (1977). The PONS test: Measuring sensitivity to nonverbal cues. *Advances in Psychological Assessment*. San Francisco, CA: Jossey-Bass.

Ross, J. A. (1992). Teacher efficacy and the effects of coaching on student achievement. *Canadian Journal of Education, 17*(1), 51–65.

Ruedy, M. C. (2008). Repercussions of MySpace teen suicide: Should anti-cyberbullying laws be created? *North Carolina Journal of Law & Technology, 9*(2), 323–346.

Russell, R. F. (2001). The role of values in servant leadership. *Leader and Organization Development, 22*(2), 78.

Sandstead, M. (2015/2016, December/January). Cutting watermelon: Lessons in instructional coaching. *Educational Leadership, 73*(4), 78–81.

Schein, E. H. (2002). Models and tools for stability and change in human systems. *Reflections, 4*(2), 36–37.

Schwartz, S. H. (2006). *Basic human values: An overview*. Retrieved from https://www.yourmorals.org/schwartz.2006.basic%20human%20values.pdf

Scott, S. (2011). *Fierce conversations*. New York, NY: Berkley Publishing Group.

Seligman, M. E. P. (1998). *Learned optimism*. New York, NY: Pocket Books.

Sinclair, L., & Kunda, Z. (1999). Reactions to a Black professional: Motivated inhibition and activation of conflicting stereotypes. *Journal of Personality and Social Psychology, 77*, 885–904.

Sisodia, R., Wolfe, D., & Sheth, J. (2014). *Firms of endearment: How world-class companies profit from passion and purpose*. Upper Saddle River, NJ: Pearson Education.

Sizemore, C. B. (2016). Compassion fatigue: The silent thief in our schools. *ASCD Express—The Working Lives of Educators 11*(18). Retrieved from http://www.ascd.org/ascd-express/vol11/1118-sizemore.aspx

Solution Tree. (n.d.). *History of PLC*. Retrieved from http://www.allthingsplc.info/about/history-of-plc

Sparks, D. (2009, Winter). Reach for the heart as well as the mind. *Journal of the National Staff Development Council, 30*(1), 48–54.

Sprick, R. (2018, October). Teaching | Learning | Coaching Conference Class. Las Vegas, NV.

Steeves, K. A., & Browne, B. C. (2000). *Preparing teachers for National Board certification: A facilitator's guide*. New York, NY: Guilford Press.

Stowe, H. B. (1869). *Oldtown folks*. (Quotation from Chapter 39; p. 507)

Strategic Data Project. (2012). *SDP Human Capital Diagnostic for Los Angeles Unified School District*. Retrieved from https://cepr.harvard.edu/publications/sdp-human-capital-diagnostic-los-angeles-unified-school-district

Strauss, V. (2015, March 10). No Child Left Behind: What standardized test scores reveal about its legacy. *Washington Post*. Retrieved from https://www.washingtonpost.com/news/answer-sheet/wp/2015/03/10/no-child-left-behind-what-standardized-test-scores-reveal-about-its-legacy

Student Learning, Student Achievement Task Force of the National Board for Professional Teaching Standards. (2011,

March). *Student learning, student achievement: How do teachers measure up?* Arlington, VA: National Board for Professional Teaching Standards.

Tajfel, H., & Turner, J. C. (1986). The social identity theory of inter-group behavior. In S. Worchel & W. Austin (Eds.), *The psychology of inter-group relations* (2nd ed., pp. 7–24). Chicago, IL: Nelson-Hall.

Tate, M. L. (2012). *"Sit & get" won't grow dendrites: 20 professional learning strategies that engage the adult brain* (2nd ed.). Thousand Oaks, CA: Corwin.

Tate, M. L. (2014). *Shouting won't grow dendrites: 20 techniques to detour around the danger zones.* Thousand Oaks, CA: Corwin.

Thinkingmaps.com. (2018). *What are Thinking Maps?* Retrieved from https://www.thinkingmaps.com/why-thinking-maps-2

U.S. Department of Education. (n.d.a). *Every Student Succeeds Act (ESSA).* Retrieved from https://www.ed.gov/essa

U.S. Department of Education. (n.d.b). *Science, technology, engineering, and math, including computer science* ("Background"). Retrieved from https://www.ed.gov/stem

U.S. Department of Education. (2015). *Teacher shortage areas nationwide listing 1990-1991-2015-2016.* Retrieved from http://www2.ed.gov/about/offices/list/ope/pol/tsa.doc

van Dierendonck, D. (2011). Servant leadership: A review and synthesis. *Journal of Management, (37),* 1228–1261.

Warner, J. (2007, August 29). Bad memories easier to remember: Negative memories may be more vivid than happy ones.

WebMD. Retrieved from https://www.webmd.com/brain/news/20070829/bad-memories-easier-to-remember

Weedn, F. (1999). *Flavia and the dream maker.* San Rafael, CA: Cedco Publishing.

Wheatley, M. J. (2006). *Leadership and the new science: Discovering order in a chaotic world* (3rd ed.). San Francisco, CA: Berrett-Koehler Publishers.

Whitehurst, G. J. (n.d.). *Evidence-based education (EBE)* [Slideshow presentation]. Retrieved from https://www2.ed.gov/nclb/methods/whatworks/eb/edlite-slide001.html

Williams, J. , & Power, K. (2010). Examining Teacher Educator Practice and Identity Through Care Reflection. *Studying Teacher Education, (6),* 115–130.

Zenger, J., & Folkman, J. (2013, March 15). The ideal praise-to-criticism ratio. *Harvard Business Review.* Retrieved from https://hbr.org/2013/03/the-ideal-praise-to-criticism

Zhang, Q. (2014). *Teaching with enthusiasm: Engaging students, sparking curiosity, and jumpstarting motivation.* Retrieved from https://www.natcom.org/communication-currents/instructors-corner-3-teaching-enthusiasm-engaging-students-sparking-curiosity

Ziglar, Z. (2017). *Born to win.* Issaquah, WA: Made for Success Publishing.

Zike, D. (2001). *Dinah Zike's Foldables: 3-dimensional interactive graphic organizers!* New York, NY: Macmillan/McGraw-Hill. Retrieved from http://www.dinah.com

Index

A SAGE Publishing Company

Helping educators make the greatest impact

CORWIN HAS ONE MISSION: to enhance education through intentional professional learning.

We build long-term relationships with our authors, educators, clients, and associations who partner with us to develop and continuously improve the best evidence-based practices that establish and support lifelong learning.

Solutions YOU WANT | Experts YOU TRUST | Results YOU NEED

EVENTS   >>> **INSTITUTES**

Corwin Institutes provide large regional events where educators collaborate with peers and learn from industry experts. Prepare to be recharged and motivated!

corwin.com/institutes

ON-SITE PD   >>> **ON-SITE PROFESSIONAL LEARNING**

Corwin on-site PD is delivered through high-energy keynotes, practical workshops, and custom coaching services designed to support knowledge development and implementation.

corwin.com/pd

>>> **PROFESSIONAL DEVELOPMENT RESOURCE CENTER**

The PD Resource Center provides school and district PD facilitators with the tools and resources needed to deliver effective PD.

corwin.com/pdrc

ONLINE   >>> **ADVANCE**

Designed for K–12 teachers, Advance offers a range of online learning options that can qualify for graduate-level credit and apply toward license renewal.

corwin.com/advance

Contact a PD Advisor at (800) 831-6640 or visit www.corwin.com for more information